Coercion, Capital, and European States, AD 990–1992

CHARLES TILLY

BLACKWELL
Cambridge MA & Oxford UK

First published 1990
Revised paperback edition, 1992
Reprinted 1993, 1994

Blackwell Publishers
238 Main Street
Cambridge, Massachusetts 02142, USA

108 Cowley Road, Oxford, OX4 1JF, UK

Library of Congress Cataloging in Publication Data
Tilly, Charles
   Coercion, capital, and European states, AD 990–1990/Charles Tilly.
p. cm.—(Studies in social discontinuity)
"20 May 1989."
Includes bibliographical references.
ISBN 1–55786–067–x
      1–55786–368–7 (Pbk)
   1. Europe – Politics and government.   2. Europe – Economic conditions.   3. Capitalism – Europe – History.   I. Title.
II. Series: Studies in social discontinuity (Basil Blackwell Publishers)
JN94.A2T54 1990
940–dc20   89–17730 CIP

British Library Cataloguing in Publication Data
A CIP catalogue record for this book is available from the British Library.

Typeset in 10 on 12 pt Ehrhardt
by Hope Services (Abingdon) Ltd.
Printed in the United States of America

This book is printed on acid-free paper

To the memory of Stein Rokkan

Intellectual enthusiast, impresario, creator, and friend

Contents

Preface

Creative neurosis, I call it: the art of directing one's compulsions and fears to productive outcomes. This book illustrates its application to writing. In this case, my compulsion to discover or invent simple symmetry in complex events combined with an urge to escape a burdensome responsibility by taking on another task that was not quite as daunting. Any reader of this book will recognize the signs of my compulsion to order and simplify. The second urge, however, takes a little explaining. Many times before I have found myself plunging into difficult work in order to avoid other work that was proving painful or difficult. This time, having started to collaborate with Wim Blockmans in the recruitment of a collection of papers on interactions of cities and states in Europe, I began an extremely ambitious book comparing the articulation of particular cities and states in several parts of Europe since AD 1000.

I meant the book to respond adequately to Perry Anderson's great challenge: "Today, when 'history from below' has become a watchword in both Marxist and non-Marxist circles, and has produced major gains in our understanding of the past, it is nevertheless necessary to recall one of the basic axioms of historical materialism: that secular struggle between classes is ultimately resolved at the *political* – not at the economic or cultural – level of society. In other words, it is the construction and destruction of States which seal the basic shifts in the relations of production, so long as classes subsist" (Anderson 1974: 11). The book, I hoped, would merge three of my career-long concerns: the history and dynamics of collective action, the process of urbanization, and the formation of national states.

Such a book, as I understood it, required a mastery of exotic sources and languages, not to mention the compilation of large catalogs and statistical series that would only fall into place an item at a time. I began writing, but soon found myself digging for new material in obscure places, and testing my ability both to learn new languages and retrieve old ones. Cornell University gave me the chance to try out some of the book's organizing ideas as its Messenger Lectures for 1987; although the discussion in Ithaca proved how ragged those ideas were, it also convinced me that the topic was important, and worth the long effort it would demand.

As I was working on that book in February and March 1988, I gave a series of lectures at the Institut d'Etudes Politiques in Paris. (I am grateful to Alain Lancelot and Pierre Birnbaum for arranging that opportunity, and to Clemens Heller for the support of the Maison des Sciences de l'Homme during my stay in Paris.) My plan was to work in Parisian archives in between the lectures. But early in the series I again lectured on European cities and states. As I reflected on the lively questioning that presentation had provoked, I suddenly realized that I had another book well underway: a much more schematic, synthetic, concise, and feasible book than the one I had already begun. Writing that book would allow me an honorable, if temporary, exit from the formidable big project. Instead of going to the archives, I stayed home at my keyboard and began tapping away excitedly at the new volume. Reworked versions of my Cornell and Institut lectures fitted into the plan, so that when I returned to New York at the end of March I had drafted major chunks of the book.

Neglecting other projects for which the Russell Sage Foundation had graciously sponsored a year's leave, I rushed to my computer and continued to write. (During that time, Pauline Rothstein and her assistants at Russell Sage provided indispensable, intelligent help with library sources, Camille Yezzi made daily routines easy, Eric Wanner and Peter de Janosi offered genial support, while Robert Merton and Viviana Zelizer encouraged my efforts to deal with big structures, large processes, and huge comparisons.) By July 1988 a complete, if uneven, draft was in circulation. It and successive drafts went the rounds under the titles *States, Coercion, and Capital, Silver, Sword, and Scepter*, and the less mellifluous but more accurate *Coercion, Capital, and European States*. (The book's present version incorporates and adapts material that previously appeared in "The Geography of European Statemaking and Capitalism Since 1500," in Eugene Genovese and Leonard Hochberg, (eds), *Geographic Perspectives in History* (Oxford: Basil Blackwell, 1989), "Warmakers and Citizens in the Contemporary World" (CSSC [Center for Studies of Social Change, New School for Social Research] Working Paper 41, 1987), "How War Made States and Vice Versa" (CSSC Working Paper 42, 1987), "States, Coercion, and Capital" (CSSC Working Paper 75, 1988), and "State and Counterrevolution in France," *Social Research* 56 (1989), 71–98.)

During the ensuing months many friends and colleagues read or heard various segments of the book; my compulsion to talk about it and to revise incessantly kept them very busy. Janet Abu-Lughod, Wim Blockmans, Bruce Carothers, Samuel Clark, Brian Downing, Carmenza Gallo, Thorvald Gran, Marjolein 't Hart, Peter Katzenstein, Andrew Kirby, John Lynn, Perry Mars,

Maarten Prak, Sidney Tarrow, Wayne te Brake, and Bin Wong gave me an inestimable gift: they criticized early drafts of the whole manuscript thoughtfully, while Richard Bensel, Robert Jervis, Jo Husbands, and David Laitin added sharp comments on particular sections. I owe Adele Rotman warm thanks for suggestions on how to get my ideas across. Nikki Aduba edited the manuscript with consummate care and intelligence. Louise Tilly was busy finishing her own books as I worked on this one, but she generously tolerated my obsession and offered strategic advice.

Audiences at the Universities of Bergen, California-Irvine, Chicago, Geneva, Leiden, and Western Ontario, at the City University of New York, Columbia University, Harvard University, and the Estonian Academy of Sciences asked pointed questions about parts of the analysis. The New School's proseminar on state formation and collective action helped me repeatedly in formulating the book's arguments. I am deeply indebted to Harrison White and his co-conspirators at Columbia University's Center for the Social Sciences (notably Lisa Anderson, David Cannadine, Martin Gargiulo, Denise Jackson, Gerald Marwell, Salvatore Pitruzzello, Kate Roberts, Hector Schamis, Kamal Shehadi, Jack Snyder, Claire Ullman, and Ronan Van Rossem) for a delightful seminar they organized to scrutinize draft chapters from this book. None of these helpful critics has seen a complete draft of the book's current version, and none therefore bears responsibility for my mistakes.

Mistakes there surely are. Stretching across a millennium, I have undoubtedly failed to consider major ideas, missed crucial events, ignored important contradictions, gotten significant facts wrong, and explained some changes incorrectly. I hope only that readers will inform me of any errors or omissions, and that they will reflect on how greatly my mistakes affect the overall argument before rejecting it out of hand. In my optimistic moods, I hope that this book will continue the work begun by the late Stein Rokkan, that it will build on the strengths and correct the errors of a work on which Stein and I collaborated, *The Formation of National States in Western Europe*, that it will exemplify the program of historically-grounded inquiry into large-scale processes of change I have advocated in earlier books such as *Big Structures, Large Processes, Huge Comparisons* and *As Sociology Meets History*, and that it will contribute to the effort to work out theories of historical contingency exemplified by recent writings of Anthony Giddens, Allan Pred, Arthur Stinchcombe, and Harrison White. If so, compulsion and phobia will once again have made a constructive contribution to knowledge. Now, of course, I face a problem: that big book still awaits me.

CHARLES TILLY

I

Cities and States
in World History

Some 3,800 years ago, the ruler of a small Mesopotamian city-state conquered all the region's other city-states, and made them subject to Marduk, his own city's god. Hammurabi, ruler of Babylon, became the supreme king of Mesopotamia. By conquering, he gained the right and obligation to establish laws for all the people. In the introduction to his famous laws, Hammurabi claimed instruction from the great gods Anu and Enlil:

> then did Anu and Enlil call me to afford well-being to the people,
> me, Hammurabi, the obedient, godfearing prince, to cause righteousness
>   to appear in the land
> to destroy the evil and the wicked, that the strong harm not the weak
> and that I rise like the sun over the black-headed people,
>   lighting up the land.
>
> (Frankfort 1946: 193)

Wrapped in a divine calling, Hammurabi could confidently call those who opposed his rule "evil" and "wicked." Vilifying victims, annihilating allies, and razing rival cities, he claimed that divine justice stood behind him. Hammurabi was building the power of his city, and founding a state; his gods and their particular vision of justice would prevail.

States have been the world's largest and most powerful organizations for more than five thousand years. Let us define states as coercion-wielding organizations that are distinct from households and kinship groups and exercise clear priority in some respects over all other organizations within substantial territories. The term therefore includes city-states, empires, theocracies, and many other forms of government, but excludes tribes, lineages, firms, and churches as such. Such a definition is, alas, controversial; while many students of politics use the term in this organizational way, some extend it to whatever structure of power exists in a large, contiguous population, and others restrict it to relatively powerful, centralized, and differentiated sovereign organizations – roughly to what I will call a national state. I will, furthermore, eventually compromise the definition by including such entities as today's Monaco and San Marino, despite their lack of "substantial" territories, on the ground that other unambiguous states treat them as fellow-states.

For the moment, let us stick with the organizational definition. By such a standard, archaeological remains first signal the existence of states as of 6000 BC, and written or pictorial records testify to their presence two millennia later. Through most of the last eight millennia, states have only occupied a minority of the earth's inhabited space. But with the passage of millennia their dominance has grown.

Cities originated in the same era. Some time between 8000 and 7600 BC, the settlement later called Jericho contained a temple and stone houses; within the next thousand years, it acquired a thick wall and differentiated buildings. By that time, one could reasonably call Jericho a city, and other Middle Eastern settlements were beginning to acquire the signs of urbanization as well. In Anatolia, Çatal Hüyük's remains include rich houses, shrines, and works of art dating to well before 6000 BC. Full-fledged cities and recognizable states, then, appeared at roughly the same point in world history, a moment of great expansion in human capacity for creativity and for destruction. For a few millennia, indeed, the states in question were essentially city-states, often consisting of a priest-ruled capital surrounded by a tribute-paying hinterland. By 2500 BC, however, some Mesopotamian cities, including Ur and Lagash, were building empires ruled by warriors and held together by force and tribute; Hammurabi's unification of southern Mesopotamia came seven centuries after the first empires formed there. From that point on, the coexistence of substantial states and numerous cities has marked the great civilizations, from Mesopotamia, Egypt, and China to Europe.

Over the eight or ten millennia since the couple first appeared, cities and states have oscillated between love and hate. Armed conquerors have often razed cities and slaughtered their inhabitants, only to raise new capitals in their place. City people have bolstered their independence and railed against royal interference in urban affairs, only to seek their king's protection against bandits, pirates, and rival groups of merchants. Over the long run and at a distance, cities and states have proved indispensable to each other.

Through most of history, *national* states – states governing multiple contiguous regions and their cities by means of centralized, differentiated, and autonomous structures – have appeared only rarely. Most states have been *non*-national: empires, city-states, or something else. The term national state, regrettably, does not necessarily mean *nation*-state, a state whose people share a strong linguistic, religious, and symbolic identity. Although states such as Sweden and Ireland now approximate that ideal, very few European national states have ever qualified as nation-states. Great Britain, Germany, and France – quintessential national states – certainly have never met the test. With militant nationalities in Estonia, Armenia, and elsewhere, the Soviet Union lived the distinction painfully to its very demise. China, with nearly three thousand years' experience of successive national states (but, given its multiple languages and nationalities, not one year as a nation-state), constitutes an extraordinary exception. Only during the last few centuries have national states mapped most of the world into their own mutually exclusive territories, including colonies. Only since World War II has almost the entire world come to be occupied by nominally independent states whose rulers recognize, more or less, each other's existence and right to exist.

As this final partitioning of the world into substantial states has proceeded, two important counter-currents have begun to flow. First, speakers for many populations that do not form distinct states have made claims to independent statehood. Not only the inhabitants of former colonies, but also minorities within old, established Western states, have demanded their own states with surprising frequency. While I write, groups of Armenians, Basques, Eritreans, Kanaks, Kurds, Palestinians, Sikhs, Tamils, Tibetans, Western Saharans, and many more stateless peoples are demanding the right to separate states; thousands have died for claiming that right. Within a Soviet Union that long seemed an unbreakable monolith, Lithuanians, Estonians, Azerbaijanis, Ukrainians, Armenians, Jews, and numerous other "nationalities" pressed successfully for varying degees of distinctness – and even, independence.

In the recent past, Bretons, Flemings, French Canadians, Montenegrins, Scots, and Welsh have also made bids for separate power, either inside or outside the states that now control them. Minorities claiming their own states have, furthermore, regularly received sympathetic hearings from third parties, if not from the states currently governing the territories they have claimed. If all the peoples on behalf of whom someone has recently made a claim to separate statehood were actually to acquire their own territories, the world would splinter from its present 160-odd recognized states to thousands of statelike entities, most of them tiny and economically unviable.

The second counter-current also runs strong: powerful rivals to states – blocs of states such as NATO, the European Economic Community or the European Free Trade Community, world-wide networks of traders in expensive, illicit commodities such as drugs and arms, and financial organizations such as giant international oil companies – have emerged to challenge their sovereignty. In 1992, members of the European Economic Community will dissolve economic barriers to a degree that will significantly limit their ability to pursue independent policies in respect of money, prices, and employment. These signs show that states as we know them will not last forever, and may soon lose their incredible hegemony.

In one of his sardonic "laws" of organizational behavior, C. Northcote Parkinson revealed that "a perfection of planned layout is achieved only by institutions on the point of collapse" (Parkinson 1957: 60). Cases in point include St Peter's basilica, and the Vatican Palace (completed during the sixteenth and seventeenth centuries, after the popes had lost most of their temporal power), the peacemaking Palace of the League of Nations (completed in 1937, just in time for the preliminaries to World War II), and the planning of colonial New Delhi, where "each phase of the [British] retreat was exactly paralleled with the completion of another triumph in civic design" (Parkinson 1957: 68). Perhaps a similar principle applies here. States may be following the old routine by which an institution falls into ruin just as it becomes complete. In the meantime, nevertheless, states remain so dominant that anyone who dreams of a stateless world seems a heedless visionary.

States form *systems* to the extent that they interact, and to the degree that their interaction significantly affects each party's fate. Since states always grow out of competition for control of territory and population, they invariably appear in clusters, and usually form systems. The system of states that now prevails almost everywhere on earth took shape in Europe after AD 990, then began extending its control far outside the continent five centuries later. It eventually absorbed, eclipsed, or extinguished all its rivals, including the systems of states that then centered on China, India, Persia, and Turkey. At the Millennium, however, Europe as such had no coherent existence; it consisted of the territory north of the Mediterranean once occupied by the Roman Empire, plus a large northeastern frontier never conquered by Rome, but largely penetrated by missionaries of the Christian churches which a disintegrating empire left as its souvenirs. At the same time Muslim empires controlled a significant part of southern Europe.

The continent we recognize today did have some potential bases of unity. An uneven network of trading cities connected much of the territory, and provided links to the more prosperous systems of production and commerce that extended from the Mediterranean to East Asia. The bulk of the region's population were peasants rather than hunters, pastoralists, or mercantile city-dwellers. Even in areas of urban concentration such as northern Italy, landlords ruled most of the population, and agriculture predominated among economic activities. Religion, language, and the residues of Roman occupation probably made the European population more culturally homogeneous than any other comparable world area outside of China. Within the area previously conquered by Rome, furthermore, traces of Roman law and political organization remained amid the splinters of sovereignty.

These features would eventually have a significant impact on Europe's history. Let us take AD 990 as an arbitrary point of reference. On the world stage the Europe of a thousand years ago was not a well-defined, unitary, independent actor. For that reason, any attempt to explain the continent's subsequent transformation in terms of its distinctive ethos or social structure runs a great risk of reasoning backwards. What is more, individual countries such as Germany, Russia and Spain simply did not exist as coherent entities; they took shape over succeeding centuries as a result of processes this book traces. Arguments that begin with the distinctive, enduring characteristics of "Germany" or "Russia" misrepresent the troubled, contingent history of European states.

So natural do the rise of national states, the growth of national armies, and the long European hegemony appear, indeed, that scholars rarely ask why plausible alternatives to them – such as the systems of loosely-articulated regional empires that thrived in Asia, Africa, and the Americas well past AD 990 – did not prevail in Europe. Surely part of the answer lies in the dialectic of cities and states that developed within a few hundred years after 990. For the coincidence of a dense, uneven urban network with a division into numerous well-defined and more or less independent states eventually set apart Europe from the rest of the world. Behind the changing geography of cities and states operated the dynamics of capital (whose preferred sphere was cities) and of coercion (which crystallized especially in states). Inquiries into the interplay between cities and states rapidly become investigations of capital and coercion.

A surprising range of combinations between coercion and capital appeared at one point or another in European history. Empires, city-states, federations of cities, networks of landlords, churches, religious orders, leagues of pirates, warrior bands, and many other forms of governance prevailed in some parts of Europe at various times over the last thousand years. Most of them qualified as states of one kind or another: they were organizations that controlled the principal concentrated means of coercion within delimited territories, and exercised priority in some respects over all other organizations acting within the territories. But only late and slowly did the national state become the predominant form. Hence the critical double question: *What accounts for the great variation over time and space in the kinds of states that have prevailed in Europe since AD 990, and why did European states eventually converge on different variants of the national state?* Why were the directions of change so similar and the paths so different? This book aims to clarify that problem, if not to resolve it entirely.

AVAILABLE ANSWERS

Established replies to the big question leave any serious student of European history unsatisfied. The alternatives now available differ especially with respect to their positions on two issues. First, to what extent, and how closely, did state formation depend on the particular form of economic change? The range runs from straightforward economic determinism to assertions of the complete autonomy of politics. Second, how strong an influence did factors exterior to any particular state have on its path of transformation? Answers vary from strongly internalist accounts to those which attach overwhelming weight to the international system. Through no coincidence, theories of war and of international relations vary in exactly the same manner: from economically determinist to politically determinist, and from internal to internationalist.

Although very few thinkers station themselves at the extremes – derive the state and its changes, for example, entirely from the economy – differences among available approaches remain impressively large. Figure 1.1 schematizes available answers to the two questions.

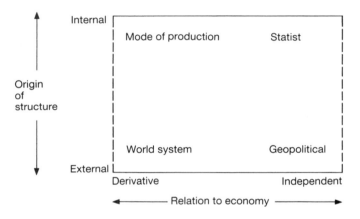

Figure 1.1   Alternative conceptions of state formation.

Statist analyses

Thus a statist model of war, international relations, and state formation treats political change as proceeding in partial independence of economic change, and presents it chiefly as a consequence of events within particular states. Many analysts of international relations have often adopted a statist perspective, assuming that individual states act on their defined interests, that the international system is anarchic, and that interactions among states ultimately reduce to the parry and thrust of self-interested actors. These days the most popular theories of the classic type bear the labels "structural realist" or "rational choice"; they allow for the effects of a hegemonic, bipolar, or multipolar international system, but ground their analyses of states' behavior in the interests and orientations of individual states (e.g. Bueno de Mesquita 1988, Gilpin 1988, Waltz 1988; for explication and criticism, see Holsti 1985, Jervis 1988a).

Among historians, sociologists, and students of comparative politics, statist accounts of states' transformations are by far the most popular. They inherit the now-discredited tradition of political development, searching for clues as to the conditions producing strong, effective, stable states, and assuming that only one such set of conditions exists. They typically take the individual state as their point of reference. When they do not reduce to particular histories of single states, they often posit a single, central path of European state formation and a set of deviations from the path explained by inefficiency, weakness, bad luck, geopolitical position, or the timing of economic growth and its concomitants; thus we have a few successful instances such as France or Britain and a great many failures, partial or total, such as Rumania or Portugal. Bertrand Badie and Pierre Birnbaum, for example, treat France as the most fully realized European state: "Prussia, Spain, and Italy followed various related paths, but the process of differentiation and institutionalization never went so far [as in France]." Great Britain they treat as "the model of under-statization" (Badie and Birnbaum 1979: 191, 217).

Samuel Huntington is a little more generous; considering Europe and the United States together, he distinguishes three patterns of modernization in governmental institutions: a Continental rationalization of authority and differentiation of structures within a unified sovereign body under the crown, a British centralization of power in a representative assembly, and an American fragmentation of sovereignty (Huntington 1968: 94–8). Soon, however, Huntington drops the distinction between Britain and the Continent in favor of a broad European–American comparison. In either analysis, Huntington singles out the effect of war on changes in state structure, but considers war to have roughly similar effects throughout Europe. His analysis emphasizes internal causes, and attributes little weight to economic determinants.

A second variant of the statist analysis stands closer to the diagram's center. This locates states in an international environment, but still treats them as acting more or less individually; its answer to questions about the diverse paths of state formation begins with sociocultural variation among the various parts of Europe – Protestant or Catholic, Slavic or German, feudal or free, peasant or pastoral – and derives differences from rulers' efforts to accomplish the same objectives in widely varying milieux. Thus in southeastern Europe theorists have repeatedly claimed to have discovered an indigenous Slavic, Magyar, or Roman village tradition distinguishing the fate of the region's states from those of Russia to the east or of capitalist states to the west (Berend 1988, Hitchins 1988, Roksandic 1988).

In a lucid and widely-read book, Paul Kennedy proposes a sophisticated variant of the statist argument, with significant economic overtones. His *Rise and Fall of the Great Powers* resembles Mancur Olson's *Rise and Decline of Nations* (which he does not cite) in more than title; both argue that the very process of economic and political expansion creates commitments that eventually slow it down. Olson, however, concentrates on the contemporary period, aims at building a general model, and singles out the coalitions – cartels, labor unions, and others – that form *within* a state to capture benefits of growth. Kennedy, in contrast, looks chiefly at a state's international position, and marks out a broad historical path.

Uneven economic growth, according to Kennedy, causes the world's leading states to acquire and lose advantages relative to other states, advantages they ordinarily seek to secure with the support of military power. States that win out in such contests, however, find that they have to commit increasing shares of their resources to armies and navies. "If, however, too large a proportion of the state's resources is diverted from wealth creation and allocated instead to military purposes, then that is likely to lead to a weakening of national power over the long term" (Kennedy 1987: xvi). Meanwhile, other states are amassing wealth, reinvesting in the creation of new wealth, and benefiting from their lesser obligation to pay for military force. Although Kennedy's initial statement renders the decline and fall merely possible, all the cases he analyzes – early imperial China, the Mughal Empire, the Ottoman Empire, the Habsburgs, Great Britain, and the United States – make it seem inevitable. In the pursuit of this argument, Kennedy provides a useful chronology of the European state system since 1519: a Habsburg bid for mastery (1519–1659), a great power struggle without primacy (1660–1815), a period of uncertain British hegemony (1815–85), another period of uneasy balance (1885–1918), the rise of the United States to temporary supremacy (1918–43), a bipolar Soviet–US system (1943–80), and another period of shifting struggle (1980–?). While Kennedy's analysis provides only vague indications of the origins of different kinds of state organization, its emphasis on the interaction of war, economic power, and international position points to factors that no treatment of the subject can afford to neglect.

William McNeill's *Pursuit of Power* brings out even more dramatically the centrality of changing forms and scales of warfare in the transformation of the European state system. McNeill's *tour de force* presents an overview of warfare – and especially its technological leading edge – in the world as a whole since AD 1000. With great clarity he traces the impact of gunpowder, siege artillery, antisiege fortifications, and other great technical innovations not only on warfare itself, but also on state finances, the introduction of time-discipline into civilian life, and much more. McNeill underestimates, I believe, the importance of such organizational innovations as the commodification of military service as well as the influence of changes in naval warfare, but he produces insight after insight into the significance of a given kind of warfare for social life and state structure. He does not, however, attempt a systematic analysis of relations between military organization and different types of state formation.

With McNeill, we reach the boundary of statist and geopolitical analyses of state formation; the sheer centrality of war in his account makes position within the international system a critical determinant of any particular state's organizational history. Most statist treatments of the subject fit the conventional use of the term much more comfortably, explaining the transformation of the French, Ottoman, or Swedish state as an outcome of events and processes within its own perimeter.

Such statist accounts of state formation – both monographic and synthetic – provide much of the raw material from which I have manufactured the argument of this book. Nevertheless, in themselves they provide no effective answer to the book's master theme: Why European states followed such diverse paths but eventually converged on the national state. They dissolve into particularisms and teleologies, explaining why the "modern" form of a given state emerged on the basis of the special character of a national population and economy. They neglect, furthermore, the hundreds of states that once flourished but then disappeared – Moravia, Bohemia, Burgundy, Aragon, Milan, Savoy, and many more. For systematic explanations, we must look beyond the statist literature.

Geopolitical analyses

If most students of state formation have adopted a statist perspective, considering the transformation of any particular state to result chiefly from noneconomic events within its own territory, each of the other three perspectives has had influential advocates. Geopolitical analyses of state formation attach great importance to the international system as the shaper of states within it. Geopolitical arguments ordinarily claim that interstate relations have a logic and influence of their own, and that state formation therefore responds strongly to the current system of relations among states. In a characteristic effort, James Rosenau distinguishes four "patterns of national adaptation" to international politics: acquiescent, intransigent, promotive, and preservative. The intransigent state, for example, "can seek to render its environment consistent with its present structures" while the promotive state "can attempt to shape the demands of its present structures and its present environment to each other" (Rosenau 1970: 4). Each of these patterns, according to Rosenau, has distinctive consequences for the character of the executive, the character of the party system, the role of the legislature, the role of the military, and much more (Rosenau 1970: 6–8). Similarly, what William Thompson calls a "global society" perspective on war and international relations attributes considerable autonomy to politics, and regards individual states as responding strongly to the structure of relations among all states; it therefore falls clearly into the geopolitical quadrant. Unsurprisingly, then, we find that geopolitical models of state formation, war, and international relations articulate closely with each other (Thompson 1988: 22–7; see also Waltz 1979). This body of work, as I read it, provides a valuable corrective to the internalism of statist analyses, but gives unclear guidance to the search for mechanisms that link particular forms of state to specific positions within the international system.

Mode of production analyses

Mode of production analyses typically spell out the logic of feudalism, capitalism, or some other organization of production, then derive the state and its changes almost entirely from that logic, as it operates within the state's territory (Brenner 1976, Corrigan 1980). "We conceive of the state," declare Gordon Clark and Michael Dear in a characteristic statement, "as deriving equally from the economic and political imperatives of capitalist commodity production. The state is ultimately implicated in the generation and distribution of surplus value as it seeks to sustain its own power and wealth" (Clark and Dear 1984: 4). It follows that explanations of state structure derive largely from the interests of capitalists who operate within the same state's jurisdictions. Marxist and *marxisant* analysts of war and international relations likewise generally deploy some version of theories of imperialism, an extension of national economic interest to the international sphere, which places them toward the diagram's mode-of-production corner.

In one of the most comprehensive and persuasive Marxist treatments, Perry Anderson proposes this formula:

The typical Western constellation in the early modern epoch was an aristocratic Absolutism raised above the social foundations of a non-servile peasantry and ascendant towns; the typical Eastern constellation was an aristocratic Absolutism erected over the foundations of a servile peasantry and subjugated towns. Swedish Absolutism, by contrast, was built on a base that was unique, because . . . it combined free peasants and nugatory towns; in other words, a set of two "contradictory" variables running across the master-division of the continent.

(Anderson 1974: 179–80)

Anderson similarly grounds the *absence* of well-developed Absolutism in Italy in the relation of town aristocracies to surrounding tributary territories in which they acted both as rulers and as predatory landlords. He complicates the picture by insisting that "It was the international pressure of Western Absolutism, the political apparatus of a more powerful feudal aristocracy, ruling more advanced societies, which obliged the Eastern nobility to adopt an equivalently centralized state machine, to survive" (Anderson 1974: 198). Thus on either side of the Elbe the full-fledged Absolutist state reflected the use of state power to fortify the positions of great feudal landlords, but military threats impinged on those positions differently in the East and the West. Anderson concentrates on the stronger, most centralized states, and aims his attention at the sixteenth to eighteenth centuries, but his general approach deserves careful attention at a European and millennial level. In the meantime, it falls far short of a comprehensive account of European state formation. While the mode-of-production literature as a whole contributes many insights into struggles for control of states, indeed, it offers only the faintest of clues to reasons for variations in form and activity among states having similar modes of production.

World system analyses

World system analyses of state formation ground the explanation of diverse paths of state formation in a characterization of the world economy. Neo-Marxist theorists such as Immanuel Wallerstein and André Gunder Frank extend the classic Marxist division between capital and labor to a world scale, thus pushing their analyses toward the world system quadrant – still deriving relations among states from economic structure, but regarding the structures of individual states as consequences of their positions within the world economy (see Taylor 1981). Wallerstein's grand survey of European history since 1500 (Wallerstein 1974–88) generally follows a spiral with respect to state formation: the mode of production in a given region creates a certain class structure, which emanates in a certain kind of state; the character of that state and the relations of the region's producers and merchants to the rest of the world economy determine the region's position – core, peripheral, or semiperipheral – in the world economy, which in turn significantly affects the state's organization. In this promising analysis, the state figures chiefly as an instrument of the national ruling class, an instrument that serves the interest of that class in the world economy. However, world system analyses have so far failed to produce a well-articulated theory linking the actual organizational structures of states to their positions within the world system. Thus Wallerstein's account of Dutch hegemony (volume II, chapter 2) in the seventeenth century provides no explanation of Dutch state structure – in particular, of the nation's prospering with a wispy national state at a time when its neighbors were creating massive civilian staffs and standing armies.

None of the four lines of explanation, much less their combination, yields a satisfactory set of answers to our pressing questions about European state formation. Most available explanations fail because they ignore the fact that many different kinds of states were viable at different stages of European history, because they locate explanations of state-to-state variation in individual characteristics of states rather than in relations among them, and because they assume implicitly a deliberate effort to construct the sorts of substantial, centralized states that came to dominate European life during the nineteenth and twentieth centuries. Geopolitical and world-system analyses provide stronger guidance, but so far they lack convincing accounts of the actual mechanisms relating position within the world to the organization and practice of particular states. In particular, they fail to capture the impact of war and preparation for war on the whole process of state formation; on that score, statist analyses do much better.

In *The Formation of National States in Western Europe*, published in 1975, my colleagues and I hoped to remedy these defects of the existing literature. In a series of historical studies emphasizing the extractive and repressive side of state formation, we looked self-consciously at war, policing, taxation, control of food supply, and related processes, and kept our distance from the models of political development that then prevailed. Our critique worked better, in retrospect, as a demonstration of the flaws in unilinear models of problem-solving political development than as an alternative account of European state formation. In fact, we implicitly substituted a new unilinear story – one running from war to extraction and repression to state formation – for the old one. We continued, more or less unthinkingly, to assume that European states followed one main path, the one marked by Britain, France, and Brandenburg-Prussia, and that the experiences of other states constituted attenuated or failed versions of the same processes. That was wrong. This book attempts to repair the errors of the previous one.

We have, fortunately, important models for the enterprise. Three great scholars – Barrington Moore, Jr, Stein Rokkan, and Lewis Mumford – escaped some of the standard literature's theoretical handicaps, even if they ultimately failed to fashion comprehensive accounts of variation in European state formation. In *Social Origins of Dictatorship and Democracy*, Barrington Moore sought to explain (as his title implies) why in the twentieth century some states sustained more or less viable representative systems while others featured one form or another of authoritarian rule. Although his accounts of individual countries were all wide-ranging and nuanced, when it came to differences among national destinies Moore used as his points of reference the forms of government that existed in the 1940s and stressed as "origins" the class coalitions that prevailed when the country's agriculture began extensive commercialization. To the extent that great, exploitative landlords survived the transition to intensive cash-crop farming, according to Moore, authoritarian government persisted into the contemporary era. To the extent that the bourgeoisie predominated, some form of democracy existed.

Moore's insightful analysis left important problems unsolved. It focused on explaining conditions of government at a single historical moment, and thus failed to explain the different forms of government experienced by the same peoples before and after the critical moment. It deliberately ignored smaller states, dependent states, and states that did not survive. It said little about the actual mechanisms that translated a certain form of class power into a specific mode of government. But it posed this book's problems with great force. It pointed toward solutions taking serious account of changes and variations in the class coalitions dominating the states of different European regions.

Early in his career, Stein Rokkan became obsessed with the variability of European political systems, and with the tendency of adjacent states to develop similar political arrangements. Eventually he came to represent variation among European states in schematic maps which included a north–south dimension reflecting the variable influence of the Roman Catholic and Orthodox churches, an east–west separation of seaward peripheries, seaward empire-nations, a city-state band, landward empire-nations, and landward buffers, plus finer variations within those two dimensions.

Rokkan died before he produced a satisfactory version of his conceptual map. As he left it, his scheme called attention to marked geographic variation in the forms of European states, singled out the distinctiveness of state-formation in Europe's central urbanized band, and hinted at the importance of long-term changes in relations among rulers, neighboring powers, dominant classes and religious institutions. But it left a muddled idea of the actual social processes connecting these changes with alternative state trajectories. It is hard to see how Rokkan could have gotten much farther without laying aside his maps and concentrating on the analysis of the mechanisms of state formation.

Lewis Mumford made a less obvious contribution. Implicitly, he fashioned a threshold-and-balance theory of urbanism. For Mumford, two great forces drive the growth of cities: the concentration of political power, and the expansion of productive means. Below a threshold combining minimum levels of power and production, only villages and bands exist. Above that threshold, the character of cities depends on the levels of power and production, relative and absolute: modest and balanced levels of power and production gave the classic *polis* and the medieval city their coherence; an excessive growth of political power informed the baroque city; the hypertrophy of production created the nineteenth century's industrial Coketowns, and huge concentrations in both directions have produced the overwhelming cities of today. Figure 1.2 diagrammatically represents the argument.

Mumford pointed to similar effects on a national scale. "There is little doubt," he wrote in 1970, "that at least in most industrially developed countries

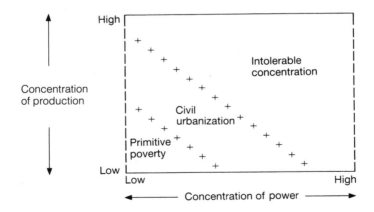

Figure 1.2   Lewis Mumford's implicit model of urbanization.

the Megatechnic Complex is now at the height of its power and authority, or is fast approaching it. In objectively measurable physical terms – units of energy, output of goods, input of 'bads,' capabilities for mass coercion and mass destruction – the system has nearly fulfilled its theoretic dimensions and possibilities; and if not judged by a more human measure, it is an overwhelming success" (Mumford 1970: 346). Mumford's prescriptions followed directly from that analysis; reduce the scale of both production and political power, he argued, and a more humane city would result.

Since Mumford never quite explicated the analytic argument, he did not spell out its implications for the formation of states. Most of the time, he treated forms of rule as outgrowths of the prevailing technology, especially the technology of war. But the logic of his analysis clearly points to alternative trajectories of state formation depending on the prevailing combination of production and power.

This book, then, takes up the problem where Barrington Moore, Stein Rokkan, and Lewis Mumford left it: at the point of recognizing decisive variations in the paths of change followed by states in different parts of Europe during successive epochs, with the realization that the class coalitions prevailing in a region at a given point in time strongly limited the possibilities of action open to any ruler or would-be ruler, and with the specific hypothesis that regions of early urban dominance, with their active capitalists, produced very different kinds of states from regions in which great landlords and their estates dominated the landscape. It goes beyond Moore, Rokkan, and Mumford most emphatically in two ways: first by placing the organization of coercion and preparation for war squarely in the middle of the analysis, arguing in its rasher moments that state structure appeared chiefly as a by-product of rulers' efforts to acquire the means of war; and second by insisting that relations among states, especially through war and preparation for war, strongly affected the entire process of state formation. Thus in this book I derive alternative histories of state formation from continuously-varying combinations of concentrated capital, concentrated coercion, preparation for war, and position within the international system.

This book's central argument does not so much synthesize as echo the analyses of Moore, Rokkan, and Mumford. Even in its simplest form, the argument is necessarily complex; it says that in European experience:

Men who controlled concentrated means of coercion (armies, navies, police forces, weapons, and their equivalent) ordinarily tried to use them to extend the range of population and resources over which they wielded power. When they encountered no one with comparable control of coercion, they conquered; when they met rivals, they made war.

Some conquerors managed to exert stable control over the populations in substantial territories, and to gain routine access to part of the goods and services produced in the territory; they became rulers.

Every form of rule faced significant limits to its range of effectiveness within a particular kind of environment. Efforts to exceed that range produced defeats or fragmentation of control, with the result that most rulers settled for a combination of conquest, protection against powerful rivals, and coexistence with cooperative neighbors.

The most powerful rulers in any particular region set the terms of war for all; smaller rulers faced a choice between accommodating themselves to the demands of powerful neighbors and putting exceptional efforts into preparations for war.

War and preparation for war involved rulers in extracting the means of war from others who held the essential resources – men, arms, supplies, or money to buy them – and who were reluctant to surrender them without strong pressure or compensation.

Within limits set by the demands and rewards of other states, extraction and struggle over the means of war created the central organizational structures of states.

The organization of major social classes within a state's territory, and their relations to the state, significantly affected the strategies rulers employed to extract resources, the resistance they met, the struggle that resulted, the sorts of durable organization that extraction and struggle laid down, and therefore the efficiency of resource extraction.

The organization of major social classes, and their relations to the state varied significantly from Europe's coercion-intensive regions (areas of few cities and agricultural predominance, where direct coercion played a major part in production) to its capital-intensive regions (areas of many cities and commercial predominance, where markets, exchange, and market-oriented production prevailed). The demands major classes made on the state, and their influence over the state, varied correspondingly.

The relative success of different extractive strategies, and the strategies rulers actually applied, therefore varied significantly from coercion-intensive to capital-intensive regions.

As a consequence, the organizational forms of states followed distinctly different trajectories in these different parts of Europe.

Which sort of state prevailed in a given era and part of Europe varied greatly. Only late in the millennium did national states exercise clear superiority over city-states, empires, and other common European forms of state.

Nevertheless, the increasing scale of war and the knitting together of the European state system through commercial, military, and diplomatic interaction eventually gave the war-making advantage to those states that could field standing armies; states having access to a combination of large rural populations, capitalists, and relatively commercialized economies won out. They set the terms of war, and their form of state became the predominant one in Europe. Eventually European states converged on that form: the national state.

Some of these generalizations (for example, the tendency for war to build state structure) hold through much of world history. Others (for example, the sharp contrast between coercion-intensive and capital-intensive regions) distinguish

Europe from many other world regions. We are pursuing a history that oscillates between the somewhat particular and the extremely general. In both regards, I will try to present enough concrete historical evidence to make the principles comprehensible and credible, but not so much as to bury them in detail.

If we explain the various paths taken by European states, we will better understand today's non-European states. Not that the states of Africa or Latin America are now recapitulating the European experience. On the contrary: the fact that European states formed in a certain way, then imposed their power on the rest of the world, guarantees that non-European experience will be different. But if we pinpoint the durable characteristics of the system Europeans first built, and identify the principles of variation within European experience, we will be better placed to specify what is distinctive about contemporary states, under what historically-imposed constraints they are operating, and what relationships among characteristics of states are likely to hold in our own time. With exactly that aim in mind, the book's final chapter turns from analyses of European experience to an examination of military power in today's Third World.

What happened in history? For the first few centuries of their existence, European states multiplied in the space left them by the large Muslim powers that ringed the Mediterranean and by the nomadic conquerors who thundered west from the Eurasian steppe. When they won territory, Muslims, Mongols, and other outsiders typically set up military rulers and systems of tribute that produced important revenues; they did not, however, intervene decisively in local social arrangements. Within their own space, Europeans farmed, manufactured, traded and, especially, fought each other. Almost inadvertently, they thereby created national states. This book tells how and why.

LOGICS OF CAPITAL AND COERCION

The story concerns capital and coercion. It recounts the ways that wielders of coercion, who played the major part in the creation of national states, drew for their own purposes on manipulators of capital, whose activities generated cities. Of course the two interacted; figure 1.3 represents the general condition.

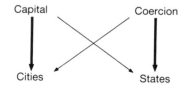

Figure 1.3   How capital and coercion generate cities and states.

Although states strongly reflect the organization of coercion, they actually show the effects of capital as well; as the rest of this book will demonstrate, various combinations of capital and coercion produced very different kinds of states. Again, cities respond especially to changes in capital, but the organization of coercion affects their character as well; Lewis Mumford's baroque city lived on capital like its cousins, but showed a clearer imprint of princely power – in palaces, parade grounds, and barracks – than they did. Over time, furthermore, the place of capital in the form of states grew ever larger, while the influence of coercion (in the guise of policing and state intervention) expanded as well.

Capital – Cities – Exploitation

Before entering into these complexities, however, it will help to explore the capital–cities and coercion–states relationships separately. Let us think of *capital* generously, including any tangible mobile resources, and enforceable claims on such resources. Capitalists, then, are people who specialize in the accumulation, purchase, and sale of capital. They occupy the realm of *exploitation*, where the relations of production and exchange themselves yield surpluses, and capitalists capture them. Capitalists have often existed in the absence of capitalism, the system in which wage-workers produce goods by means of materials owned by capitalists. Through most of history, indeed, capitalists have worked chiefly as merchants, entrepreneurs, and financiers, rather than as the direct organizers of production. The system of capitalism itself arrived late in the history of capital. It grew up in Europe after 1500, as capitalists seized control of production. It reached its apex – or, depending on your perspective, its nadir – after 1750, when capital-concentrated manufacturing became the basis of prosperity in many countries. For millennia before then, capitalists had flourished without much intervening in production.

The processes that accumulate and concentrate capital also produce cities. Cities figure prominently in this book's analyses, both as favored sites of capitalists and as organizational forces in their own right. To the extent that the survival of households depends on the presence of capital through employment, investment, redistribution or any other strong link, the distribution of population follows that of capital. (Capital, however, sometimes follows cheap labor; the relationship is reciprocal.) Trade, warehousing, banking, and production that depends closely on any of them all benefit from proximity to each other. Within limits set by the productivity of agriculture, that proximity promotes the formation of dense, differentiated populations having extensive outside connections – cities. When capital both accumulates and concentrates within a territory, urban growth tends to occur throughout the same territory – more intensely at the greatest point of concentration, and secondarily elsewhere (see figure 1.4). The form of urban growth, however, depends on the balance between concentration and accumulation. Where capital accumulation occurs

Figure 1.4   How capital generates urban growth.

quite generally, but concentration remains relatively low, many smaller centers develop. Where a single concentration of capital emerges, urban population concentrates around that center.

Properly speaking, then, cities represent regional economies; around every city or urban cluster lies a zone of agriculture and trade (and sometimes of manufacturing as well) that interacts closely with it. Where accumulation and concentration occur in tandem, a hierarchy from small centers to large tends to take shape (see figure 1.5). These tendencies have always operated within important limits. City people normally depend on others to raise most or all of their food and fuel; the transportation and preservation of these requisites for large cities consumes a great deal of energy. Until very recently, most of the world's agricultural areas, including those of Europe, were too unproductive to permit much more than a tenth of the nearby population to live off the land. Cities that could not reach agricultural areas conveniently by means of low-cost water transportation, furthermore, faced prohibitively high food costs. Berlin and Madrid provide good examples: except as their rulers force-fed them, they did not grow.

Health mattered as well. Through almost all of the last thousand years, despite their disproportionate recruitment of vigorous migrants of working age, cities have had significantly higher death rates than their hinterlands. Only after 1850, with improvements in urban sanitation and nutrition, did the balance shift in favor of city-dwellers. As a result, cities have only grown rapidly when

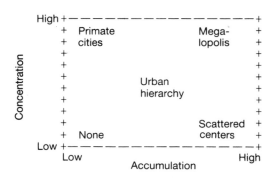

Figure 1.5   Alternative forms of urban growth as functions of capital accumulation and concentration.

agriculture and transportation were becoming relatively efficient or when powerful pressures were driving people off the land.

The sheer growth of cities, however, produced a spiral of change in all these regards. In the vicinity of active cities, people farmed more intensively and devoted a higher proportion of their farming to cash crops; in Europe of the sixteenth century, for example, highly productive agriculture concentrated in the two most urbanized regions, northern Italy and Flanders. Similarly, urban growth stimulated the creation and improvement of transportation by water and land; the Netherlands' superb system of canals and navigable streams brought down the cost, and brought up the speed, of communication among its swarm of cities, thus serving as both cause and effect of urbanization (de Vries 1978). The pressures that drove people off the land, furthermore, often resulted in part from urbanization, as when urban landlords drove smallholders from the hinterland or urban demand fostered the capitalization of the hinterland's agriculture. Accumulation and concentration of capital fostered urban growth, while transforming the regions surrounding new clusters of cities.

Coercion – States – Domination

What of coercion? Coercion includes all concerted application, threatened or actual, of action that commonly causes loss or damage to the persons or possessions of individuals or groups who are aware of both the action and the potential damage. (The cumbersome definition excludes inadvertent, indirect, and secret damage.) Where capital defines a realm of exploitation, coercion defines a realm of domination. The means of coercion center on armed force, but extend to facilities for incarceration, expropriation, humiliation, and publication of threats. Europe created two major overlapping groups of specialists in coercion: soldiers and great landlords; where they merged and received ratification from states in the form of titles and privileges they crystallized into nobilities, who in turn supplied the principal European rulers for many centuries. Coercive means, like capital, can both accumulate and concentrate: some groups (such as monastic orders) have few coercive means, but those few are concentrated in a small number of hands; others (such as armed frontiersmen) have many coercive means that are widely dispersed. Coercive means and capital merge where the same objects (e.g. workhouses) serve exploitation and domination. For the most part, however, they remain sufficiently distinct to allow us to analyze them separately.

When the accumulation and concentration of coercive means grow together, they produce states; they produce distinct organizations that control the chief concentrated means of coercion within well-defined territories, and exercise priority in some respects over all other organizations operating within those territories (see figure 1.6). Efforts to subordinate neighbors and fight off more distant rivals create state structures in the form not only of armies but also of

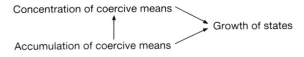

Figure 1.6   How coercion generates the growth of states.

civilian staffs that gather the means to sustain armies and that organize the ruler's day-to-day control over the rest of the civilian population.

WAR DRIVES STATE FORMATION AND TRANSFORMATION

The deployment of coercive means in war and domestic control presents warriors with two dilemmas. First, to the extent that they are successful in subduing their rivals outside or inside the territory they claim, the wielders of coercion find themselves obliged to administer the lands, goods, and people they acquire; they become involved in extraction of resources, distribution of goods, services, and income, and adjudication of disputes. But administration diverts them from war, and creates interests that sometimes tell against war. We can see the dilemma in the five-century conquest of Muslim Spain by Christian warriors. Starting with the taking of Coimbra in 1064, standard siege practice ran like this:

> Residents of a town under siege who surrendered promptly could remain with full freedoms after the conquest. If the Muslims surrendered after having been under siege for some time, they could leave with only those goods they could carry. If they waited for the town to fall by force, they faced death or enslavement.
>
> (Powers 1988: 18)

Any of the three responses set a problem for conquerors. The first imposed the obligation – at least temporarily – to establish a system of parallel rule. The second called for a redistribution of property as well as the settlement and administration of a depopulated town. The third left slaves in the hands of the victors, and posed even more sharply the challenge of reestablishing production and population. In one way or another, conquest entailed administration. On a larger scale, these problems dogged the whole reconquest of Iberia. In different forms, they marked the history of conquest throughout Europe.

The second dilemma parallels the first. Preparation for war, especially on a large scale, involves rulers ineluctably in extraction. It builds up an infrastructure of taxation, supply, and administration that requires maintenance of itself and often grows faster than the armies and navies that it serves; those who run the infrastructure acquire power and interests of their own; their interests and power limit significantly the character and intensity of warfare any particular state can carry on. Europe's Mongol and Tatar states resolved the dilemmas by raiding and looting without building much durable administration, but their strategy put inherent limits on their power, and eventually made them vulnerable to well-financed mass armies. In contrast highly commercial states such as Genoa resolved the dilemmas by borrowing or contracting out the structure necessary to extract the means of war. Between the two extremes, European states found a number of other ways of reconciling the demands of warmaking, extraction, and other major activities.

European states differed significantly, indeed, with respect to their salient activities and organizations. Three different types of state have all proliferated in various parts of Europe during major segments of the period since 990: tribute-taking empires; systems of fragmented sovereignty such as city-states and urban federations, and national states. The first built a large military and extractive apparatus, but left most local administration to regional powerholders who retained great autonomy. In systems of fragmented sovereignty, temporary coalitions and consultative institutions played significant parts in war and extraction, but little durable state apparatus emerged on a national scale. National states unite substantial military, extractive, administrative, and sometimes even distributive and productive organizations in a relatively coordinated central structure. The long survival and coexistence of all three types tells against any notion of European state formation as a single, unilinear process, or of the national state – which did, indeed, eventually prevail – as an inherently superior form of government.

Over the centuries, tribute-taking empires have dominated the world history of states. Empires appeared mainly under conditions of relatively low accumulation of coercive means with high concentration of the available means. When anyone other than the emperor accumulated important coercive means, or the emperor lost the ability to deploy massive coercion, empires often disintegrated. For all its appearance of massive durability, the Chinese Empire suffered incessantly from rebellions, invasions, and movements for autonomy, and long spent a major part of its budget on tribute to Mongols and other nomadic predators. Nor did Europe's empires enjoy greater stability. Napoleon's 1808 invasion of the Iberian peninsula, for instance, shattered much of the Spanish overseas empire. Within months, movements for independence formed in most of Spanish Latin America, and within ten years practically all of the region had broken into independent states.

Federations, city-states, and other arrangements of fragmented sovereignty differed from empires in almost every respect. They depended on relatively high accumulations, and relatively low concentrations, of coercion; the widespread urban militias of fourteenth-century western Europe typify that combination. In such states, a relatively small coalition of nominal subjects could equal the ruler's forces, while individuals, groups, and whole populations had abundant opportunities for defection to competing jurisdictions.

Fourteenth-century Prussia and Pomerania offer a telling contrast: in Prussia, then dominated by the Teutonic Knights, no great princes rivalled the Knights' Grand Master, and towns wielded little power. But the landlords installed by the Knights had wide discretion within their own extensive domains, just so long as revenues flowed to the Knights. In nearby Pomerania, a duchy established simultaneously by smaller-scale German conquests and alliances, many armed rivals to the duke arose, and smaller lords took to outright banditry, as towns dominated the duchy's Estates and provided major military forces in time of war.

During the 1326–8 war between the dukes of Pomerania and Mecklenburg, Pomerania's towns generally sided with their duke while nobles aligned themselves with Mecklenburg. When the Pomeranian house won, the Estates, in which the cities had much say, "were granted far-reaching privileges: the guardianship over minor dukes, the decision whether new ducal castles should be built or pulled down, the right to choose a new master if ever the duke broke his promises or wronged his subjects" (Carsten 1954: 90). The cities' ability to give or withhold support afforded them great bargaining power.

In between tribute-taking empires and city-states stand national states – built around war, statemaking, and extraction like other states, but compelled by bargaining over the subject population's cession of coercive means to invest heavily in protection, adjudication, and sometimes even production and distribution. The later history of Prussia illustrates the process by which national states formed. During the fourteenth century, as we have seen, the Teutonic Knights established a centralized empire there. During the fifteenth century, the Knights, shaken by plague, out-migration of peasants, and military defeat, began to disintegrate, and the regional magnates they had previously controlled became Prussian political powers in their own right. They used their power to impose greater and greater restrictions on the peasants who remained on their estates; with coerced labor the increasingly powerful landlords shifted toward demesne farming and the export of grain to western Europe.

At the same time, the rulers of Brandenburg and Pomerania, previously weakened by alliances of their dukes with prosperous burghers, began to win their incessant struggles with the towns, as the towns' position in international trade declined and the ability of the Hanseatic League to intercede on their behalf weakened. The rulers then had to bargain with noble-dominated Estates, which acquired the fundamental power to grant – or deny – royal revenues for war and dynastic aggrandizement. Over the next few centuries the Hohenzollern margraves of Brandenburg fought their way to pre-eminence in what became Brandenburg-Prussia, absorbing much of old Pomerania in the process; they contracted marriage and diplomatic alliances that eventually expanded their domains into adjacent areas and into the capital-rich areas of the lower Rhine; and they negotiated agreements with their nobility that ceded privileges and powers to the lords within their own regions, but gave the monarch access to regular revenues.

Out of battles, negotiations, treaties, and inheritances emerged a national state in which the great landlords of Prussia, Brandenburg, and Pomerania had great power within domains the crown had never wrested from them. During the eighteenth century, such monarchs as Frederick the Great locked the last pieces of the structure into place by incorporating peasants and lords alike into the army, the one under the command of the other. Prussia's army mimicked the countryside, with nobles serving as officers, free peasants as sergeants, and serfs as ordinary soldiers. Peasants and serfs paid the price: many peasants fell into serfdom, and "In war and peace Old Prussia's military obligations weakened the social position, the legal rights, and the property holding of serfs vis à vis the noble estate" (Busch 1962: 68). In this respect, Prussia followed a different path from Great Britain (where peasants became rural wage-workers) and France (where peasants survived with a fair amount of property into the nineteenth century). But Prussia, Great Britain, and France all trembled with struggles between monarch and major classes over the means of war, and felt the consequent creation of durable state structure.

As military allies and rivals, Prussia, Great Britain, and France also shaped each other's destinies. In the nature of the case, national states always appear in competition with each other, and gain their identities by contrast with rival states; they belong to *systems* of states. The broad differences among major types of state structure are schematized in figure 1.7. Well developed examples of all four kinds of state existed in different parts of Europe well after AD 990. Full-fledged empires flourished into the seventeenth century, and the last major zones of fragmented sovereignty only consolidated into national states late in the nineteenth.

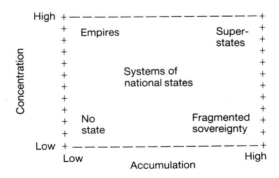

Figure 1.7   Alternative conditions of state growth as functions of accumulation and concentration of coercion.

Rulers of the three types faced some common problems, but faced them differently. Of necessity, they distributed means of coercion unevenly through the territories they sought to control. Most often they concentrated force at the center and at the frontiers, attempting to maintain their authority in between by means of secondary coercive clusters, loyal local wielders of coercion, roving patrols, and widespread collection of intelligence. The Ottoman Empire, for example, created two overlapping systems, one consisting of the *kazas* and other units of civil administration, governed by kadis, the other composed of *sancaks* and other districts of the feudal cavalry, governed by a military commander; in time of conquest, the military system tended to absorb the civilian, at the cost of losses in revenue (Pitcher 1972: 124).

The larger the state and the greater the discrepancy between the distribution of coercion and that of capital, however, the stronger the incentives to resist central control, and for alliances to form among different enemies of the state, whether inside or outside its territory. In the *sancak* of Belgrade, part of nineteenth-century Ottoman Serbia, the empire-serving notables (*avan*)

logically concluded that they could enrich themselves more easily by creating their own redistributive system than by serving simply as the stewards of redistribution. They seized a share in the production of the peasantry, levied illegal tolls on the passage of livestock, and retained a portion of the fees collected at the customs stations of the Sava and Danube entrepôts, especially Belgrade, through which passed the cotton exports of Serres and Salonika destined for Vienna and Germany. In particular, they asserted their right to the *deveto*, ostensibly an illegal tribute of one-ninth of a peasant's harvest after the collection by the timariot (in return for cavalry service to the state) of the *deseto* or tenth. By this action and other acts of violence against person or property, the dues in kind exacted from many Serbian peasants were suddenly doubled, sometimes tripled.

(Stoianovitch 1989: 262–3)

This sort of devolution of power occurred widely in the disintegrating Ottoman Empire of the nineteenth century. But in one version or another, agents of indirect rule everywhere in Europe faced temptations to emulate their Serbian cousins. Given the costs of communication and the advantages regional agents of the crown could gain by evading demands from the center or by using delegated national means for local or individual ends, all rulers faced repeated challenges to their hegemony.

Rulers of empires generally sought to co-opt local and regional powerholders without utterly transforming their bases of power and to create a distinctive corps of royal servants – often present or former comrades in arms – whose fate depended on that of the crown. Mamluk sultans, to take an extreme case, maintained a whole caste of enslaved foreigners who became warriors and administrators; except for fiefs directly supporting officials, however, the Mamluks left local magnates in place within their domains. With such a system, slaves actually ruled Egypt and adjacent areas of the Middle East from 1260 to 1517 (Garcin 1988). Rulers of national states usually tried harder to create a complete administrative hierarchy and to eliminate autonomous bases of power. The Electors and kings of Brandenburg-Prussia, for example, ceded great power to the landholding Junkers, but tied them closely to the crown by means of offices, tax exemptions, and military service.

Those who ruled, or claimed to rule, in city-states, federations, and other states of fragmented sovereignty often managed to exercise tight control over a single city and its immediate hinterland. Beyond that scale, however, they had no choice but to bargain with the authorities of competing centers. The local control usually depended not only on the city's coercive forces, but also on extensive rural landholding by the urban ruling class. Once Florence began its aggressive expansion beyond the municipal level during the fourteenth century, its tyrants replaced the rulers of conquered cities with their own men as much as possible, but selected the replacements from among the local patricians.

All these arrangements left considerable power and discretion in the hands of local potentates, just so long as they contained the monarch's enemies and kept the revenues flowing to the national capital. On a national scale, in fact, no European state (except, perhaps, Sweden) made a serious attempt to institute direct rule from top to bottom until the era of the French Revolution. Before then all but the smallest states relied on some version of indirect rule, and thus ran serious risks of disloyalty, dissimulation, corruption, and rebellion. But indirect rule made it possible to govern without erecting, financing, and feeding a bulky administrative apparatus.

The transition to direct rule gave rulers access to citizens and the resources they controlled through household taxation, mass conscription, censuses, police systems, and many other invasions of small-scale social life. But it did so at the cost of widespread resistance, extensive bargaining, and the creation of rights and perquisites for citizens. Both the penetration and the bargaining laid down new state structures, inflating the government's budgets, personnel, and organizational diagrams. The omnivorous state of our own time took shape.

It is all too easy to treat the formation of states as a type of engineering, with kings and their ministers as the designing engineers. Four facts compromise the image of confident planning.

1   Rarely did Europe's princes have in mind a precise model of the sort of state they were producing, and even more rarely did they act efficiently to produce such a model state. As the Norman Roger de Hauteville wrested Sicily from Arab control between 1060 and 1075, for example, he improvised a government by incorporating segments of the existing Muslim administration, drew Muslim soldiers into his own army, and maintained Muslim, Jewish, and Greek Christian churches, but took over large tracts of land as his own domain and parceled out other lands to his followers. Calabria, which belonged to Sicily, remained very Greek in culture and political style, with Byzantine offices and rituals brought wholesale into Norman government. But Arab institutions also had their place: Roger's chief minister bore the wonderful title Emir of

Emirs and Archonte of Archontes. The resulting state was certainly distinctive and new, but it did not emanate from a coherent plan. Roger de Hauteville and his followers created a mosaic of adaptations and improvisations (Mack Smith 1968a: 15–25).

2   No one designed the principal components of national states – treasuries, courts, central administrations, and so on. They usually formed as more or less inadvertent by-products of efforts to carry out more immediate tasks, especially the creation and support of armed force. When the French crown, greatly expanding its involvement in European wars during the 1630s, stretched its credit to the point of bankruptcy, the local authorities and officeholders on whom the king's ministers ordinarily relied for the collection of revenues ceased cooperating. At that point chief minister Richelieu, in desperation, began sending out his own agents to coerce or bypass local authorities (Collins 1988). Those emissaries were the royal intendants, who became the mainstays of state authority in French regions under Colbert and Louis XIV. Only in faulty retrospect do we imagine the intendants as deliberately designed instruments of Absolutism.

3   Other states – and eventually the entire system of states – strongly affected the path of change followed by any particular state. From 1066 to 1815, great wars with French monarchs formed the English state, French intervention complicated England's attempts to subdue Scotland and Ireland, and French competition stimulated England's adoption of Dutch fiscal innovations. From the sixteenth century onward, settlements of major wars regularly realigned the boundaries and the rulers of European states, right up to World War II; the division of Germany, the incorporation of Estonia, Latvia, and Lithuania into the Soviet Union, and the dismantling of most European overseas empires all stemmed more or less directly from the settlements of World War II. In none of these cases can we reasonably think of a self-guided state acting on its own.

4   Struggle and bargaining with different classes in the subject population significantly shaped the states that emerged in Europe. Popular rebellions, for example, usually lost, but each major one left marks on the state in the form of repressive policies, realignments of classes for or against the state, and explicit settlements specifying the rights of the affected parties. During the fierce revolt of the Florentine workers (the Ciompi) in 1378, two of the three new woolworkers' guilds formed during the rebellion defected to the government and thereby destroyed a front that had seized effective power in the city; in the settlement, the still-insurrectionary (and more proletarian) guild lost its right to exist, but the two collaborators joined the guilds that paraded and deliberated as part of the official municipal government (Schevill 1963: 279; Cohn 1980: 129–54).

On a smaller scale, both the resistance and the cooperation of knights, financiers, municipal officers, landlords, peasants, artisans, and other actors created and recreated state structure over the long run. Thus the class structure of the population that fell under the jurisdiction of a particular state significantly affected the organization of that state, and variations in class structure from one part of Europe to another produced systematic geographic differences in the character of states. Not only the ruling classes, but all classes whose resources and activities affected preparation for war, left their imprint on European states.

Twin facts, for example, strongly affected the path of Swedish state formation: first, the overwhelming presence of a peasantry that held plenty of land well into the eighteenth century; second, the relative inability of landlords either to form great estates or to coerce peasant labor on their lands. That exceptional rural class structure prevented the royal strategy of granting nobles fiscal and judicial privileges and assistance in bending peasants to their will in return for collaboration in extracting revenues and military service from the peasantry – even though such a strategy prevailed in nearby areas such as Prussia and Russia. It also helps explain the survival of a separate peasant Estate which actually had some power over governmental action, and the fact that in its period of imperial expansion Sweden turned rapidly from the hiring of mercenaries on the European market to the creation of militias whose members received land, or the income from land, in return for their service. In Sweden as elsewhere, the ambient class structure constrained rulers' attempts to create armed force, and therefore left its impact on the very organization of the state.

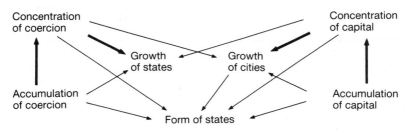

Figure 1.8　Relations among coercion, capital, states, and cities.

A more general and schematic statement of the essential relationships is given in figure 1.8. The diagram takes this shape for the reasons we surveyed earlier: war and preparation for war involved rulers in extracting the means of war from others who held the essential resources – men, arms, supplies, or money to buy them – and were reluctant to surrender them without strong pressure or compensation. The organization of major social classes within a state's territory, and their relations to the state, significantly affected the strategies rulers employed to extract resources, the resistance they met, the struggle that resulted, the sorts of durable organization extraction and struggle laid down, and therefore the efficiency of resource extraction. Within limits set by the demands and rewards of other states, extraction and struggle over the means of war created the central organizational structures of states. The organization of major social classes, and their relations to the state varied significantly from Europe's coercion-intensive regions (areas of few cities and agricultural predominance, where direct coercion played a major part in production) to its capital-intensive regions (areas of many cities and commercial predominance, where markets, exchange, and market-oriented production prevailed). Demands major classes made on the state, and the influence of those classes over the state, varied correspondingly. The relative success of different extractive strategies, and the strategies rulers actually applied, therefore varied significantly from coercion-intensive to capital-intensive regions. As a consequence, the organizational forms of states followed distinctly different trajectories in these different parts of Europe. Such circumstances belie any idea that European monarchs simply adopted a visible model of state formation and did their best to follow it.

LONG TRENDS AND INTERACTIONS

Another illusion must also disappear. So far I have presented the relationships as though capital and coercion always moved toward greater accumulation and concentration. For the thousand years that concern us here, those have been the main trends. Yet even within the European experience many states have undergone deflation in both regards; Poland endured many reversals in capital and coercion, successive Burgundian and Habsburg empires collapsed, and the sixteenth-century religious wars seriously depleted Europe's stocks of capital and coercive means. The history of European state formation runs generally upward toward greater accumulation and concentration, but it runs across jagged peaks and profound valleys.

Accumulation probably made the larger long-term difference to the history of the European economy. But concentration, deconcentration, and reconcentration of coercion mark off major chapters in the story of state formation; the concentration came to depend in important degree on the availability of concentrated capital. Exactly why and how that was so will preoccupy this book's later sections and take us into complicated questions of fiscal policy. Yet the central link is simple: over the long run, far more than other activities, war and preparation for war produced the major components of European states. States that lost wars commonly contracted, and often ceased to exist. Regardless of their size, states having the largest coercive means tended to win wars; efficiency (the ratio of output to input) came second to effectiveness (total output).

Through the interplay of competition, technological change, and the sheer scale of the largest belligerent states, war and the creation of coercive means became immensely more expensive over time. As that happened, fewer and fewer rulers could create military means from their own routine resources; more and more they turned to short-term borrowing and long-term taxation. Both activities went more easily where concentrations of capital already existed. But everywhere they produced changes in governmental organization.

How did changes in warfare and state organization relate to each other? As a first approximation, we can divide the years since AD 990 into four segments, with varying temporal limits from one part of Europe to another:

1   *patrimonialism*: a time (up to the fifteenth century in much of Europe) when tribes, feudal levies, urban militias, and similar customary forces played the major part in warfare, and monarchs generally extracted what capital they needed as tribute or rent from lands and populations that lay under their immediate control;

2   *brokerage*: an era (roughly 1400 to 1700 in important parts of Europe) when mercenary forces recruited by contractors predominated in military activity, and rulers relied heavily on formally independent capitalists for loans, for management of revenue-producing enterprises, and for installation and collection of taxes;

3   *nationalization*: a period (especially 1700 to 1850 or so in much of Europe) when states created mass armies and navies drawn increasingly from their own national populations, while sovereigns absorbed armed forces directly into the state's administrative structure, and similarly took over the direct operation of the fiscal apparatus, drastically curtailing the involvement of independent contractors;

4   *specialization*: an age (from approximately the mid-nineteenth century to the recent past) in which military force grew as a powerful specialized branch of national government, the organizational separation of fiscal from military activity increased, the division of labor between armies and police sharpened, representative institutions came to have a significant influence over military expenditures, and states took on a greatly expanded range of distributive, regulatory, compensatory, and adjudicative activities.

Clearly the relations between capital and coercion changed significantly from one period to the next.

The transformation of states by war, in its turn, altered the stakes of war. Through the period of patrimonialism, conquerors sought tribute much more than they sought the stable control of the population and resources within the territories they overran; whole empires grew up on the principle of extracting rents and gifts from the rulers of multiple regions without penetrating significantly into their systems of rule. In the move to brokerage and then to nationalization, a closely administered territory became an asset worth fighting for, since only such a territory provided the revenues to sustain armed force. But in the age of specialization, states accumulated claimants to their services so rapidly that war became, even more than before, a means of satisfying the economic interests of the ruling coalition by gaining access to the resources of other states. Since World War II, with the extension of the European state system to the entire world and the accompanying rigidification of national boundaries, that has increasingly meant exercising influence over other states without actually incorporating their territory into that of the more powerful state.

Those were the broad trends. Yet more than one combination of capital and coercion appeared at each stage in the growth of European states. We might distinguish a coercion-intensive, a capital-intensive, and a capitalized coercion path to state formation. They do not represent alternative "strategies" so much as contrasting conditions of life. Rulers pursuing similar ends – especially successful preparation for war – in very different environments responded to those environments by fashioning distinctive relations to the major social classes within them. The reshaping of relations between ruler and ruled produced new, contrasting forms of government, each more or less adapted to its social setting.

In the *coercion-intensive* mode, rulers squeezed the means of war from their own populations and others they conquered, building massive structures of extraction in the process. Brandenburg and Russia – especially in their phases as tribute-taking empires – illustrate the coercion-intensive mode. At the very extreme of the mode, however, armed landlords wielded so much power that no one of them could establish durable control over the rest; for several centuries, the Polish and Hungarian nobilities actually elected their own kings, and struck them down when they strove too hard for supreme power.

In the *capital-intensive* mode, rulers relied on compacts with capitalists – whose interests they served with care – to rent or purchase military force, and thereby warred without building vast permanent state structures. City-states, city-empires, urban federations, and other forms of fragmented sovereignty commonly fall into this path of change. Genoa, Dubrovnik, the Dutch Republic, and, for a time, Catalonia, exemplify the capital-intensive mode. As the history of the Dutch Republic illustrates, at the extreme this mode produced federations of largely autonomous city-states, and constant negotiation among them over state policy.

In the intermediate *capitalized coercion* mode, rulers did some of each, but spent more of their effort than did their capital-intensive neighbors on incorporating capitalists and sources of capital directly into the structures of their states. Holders of capital and coercion interacted on terms of relative equality. France and England eventually followed the capitalized coercion mode, which produced full-fledged national states earlier than the coercion-intensive and capital-intensive modes did.

Driven by the pressures of international competition (especially by war and preparation for war) all three paths eventually converged on concentrations of capital and of coercion out of all proportion to those that prevailed in AD 990. From the seventeenth century onward the capitalized coercion form proved more effective in war, and therefore provided a compelling model for states that had originated in other combinations of coercion and capital. From the nineteenth century to the recent past, furthermore, all European states involved themselves much more heavily than before in building social infrastructure, in providing services, in regulating economic activity, in controlling population movements, and in assuring citizens' welfare; all these activities began as by-products of rulers' efforts to acquire revenues and compliance from their subject populations, but took on lives and rationales of their own. Contemporary socialist states differ from capitalist states, on the average, in exerting more direct, self-conscious control over production and distribution. As compared with the range of states that have existed in Europe over the last thousand years, nevertheless, they belong recognizably to the same type as their capitalist neighbors. They, too, are national states.

Before their recent convergence, the coercion-intensive, capital-intensive and capitalized coercion paths led to very different kinds of states. Even after convergence, states retained some features – for example, the character of their representative institutions – that clearly reflected their earlier historical experiences. All three types of state were quite viable under certain conditions that actually prevailed in Europe at various times before the present. Indeed, at the abdication of Charles V in 1555, the major part of Europe lay under imperial hegemony, rather than under the control of national states in any strong sense of the term.

At that point, Suleyman the Magnificent's Ottoman Empire (in addition to dominating Anatolia and much of the Middle East) occupied most of the Balkans and held in vassalage states from the Volga to the Adriatic. Charles V, as Holy Roman Emperor, Emperor of Spain, and Elder of the Habsburgs, then claimed rule over Spain, the Netherlands, Milan, Naples, Sicily, Sardinia, Austria, Bohemia, Burgundy, Franche-Comté and (more contestably) the swarm of states in the territory we now call Germany. Further east, Poland, Lithuania, Muscovy, and the Don Cossacks also organized in imperial style. In 1555, northern Italy, Switzerland, and significant parts of the Holy Roman Empire remained areas of intensely fragmented sovereignty, while only France and England resembled our conventional models of national states. By that time, city-states and other small-scale organizations were losing ground relative to other forms of state. Yet the Dutch Republic was soon to prove that federations of cities and adjacent territories could still hold their own as world powers. Empires, furthermore, were advancing. Nothing then assured the ultimate victory of the national state.

The lesson is clear. To use twentieth-century strength as the main criterion of effective state formation (as many analysts do) means succumbing to the temptations of teleology, misconceiving the relations among cities, states, capital, and coercion in the European past. We can avoid these pitfalls by following the choices of statemakers, and the consequences of those choices, forward from an early date – here set arbitrarily at AD 990 – to the present.

That forward-looking strategy will allow us to reach some tentative answers to this book's crucial question: *What accounts for the great variation over time and space in the kinds of states that have prevailed in Europe since AD 990, and why did European states eventually converge on different variants of the national state?* Although the question is formidably broad, it translates into narrower, more manageable problems such as:

1   What accounts for the roughly concentric pattern of state formation in Europe as a whole, with large but thinly-controlled states as the Ottoman Empire and Muscovy forming early around the periphery, smaller but more tightly governed states such as France and Brandenburg grouped in a rough intermediate zone, and a central band of city-states, principalities, federations, and other varieties of intensely fragmented sovereignty that only after 1790 consolidated into larger states?

2   Why, despite obvious interests to the contrary, did rulers frequently accept the establishment of institutions representing the major classes within the populations that fell subject to the state's jurisdiction?

3   Why did European states vary so much with respect to the incorporation of urban oligarchies and institutions into national state structure, with the Dutch Republic's state practically indistinguishable from its cluster of municipal governments, the Polish state almost oblivious to urban institutions, and a dozen other variants in between those extremes?

4   Why did political and commercial power slide from the city-states and city-empires of the Mediterranean to the substantial states and relatively subordinated cities of the Atlantic?

5   Why did city-states, city-empires, federations, and religious organizations lose their importance as prevailing kinds of state in Europe?

6   Why did war shift from conquest for tribute and struggle among armed tribute-takers to sustained battles among massed armies and navies?

The questions remain large, but not so large as the demand for a general explanation of the alternative trajectories taken by European states. The challenge, then, is to address this huge problem and its more manageable subsidiaries by close examination of the various paths that states actually took in different parts of Europe after AD 990. That will involve identifying the main processes transforming states, and sorting them out into their coercion-intensive, capital-intensive, and capitalized-coercion variants.

A book on these questions must steer a narrow road between randomness and teleology. On one side, the blank wall of randomness, in which every history seems *sui generis*, one king or battle after another. On the other, the crevasse of teleology, in which the outcome of state formation seems to explain its entire course. I will try to avoid the blank wall and the crevasse by pointing out that the paths of state formation were multiple but not infinite, that at any particular historical juncture several distinctly different futures were possible, that states, rulers, and citizens influenced each other profoundly, that systematic problems and processes connected the histories of all European states, hence the relations among them. If successful, the chapters to come will tell a tale of diversity in unity, of unity in diversity, of choice and consequences.

PROSPECTS

Let me confess at once: my reading of the European past is unconventional, unproved, and riven with gaps. On the whole, students of European states have prudently avoided syntheses on the scale of a thousand years. Those who have made the leap have generally either sought to explain what was distinctive about the West as a whole, or proposed a single standard path of state formation, or both. They have usually proceeded retrospectively, seeking the origins of the states we now know as Germany or Spain and ignoring states that disappeared along the way rather than trying to chart the whole range of state formation.

By claiming the existence of multiple paths as a function of the relative ease with which capital and coercion concentrated, in arguing a strong interdependence between the form of a state and its previous access to capital, and by seeking to replace a retrospective with a prospective analysis of transformations in state structure I am abandoning the solid ways of established scholarship for an adventure in rethinking the past. By discussing a thousand years in little more than two hundred pages, furthermore, I can hope to do no more than identify some important relationships, and illustrate how they worked.

A fully expanded version of the book's argument would give far greater weight to the dynamics of the European economy than the following pages do. First of all, I will say far too little about swings in prices, productivity, trade and population growth, neglecting among other things the probable importance of price rises in the thirteenth, sixteenth, and eighteenth centuries and of depressions in between for the viability of different kinds of states and the relative power of merchants, peasants, landlords, officials, and other social classes (Abel 1966, Frank 1978, Kriedte 1983, Wallerstein 1974–88).

Second, I will treat the changing organization of production and the resulting class structure only cursorily. That is not because I think it negligible. On the contrary: relations between landlords and cultivators made an enormous difference to the consequences of statemaking, protection, and extraction, as contrasts among Hungary, Florence, and England instantly demonstrate. The seventeenth-century Prussian state, for example, bore the marks of Prussia's earlier history: during the thirteenth and fourteenth centuries a crusading order, the Teutonic Knights, extended military control over that thinly-settled region, subdued the Slavs who had previously occupied it, induced German knights to come in and organize large estates, and encouraged cultivation by those knights' recruitment of peasants to clear and farm land that would be theirs in return for dues and service. Such arrangements at the level of household, village, or region clearly affected the viability of different kinds of taxation, conscription, and surveillance. But my assignment is already complicated enough. In order to concentrate on mechanisms of state formation I will repeatedly stereotype or take for granted the relations among landlords, peasants, agricultural proletarians, and other major rural actors.

In attempting to close in on the crucial relationships, furthermore, I will make no effort to review alternative theories of state formation, past or present. Nor will I try to state the pedigrees of the book's organizing ideas. Let us take for granted the existence of analyses by Karl Marx, Max Weber, Joseph Schumpeter, Stein Rokkan, Barrington Moore, Gabriel Ardant, and others that obviously bear on the book's subject matter; *cognoscenti* will surely notice their influence on almost every page, and reviewers will no doubt waste many of their words trying to pigeonhole the book into one school or another. To deal with those analyses, the theories behind them, and the historical phenomenon of state formation at the same time would blunt the analysis and double its length without advancing it greatly. Instead, the book will focus on the actual processes of state formation.

In the interests of compact presentation, I will likewise resort to metonymy and reification on page after page. Metonymy, in that I will repeatedly speak of "rulers," "kings," and "sovereigns" as if they represented a state's entire decision-making apparatus, thus reducing to a single point a complex, contingent set of social relations. Metonymy, in that cities actually stand for regional networks of production and trade in which the large settlements are focal points. Reification, in that I will time and again impute a unitary interest, rationale, capacity, and action to a state, a ruling class, or the people subject to their joint control. Without a simplifying model employing metonymy and reification, we have no hope of identifying the main connections in the complex process of European state formation.

Most of the time the implicit model will contain these elements: a *ruler* summing up the joint decision-making of a state's most powerful officers; a *ruling class* allied with the ruler and controlling major means of production within the territory under the state's jurisdiction; other *clients* enjoying special benefits from their association with the state; *opponents, enemies, and rivals* of the state, its ruler, its ruling class, and its clients, both within and outside the state's own area; the remainder of the *population* falling under the state's jurisdiction; a *coercive apparatus* including armies, navies, and other organized, concentrated means of force that operate under the state's control; and the *civilian apparatus* of the state, consisting especially of distinctive fiscal, administrative, and judicial organizations that operate under its control.

Most of the arguments to come entail the description and explanation of the different ways that rulers, ruling classes, clients, opponents, general populations, coercive organizations, and civil administrations articulated in European history from AD 990 onward. Occasionally they unpack one or another of these reified categories – most notably by specifying when, why, and with what effects capitalists (themselves, to be sure, a reified class of people) fell into one or another of the categories. But usually the arguments proceed as if each category were real, unitary and unproblematic. We pay that price for operating on the scale of a continent and a thousand years.

A final apology. On such a scale, I must deal with historical facts like a rock skipping water; spinning quickly from high point to high point without settling for more than an instant at a time. I do not know all the history one would need to write this book fully, and to supply all the documentation for the history I think I do know would burden the text immeasurably. On the recent growth of state activity, for example, any responsible author would want to cite Reinhard Bendix, Walter Korpi, Theda Skocpol, Goran Therborn, and many more. I do nothing of the sort, generally reserving citations for direct quotations and esoteric or controversial information. Clearly, experts will have to scrutinize my rendering of European histories, and ponder whether its errors vitiate its arguments.

Given their broad, synthetic, and speculative character, this book's arguments do not lend themselves immediately to verification or refutation. Yet we can judge them wrong to the degree that:

1   rulers having very different relations to capital and coercion nevertheless pursued similar strategies, with similar effects, when they tried to build armed force and state power;

2   major moments in the growth and transformation of particular states, and of the European state system as a whole, did *not* correspond to war and preparation for war;

3   efforts to amass the means of armed force did *not* produce durable features of state structure;

4   rulers deliberately set out to construct states according to preconceived designs, and succeeded in following those designs;

5   some or all of the empirical regularities I have claimed – especially (a) state formation's geography, (b) differential incorporation of urban oligarchies and

institutions into national state structure, (c) development of representative institutions despite rulers' contrary interests, (d) movement of political and commercial power from Mediterranean to Atlantic, (e) decline of city-states, city-empires, federations, and religious organizations, and (f) shift of war to sustained battles among massed armies and navies – do not, in fact, hold up to historical scrutiny;

6   alternative explanations provide more economical and/or convincing accounts of those empirical regularities that *do* hold up to scrutiny.

If any of these holds true, my argument faces a serious challenge. If all of them hold true, it is clearly wrong.

Important theoretical issues are at stake. One might expect a follower of Joseph Strayer, for example, to hold that the domestic peacemaking activities of monarchs began much earlier and played a much larger part in people's acceptance of the state than my account implies, and therefore to uphold most of the checklist's charges against the book's analysis. One might expect a follower of Douglass North to claim that the state's construction and protection of property rights underlay many of the changes I have attributed to preparation for war. One might expect a follower of Immanuel Wallerstein to insist that the activities of states forwarded the interests of capitalists to an even larger degree than I have allowed, and a follower of Perry Anderson to counter (at least for the middle period of my analysis) that the argument greatly underestimates the weight of European nobilities in the creation of bulky "absolutist" states. Thus the ways in which my arguments are right or wrong bear on widely-discussed disagreements concerning European state formation.

The checklist provides a means of sorting possible criticisms of the book into legitimate, semi-legitimate, and illegitimate. It would be fully legitimate, and quite illuminating, to establish that one of the conditions just listed, or a similar condition implied by the book's arguments did, indeed, hold for some substantial block of European experience. It would be semi-legitimate to show that the argument did not account for certain major, durable features of particular states. (The criterion would be only semi-legitimate because it would show that the argument was incomplete – which I concede readily in advance – but not that it was wrong.)

It would be illegitimate to complain that the argument neglects variables the critic happens to regard as important: physical environment, ideology, military technology, or something else. The missing-variable criticism only becomes legitimate when the critic shows that neglect of the variable causes a false reading of relationships among variables that *do* appear in the argument. The point is not to give a "complete" account (whatever that might be), but to get the main connections right.

In pursuit of that goal, the next chapter concentrates on the changing geography of cities and states in Europe over the inquiry's thousand years. Chapter 3 takes up the mechanisms by which the rulers of states acquired the means to carry on their major activities – especially the creation of armed force – and the implications of those mechanisms for state structure. Chapter 4 concentrates on relations between states and citizens, tracing the formation through bargaining of massive, multi-function states. Chapter 5 deals with alternative paths of state formation, tracing out the effects of varying relationships to capital and coercion. Chapter 6 examines European states as a set of interacting parties, a system whose operation constrains the actions of its members. Chapter 7 brings the story up to the present, reflecting on contemporary relationships between capital and coercion in an effort to understand why military men have gained power in so many states since World War II, and in the hope of discerning in what ways European experience helps us understand the troubled states of our own time.

2

European Cities and States

A thousand years ago, Europe did not exist. A decade before the Millennium, the roughly thirty million people who lived at the western end of the Eurasian land mass had no compelling reason to think of themselves as a single set of people, connected by history and common fate. Nor did they. The disintegration of the Roman Empire, it is true, had left a significant part of what we now call Europe connected by roads, trade, religion, and collective memory. But that once-Roman world omitted much of the area east of the Rhine and north of the Black Sea. Nor was the late empire exclusively European; it had extended all around the Mediterranean into Asia and Africa.

From the viewpoint of trade and cultural contact, Millennial "Europe" broke into three or four loosely connected clusters: an eastern band corresponding roughly to today's European Russia, which maintained strong connections to Byzantium and to the major trade routes across Asia; a Mediterranean shared by Muslims, Christians, and Jews that was even more strongly linked to the great metropolises of the Middle East and Asia; a post-Roman system of cities, towns, roads, and rivers that was densest in an arc from central Italy to Flanders, but radiated into Germany and France; perhaps a distinct northern cluster including Scandinavia and the British Isles. (Many of these labels, to be sure, commit the crime of anachronism; short of adopting a ponderous set of geographic conventions, we have no alternative to using such designations as "Germany" and "British Isles" with a loud warning that they do not imply political or cultural connectedness.)

In the year 990 Muslim dominions controlled a major share of the Roman Empire's former space: all of the Mediterranean's southern shores and most of the Iberian peninsula, not to mention numerous Mediterranean islands and a

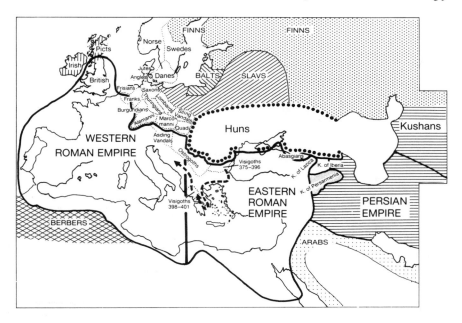

Figure 2.1   Europe in AD 406 (adapted from Colin McEvedy, *The Penguin Atlas of Medieval History*, Penguin Books, 1961. Copyright © 1961 Colin McEvedy).

few points along its northern coast. A loosely linked Byzantine empire extended from eastern Italy to the Black Sea's eastern end, while to its north an even more indefinite Russian state stretched to the Baltic. A Danish kingdom wielded power from the western Baltic over to the British Isles, while shifting Polish, Bohemian, and Hungarian principalities controlled the territory south of the Baltic. To their west lay a Saxon empire, claimant to the heritage of Charlemagne, while still farther in the same direction Hugh Capet ruled the kingdom of France.

None of these half-familiar place names, however, should disguise the enormous fragmentation of sovereignty then prevailing throughout the territory that would become Europe. The emperors, kings, princes, dukes, caliphs, sultans, and other potentates of AD 990 prevailed as conquerors, tribute-takers, and rentiers, not as heads of state that durably and densely regulated life within their realms. Inside their jurisdictions, furthermore, rivals and ostensible subordinates commonly used armed force on behalf of their own interests while paying little attention to the interests of their nominal sovereigns. Private armies

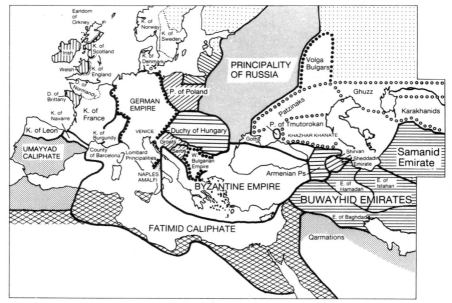

Figure 2.2   Europe in 998 (adapted from Colin McEvedy, *The Penguin Atlas of Medieval History*, Penguin Books, 1961. Copyright © 1961 Colin McEvedy).

proliferated through much of the continent. Nothing like a centralized national state existed anywhere in Europe.

Within the ring formed by these sprawling, ephemeral states sovereignty fragmented even more, as hundreds of principalities, bishoprics, city-states, and other authorities exercised overlapping control in the small hinterlands of their capitals. At the Millennium the pope, the Byzantine emperor and the Holy Roman emperor claimed most of the Italian peninsula, but in fact almost every important city and its hinterland operated as a political free agent. (In AD 1200, the Italian peninsula alone hosted two or three hundred distinct city-states: Waley 1969: 11.) Except for the relative urbanization of Muslim lands, the correlation between size of states and density of cities was negative: where cities swarmed, sovereignty crumbled.

Soon a rough chronology of changes in cities and states over the last thousand years will start to fall into place. In the meantime, however, let us settle for an arbitrary comparison at 500-year intervals, just to get a sense of how much changed. By 1490, the map and the reality had altered greatly. Armed Christians were driving Muslim rulers from their last major territory on the continent's western half – Granada. An Islamic Ottoman empire had displaced the Christian Byzantines between the Adriatic and Persia. The Ottomans were grinding away at Venetian power in the eastern Mediterranean and advancing into the Balkans. (In alliance with threatened Granada, they were also pursuing their first adventures in the western Mediterranean.) After centuries during which European wars had remained regional, and only an occasional crusade had involved the transalpine states militarily in the Mediterranean, furthermore, the kings of France and Spain were beginning to struggle for hegemony in Italy.

Figure 2.3   Europe in AD 1478 (adapted from Colin McEvedy, *The Penguin Atlas of Medieval History*, Penguin Books, 1961. Copyright © 1961 Colin McEvedy).

Around Europe's periphery, in 1490, stood rulers who dominated substantial territories: not only the Ottoman Empire, but also Hungary, Poland, Lithuania, Muscovy, the lands of the Teutonic Order, the Scandinavian Union, England, France, Spain, Portugal, Naples. Those powers lived largely from rents and tributes, and ruled through regional magnates who enjoyed great autonomy within their own terrains; the magnates frequently resisted or even rejected royal power. Yet the great kings and dukes of 1490 were, on the whole, consolidating and extending their domains.

Inside the broken circle of larger states, then, Europe remained a land of intensely fragmented sovereignty. A scattered Habsburg empire, it is true, was beginning to reach across the continent, while Venice dominated an important arc of the Adriatic. But the zone from northern Italy to Flanders, and east to the uncertain borders of Hungary and Poland, broke into hundreds of formally independent principalities, duchies, bishoprics, city-states, and other political

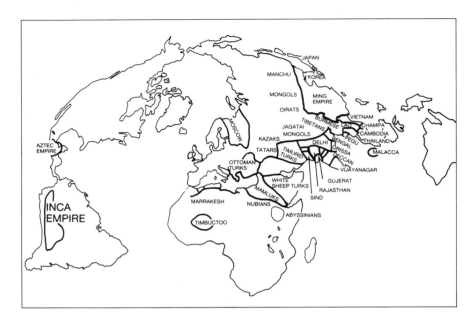

Figure 2.4   The world in AD 1490 (adapted from Colin McEvedy, *The Penguin Atlas of Modern History to 1815*, Penguin Books, 1972. Copyright © 1972 Colin McEvedy).

entities that generally could use force only in the immediate hinterlands of their capitals; south Germany alone included 69 free cities in addition to its multiple bishoprics, duchies, and principalities (Brady 1985: 10). "In spite of the border which a cartographer can draw around the area which opinion in the mid-fifteenth century accepted as within the Holy Roman Empire, that is the chiefly Germanic zone between France and Hungary, and Denmark and northern Italy," muses J. R. Hale, "he cannot colour in the multitude of cities, princely enclaves and militant ecclesiastical territories that saw themselves as actually or potentially independent, without giving the reader an impression that he is suffering from a disease of the retina" (Hale 1985: 14). Europe's 80 million people divided into something like 200 states, would-be states, statelets, and statelike organizations.

By 1990, another five centuries later, Europeans had greatly extended the work of consolidation. Six hundred million people now lived within the continent's perimeter. No Muslim state remained on the continent, although a powerful Islamic world thrived contentiously to the south and southeast of Europe and impressive residues of Muslim culture survived in Spain, the Balkans, and Turkey. A giant Russian state had taken shape on the east and stretched all the way to the Arctic and the Pacific, while a spacious Turkey crossed the Asian border to the southeast. Much of the continent had settled into states that occupied at least 40,000 square miles, not including colonies and dependencies: Bulgaria, Czechoslovakia, Finland, France, each of the two Germanies, Greece, Italy, Norway, Poland, Romania, Spain, Sweden, Turkey, the United Kingdom, and the not yet splintered USSR. Microstates such as Luxembourg and Andorra, although larger than many of the political entities that existed in 1490, had become curiosities. Depending on the rules for counting, the whole of Europe divided into a mere 25 to 28 states.

It took a long time for national states – relatively centralized, differentiated, and autonomous organizations successfully claiming priority in the use of force within large, contiguous, and clearly bounded territories – to dominate the European map. In 990 nothing about the world of manors, local lords, military raiders, fortified villages, trading towns, city-states, and monasteries foretold a consolidation into national states. In 1490 the future remained open; despite the frequent use of the word "kingdom," empires of one sort or another

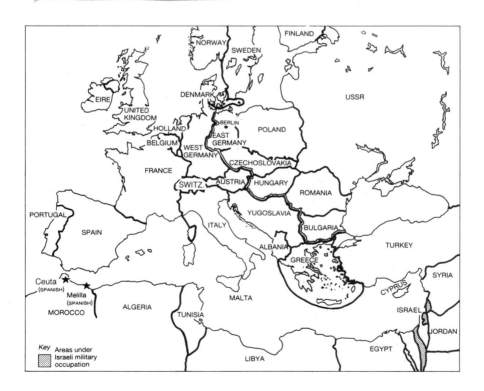

Figure 2.5   Europe in AD 1990.

claimed most of the European landscape, and federations remained viable in some parts of the continent. Some time after 1490 Europeans foreclosed those alternative opportunities, and set off decisively toward the creation of a system consisting almost entirely of relatively autonomous national states.

States, on the other hand, diminished in number and increased in area. In order to draw the changing map, we must apply the term "state" generously, to include any organization that commanded substantial means of coercion and successfully claimed durable priority over all other users of coercion within at least one clearly bounded territory. In the year 990 relatively large Muslim states dominated much of the western Mediterranean, including southern Spain and Africa's north coast. Other sizeable states included the kingdom of France, the Saxon empire, the Danish kingdom, Kievan Russia, Poland, Hungary, Bohemia, and the Byzantine Empire. On the whole, the rulers of these political entities drew tribute from the territories nominally under their control. But outside their home regions they barely administered their supposed domains, and saw their authority continually contested by rival potentates, including their own putative agents and vassals.

Consider Hungary, a state that grew from conquest by Magyars, one of many armed nomadic peoples who invaded Europe from the Eurasian steppe. During the tenth century, the bulk of the Magyars migrated from the Volga and overwhelmed the smaller number of tilling and forest-dwelling Slavs who inhabited the Carpathian Basin, which we now call Hungary (Pamlenyi 1975: 21–5). Once they moved west of the Carpathians, the shortage of natural pasture forced any predatory nomads to withdraw, thin their numbers, or dismount (Lindner 1981). After a century of marauding, the now-Christianized Hungarians settled increasingly into agriculture inside a territory almost without cities.

Their agricultural base did not prevent the Hungarian nobility from warring with their neighbors, struggling over the royal succession, or playing the European game of marriages and alliances. Their control of armed force, furthermore, permitted them to drive slaves and freemen alike toward a common serfdom. Towns grew up as feudal agriculture prospered, mines exported metals to the rest of Europe, and the region's trade routes knitted together with those of central and western Europe. German capital came to dominate Hungarian commerce and industry. Hungary's towns, however, remained tightly subordinate to their noble lords until, during the fifteenth century, the crown began to exert control over them.

During the later fifteenth century, King Janos Hunyadi and his son, King Matthias Corvinus built a relatively centralized and effective war machine, fighting off both the warlike Turks to their southeast and the hungry Habsburgs to their west. With the death of Matthias, however, the nobility counter-attacked, depriving his successor Ladislas of the means to keep his own army. In 1514 the effort to mount yet another crusade against the Turks incited a huge peasant rebellion, whose repression in turn definitively reduced the peasantry to servitude and abolished their right to change masters. In the struggle among magnates that accompanied the settlement of the peasant war, lawyer Istvan Verböczi set down the nobles' view of Hungarian customs, including the retributive laws against the peasantry and the provisions that

nobles enjoyed immunity from arrest without prior legal judgment, were subject only to a legally crowned king, paid no taxes whatsoever, and could be required to render military service only for the defense of the realm. Finally, the right of rebellion was guaranteed against any king who infringed upon the rights of the nobility in any way.

(McNeill 1975 [1964]: 17)

Verböczi's treatise became the standard authority for Hungarian law and "the bible of the nobility" (Pamlenyi 1975: 117). By 1526, Hungary had not one but two elected kings, and the two were at war with each other. Small wonder that in the following half-century Turks were able to capture half the territory of Hungary! In that era, clearly, large states were not necessarily strong states.

STATES AND COERCION

By 1490 Muslims were retreating from their last Iberian outpost, Granada, but building a substantial empire around the eastern Mediterranean and making inroads to the Balkans. States fielding large armies and extending some judicial and fiscal control over good-sized territories were beginning to appear around Europe's edges, and city-states were arming for land war as never before. The European map of 1490 assigns large areas to England, Sweden, Poland, Russia, and the Ottoman Empire, but also marks off dozens of duchies, principalities, archbishoprics, city-states, and other miniature states.

How many European states we distinguish depends on contestable decisions bearing on the very nature of the era's states: whether the 13 Swiss cantons (as of 1513) and the 84 free cities of the Ottoman Empire (as of 1521) count as separate entities, whether such technically autonomous dependencies of Aragon and Castile as Catalonia and Granada deserve recognition, whether the entire patchwork of the Low Countries constituted a single state (or only part of a state) under Habsburg hegemony, whether the tributary states under Ottoman control belonged individually to the European state system of the time. No plausible set of definitions yields fewer than 80 distinct units or more than 500. We might arbitrarily take 200 as the median number. The roughly 200 formally autonomous European political entities of the time controlled an average of 9,500 square miles, roughly the size of today's El Salvador, Lesotho, and Qatar.

Europe's population of approximately 62 million in 1490 divided up into an average of some 310,000 persons per state. Of course, averages obscure enormous variations: scores of Europe's smaller states and their populations would have fitted easily into Russia's vast territory. Nevertheless, Europe was beginning to consolidate into territorially distinct states organized around permanent military establishments, and military superiority was starting to give the larger states better chances of survival.

Only starting, to be sure. In 1490, armies consisted largely of mercenaries hired by the campaign, clients of great lords, and citizen militias. Standing armies had displaced urban militias in France and Burgundy, but few other realms. Tribute and personal rents still bulked large in royal revenues. Within the larger states, communities, guilds, churches, and regional magnates retained large areas of immunity and self-government. Administration chiefly concerned military, judicial and fiscal affairs. Europe's central zone continued to teem with tiny jurisdictions. Since city-states, leagues of cities, dynastic empires, principalities having only nominal bonds to larger monarchies or empires, and ecclesiastical entities such as the Teutonic Order all coexisted (however contentiously) on the continent, it was not clear that national states as we know them would become Europe's dominant organizations. Not until the nineteenth century, with Napoleon's conquests and the subsequent unifications of Germany and Italy, would almost all of Europe consolidate into mutually exclusive states having permanent, professional armed forces and exercising substantial control over people in areas of 40,000 square miles or more.

Over the next four centuries, many war settlements and a few deliberate federations drastically reduced the number of European states. During the nineteenth century, the number stabilized. At the beginning of 1848, for instance, Europe hosted from 20 to 100 states, depending on how one counts the 35 members of the German Confederation, the 17 papal states, the 22 technically autonomous segments of Switzerland, and a few dependent but formally distinct units such as Luxembourg and Norway: in the Almanach de Gotha, that directory of nobles and statesmen, the full alphabetical list then began with tiny Anhalt-Bernburg, Anhalt-Dessau and Anhalt-Kothan before getting to more substantial Austria, Baden, and Bavaria.

Major consolidations occurred with the formation of the German Empire and the kingdom of Italy. By the start of 1890, the roster of states had declined to about 30, of which nine were members of the German Empire. At the end of 1918, the count stood at around 25 separate states. Although boundaries changed significantly with the settlements of World Wars I and II, the number and size of European states did not change dramatically during the twentieth century. If, following Small and Singer, we count only those states large enough to make an independent military difference, we actually detect a slight reversal of the long-term trend: 21 contenders at the end of the Napoleonic Wars, 26 in 1848, 29 (now including Malta, Cyprus, and Iceland) in 1980 (Small and Singer 1982: 47–50).

In contrast to the 9,500 square miles of 1490, the 30 states of 1890 controlled an average of 63,000 square miles, which put them in the class of today's Nicaragua, Syria, and Tunisia. Instead of the 310,000 inhabitants of 1490, the average state of 1890 had about 7.7 million. Imagined as circles, states rose from an average radius of 55 miles to 142 miles. At a 55-mile radius, direct control of the hinterland by a single city's rulers was often feasible; at 142 miles, no one governed without a specialized apparatus of surveillance and intervention. Although such microstates as Andorra (175 square miles), Liechtenstein (61), San Marino (24) and even Monaco (0.7) survived the great consolidation, furthermore, inequalities of size declined radically over time.

Generally speaking, the last part of Europe to consolidate into substantial national states was the city-state band running from northern Italy, around the Alps, and down the Rhine to the Low Countries. The successive creations of Germany and Italy brought those prosperous but cantankerous little municipalities and their hinterlands under national control. It is as if Europeans discovered that under the conditions prevailing since 1790 or so, a viable state required a radius of at least 100 miles, and could not easily dominate more than a 250-mile radius.

CITIES AND CAPITAL

To see the geographic pattern more clearly, we should distinguish between city systems and systems of states. Europe's systems of cities represented the changing relations among concentrations of capital, its systems of states the changing relations among concentrations of coercion. European cities formed a loose hierarchy of commercial and industrial precedence within which at any point in time a few clusters of cities (usually grouped around a single hegemonic center) clearly dominated the rest. (The European hierarchy, to be sure, formed only part of a vaster urban network that reached far into Asia at the start of the period, and extended to Africa and the Americas as time went on.) In Fernand Braudel's useful simplification, Venice, Antwerp, Genoa, Amsterdam, London, and New York successively topped the European system of cities from the fourteenth century to the twentieth.

For dominance, the crucial matter was not so much size as centrality in the European network of trade, production, and capital accumulation. Nevertheless, the concentrations of capital and urban population corresponded closely enough for the dominant *cluster* of cities to be always also one of the largest. Using a rank–size criterion and some rather arbitrary blocking out of boundaries, J. C. Russell delineates medieval regions centering on Florence, Palermo, Venice, Milan, Augsburg, Dijon, Cologne, Prague, Magdeburg, Lübeck, Ghent, London, Dublin, Paris, Toulouse, Montpellier, Barcelona, Córdoba, Toledo, and Lisbon. The cities were denser and the regions correspondingly smaller in the band from Florence to Ghent, especially at its Italian end; as gauged by the total population of their ten largest cities, the regions of Venice (357,000), Milan (337,000), and Florence (296,000) led the pack (Russell 1972: 235). In 1490, Jan de Vries' more precise computation of "urban potential" singles out regions centering approximately on Antwerp, Milan, and Naples as the peaks of the European urban system, while in 1790 the one zone around London (including areas across the English Channel) clearly predominated (de Vries 1984: 160–4).

City system and state system spread very unevenly, and in contrasting ways, across the European map. In the year 990, cities were small and scattered almost everywhere north of the Alps. They were nevertheless denser, and relations among them more intense, in a band extending north from Bologna and Pisa across the Alps to Ghent, Bruges, and London. Secondary zones of urban concentration appeared in southern Spain and southern Italy. The Mediterranean lands hosted significantly more cities than those bordering the Atlantic or the Baltic. Europe's two largest cities were then Constantinople and Córdoba, not only major centers of trade but seats respectively of the Byzantine Empire and the Umayyad caliphate; each had a population approaching half a million (Chandler and Fox 1974: 11). Over the next millennium the central band remained Europe's most intensely urban zone, but it widened, and its center of gravity shifted northward toward the great Atlantic ports. From 1300 onward, the band of connected cities north of the Alps grew disproportionately.

The presence or absence of urban clusters made a profound difference to regional social life, and significantly shaped the possibilities for state formation. Under the conditions of production and transportation prevailing in Europe before the nineteenth century, substantial cities stimulated cash-crop agriculture in tributary areas reaching many miles into the countryside. Commercial agriculture, in its turn, generally promoted the prosperity of merchants, larger peasants, and smaller landlords while reducing the ability of great landholders to dominate the people in their rural surroundings. (A significant exception occurred, however, where the city's ruling class also held extensive land in the hinterland, as was frequently the case in Italian city-states; there the peasantry felt the full weight of lordly control.)

In addition, cities deeply affected the demography of surrounding regions. Until recently, most European cities experienced natural decrease: their death rates exceeded their birth rates. As a result, even stagnant cities drew considerable numbers of migrants from nearby towns and villages, while growing cities generated large migrant streams. The streams were much larger than the urban deficit of births plus the urban rate of growth, since all migration systems involved a great deal of movement back and forth; peddlers, merchants, servants, and artisans frequently oscillated between city and country from year to year or season to season. The net flow from country to city usually included more women than men, with the result that sex ratios (males per 100 females) ran characteristically high in the countryside and low in the city. Thus the city imprinted itself on the very opportunities for marriage of villagers in its surroundings.

The commercial and demographic impact of cities made a significant difference to state formation. Let us leave aside momentarily the importance of urban ruling classes and city-based capitalists as supporters or opponents of efforts to expand state power; they will get plenty of attention later on. The existence of intensive rural–urban trade provided an opportunity for rulers to collect revenues through customs and excise taxes, while the relatively commercialized economy made it easier for monarchs to bypass great landlords as they extended royal power to towns and villages.

Relations between city and country, furthermore, affected the potential supply of soldiers: would they be the serfs and tenants of rural magnates, mercenaries from regions of high mobility and low nuptiality, urban militias, or landless workers swept up by pressing squads? Opportunities for taxation, the power of landlords, and the supply of troops deeply affected how states took shape. Through food supply, migration, trade, communications, and opportunities for employment, large urban clusters stamped their mark on the social life in surrounding regions, and thereby influenced the strategies of rulers who attempted to extend state power into those regions. Periods of urban growth only accentuated these effects.

With some risk, and great disregard of regional variation, we can divide European urban growth since 1000 into five phases: a period of considerable expansion to about 1350; a time of depression and then of trendless fluctuation between 1350 and 1500; a sixteenth-century acceleration; a seventeenth-century slowdown, and finally an enormous acceleration after 1750 (Hohenberg and Lees 1985: 7–9). The devastating fourteenth-century spread of plague marks the transition from the first phase to the second, Iberian navigation to America the start of the third phase, the growth of cottage industry after 1600 the launching of the fourth; the implosion of capital, manufacturing, services, and trade into cities the movement from the fourth to the fifth.

From the sixteenth to eighteenth centuries, many European regions, including the hinterlands of Milan, Lyon, and Manchester, experienced protoindustrialization: the multiplication of small manufacturing units, including households, and of small merchants who linked them with distant markets. During that great industrial expansion, capital went to labor rather than vice versa; rural labor proletarianized, in the sense of shifting decisively toward work for wages using means of production owned by capitalists, but remained in households and small shops. Capital then accumulated grandly, but did not concentrate enormously. During the nineteenth and twentieth centuries an inverse movement occurred: capital imploded, manufacturing and workers moved to cities, and vast areas of the countryside deindustrialized. Increasingly, manufacturers located where they could minimize the costs of getting to their raw materials and to the markets for their goods, assuming correctly that workers would come to them at someone else's expense. The last burst of concentration greatly accelerated European urbanization, and produced the citified continent we know today.

Cities grew with the European population as a whole, and the number of urban places therefore multiplied even when the urban share of the population was constant; on present evidence, we simply do not know whether the European population actually became more urban before 1350. In any case, the proportion living in cities did not rise dramatically until the nineteenth century. According to the best available estimates, the share in places of 10,000 people or more ran at around 5 percent in 990, 6 percent in 1490, 10 percent in 1790, and 30 percent in 1890, as compared with nearly 60 percent today (Bairoch 1985: 182, 282; de Vries 1984: 29–48).

The timetable of urbanization reflected the history of European capital. For centuries, the bulk of Europe's liquid capital lay in the hands of small merchants who worked scattered through the continent, either trading goods produced elsewhere or guiding manufacturing by formally independent producers in villages, towns, and small cities. Great capitalists like those of Genoa, Augsburg and Antwerp played a crucial part in linking Europe together and with the rest of the world, but held only a small share of all the capital that was in motion.

Before 1490, the scattered evidence makes it difficult to offer any more detailed quantitative statements. Paul Bairoch's estimates and Jan de Vries's recent compilation of evidence concerning European urbanization since 1500 nevertheless make possible some simple but telling computations. Table 2.1 shows the trivial long-run rate of urban growth before 1490, the acceleration of the sixteenth century, the slowdown of the seventeenth, and the exceptional urbanization after 1790. By 1980, the barrier of 10,000 had lost its meaning (hence the speculative numbers in the table), and a full 390 cities had 100,000 inhabitants or more. In fact, the 1980 statistics locate 34.6 percent of the population in cities of at least 100,000. The great acceleration of urban growth arrived after 1790, with the nineteenth-century concentration of capital,

Table 2.1   Urbanization from 990 to 1980 in Europe west of Russia

	990	1490	1590	1690	1790	1890	1980
number of cities of 10,000 or more	111	154	220	224	364	1709	5000?
population in cities of 10,000 or more (millions)	2.6	3.4	5.9	7.5	12.2	66.9	250?
annual percent rate of growth since previous date	—	0.1	0.6	0.2	0.5	1.7	1.5?
percentage of population in cities of 10,000 +	4.9	5.6	7.6	9.2	10.0	29.0	55?
square miles per city (thousands)	17.1	12.3	8.6	8.5	5.2	1.1	0.4?

Source: de Vries 1984: 29–48, Bairoch 1985: 182

increase in scale of workplaces, and creation of mass transport. But through most of the period after 1490, the exclusive hinterlands available to most cities were shrinking in size.

CITY–STATE INTERACTION

The diverging trends of cities and states changed some critical ratios. In AD 990, with thousands of statelike units, Europe may well have had only one city of 10,000 for every twenty or thirty "states." In 1490, one such city existed for every one or two states. In 1890, the mythical average state had about sixty cities of 10,000 or more. That change alone implied fundamental alterations in the relations between rulers and ruled: altered techniques of control, altered fiscal strategies, altered demands for services, altered politics.

Cities shape the destinies of states chiefly by serving as containers and distribution points for capital. By means of capital, urban ruling classes extend their influence through the urban hinterland and across far-flung trading networks. But cities vary in how much capital their oligarchies control; seventeenth-century Amsterdam made once-glorious Bruges look puny. The fact that cities are loci of capital accumulation, furthermore, gives their political authorities access to capital, credit, and control over hinterlands that, if seized or co-opted, can serve the ends of monarchs as well. Adam Smith stated the central fact forcefully:

A country abounding with merchants and manufacturers . . . necessarily abounds with a set of people who have it at all times in their power to advance, if they choose to do so, a very large sum of money to government.

(Smith 1910 [1778]: II, 392)

If they choose to do so: behind that qualifier hide centuries of contention between capitalists and kings. Yet Adam Smith was absolutely right to stress the financial advantages of states that operated in regions of abundant capital.

States themselves operate chiefly as containers and deployers of coercive means, especially armed force. Nowadays the development of welfare states, of regulatory states, of states that spend a great deal of their effort intervening in economic affairs, has mitigated and obscured the centrality of coercion. Over the millennium of European history we are surveying, however, military expenditure has usually consumed the majority of state budgets, and armed forces have typically constituted the largest single branch of government.

Differences between the geographies of European state formation and city-building presented an acute problem for any would-be ruler. Borrowing from Paul Hohenberg and Lynn Lees, we can make a rough distinction between cities as *central places* and as points in *urban networks*; all cities belong to both systems, but the relative importance of the two sets of relations varies dramatically from one city to another (Hohenberg and Lees 1985: chapter 2). The hierarchical central place system mediates the flow of ordinary goods such as food and clothing among the settlements of a contiguous region; raw materials and rough goods tend to move up the hierarchy of central places toward larger settlements that serve more extensive markets, while fine and specialized goods – especially those produced outside the regional system – tend to move downward from larger places to smaller ones. Over much of the history we are examining, primary producers, local merchants, peddlers, and recurrent public markets brought a major part of the goods sold to their consumers.

Urban networks, on the other hand, link higher-level centers in separate regional systems, sometimes removed from each other by thousands of kilometers. Although timber, wheat, salt, and wine traveled great distances in Europe well before 1500, urban networks long specialized in the exchange of light, expensive goods such as spices and silks. Merchants and financiers with substantial capital at their disposal figured importantly in Europe's urban networks. For centuries, what Philip Curtin calls trade diasporas had a crucial role; geographically dispersed mercantile groups such as Jews, Armenians, or Genoese, who shared language, religion, kinship, and (sometimes) geographic origin reduced the uncertainties of international trade by extending each other credit, market information, and preferential treatment (Curtin 1984). Even where trade diasporas did not make the crucial links among distant centers, dispersed merchants commonly maintained acquaintance with their colleagues by means of voyages, personal correspondence, maintenance of local representatives, and contact with mutual acquaintances.

A coercion-wielding ruler can, with a certain amount of effort, capture the entire territory of one or more central-place hierarchies, and even reshape a hierarchy to correspond approximately with the limits of his state; by the sixteenth century, a rough correspondence had emerged between England and the central-place system of London, between France and the central-place system of Paris. But it is rare and difficult to match a state to the contours of a long-distance urban network. Federations such as the Hanseatic League and maritime empires such as those of Venice and Portugal came close for a time, but always found themselves competing or bargaining with territorial rulers who laid claim on one or another of their trading outposts; the consolidation of an Ottoman empire athwart Venice's most lucrative trade routes doomed the spectacular mercantile empire Venetians had stitched together during the twelfth and thirteenth centuries. Territorial states whose merchants devoted themselves to long-distance trade, on the other hand, always found themselves confronted with powerful economic actors whose external relations they could never entirely control, and who found it relatively easy to escape with their capital to another business site if the ruler's demands became unbearable. The long-lasting discrepancy between the geographies of coercion and of capital guaranteed that the social relations organized around them would evolve in distinctive ways.

Over Europe as a whole, alterations in state control of capital and of coercion between AD 900 and the present have followed two parallel arcs. At first, during the age of *patrimonialism*, European monarchs generally extracted what capital they needed as tribute or rent from lands and populations that lay under their immediate control – often within stringent contractual limits on the amounts they could demand. In the time of *brokerage* (especially between 1400 and 1700 or so), they relied heavily on formally independent capitalists for loans, for management of revenue-producing enterprises, and for collection of taxes. By the eighteenth century, however, the time of *nationalization* had come; many sovereigns were incorporating the fiscal apparatus directly into the state structure, and drastically curtailing the involvement of independent contractors. The last century or so, the age of *specialization*, has brought a sharper separation of fiscal from military organization and an increasing involvement of states in the oversight of fixed capital.

On the side of coercion, a similar evolution took place. During the period of patrimonialism, monarchs drew armed force from retainers, vassals, and militias who owed them personal service – but again within significant contractual limits. In the age of brokerage (again especially between 1400 and 1700) they turned increasingly to mercenary forces supplied to them by contractors who retained considerable freedom of action. Next, during nationalization, sovereigns absorbed armies and navies directly into the state's administrative structure, eventually turning away from foreign mercenaries and hiring or conscripting the bulk of their troops from their own citizenries. Since the mid-nineteenth century, in a phase of specialization, European states have consolidated the system of citizen militias backed by large civilian bureaucracies, and split off police forces specialized in the use of coercion outside of war.

By the nineteenth century, most European states had internalized both armed forces and fiscal mechanisms; they thus reduced the governmental roles of tax farmers, military contractors, and other independent middlemen. Their rulers then continued to bargain with capitalists and other classes for credit, revenues, manpower, and the necessities of war. Bargaining, in its turn, created numerous new claims on the state: pensions, payments to the poor, public education, city planning, and much more. In the process, states changed from magnified war machines into multiple-purpose organizations. Their efforts to control coercion and capital continued, but in the company of a wide variety of regulatory, compensatory, distributive, and protective activities.

Before the nineteenth century, states differed markedly in the relative timing and intensity of the two main processes of change. The Dutch state rented large armies and navies for a century or more, adopted state management of finances precociously, yet long remained beholden to the capitalists of Amsterdam and other commercial cities. At moments, indeed, the Dutch state dissolved into the governments of its major municipalities. In Castile, on the other hand, land forces – often hired outside of Spain – prevailed; there the monarchy captured the credit of merchants by turning them into rentiers and by relying on colonial revenues for their reimbursement. Portugal, Poland, Italian city-states, and the states of the Holy Roman Empire followed other combinations of the two arcs, and thereby created distinctly different state structures.

STATE PHYSIOLOGIES

Why did European states follow such different trajectories, yet almost all head in the direction of greater concentration with respect to capital and coercion? Two secrets account for most of the complexity. The first is the continuous, aggressive competition for trade and territory among changing states of unequal size, which made war a driving force in European history. The second lies in what Gabriel Ardant called the "physiology" of states: the processes by which they acquire and allocate the means of carrying on their major activities. For most of the history that concerns us here, the crucial means were especially coercive, the means of war. Coercive means obviously played a part in warmaking (attacking external rivals), statemaking (attacking internal rivals), and protection (attacking the enemies of the state's clients). Coercive means also came into play in a state's exercise of extraction (drawing the means of state activity from its subject population) and adjudication (settling disputes among members of that population). Only when it came to production and distribution were coercive means not major supports of the state's activity – and even there the degree of coercion varied from state to state. Where states established their own monopolies over the production of salt, arms, or tobacco products, for example, they typically did so by force of arms; contraband usually becomes contraband when rulers decide to monopolize the distribution of the commodity in question.

Coercive means combine weapons with men who know how to use them. (I do mean *men*; in Western experience, women have played an amazingly small part in the construction and use of coercive organization, a fact that surely helps account for their subordinate position within states.) Agents of states have an easier time concentrating coercion, and keeping others from doing so, to the extent that (a) production of weapons involves esoteric knowledge, rare materials, or substantial capital, (b) few groups have the independent capacity to mobilize large numbers of men and (c) few people know the secrets of combining weapons with men. Over the long run, the rulers of European states took advantage of all these conditions to move toward monopolies of the larger concentrations of coercive means within their territories: armies, police forces, weapons, prisons, and courts.

States used concentrated coercion in a number of different ways. During the first few centuries after AD 990, kings rarely had much more armed force under their direct control than did their chief followers. The logistics of feeding and maintaining armed men made the establishment of standing armies prohibitively expensive. A royal army normally consisted of the king's small permanent force plus troops who came only temporarily from civilian life at his followers' call. The king's presence reinforced the personal connections among warriors: "It was a general rule that the king should command in person every important campaign. Age did not matter; Otto III was 11 when he led his army against the Saxons (991) and Henry IV 13 when he went to war against the Hungarians in 1063" (Contamine 1984: 39). Royal armies on the move lived largely from requisition (which was theoretically to be repaid from the royal treasury) and plunder (which was not); the distinction, to be sure, remained unclear for centuries.

Cities commonly organized citizen militias which guarded walls, patrolled streets, intervened in public conflicts, and now and then fought battles against enemies of city or of the kingdom. Spanish municipal militias were exceptional; they played the central part in the conquest of Muslim Iberia by Christian kings, a fact reflected in the great powers vested in the noble-dominated municipalities after the Reconquista, and in the crystallization of the distinction between *caballero* (horseman) and *péon* (foot soldier) into an enduring and general social division (Powers 1988). Elsewhere, kings generally sought to limit the independent armed force at the disposition of townsmen, for the very good reason that townsmen were quite likely to use force in their own interest, including resistance to royal demands.

These various military forces confronted many groups of armed men who did not operate under direct royal control: among others, the retainers of particular lords who were not currently mobilized for royal service, bandits (who were often demobilized soldiers, continuing their plunder without royal assent), and pirates (who frequently worked with royal or civic protection). Accumulations of coercive means were modest but very widely spread; concentration was slight. Even so, rulers were doing more to concentrate coercion than was anyone else.

Eventually states came to operate multiple armed forces, all of them bureaucratized and more or less integrated into the national administration. Even Spain, notorious for the repeated devolution of state powers to its agents and grandees, made repeated efforts to detach its armed forces from their civilian surroundings. Philip II, for example, deliberately placed under direct government control armed forces whose commands had almost been private possessions of grandees during the reign of his father, Charles V. By 1580,

the entire military establishment had been restored to the Crown and was being run by royal ministers; the galleys of Spain, Naples and Sicily, after a brief and unsuccessful return to contracting in 1574–6, were back in *administración*, the provisioning of the Mediterranean fleets and the garrisons of north Africa was controlled by the royal commissariat in Seville, the arms industries and the saltpetre makers were under strict royal supervision, and the manufacture of gunpowder was a royal monopoly.

(Thompson 1976: 6–7)

During the next half-century the exigencies of financing and administration led Spain back to extensive contracting and local control; nevertheless, the armed forces henceforth operated as distinct, differentiated branches of the national state. Indeed by the nineteenth century the Spanish army acquired such distinctness and autonomy as to intervene repeatedly as a separate force in national politics (Ballbé 1983).

In Spain and elsewhere, a sharp division between armies and navies emerged early, and endured. At a national scale, the division between armies (generally specialized in combatting other armed forces) and police forces (generally specialized in the control of unarmed or lightly-armed individuals and small groups) only became general quite late – in most countries, during the nineteenth century. By that time accumulations of coercive force were large, concentrated, and therefore very unequal. By the nineteenth century, states had succeeded in arming themselves impressively, and in almost disarming their civilian populations.

Figure 2.6 schematizes the relationship between cities and states as an interaction of capital and coercion. Above the diagonal, coercion outran capital; below it, capital outstripped coercion. The distinction applies to individual cities; European ports such as Amsterdam and Barcelona typically wallowed in capital while having relatively thin coercive apparatuses; seats of monarchs such as as Berlin and Madrid, on the other hand, stood much higher with respect to coercion than to capital.

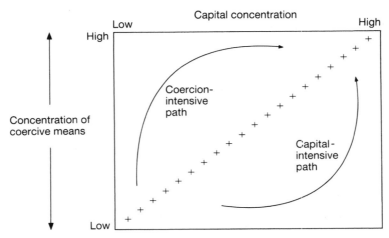

Figure 2.6   Alternative paths of change in concentrated capital and concentrated coercive power in Europe, 1000–1800.

The distinction also applies to the environments of states. The general direction of European change over the millennium undoubtedly ran up the diagonal, toward greater and greater concentrations of both capital and coercion. But different states followed different paths in the same general direction. Brandenburg-Prussia grew up in a coercion-rich, capital-poor environment, and bore the marks of its early environment even when it extended its control to the capitalist cities of the Rhineland. Denmark usually had greater concentrations of capital at its disposal than the rest of Scandinavia, and invested less of its state effort in the building up of military might.

The Teutonic Knights (the Order of St Mary's Hospital at Jerusalem) took an irregular path: from freebooting crusaders in the Holy Land (hence heavily involved in the piratical world of oceanic commerce) at the end of the twelfth century to governors of a large piece of Transylvania during the thirteenth century to conquerors and colonizers of pagan Prussia, where they ruled in the style of great landlords from about 1300 into the sixteenth century. The Knights crossed the line from capital-intensive to coercion-intensive state formation in about thirty years. The Knights of Malta (also known successively as the Knights Hospitallers of St John of Jerusalem and the Knights of Rhodes) likewise zigged and zagged, but ended up in a very different location:

. . . a religious order born in the Holy Land toward 1100, but almost immediately transformed into a military order in defense of the East's Latin states, then moving to a maritime career in its retreat to Cyprus (1291) and then Rhodes (1309), and finally forced to devote itself full time to that calling at its installation in Malta as a sovereign state under the suzerainty of the King of Sicily in 1530.

(Fontenay 1988a: 362)

By devoting themselves to legalized piracy from their Maltese base, the Knights followed a more capital-intensive course than their onetime neighbors in the Holy Land. Thus we can think of the diagram as a map of the multiple paths taken by different European states in their various interactions with the cities in their territories.

The capital–coercion diagram embodies the argument I sketched in the first chapter: the most powerful rulers in any particular region set the terms of war for all; smaller rulers faced a choice between accommodating themselves to the demands of powerful neighbors and putting exceptional efforts into preparations for war. War and preparations for war involved rulers in extracting the means of war from others who held the essential resources – men, arms, supplies, or money to buy them – and who were reluctant to surrender them without strong pressure or compensation. Within limits set by the demands and rewards of other states, extraction and struggle over the means of war created the central organizational structures of states. The organization of major social classes within a state's territory, and their relations to the state, significantly affected the strategies rulers employed to extract resources, the resistance they met, the struggle that resulted, the sorts of durable organization that extraction and struggle laid down, and therefore the efficiency of resource extraction.

The organization of major social classes, and their relations to the state varied significantly from Europe's coercion-intensive regions (areas of few cities and agricultural predominance, where direct coercion played a major part in production) to its capital-intensive regions (areas of many cities and commercial predominance, where markets, exchange, and market-oriented production prevailed). The demands major classes made on the state, and their influence over the state, varied correspondingly. The relative success of different extractive strategies, and the strategies rulers actually applied, therefore varied significantly from coercion-intensive to capital-intensive regions.

As a consequence, the organizational forms of states followed distinctly different trajectories in these different parts of Europe. Which sort of state prevailed in a given era and part of Europe varied greatly. Only late in the millennium did national states exercise clear superiority over city-states, empires, and other common European forms of state. Nevertheless, the increasing scale of war and the knitting together of the European state system through commercial, military, and diplomatic interaction eventually gave the warmaking advantage to those states that could field great standing armies; states having access to a combination of large rural populations, capitalists, and relatively commercialized economies won out. They set the terms of war, and their form of state became the predominant one in Europe. Eventually European states converged on that form: the national state.

Within each path marked out in the capital–coercion diagram, earlier steps constrained later ones. If urban ruling classes played important parts in the initial consolidation of a given state (as they did in Holland), long afterward the state bore their imprint in the form of bourgeois institutions. If a state originated in conquest of largely rural populations (as did successive Russian empires) it continued to offer little scope to such cities as grew up in its midst; in such regions, large nobilities grew up as monarchs granted fiscal privileges and substantial local jurisdictions to arms-bearing landlords in return for their intermittent military service.

LIAISONS DANGEREUSES

Through most of the last millennium, European cities and states have carried on a series of *liaisons dangereuses*, love–hate affairs in which each became at once indispensable and insufferable to the other. Cities and their capitalists drew indispensable protection for their commercial and industrial activity from the specialists in coercion who ran states, but rightly feared interference in their money-making and diversion of their resources to war, preparation for war, or payment for past wars. States and military men depended on city-based capitalists for the financial means to recruit and sustain armed force, yet properly worried about the resistance to state power engendered by cities, their commercial interests, and their working classes. Cities and states found the grounds for uneasy bargains in the exchange of protection for access to capital, but until the nineteenth century such bargains remained fragile.

These days it is hard to imagine the seventeenth-century machinations of Messina, Sicily's most mercantile city. Sicily has become such an emblem for backwardness that we easily forget the many centuries of Sicilian glory as a seat of brilliant kingdoms, a breadbasket for the Mediterranean, and an object of competition among great powers. Sicily – once Muslim, and then Norman – had come under Aragonese rule in 1282, and had become a property of Spain with the sixteenth-century formation of a unified monarchy. The merchant-oligarchs of Messina chafed under Spanish rule, which cramped their access to foreign markets, and especially their control over the export of Sicilian silk, in favor of dynastic interests. In 1674, Spain (loosely allied with Holland) was at war with France (loosely allied, for the moment, with England). Messina's leaders closed their gates to Spanish troops, appealed for help to France, England, and the Ottoman Empire, bid for an independent Sicily ruled from Messina by a foreign king, asked for their port to be free of customs, and welcomed a French governor of Sicily with his troops.

After three years, however, the Messinans tired of French occupation as the French lost their enthusiasm for maintaining a military establishment amid a perfidious population. When the French withdrew and the leading families fled, the remaining merchants formed a civic guard and cheered the return of Spanish rule (Mack Smith 1968a: 225–30). In Sicily and elsewhere, state–city compacts broke easily when external events altered the state's military position or the cities' commercial position, and when one side or the other pushed its advantage too far. Rulers and capitalists constantly renegotiated their relative positions.

Not every state–city pair, however, maintained the same relationship. Far from it: the pattern varied sharply from one part of Europe to another, and changed dramatically over the centuries. Venice created its own commercial empire and only later undertook the conquest of mainland territory, Polish lords stunted the growth of their cities, while Paris, for all its rebellions, served the French monarchy well.

Returning to the capital–coercion diagram, we might sketch the stories of a number of different European areas as in figure 2.7. Thus, according to the diagram, the Polish state lived in a coercion-rich, capital-poor environment, and actually faced a decline in the concentrations of both as great nobles seized their shares of coercion and capital. Scandinavian states generally began amid substantial concentrations of coercion, and eventually moved toward higher levels of control over concentrated capital. Small German states, Italian city-states,

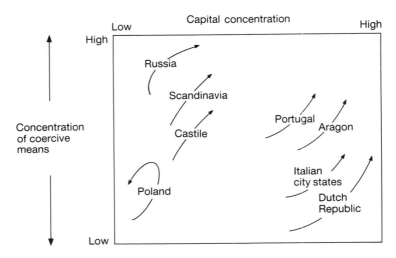

Figure 2.7 Hypothetical trajectories of different states.

and the Dutch Republic, in contrast, began their trajectories in the presence of substantial concentrations of capital but weak, intermittent armed force, only gradually moving toward permanent, concentrated military establishments.

The positions of cities within market hierarchies (international markets, regional markets, exclusively local markets, and so on) correlated approximately with their size, their demographic impact on their hinterlands, the extent of their capital accumulation and their ability to build up and control an extended sphere of influence. These in turn strongly affected the relative attractiveness of different cities as sources of capital for the building of armies and state formation, the autonomy of their ruling classes with respect to would-be and actual statemakers, and the strength of their representative institutions. The higher its market position, on average, the more likely that within their relations with national rulers a city's oligarchy acted as indispensable equals having extensive rights of representation.

As a consequence, major trading cities and city-states mounted more effective resistance to the penetration of national states than did cities in mainly agrarian regions. Most often national states only gained genuine control over major trading cities when the cities had begun to lose their predominant positions in international markets. Even then, important trading cities managed to build into the state apparatus more of their municipal power structures than did local and regional market centers, and their presence in great numbers generally slowed down the formation of national states. In the absence of ready capital, on the other hand, rulers built massive apparatuses to squeeze resources from a reluctant citizenry.

With important exceptions, the Protestant Reformation concentrated in Europe's city-state band, and at first offered a further base for resistance to the authority of centralizing states. The exceptions include Catholic northern Italy, where the Roman church never lost its great influence, as well as Protestant Bohemia and Hungary, profoundly rural areas that were already producing populist variants of Christianity well before the Reformation. In many places, notably England and the Nordic countries, rulers promoted and co-opted their own versions of the Reformation, which established extensive state control over the religious apparatus and close cooperation between clergy and lay officials in local administration. Elsewhere (as in the Netherlands) Protestantism provided an attractive doctrinal basis for resistance to imperial authority, especially authority buttressed by claims of divinely-sanctioned royal privilege. Confronted with the spread of popular Protestantism, a ruler had three choices: embrace it, co-opt it, or fight it.

Within the Holy Roman Empire, the division between officially Protestant and Catholic principalities and the threat that a ruler – seeking either dynastic ends, religious solace, or a ground for resistance to the emperor – would change faith, became constant sources of contention during the sixteenth century. The Treaty of Westphalia, ending the Thirty Years' War in 1648, featured a provision that any ruler who switched faiths would forfeit his or her claim to the crown. From that point on, religious differences remained important in European domestic politics, but declined rapidly as a stake of war.

On the whole, bulky state churches (whether Protestant, Catholic, or Orthodox) came into being where the state itself built large civilian and military bureaucracies in the process of massing armed force. People in areas of concentrated capital generally resisted the imposition of state-prescribed forms of worship as successfully as they blocked the early development of national states.

London and England constitute the obvious challenge to the theoretical opposition of capitalist activity and state power. In England, a substantial state formed relatively early despite the presence of a formidable trading city and maintained a hegemonic state church into the nineteenth century. Note, however, several crucial features of the English experience. The monarchy acquired extensive powers before London became a major international center; in that regard, England resembled Scandinavia more closely than it did the Netherlands. Kinship, trade, and finance, however, gave London's merchants close ties to the country's nobility and gentry; the City of London gained direct representation in Parliament and, through the Livery, a semi-autonomous voice in royal affairs. In those regards, England resembled the Netherlands more closely than it did Scandinavia. From the seventeenth century onward, finally, the state that emerged saw royal power increasingly contained by the joint representative of landowners and bourgeoisie, Parliament. Thus England managed to travel a certain distance on both the major paths to state formation.

The experiences of other areas indicate that the focus of bargaining over the wherewithal of war strongly affected the forms of representation that emerged. In Portugal, with strong reliance on overseas trade for royal income, we see few representative institutions of any kind except for the strong presence of Lisbon's municipal government as interlocutor. In sixteenth-century Aragon, we observe Barcelona in a similar relation to the crown; its puissant *Consell de Cent* could bypass the viceroy and speak directly to the king in Madrid, yet it never had the power to dominate the whole of Aragon, much less of all Spain. In Castile, we witness the power invested in the Cortes, an instrument of great landlords and of eighteen cities' oligarchies. On the whole, urban institutions themselves seem to have become part of state structure more readily where capitalists predominated.

States in which capitalists and bourgeois institutions played commanding roles had great advantages when it came to the rapid mobilization of capital for expensive wars. But they remained vulnerable to withdrawals of capital and demands for commercial protection. The Dutch Republic illustrates clearly the costs and benefits of capitalist dominance. On the one hand, the Dutch could easily raise revenues for warfare – in the short run by means of loans from its richer citizens, in the long run by means of customs duties and sales taxes on everything from ivory to spirits ('t Hart 1986, 1989a, 1989b, Schama 1975); they did so without creating much permanent state structure. Large Dutch fleets, including the private navies of the East and West India Companies, converted quickly into a formidable navy. But only when the major provinces (especially Holland) agreed to pay could the republic undertake a war, or any other large effort; they often disagreed. The military advantage of such states varied with the prevailing type of warfare: it was historically great for naval warfare, less so for artillery and cavalry, and a long-term drawback in mass-army tactics.

Permanent military forces reduced (but by no means eliminated) surges in the demand for military means, and thereby increased the advantage of states having long-term credit and large tax bases. States such as Prussia, France, and Britain – often considered models of effective state formation – combined the co-optation of landlords and merchants, built standing armies (and navies) in the time of mass-army tactics from the Thirty Years' War to the Napoleonic Wars, and as a consequence created substantial central bureaucracies. Contrasts among these textbook examples, however, occupied only a narrow band in the whole spectrum of European state formation.

As they mobilized for the French Revolutionary and Napoleonic wars, most European states expanded and centralized. At war's end they all contracted somewhat – if only through the demobilization of the millions of troops who were under arms by 1815 – but their budgets, personnel, and levels of activity remained much higher than they had been in 1790. War in Europe and abroad continued to provide the greatest stimulus to increases in state expenditure. Yet during the nineteenth century several crucial changes in state formation occurred. The great implosion of capital and labor into cities and towns presented rulers with threats and opportunities they had not previously faced: threats of concentrated working-class collective action, opportunities to extract and control as never before. The scope of state activity broadened immensely throughout Europe; improving navigation, building roads and railroads, policing, creating schools, establishing post offices, regulating relations between capital and labor all became regular activities of states, and occasions to add specialists to the state service. Professional civil services formed and multiplied.

Simultaneously, as rulers bargained directly with their subject populations for massive taxes, military service, and cooperation in state programs, most states took two further steps of profound importance: a movement toward direct rule that reduced the role of local or regional patrons and placed representatives of the national state in every community, and expansion of popular consultation in the form of elections, plebiscites, and legislatures. Together they promoted nationalism both in the sense of popular identification with state ends (for the majority) and (for the minorities) in the sense of resistance to demands for uniformity and integration, resistance in the name of distinctive linguistic and cultural groups. The omnipresent state, the struggles over its rulers and policies, the formation of serious budgetary competitors to the armed forces, and many other features of states we now take for granted emerged in the nineteenth-century absorption of the general population into the state. European states, for all their differences in relations between state and economy, began to converge on a model of bureaucracy, intervention, and control.

The analysis embedded in the capital–coercion diagram shows us multiple paths of state formation and an ultimate convergence on states with high concentrations of both capital and coercion. The analysis helps rephrase and answer the initial question: *What accounts for the great variation in time and space in the kinds of states that have prevailed in Europe since AD 990, and why did European states eventually converge on different variants of the national state?* There are three answers: the relative availability of concentrated capital and concentrated means of coercion in different regions and periods significantly affected the organizational consequences of making war; until recently only those states survived that held their own in war with other states; and finally, over the long run the changing character of war gave the military advantage to states that could draw large, durable military forces from their own populations, which were increasingly national states.

The capital–coercion reasoning also suggests some possible solutions to the historical problems that flow from this general question. *What accounts for the roughly concentric pattern of European state formation?* It reflects the uneven spatial distribution of capital, and therefore sets off the relatively large but capital-poor states that ringed the continent from the swarm of smaller, capital-rich statelike entities that proliferated near its center. The contrast distinguishes exterior states, such as Sweden and Russia, that went through their formative years with relatively large concentrations of coercion and relatively small concentrations of capital, from interior states, such as Genoa and Holland, for which the opposite was true, and intermediate states, such as England and France, in which concentrations of capital and of coercion grew up side by side.

Why, despite obvious interests to the contrary, did rulers frequently accept the establishment of institutions representing the major classes within their jurisdictions? In fact, rulers attempted to avoid the establishment of institutions representing groups outside their own class, and sometimes succeeded for considerable periods. In the long term, however, those institutions were the price and outcome of bargaining with different members of the subject population for the wherewithal of state activity, especially the means of war. Kings of England did not *want* a Parliament to form and assume ever-greater power; they conceded to barons, and then to clergy, gentry, and bourgeois, in the course of persuading them to raise the money for warfare.

Why did European states vary so much with respect to the incorporation of urban oligarchies and institutions? States that had to contend from the start with urban oligarchies and institutions generally incorporated those oligarchies and institutions into the national structure of power. Representative institutions generally first appeared in Europe when local, regional, or national governments bargained with groups of subjects who had enough power to inhibit the governments' operation but not enough power to take them over (Blockmans 1978). Where the governments in question were more or less autonomous states and the groups of subjects were urban oligarchies, municipal councils and similar institutions commonly became integral elements of the state structure. Where a single city predominated, a very effective form of state – the city-state or city-empire – emerged. The city-state and city-empire lost out, however, once mass armies recruited from the state's own population became crucial to successful warfare.

Why did political and commercial power slide from the city-states and city-empires of the Mediterranean to the substantial states and relatively subordinated cities of the Atlantic? They lost out not only because the Atlantic and Baltic trade eclipsed that of the Mediterranean but also because control of massive, permanent armed force became increasingly crucial to a state's success in politics and economics alike. When, in the late sixteenth century, Spain, England, and Holland all started to send large armed vessels into the Mediterranean for trade and piracy (the two were not so distinct), city-states such as Ragusa, Genoa, and Venice found that their previous reliance on speed, connections, and craftiness was no longer enough to evade massive commercial losses. The owners of big ships that were suitable for long ocean voyages won out in both commercial and military terms (see Guillerm 1985, Modelski and Thompson 1988).

Why did city-states, city-empires, federations, and religious organizations lose their importance as prevailing kinds of state in Europe? Two things happened. First, commercialization and capital accumulation in the larger states reduced the advantage enjoyed by small mercantile states, which had previously been able to borrow extensively, tax efficiently, and rely on their own seapower to hold off large landbound states. Second, war eventually changed in a direction that made their small scale and fragmented sovereignty a clear disadvantage, and they lost to large states. Florentine and Milanese republics crumbled under the weight of the fifteenth and sixteenth century's military requirements. Indeed a professional organizer of mercenary armies, Francesco Sforza, became duke of Milan in 1450 before his descendants lost their duchy to France (1499) and then to Spain (1535).

In Florence, a revived republic lasted until 1530, but then the combined forces of the pope and Emperor Charles V occupied its *contado*, forced a surrender of the city (despite fortifications recommended by a commission headed by Nicolò Macchiavelli and built under the direction of Michelangelo Buonarotti), and installed the Medicis as dukes. With the partial exceptions of Venice and Genoa, which retained some distinction as maritime powers, that era of large armies, heavy artillery, and extensive fortifications relegated all the Italian city-states to extinction, subordination, or perilous survival in the interstices of great powers.

Why did war shift from conquest for tribute and struggle among armed tribute-takers to sustained battles among massed armies and navies? For essentially the same reasons: with the organizational and technical innovations in warfare of the fifteenth and sixteenth centuries, states with access to large numbers of men and volumes of capital gained a clear advantage, and either drove back the tribute-takers or forced them into patterns of extraction that built a more durable state structure. During the fifteenth and sixteenth centuries, the Russian state made the transition as Ivan III and Ivan IV used awards of land to tie bureaucrats and soldiers to long-term service of the state. During the eighteenth century, the ability of populous states such as Great Britain and France to draw mass armies from their own citizens gave them the means to overpower small states.

If this analysis is correct, it creates its own puzzles: why, for example, the fragmented Holy Roman Empire lasted so long in the midst of consolidating, bellicose monarchies. Why didn't it disappear into the maws of large, powerful states? Again, what logic would have predicted that commercial Novgorod, a trading city whose patricians exercised control over their own large hinterland, would give way to princely Moscow? Geopolitical position and stand-offs among major powers surely played a larger part than my simple formulation implies. They figure importantly in later chapters. Nevertheless, the line of reasoning summarized in the capital–coercion diagram invites us to rethink European state formation in terms of the interplay of cities and states, and thereby captures some broad regularities in state formation. It clearly improves on the portrayal of English, French, or Prussian state formation (or some generalization of the three) as the core process, and all others as attenuated or failed attempts to follow the same path.

Over the centuries before the nineteenth, however, states had long diverged as they fashioned military forces in situations of very different relations between capital and coercion. Alternative paths of state formation, in their turn, led to different forms of resistance and rebellion, different state structures, and different fiscal systems. If so, standard debates about the transition from feudalism to capitalism and the rise of national states have concentrated too heavily on the experiences of France, England, and a few other massive states, while neglecting a major determinant of the actual character of states. Great landlords overwhelmed both capitalists and kings in Poland, but were practically nonexistent in Holland. The "feudalism" of Florence and its *contado* differed so greatly from the "feudalism" of Hungary that it hardly seems worthwhile to cover them both by the same term.

More than anything else, the relative importance of cities, financiers, and capital in a zone of state formation significantly affected the kinds of states that took shape there. Mobilizing for war had significantly different effects depending on the presence or absence of substantial capital and capitalists. A closer look at the actual operation of European states – the business of the next chapter – will clarify how the availability and form of capital made such a difference to preparation for war, and how war, in its turn, shaped the durable organizational structure of states.

Chapters 3 and 4 will neglect geographic variation within Europe in favor of placing major changes in war, political structure, and domestic struggle firmly in time. Chapters 5 and 6 (on alternative paths of state formation and the evolution of the international state system) will, in contrast, pay great attention to variation among different kinds of states, before chapter 7 confronts European historical experience with the character of state formation in the contemporary world.

3
How War Made States, and Vice Versa

A BIFURCATION OF VIOLENCE

Despite the current forty-year lull in open war among the world's great powers, the twentieth century has already established itself as the most bellicose in human history. Since 1900, by one careful count, the world has seen 237 new wars – civil and international – whose battles have killed at least 1,000 persons per year; through the year 2000, the grim numbers extrapolate to about 275 wars and 115 million deaths in battle. Civilian deaths could easily equal that total. The bloody nineteenth century brought only 205 such wars and 8 million dead, the warlike eighteenth century a mere 68 wars with 4 million killed (Sivard 1986: 26; see also Urlanis 1960). Those numbers translate into death rates per thousand population of about 5 for the eighteenth century, 6 for the nineteenth century, and 46 – eight or nine times as high – for the twentieth. From 1480 to 1800, a significant new international conflict started somewhere every two or three years, from 1800 to 1944 every one or two years, since World War II every fourteen months or so (Beer 1974: 12–15; Small and Singer 1982: 59–60; Cusack and Eberwein 1982). The nuclear age has not slowed the centuries-old trend toward more frequent, deadlier wars.

That Westerners commonly think otherwise probably results from the fact that war has become rarer among the great powers: France, England, Austria, Spain, and the Ottoman Empire in 1500; France, the United Kingdom, the Soviet Union, West Germany, the United States, and China in the recent past; other sets in between. Wars directly involving great powers have, on the average, declined in frequency, duration, and number of participating states since the sixteenth century. They have also, in bitter compensation, become much more severe – especially if we count the number of deaths per month or per year (Levy 1983: 116–49). Among lesser powers, more and more wars, but fairly small ones; among the great powers, fewer and fewer wars, but increasingly deadly ones.

We can read the contrast between great power experience with war and that of other states optimistically or pessimistically. Optimistically, we might suppose that the great powers eventually found less costly ways of settling their differences than incessant wars, and that the same thing will eventually happen to other states. Pessimistically, we might conclude that the great powers have exported war to the rest of the world, and have saved their own energy for destroying each other in concentrated bursts. In either mood, we see an increasingly belligerent world in which the most powerful states enjoy a partial exemption from war on their own terrains and therefore, perhaps, become less sensitive to the horrors of war.

The problem is not, however, that people in general have become more aggressive. As the world has grown more warlike, interpersonal violence outside of the state's sphere has generally declined (Chesnais 1981, Gurr 1981, Hair 1971, Stone 1983). At least that seems to be true of Western countries, the only ones so far for which we have long series of evidence. Although the reports of murders, rapes, and collective violence in our daily newspapers may suggest otherwise, the chances of dying a violent death at some other civilian's hand have diminished enormously.

Homicide rates in thirteenth-century England, for example, were about ten times those of today, and perhaps twice those of the sixteenth and seventeenth centuries. Rates of murder declined with particular rapidity from the seventeenth to the nineteenth centuries. (Because the United States has by far the highest national homicide rate in the Western world, it may be harder for Americans than for others to appreciate how rare interpersonal violence has become elsewhere; in most Western countries suicide is ten or twenty times as common as murder, while the American population's homicide rate approaches its rate of suicide.) If it were not for war, state repression, the automobile, and suicide, the odds of violent death of any kind would be incomparably slimmer in most of the Western world today than they were two or three hundred years ago.

Such thinkers as Michel Foucault and Marvin Becker may be right to attribute part of the change to massive shifts in mentality. But surely a significant contribution came from the increasing tendency of states to monitor, control, and monopolize the effective means of violence. In most of the world, the activity of states has created a startling contrast between the violence of the state's sphere and the relative non-violence of civilian life away from the state.

HOW STATES CONTROLLED COERCION

European states led the construction of that contrast. They did so by building up fearsome coercive means of their own as they deprived civilian populations of access to those means. For the most part, they relied heavily on capital and capitalists as they reorganized coercion. Yet different states did so in strikingly different ways.

Do not underestimate the difficulty or importance of the change. Over most of European history, ordinary men (again, the masculine form of the word matters) have commonly had lethal weapons at their disposal; within any particular state, furthermore, local and regional powerholders have ordinarily had control of concentrated means of force that could, if combined, match or even overwhelm those of the state. For a long time, nobles in many parts of Europe had a legal right to wage private war; the twelfth-century *Usatges*, or Customs, of Catalonia specifically recorded that right (Torres i Sans 1988: 13). Bandits (who often consisted of disbanded segments of private or public armies) flourished in much of Europe through the seventeenth century. In Sicily, those controlled and protected entrepreneurs of violence called *mafiosi* have terrorized rural populations into our own time (Blok 1974, Romano 1963). People outside the state have often profited handsomely from their private deployment of violent means.

Since the seventeenth century, nevertheless, rulers have managed to shift the balance decisively against both individual citizens and rival powerholders within their own states. They have made it criminal, unpopular, and impractical for most of their citizens to bear arms, have outlawed private armies, and have made it seem normal for armed agents of the state to confront unarmed civilians. By clinging to civilian possession of firearms, the United States now sets itself apart from all other Western countries, and pays the price in rates of death by gunshot hundreds of times higher than its European counterparts; in the proliferation of private weaponry, the United States resembles Lebanon and Afghanistan more than Great Britain or the Netherlands.

Disarmament of the civilian population took place in many small steps: general seizures of weapons at the ends of rebellions, prohibitions of duels, controls over the production of weapons, introduction of licensing for private arms, restrictions on public displays of armed force. In England, the Tudors suppressed private armies, reduced the princely power of great lords along the Scottish border, contained aristocratic violence, and eliminated the fortress-castles that once announced the power and autonomy of the great English magnates (Stone 1965: 199–272). Louis XIII, the seventeenth-century monarch who with the aid of Richelieu and Mazarin rebuilt the armed force of the French state, probably tore down more fortresses than he constructed. But he built at the frontiers, and destroyed in the interior. In subduing magnates and cities that resisted his rule, he commonly demolished their fortifications, reduced their rights to bear arms, and thereby decreased the odds of any serious future rebellion.

At the same time, the state's expansion of its own armed force began to overshadow the weaponry available to any of its domestic rivals. The distinction between "internal" and "external" politics, once quite unclear, became sharp and fateful. The link between warmaking and state structure strengthened. Max Weber's historically contestable definition of the state – "a state is a human community that (successfully) claims the *monopoly of the legitimate use of physical force* within a given territory" (Gerth and Mills 1946: 78) – finally began to make sense for European states.

Exactly how civilian disarmament proceeded depended on its social setting: in urban regions, the installation of routine policing and the negotiation of agreements between municipal and national authorities played a major part, while in regions dominated by great landlords the disbanding of private armies, the elimination of walled, moated castles, and the interdiction of vendettas alternated between co-optation and civil war. Coupled with the continued buildup of the state's armed force, the disarmament of civilians enormously increased the ratio of coercive means in state hands to those at the disposal of domestic rivals or opponents of those currently holding state power. As a result, it has become almost impossible for a dissident faction to seize power over a Western state without the active collaboration of some segments of the state's own armed forces (Chorley 1943, Russell 1974).

A ruler's creation of armed force generated durable state structure. It did so both because an army became a significant organization within the state and because its construction and maintenance brought complementary organizations – treasuries, supply services, mechanisms for conscription, tax bureaux, and much more – into life. The Prussian monarchy's chief tax-collection agency came into being as the General War Commissariat. During the later seventeenth century, England's successive republican and monarchical governments, intent on countering French and Dutch naval power, built royal shipyards into the country's largest concentrated industry. Such empire-building organizations as the Dutch East India Company became enormously influential elements of their national governments (Duffy 1980). From AD 990 onward, major mobilizations for war provided the chief occasions on which states expanded, consolidated, and created new forms of political organization.

WARS

Why did wars occur at all? The central, tragic fact is simple: coercion *works*; those who apply substantial force to their fellows get compliance, and from that compliance draw the multiple advantages of money, goods, deference, access to pleasures denied to less powerful people. Europeans followed a standard war-provoking logic: everyone who controlled substantial coercive means tried to maintain a secure area within which he could enjoy the returns from coercion, plus a fortified buffer zone, possibly run at a loss, to protect the secure area. Police or their equivalent deployed force in the secure area, while armies patrolled the buffer zone and ventured outside it; the most aggressive princes, such as Louis XIV, shrank the buffer zone to a thin but heavily-armed frontier, while their weaker or more pacific neighbors relied on larger buffers and waterways. When that operation succeeded for a while, the buffer zone turned into a secure area, which encouraged the wielder of coercion to acquire a new buffer zone surrounding the old. So long as adjacent powers were pursuing the same logic, war resulted.

Some conditions for war varied, however. Every state's particular brand of warmaking depended on three closely-related factors: the character of its major rivals, the external interests of its dominant classes, and the logic of the protective activity in which rulers engaged on behalf of their own and dominant classes' interests. Where rivals were commercial seafarers, piracy and privateering simply continued, regardless of the formal state of war and peace, while where landlord-dominated agrarian powers lived shoulder to shoulder, disputes over control of land and labor – especially at moments of disputed succession – precipitated resort to arms much more frequently. When small maritime powers owned large overseas empires, protection of interests drew them into the patrolling of sea lanes, and therefore into inevitable battles with others who coveted the same trade. Because the constellation of rivalries, the nature of dominant classes, and the demands of protection changed fundamentally over the thousand years we are surveying, the characteristic causes of war changed as well.

Coercion is always relative; anyone who controls concentrated means of coercion runs the risk of losing advantages when a neighbor builds up his means. In Europe before 1400, the control of most states by kin groups compounded the competition. Where rulers formed a kin group, the tendency of prospering kin groups to expand and to seek places for growing numbers of heirs incited conquest, and therefore sharpened rivalries. Intermarriage among ruling families, furthermore, multiplied the claims of powerful dynasties to vacated thrones. In the fragmented sovereignty of Europe, rivals – whether kinsmen or not – were always close at hand, but so was a coalition nearly always available to keep any particular center from expanding indefinitely.

For a long time, furthermore, larger states such as Burgundy and England always harbored *internal* rivals to the current sovereign, armed groups who had also some claim to rule, and who sometimes served as implicit or explicit allies of external enemies. In China, once the vast imperial apparatus formed, a waxing empire had plenty of enemies, but no real rivals inside or outside its territories. Mongols constantly threatened along China's northern border, and intermittently staged devastating raids into the empire, but only once actually took it over. In general, the Mongols were better at exacting tribute than they would have been at running the state apparatus themselves. Chinese dynasties collapsed when the empire's administrative reach exceeded its grasp, when warlords organized in the empire's interstices, and when mobile invaders (especially Manchus) swept into imperial territory and seized the levers of power. China became the great land of rebellions and civil war, but not of war among multiple states. For that, Europe held the record.

Over the long run, European wars became more lethal and less frequent. Drawing on the pioneer work of Pitirim Sorokin, Jack Levy has compiled a catalog of larger wars involving great powers – European or otherwise – from 1495 through 1975 (see table 3.1). His catalog, which requires at a minimum 1,000 battle deaths per year, is much smaller than Evan Luard's attempt at a comprehensive listing of all substantial wars over a comparable period, but Levy sets clearer criteria for inclusion and provides more detail on the wars he does include (see Levy 1983, Luard 1987). Over the centuries, the number of great power wars, their average duration, and the proportion of all years in which such wars were in progress all dropped dramatically (Levy 1983: 88–91, 139). William Eckhardt's list of all wars – great power and other, international and civil, combined – includes 50 for the eighteenth century, 208 for the nineteenth, and 213 for the twentieth through 1987 (Eckhardt 1988: 7; Sivard 1988: 28–31).

Table 3.1   Wars involving great powers

Century	Number of wars	Average duration of wars (years)	Proportion of years war underway (%)
16th	34	1.6	95
17th	29	1.7	94
18th	17	1.0	78
19th	20	0.4	40
20th[a]	15	0.4	53

[a] through 1975
Source: Levy 1983, Luard 1987

In addition, the intensity of war altered significantly. Figure 3.1 captures some of the alteration by means of a device borrowed from the analysis of strikes: a solid whose volume represents the total number of battle deaths incurred by great powers per year, and whose three dimensions show the components of total battle deaths. The three components are: number of battle deaths per state participating in great power wars during the average year; number of states participating in those wars during the average year; and average number of wars per state-year of participation. Thus

battle deaths per year =
battle deaths per state × *state-years per war* × *wars per year*

which is what the solid shows.

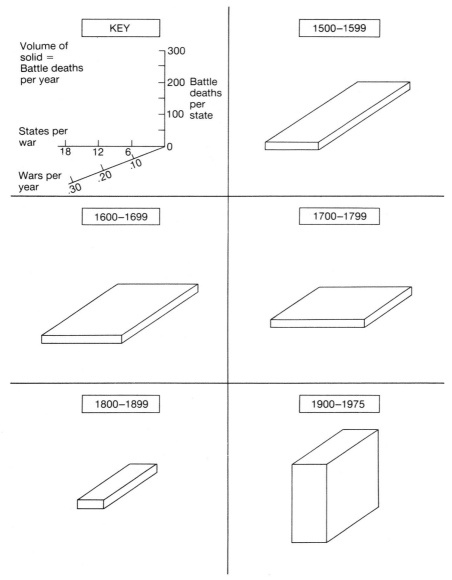

Figure 3.1   Magnitudes of great power war by century, 1500–1975.

Moving from century to century, we see the number of great power battle deaths per state rising from just under 3,000 per year during the sixteenth century to more than 223,000 during the twentieth. The average number of states involved in great power wars rose from 9.4 in the sixteenth century to

17.6 in the eighteenth century, only to fall back to 6.5 in the twentieth. (The rise and fall reveals the development of the general war among most or all of the great powers, counterbalanced in the nineteenth and twentieth centuries by the tendency of Western states to start or intervene in local conflicts outside of the West.) Finally, the number of wars going on in a given year per warmaking state dropped from the sixteenth to eighteenth centuries, then held steady: 0.34, 0.29, 0.17, 0.20, and 0.20. During the sixteenth century, that is, states that ever participated in great power wars were at war during about one year in three (0.34); during the twentieth, one year in five (0.20).

As a result of these changes, the sheer volume of great power deaths per year soared from 9,400 during the sixteenth century to 290,000 during the twentieth. If we could include deaths of civilians and among troops of minor powers, the inflation would surely be even more rapid. With aircraft, tanks, missiles, and nuclear bombs, the death toll of twentieth-century wars far outshadows those of previous centuries.

The numbers are only approximate, but they establish the heavy involvement of European states (which, from the sixteenth to the nineteenth centuries constituted almost all the world's great powers) in warfare, century after century. They also suggest that preparation for war, paying for it, and mending its damage preoccupied rulers throughout the five centuries under scrutiny. In the five centuries before 1500, furthermore, European states concentrated even more exclusively on the making of war. Over the millennium as a whole, war has been the dominant activity of European states.

State budgets, taxes, and debts reflect that reality. Before 1400, in the era of patrimonialism, no state had a national budget in the understood sense of the word. Taxes existed in Europe's more commercialized states, but rulers everywhere acquired most of their revenues from tribute, rents, dues, and fees. Individual sovereigns borrowed money, but usually in their own names and against real collateral. During the sixteenth century, as war multiplied state expenditures through most of the continent, European states began to regularize and expand budgets, taxes, and debts alike. States' future revenues began to serve as security for long-term debt.

France's public debt took on serious proportions when Francis I started borrowing from Parisian businessmen in the 1520s, offering the city's future revenues as security (Hamilton 1950: 246). He spent the money on his great campaigns against Habsburg Emperor Charles V. Although the French national debt fluctuated as a function of war efforts and fiscal policies, in general it galloped upward – to the point at which borrowing for eighteenth-century wars swamped the state, ruined its credit, and led directly to the fateful calling of the Estates General in 1789. Budgets and taxes swelled accordingly: French taxes rose from the equivalent of about 50 hours of an ordinary laborer's wages per capita per year in 1600 to almost 700 hours per capita in 1963 (Tilly 1986: 62).

Great Britain survived without large state debts until the reign of William and Mary. The War of the League of Augsburg (1688–97) elevated the long-term British debt to £22 million. By 1783, after the Seven Years' War and the War of American Independence, it had increased tenfold, to £238 million. In 1939, as Britain rearmed, the public debt reached £8,300 million (Hamilton 1950: 254–7). From the late seventeenth century onward budgets, debts, and taxes arose to the rhythm of war. All of Europe's warmaking states had the same experience.

If war drove states, it did not exhaust their activity. On the contrary: as a by-product of preparations for war, rulers willy-nilly started activities and organizations that eventually took on lives of their own: courts, treasuries, systems of taxation, regional administrations, public assemblies, and much more. Writing of the sixteenth century, J. H. Elliott notes:

> If warfare was a dominant theme in the history of Spain under Charles V and Philip II, bureaucratization was another . . . The replacement of the warrior-king Charles V by a sedentary Philip II, who spent his working day at his desk surrounded by piles of documents, fittingly symbolized the transformation of the Spanish Empire as it passed out of the age of the *conquistador* into the age of the Civil Servant.
>
> (Elliott 1963: 160)

The tasks of fitting out armies and navies were not the only ones which resulted in an expanding governmental structure. No monarch could make war without securing the acquiescence of nearly all of his subject population, and the active cooperation of at least a crucial few. Over and over, rulers sent troops to enforce the collection of tribute, taxes, and levies of men or materials. But they also allowed localities to buy off the costly imposition of troops by timely payments of their obligations. In this regard, rulers resembled racketeers: at a price, they offered protection against evils that they themselves would otherwise inflict, or at least allow to be inflicted.

At the level of the state, the organizational division between armed forces oriented to attacks on external enemies (armies) and those oriented to control of the national population (police) developed only slowly, and never became complete. Problems of policing differ systematically between rural areas (where, among other things, large proportions of land tend to be in private space, forbidden to public authorities) and urban areas (where much land is public space, accessible to anyone); a military style of policing on call suits most rural areas, while systematic patrolling and surveillance becomes possible in urban areas (Stinchcombe 1963). As a consequence of these and other differences, cities generally developed distinct police forces well before the countryside, and the separation of police forces from other military organizations occurred earlier in relatively urban states.

Well into the seventeenth century, most large European states, by virtue of their reliance on armed and partly autonomous regional magnates for domestic rule, faced recurrent threats of civil war as magnates took up arms against rulers. During the critical centuries from 1400 to 1700, rulers spent much of their effort disarming, isolating, or co-opting rival claimants to state power. Although municipalities and rural jurisdictions had created their own small police forces long before, only during the nineteenth century did European states establish uniformed, salaried, bureaucratic police forces specialized in control of the civilian population. They thus freed their armies to concentrate on external conquest and international war.

TRANSITIONS

War wove the European network of national states, and preparation for war created the internal structures of the states within it. The years around 1500 were crucial. Europeans had started using gunpowder seriously in warfare toward the middle of the fourteenth century. Over the following 150 years, the invention and diffusion of firearms had tipped the military advantage toward monarchs who could afford to cast cannon and build the new kinds of fortresses that cannon could not easily shatter. Warfare shifted from battles fought on open plains toward sieges of important cities. Around 1500 costs rose again as mobile siege artillery, and infantry to accompany it, came into widespread use; the development of portable musketry in the early sixteenth century further enhanced the importance of trained, disciplined infantry. At the same time, sailing vessels carrying big guns started to predominate in naval warfare. The larger states north of the Alps, especially France and the Habsburg empire, had the scale to absorb the increased costs, and took advantage of it.

For two more centuries, it is true, some states that concentrated on navies continued to thrive; by some standards the Dutch Republic, with very small land forces, became Europe's leading state during the seventeenth century. Portugal and Venice likewise held their own into the seventeenth century. Insular England prospered as a maritime power before building up its armies during the eighteenth century (Modelski and Thompson 1988: 151–244). Such states drew riches from their colonies, profited from intensive international trade, and took advantage of home bases that seapower could easily defend. Eventually, however, those states that recruited and maintained huge armies from their own national resources – France, Great Britain, and Prussia are the preponderant models – prevailed over all the rest.

On a European scale, then, the late fifteenth century marked an important transition: as the large military states began to feel the stimulus of capitalist expansion, the advantages of the small mercantile states began to disappear. Geopolitics played its part: the end of the Hundred Years' War freed a relatively unified France to look around for spaces to conquer. The multiple states of

Iberia, which were completing the expulsion of Muslim powers from the peninsula, felt the French pressure; in 1463, Louis XI actually annexed the Catalan counties of Roussillon and Cerdagne. The marriage of Ferdinand and Isabella (1474), by joining the crowns of Aragon and Castile, replied to the French threat, and threatened France in its turn. The rivalry of France and Spain then began to reverberate through European politics.

Italy felt the impact of that change first. The papal states, the republics, and the small monarchies of Italy had, of course, long involved themselves in politics outside of the peninsula. Delicately balanced alliances, appeals to outside mediators, and timely marriages played significant parts in their politics. During the eleventh to fourteenth centuries, popes had devoted much of their energy to checking, controlling, or even engineering the elections of German-based Holy Roman emperors. The emperors, in their turn, had typically claimed suzerainty over much of Italy. In short, Italian politics had long connected with politics elsewhere.

Nor were war and international rivalry novelties in the peninsula. During the thirteenth century, Aragon, the Holy Roman Empire, France, and the papacy had all contended for priority in Italy. Many of the century's major battles occurred there. By the 1490s, furthermore, the major powers of Italy – Venice, Milan, Florence, Naples, and the papal states – had been warring with each other intermittently for decades. Their wars, however, had proceeded in a genteel, limited way. Then the usurper-duke Ludovico Sforza of Milan invited Charles VIII of France to press his family's claims to the kingdom of Naples.

With Charles VIII's siege of Naples, not one scourge but two entered Italy. Before 1494, syphilis probably did not exist in Europe; returnees from Columbus's first voyage to America, who had contracted the disease in America, very likely introduced the disease to Spain. Spanish mercenaries at the siege of Naples (1494–5) suffered an epidemic that was almost certainly syphilis, whence it spread throughout the continent. As the plague spread, the French commonly called it "Neapolitan disease," while Neapolitans preferred to call it "the French disease" (Baker and Armelagos 1988). Whatever the precise origin of that first epidemic, Italians soon knew that the French and their mercenaries had returned to the peninsula, with a vengeance. If the French arrived, the Spanish would follow.

The 1490s therefore differed from the past. They differed in bringing not just ambassadors, princes, and imperial forces, but large armies from the waxing national states across the Alps, into city-state Italy. The northerners arrived, furthermore, with mobile siege guns and tactics to accompany them, which multiplied the scale and destructiveness of warfare. The French invasion of 1494 made the peninsula Europe's battleground, ended the round of small-scale wars among autonomous city-states, and shocked Italian thinkers.

Their shock resulted from the fact that barbarian forces had once again overrun the homeland of civilization. As J. R. Hale puts it:

The change that came over the nature of warfare after 1494 was overstressed by Machiavelli in the interest of proving a thesis about the relative merits of militiamen to *condottieri*, as it was by Guicciardini in the interest of turning the knife in the wound to Italy's self-esteem, but a change there certainly was, and it was greeted with widespread horror. This horror, however, was not directed against large-scale war as such, as opposed to earlier small-scale wars, nor even against a long period of such wars; nor was it directed to any important extent against the changed nature of war – more bloody, more total, more expensive. It was caused by the evidence provided by these wars of a failure of morale, a failure of the Italian character to meet their challenge.

(Hale 1983: 360)

A significant portion of Machiavelli's writing about military affairs stemmed from his effort to think through what was happening to the Italian state system, and what to do about it.

What *was* happening to the Italian state system? The national states in formation north of the Alps, by competing for hegemony in Italy, were forcibly integrating it into a larger system spanning much of Europe. Soon after, the Ottoman Empire was expanding deep into European territory, and putting pressure on Italy from the southeast; the reign of Suleyman the Magnificent (1520–66) brought the Turks to the summit of their European power. The Ottoman advance, in its turn, started a four-century struggle with Russia, aligning the strategically-located Crimean Tatars with the Ottomans and against the Russians for the first time.

In Italy, the alteration of warfare had devastating consequences. By the 1520s, Habsburgs and Valois were fighting their dynastic wars on Italian territory. In 1527, the Habsburg emperor's mercenaries sacked Rome. As of 1540, Milan and Lombardy had fallen under Spanish rule, France occupied much of Savoy and Piedmont, Florence had become a Medici-ruled duchy nominally subject to the empire, and Naples was an appanage of the Spanish crown. Of the greater Italian powers, only the most maritime, Venice and Genoa, had maintained their oligarchic institutions. Even they lost their pre-eminence in the Mediterranean.

As the northern states generalized their wars and drew Italy into their struggles, war on land became more important, and the ability to field large armies more critical to a state's success. France had 18,000 troops under arms in 1494, 32,000 in 1525, and 40,000 in 1552. Spain's forces expanded much faster: from 20,000 soldiers in 1492 to 100,000 in 1532. By 1552, Emperor Charles V had some 148,000 men under arms, a total unprecedented since Roman times (Parker 1988: 45). At Spain's peak, around 1630, 300,000 men served under its banners. The ratio of troops to total population rose significantly. The figures in table 3.2 require many qualifications. The dates are approximate, "England and Wales" means England and Wales through 1600, Great Britain in 1700, and the United Kingdom thereafter, the boundaries of all these states changed continually throughout the period, and the frequent

Table 3.2   Men under arms, Europe 1500–1980

Country	Thousands of troops under arms					Troops as percent of national population				
	1500	1600	1700	1850	1980	1500	1600	1700	1850	1980
Spain	20	200	50	154	342	0.3	2.5	0.7	1.0	0.9
France	18	80	400	439	495	0.1	0.4	2.1	1.2	0.9
England/Wales	25	30	292	201	329	1.0	0.7	5.4	1.1	0.6
Netherlands		20	100	30	115		1.3	5.3	1.0	0.8
Sweden		15	100	63	66		1.5	7.1	1.8	0.8
Russia		35	170	850	3663		0.3	1.2	1.5	1.4

Source: Compiled from Ballbé 1983, Brewer 1989, Corvisier 1976, Flora 1983, Jones 1988, Lynn 1989, Mitchell 1975, Parker 1976, Parker 1988, Reinhard, Armengaud and Dupâquier 1968, Sivard 1983, de Vries 1984, Wrigley and Schofield 1981.

employment of foreign mercenaries meant that between 1500 and 1700 the figures shown here were in most cases much higher than the proportion of the national population under arms. Furthermore, the official and real strengths of armies often differed significantly, especially before 1800. Finally, for reasons this chapter explores, numbers of troops fluctuated dramatically from year to year, depending on public finances and the state of war; in France toward 1700, for example, the peacetime army ran to around 140,000 men, but Louis XIV brought it up to 400,000 in the midst of his great campaigns (Lynn 1989). Nevertheless, the figures make their main point eloquently. During the sixteenth and seventeenth centuries, especially, armies expanded. They became big business.

State budgets, taxes, and debt rose accordingly. Castile's tax revenues rose from less than 900,000 *reales* in 1474 to 26 million in 1504 (Elliott 1963: 80). At the same time, Ferdinand and Isabella borrowed to pay for their wars in Granada and Italy. As Spanish control over Italy deepened, Italian taxation became a prime source of crown income; the Netherlands likewise yielded an important share of Castile's revenue. The Cortes of Catalonia, Aragon, and Valencia, in contrast, successfully resisted royal demands to increase their contributions to the state's warmaking. By the middle of the sixteenth century, Spain's Italian and Dutch provinces ceased to yield substantial increases; Charles V and Philip II turned increasingly to Castile (where their predecessors had more effectively subjugated nobility, clergy, and cities to royal will) and to America for financial aid (Elliott 1963: 192–3). They also borrowed through anticipations of revenue from both Castile and America, with the result that by 1543, 65 percent of the crown's regular revenues went to payment of annuities (Elliott 1963: 198; for more detail, see Fernandez Albaladejo 1989). Unsurprisingly, the crown went bankrupt, repudiating its debts in 1557.

At the same time, the Swiss – still, at that time, a conquering people – developed new, highly-disciplined infantry tactics that rapidly proved their superiority. The Swiss had established their military mettle in defeating

Burgundy's Charles the Bold repeatedly during the 1470s. Soon almost every power needed its own Swiss soldiers, and the Swiss began substituting the training and export of mercenaries for the conduct of their own wars (Fueter 1919: 10). In the process, the Swiss cantons themselves entered the business of supplying soldiers for pay (Corvisier 1976: 147). Like other exporters of mercenaries, Switzerland already had a substantial number of poor, mobile, semi-proletarianized and late-marrying highlanders who became attractive candidates for military service away from home (Braun 1960). Mercenaries, Swiss and otherwise, displaced armies of clients and citizen militias.

On a small scale, mercenaries had played their part in European wars for centuries. From the time of the crusades, freebooting soldiers from north of the Alps had sold their services to princes, actual and aspiring, all through the Mediterranean. When no one employed them, they extorted and pillaged on their own account (Contamine 1984: 158). During the fourteenth century, Italian city-states started employing small bodies of hired troops. As it accelerated its forcible annexation of adjacent territory in the 1320s, for example, Florence began relying regularly on mercenary cavalry. In the 1380s, democratic Florence engaged – or bought off – the great English mercenary Sir John Hawkwood, who had been pillaging Tuscany since the end of a war between Milan and the papacy left his company jobless. Hawkwood had previously served England, Savoy, Milan, Pisa and the papacy. Unfortunately for Florentine democrats, Hawkwood backed the oligarchy in their successful rising of 1382; Hawkwood "was accorded the rare favor of Florentine citizenship together with a pension for life and exemption from taxation; and when he died in 1394 the grateful government not only honored him with a splendid funeral at public expense, but also commemorated his services by having him painted on the wall of the inner façade of the cathedral mounted on horseback in full panoply of war" (Schevill 1963: 337). Today's tourists still see the curiously secular mural.

In Venice, that great maritime power, the resident nobility long provided its own military commanders on sea and land; they recruited their soldiers and sailors, furthermore, largely from the Venetian population. But by the end of the fourteenth century Venice, like its Italian neighbors, was hiring mercenary captains, *condottieri*, who recruited their own troops and fought the city-state's wars for a handsome price. Since a *condotta* was a contract to make war for a particular sovereign, *condottiere* meant, essentially, contractor. The German word *Unternehmer* conveys the same commercial tone. The *condottieri* were the oilmen of their time, shifting allegiances from deal to deal and sometimes accumulating great wealth; when the mercenary entrepreneur Bartolomeo Colleoni died in 1475, his fortune was "comparable to the riches of the leading banker of the age, Cosimo de'Medici" (Lane 1973a: 233). By 1625 Wallenstein, Duke of Friedland, ran his own domain of 2,000 square miles and used it as a supply base for troops he deployed – at a profit – on behalf of the

Holy Roman Emperor. Instead of allowing his troops to loot indiscriminately, he organized a protection racket, forcing occupied cities to pay lest the soldiers be let loose (Maland 1980: 103). Under Wallenstein, war became a well-oiled business.

War did not merely entail recruiting and paying troops. Warmaking states had to supply them as well. During the later seventeenth century, a typical army of 60,000 men, with its 40,000 horses, consumed almost a million pounds of food per day – some carried with the army, some stored in magazines, the great bulk procured wherever the army was located, but all of it requiring massive expenditure and organization (Van Creveld 1977: 24). At the prices and wages of the time, a million pounds of grain cost the equivalent of the daily wages of about 90,000 ordinary laborers (calculated from Fourastié 1966: 423). In addition to food, armies had to acquire weapons, horses, clothing, and shelter; the larger the armies, the less feasible to have each individual supply his own. From Wallenstein to Louvois, the great seventeenth-century organizers of war involved themselves in supply as much as in battle. That made their big business even bigger.

From the fifteenth to seventeenth centuries – the critical period for European state formation – armies deployed through much of Europe consisted largely of mercenaries recruited by great lords and military entrepreneurs. Similarly, national navies (especially the corsairs who preyed on enemy shipping with authorization from a protector state) commonly grouped hired sailors from all over the continent (Fontenay 1988b). True, states varied in how much, and how long, they relied on mercenaries. Rulers of larger, more powerful states strove to limit their dependence: France, Spain, England, Sweden, and the United Provinces kept their own generals in place while hiring regiments and companies, but smaller states commonly rented whole armies from generals on down. The German Habsburgs relied on local levies until the Thirty Years' War, engaged the great but demanding *condottiere* Wallenstein during the war and then moved to create a standing army during the latter half of the seventeenth century.

Since battles pay off on the size of armies relative to each other rather than on the per capita effort behind them, one can see why relatively prosperous smaller states often rented their armies on the international market. Navies, too, mixed private and public forces. "Until the 1660s," remarks M. S. Anderson,

a considerable proportion of the French galley-fleet was provided by private entrepreneurs (often Knights of Malta) who owned the galleys they commanded and served the king under contract for a fixed period in return for a specified sum. In Spain in 1616, when the navy was at a very low ebb, of the seventeen vessels in the fleet five were privately owned, hired merely for the summer (the campaigning season at sea as on land), while in the following year another six or seven had to be hired to provide an escort to bring the silver flotas from America into port. In England, of the twenty-five ships which had made up Drake's expedition to the West Indies in 1585 only two were supplied by the queen; and though he sailed as Elizabeth's admiral and had official instructions, only about a third of the cost of fitting out the expedition was met by the government.

(Anderson 1988: 27; see also Fontenay 1988a, 1988b)

Privateers, who thrived in seventeenth-century sea warfare, came by definition from licensed non-governmental forces.

Rented armies and leased navies lived chiefly on payments made or authorized by agents of the crowns they served. Etymologically, after all, "soldier" carries the meaning "he who fights for pay." The *Söldner* and the *Unternehmer* complemented each other. The peculiarity of the system became clear early on, when in 1515 "two Swiss armies, one in the service of the French king and one in the service of an Italian baron, met on opposing sides in a battle at Marignano in northern Italy and almost completely annihilated each other" (Fischer 1985: 186). The event helped persuade the Swiss to avoid wars of their own, but it did not keep them from shipping mercenaries to other people's battles.

For several centuries, European states found the system of hire-purchase through returns from taxation a convenient way to build armed force. The extreme case of state specialization in the production of mercenaries was no doubt Hesse-Cassel, a small eighteenth-century state that maintained a full 7 percent of its entire population under arms – 12,000 in domestic garrisons that participated in the local economy, and another 12,000 in a well-trained army that the Landgrave rented out for profit (Ingrao 1987: 132). When Britain needed extra troops for its war against rebellious Americans, it turned to Hesse. As a result, in American folk history "Hessian" signifies crass and unpatriotic – in short, mercenary. On the basis of military business, Frederick II (1760–85) built an enlightened despotism complete with poor relief and maternity hospital; most of the programs, however, collapsed as the American war ended and as Europe's states turned to recruiting their own national armies (Ingrao 1987: 196–201). The age of mercenaries was then ending.

Europe's larger states had long struggled to contain mercenaries within armies commanded by their own nationals and controlled by their own civilians. With the eighteenth century, furthermore, the costs and political risks of large-scale mercenary forces led those states' rulers to enlist more and more of their own citizens, and to substitute them for foreign mercenaries where possible. In the early stages of military expansion by means of rented armies, rulers found the raising of armies from their own populations costly and politically risky; the danger of domestic resistance and rebellion remained large. The wars of the French Revolution and Empire capped the trend, and ended the dominance of mercenary armies. As Carl von Clausewitz reflected after Napoleon's defeat:

Whilst, according to the usual way of seeing things, all hopes were placed on a very limited military force in 1793, such a force as no one had any conception of made its appearance. War had again suddenly become an affair of the people, and that of a people numbering thirty millions, every one of whom regarded himself as a citizen of the State . . . By this participation of the people in the War instead of a Cabinet and an Army, a whole Nation with its natural weight came into the scale. Henceforth, the means available – the efforts which might be called forth – had no longer any definite limits; the energy with which the War itself might be conducted had no longer any counterpoise, and consequently the danger for the adversary had risen to the extreme.

(Clausewitz 1968 [1832]: 384–5)

With a nation in arms, a state's extractive power rose enormously, as did the claims of citizens on their state. Although a call to defend the fatherland stimulated extraordinary support for the efforts of war, reliance on mass conscription, confiscatory taxation, and conversion of production to the ends of war made any state vulnerable to popular resistance, and answerable to popular demands, as never before. From that point onward, the character of war changed, and the relationship between warmaking and civilian politics altered fundamentally.

Given the general move toward monetization and commodification, the disappearance of mercenary armed forces comes as a surprise. Why on earth would states stop buying their soldiers and sailors and substitute for them standing armies based on conscription? Several factors converged on that outcome. The creation of immense armed forces whose obligation to the crown was purely contractual raised the dangers of foot-dragging, rebellion, and even rivalry for political power; a state's own citizens, commanded by members of its own ruling classes, often fought better, more reliably, and more cheaply. The power over the domestic population that rulers gained through the construction of mercenary armies and the infrastructure to support them eventually shifted the balance; as mercenaries became expensive and dangerous in their own right, the chances of effective resistance on the part of the national population declined. As wars became more expensive, the sheer cost of warfare on the scale established by their large rivals overwhelmed the financial resources of all but the most commercialized states. During the eighteenth century, the vast expansion of rural industry opened up alternative economic opportunities to the people of major regions, such as highland Switzerland, that had been exporting soldiers and domestic servants to the rest of Europe, and thus squeezed the supply of mercenaries. The French Revolution and Napoleon gave the *coup de grâce* to the mercenary system by raising huge, effective armies chiefly from France's own expanding territory. By that time, however, even domestically recruited standing armies had to be paid and supplied. From the fifteenth century onward, European states moved decisively toward the creation of paid forces supported by loans and taxes.

The mercenary system had, indeed, a great weakness: when pay came too slowly or not at all, mercenaries commonly mutinied, lived off the land, became bandits, or all three at once; local people paid the price (see Gutmann

1980: 31–71). In the wars of the sixteenth and seventeenth centuries, booty supplemented military income, but fell far short of allowing armies to support themselves. With great variability from state to state, the leasing of armed force from more or less independent entrepreneurs peaked in the seventeenth century, and began to recede during the eighteenth. Over three or four centuries, nevertheless, mercenaries set the European standard of military performance. For the most part, entrepreneurs who served armies bought food, arms, uniforms, shelter, and means of transport either directly or through allowances to subordinate officers. For that, they needed money, and plenty of it. In 1502 Robert de Balsac, veteran of the Italian campaigns, concluded a treatise on the art of war with advice to any prince: "most important of all, success in war depends on having enough money to provide whatever the enterprise needs" (Hale 1967: 276).

SEIZING, MAKING, OR BUYING COERCION

By 1502, most European princes already knew de Balsac's lesson by heart. Roughly speaking, rulers had three main ways of acquiring concentrated means of coercion: they could seize them, make them, or buy them. Before the twentieth century, few European states ever manufactured a major share of their own coercive means; they rarely possessed the necessary capital or expertise. Such expensive and dangerous manufactures as gunpowder and cannon constituted the chief exceptions. Increasingly after AD 990, European states moved away from direct seizure and toward purchase.

Several important changes pushed them in the same direction. First, as war became more complex and capital-intensive, fewer and fewer people in the civilian population had the means of war; every thirteenth-century noble household owned swords, but no twentieth-century household owns an aircraft carrier. Second, rulers deliberately disarmed their civilian populations as they armed their troops, thus sharpening the distinction between those who controlled the means of war and those whom the monarch ordinarily wanted to pay for war. Third, states involved themselves increasingly in producing the means of warfare, which restated the question as a choice between seizing and buying the means of production instead of the products themselves. Fourth, the mass of the subject population resisted direct seizure of men, food, weapons, transport, and other means of war much more vigorously and effectively than they fought against paying for them. Although various forms of conscription have continued to our own time, European states generally moved toward a system of collecting taxes in money, paying for coercive means with the money thus collected, and using some of the coercive means to further the collection of taxes.

Such a system only worked well under two very demanding conditions: a relatively monetized economy, and the ready availability of credit. In an economy where only a small share of goods and services are bought and sold, a number of conditions prevail: collectors of revenue are unable to observe or evaluate resources with any accuracy, many people have claims on any particular resource, and the loss of that resource is hard for the loser to repair. As a result, any taxation imposed is inefficient, visibly unjust, and quite likely to stir up resistance. When little credit is available, even in a monetized economy, current spending depends on cash on hand, and surges in spending can only occur after careful hoarding. In these circumstances, any ruler who cannot seize the means of war directly from his subject population or acquire it without payment elsewhere is hard pressed to build up his state's armed force. After 1500, as the means of successful warfare became more and more expensive, the rulers of most European states spent much of their time raising money.

Where did the money come from? In the short run, typically from loans by capitalists and levies on local populations unlucky enough to have troops in their vicinity. In the long run, from one form of taxation or another. Norbert Elias sees an intimate relationship between taxation and military force:

The society of what we call the modern age is characterized, above all in the West, by a certain level of monopolization. Free use of military weapons is denied the individual and reserved to a central authority of whatever kind, and likewise the taxation of the property or income of individuals is concentrated in the hands of a central social authority. The financial means thus flowing into this central authority maintain its monopoly of military force, while this in turn maintains the monopoly of taxation. Neither has in any sense precedence over the other; they are two sides of the same monopoly. If one disappears the other automatically follows, though the monopoly rule may sometimes be shaken more strongly on one side than on the other.

(Elias 1982: II, 104)

Elias's duo, however, actually forms two voices of a trio. The missing member, credit, links the military monopoly to the monopoly of taxation.

Historically, few large states have ever been able to pay for their military expenditures out of current revenues. Instead, they have coped with the shortfall by one form of borrowing or another: making creditors wait, selling offices, forcing loans from clients, borrowing from bankers who acquired claims on future governmental revenues. If a government and its agents can borrow, they can separate the rhythm of their expenditures from that of their income, and spend ahead of their income. Spending ahead of income makes expensive warmaking easier, since expenditures for men, arms, and other requisites of war usually come in surges, while potential and actual state revenues ordinarily fluctuate much less from one year to the next. A state that borrows quickly, furthermore, can mobilize faster than its enemies, and thus increase its chances of winning a war.

The availability of credit depends on a state's previous repayment of its debts, to be sure, but it depends even more on the presence of capitalists. Capitalists serve states, when they are willing to do so, as lenders, as mobilizers of loans, and as managers or even collectors of revenues to repay the loans. European capitalists sometimes combined all these activities in the much-hated figure of the tax farmer, who advanced money to the state in anticipation of taxes he himself collected with the authority and military force of the state, and charged a handsome cut of the taxes as his payment for credit, risk, and effort. But even more often capitalists served as major organizers and holders of public debt. Their activity also promoted monetization of a state's economy; some of the crucial relationships are summarized in figure 3.2. These are not the only relationships affecting the variables in the scheme. A crown's direct access to easily sold resources, for example, made it more attractive to creditors, and occasionally provided an alternative to borrowing. So long as gold and silver flowed in from the Americas, Spanish kings found willing lenders in Augsburg, Antwerp, Amsterdam, and elsewhere. In the age of mass mobilization and huge citizen armies that began with the French Revolution, the sheer size of a state's population began to figure very largely in the ease of warmaking. Even then the relationships among capitalist activity, monetization, available credit, and ease of warmaking made a major difference among the states of Europe; they gave states that had ready access to capitalists signal advantages in moving quickly to a war footing.

Figure 3.2   How the presence of capital facilitates warmaking.

The relative presence or absence of commercial cities within a state's territories therefore strongly affected the ease of its mobilization for war. Not only did loans and taxes flow more readily into state coffers where cities abounded – given sufficient state attention to the burghers' interests inside and outside the territory – but also urban militias and commercial fleets lent themselves readily to adaptation for defense and military predation. Where cities were weak and rare, rulers either went without large loans or resorted to foreign bankers who exacted high prices for their services, enlisted the cooperation of magnates who controlled armed force and likewise demanded privileges in return, and built up cumbersome fiscal apparatuses in the process of taxing a resistant, penniless population.

During the sixteenth century, as the scale of war expanded and the use of mercenaries generalized, the ability to borrow became more and more crucial to military success. South German merchants such as the Fuggers of Augsburg joined their Italian colleagues in lending to kings; the Fuggers borrowed in

Antwerp, for example, to finance Spanish wars, with future deliveries of American silver as collateral. Long-range borrowing obligated monarchs to foreigners they could not easily control, but allowed them to repudiate their debts with less catastrophic effects on their local economies. Eventually the disadvantages outweighed the advantages, and those monarchs who could moved toward domestic borrowing. Those who could borrow at home were, of course, especially those whose states included important zones of capitalist enterprise. Around the time of Henry IV (1598–1610), France moved rapidly from dependency on other centers of capital (notably Lyon, a conduit for Italian capital) to Parisian financial dominance, from foreign to French financiers, and from negotiation to enforced payment of taxes (Cornette 1988: 622–4). Although insolvency threatened the crown repeatedly during the following two centuries, that consolidation of fiscal power gave France an enormous advantage in the wars to come.

PAYING THE DEBTS

Whether they borrowed heavily or not, all rulers faced the problem of paying for their wars without destroying the ability of their sources to pay again in the future. They adopted very different fiscal strategies. Governmental revenues in general ("taxes," in a loose sense of the word) fall into five broad categories: tributes, rents, payments on flows, payments on stocks, and income taxes. *Tributes* include arbitrary payments levied on individuals, groups, or localities; head taxes which are equal across the population or across its major categories constitute a special kind of tribute. *Rents* consist of direct payments for lands, goods, and services supplied contingently to particular users by the state. (Some states – Russia, Sweden, and the Ottoman Empire, for example – gave a special twist to rents by assigning some military officers and civilian officials the rents from crown lands the officers held so long as they remained in royal service.)

Both rents and tributes can easily be collected in kind. Payments on flows and stocks cannot. *Payments on flows* cover excise, customs, tolls, transaction charges, and other collections on transfers or movements; specialists often call them indirect taxes, because they reflect only quite indirectly the taxpayer's ability to pay. *Payments on stocks* divide chiefly into land and property taxes; specialists often call them direct taxes. *Income taxes* (actually a special case of payments on flows) touch current revenues, especially salaries and other monetary revenues.

The five kinds of taxes form a kind of continuum with respect to their dependence on monetization of the ambient economy. They also differ in terms of the amount of continuous surveillance the collector must apply (see figure 3.3). In general, taxes that require little surveillance rely on open use of force more frequently than those that entail continuous surveillance, and

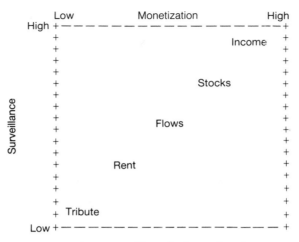

Figure 3.3   Alternative forms of taxation.

therefore promote the development of specialized staffs for evaluation and collection. Governments that have plenty of force at their disposition can collect tributes and rents in relatively unmonetized economies, although even there people's ability to pay cash still depends on their ability to sell goods or services for cash. Even customs revenues depend on the existence of well-defined and well-defended borders; smuggling – the evasion of internal or external customs duties – became a crime precisely to the extent that European states attempted to define and defend their boundaries. In the ages of patrimonialism and brokerage, indeed, states often relied on tolls collected at strategic roads, ports, or waterways instead of customs collected all round a monitored frontier (Maravall 1972: I, 129–33).

Payments on flows depend heavily on monetization, because monetization increases such flows, eases assessors' evaluations of flows, and increases the ability of those who are liable to pay in cash. Payments on stocks, counter-intuitively, also depend heavily on monetization, since in the absence of an active market for the land or property in question assessors lack the means to match tax with value; when the match is poor, the tax is inefficient (see Ardant 1965). Thus monetization strongly affects the effectiveness with which a state can finance its war effort by means of taxation, instead of wresting the means of war directly from its citizenry. The income tax is an extreme case, one that only becomes a durable and effective source of governmental revenue in economies where practically everyone is involved in the money economy and most workers toil for wages.

Highly commercialized states, however, draw some important advantages from these relationships. Given an appropriate level of monetization, the taxes toward the upper end of the continuum are relatively efficient. They build on the measurement and visibility a commercial economy applies to property, goods, and services. Participants in markets already do a significant share of the requisite surveillance through the recording of prices and transfers. Properly socialized citizens, furthermore, come to attach moral value to the payment of taxes; they monitor themselves and each other, blaming tax evaders as free riders. Taxes on flows, stocks, and especially income therefore yield a high return for a given amount of effort at collection, and adapt more readily than tribute or rents to alterations in state policy. A state attempting to collect exactly the same amount from the same tax in a less commercialized economy faces greater resistance, collects less efficiently, and therefore builds a larger apparatus of control in the process. If two states of similar size but different degrees of commercialization go to war and attempt to extract comparable sums of money from their citizens by means of the same sorts of taxes, the less commercialized state creates a bulkier state structure as it wars and pays for war. The more commercialized state, on the average, makes do with a slimmer administrative organization.

The direct supplying of armies, the imposition of taxes, and the management of royal credit all went more easily in commercialized, capital-rich economies. Wherever they occurred, however, they multiplied the state's civilian servants. A major war effort generally produced a permanent expansion of the state's central apparatus – the number of its full-time personnel, the scope of its institutions, the size of its budget, the extent of its debt. When Holland and Spain reached a truce in their draining war over Dutch claims to independence in 1609, many observers on both sides expected relief from the extraordinary taxation that had beset them during the previous decade. As it turned out, debt service, building of fortifications, and other state activities easily absorbed the revenues freed by military demobilization. Taxes did not decline significantly in either country (Israel 1982: 43–4).

Some historians speak of a "ratchet effect" by which an inflated wartime budget fails to return to its prewar level (Peacock and Wiseman 1961; Rasler and Thompson 1983, 1985a). The ratchet does not occur universally, but it does appear quite often, especially in states that have not suffered great losses in the war at hand. It occurs for three reasons: because the wartime increase in state power gives officials new capacity to extract resources, take on new activities, and defend themselves against cost-cutting; because wars either cause or reveal new problems that call for state attention; and because the wartime accumulation of debt places new burdens on the state.

National debts arose largely from borrowing for and during wars. The ability to borrow for military expenditure strongly affected a state's ability to mount effective military campaigns. The seventeenth-century claims of the Dutch Republic on the financiers of Amsterdam and other major trading cities allowed a small state to raise enormous sums rapidly for its armies and navies, and to become the dominant European power for a time. The critical innovations had occurred between 1515 and 1565, when the States General of the Habsburg Netherlands (of which the northern provinces, after their rebellion of 1568, would eventually become the Dutch Republic) took steps toward issuing state-backed annuities secured by specific new taxes and bearing attractive interest (Tracy 1985). As a result, "in an emergency, the Dutch Republic could raise a loan of 1 million florins at only 3 percent in two days" (Parker 1976: 212–13). State securities became a favorite investment for Dutch rentiers, whose representatives taxed the entire economy for their benefit. Indeed, the word "capitalist" in its modern use seems to have come from the word for those Dutch citizens who paid the highest per capita tax rate, thereby advertising their wealth and creditworthiness.

Dutch bankers were so affluent, adept, and independent that after 1580, as the war of the northern Netherlands against their former Spanish masters continued, the bankers were able to make money by shipping silver diverted from the Spanish fleet to Antwerp, where it paid for Spanish expenses of the war (Parker 1972: 154–5). When in 1608 Spain proposed to recognize Dutch independence if Holland withdrew from the East and West Indies, Dutch negotiator Oldenbarnevelt "retorted that too many prominent personages in the Republic were involved in the East India Company for it to be disbanded" (Israel 1982: 9). On the whole, however, the merchants' affluence worked to the advantage of their own Dutch state. An intensely commercial economy permitted the seventeenth-century Dutch state to follow a path that the neighboring Prussians found barred and that the English, newly blessed with a Dutch king, borrowed in the 1690s. By adopting Dutch fiscal techniques, the English managed to reduce their previous dependence on Dutch bankers, and eventually to best the Dutch at war.

The seventeenth-century Dutch occupied an extreme position on the axis of commercialization. Other capital-intensive states, such as the Italian commercial powers of Genoa and Venice, adopted similar approaches to the raising of military force through public credit and taxation on flows of goods. In coercion-intensive regions, resources that might be used for war remained embedded in agriculture, and in the hands of magnates who wielded considerable autonomous force; there, the extraction of military resources obviously took very different forms: various combinations of expropriation, co-optation, clientage, conscription, and heavy-handed taxation. In between the two extremes, in areas of capitalized coercion, the more even balance of capital and coercion allowed rulers to play one against the other, using purchased force to check the holders of private armies and national armies to persuade the holders of private capital; in the long run, as the sheer bulk of military requirements rose, the combination gave rulers of capitalized-coercion states the decisive advantage in warfare; as a consequence, their sort of state – the national state –

won out over city-states, empires, urban federations, and other forms of state that had sometimes prospered in Europe.

THE LONG, STRONG ARM OF EMPIRE

By the end of the seventeenth century, a significant part of European war – including war between neighboring Holland and England – was taking place at sea, far from the continent. The struggle for maritime empire complemented European land warfare in shaping distinctive kinds of European states. Before they created national states, Europeans had plenty of experience with empires. Norsemen constructed fleeting empires well before the Millennium. Mongol, Russian, Ottoman, Swedish, Burgundian, and Habsburg empires long dominated significant parts of Europe. Great trading cities such as Genoa and Venice conquered or purchased their own scattered empires. Napoleon built a vast, if short-lived European empire. Ottoman, Austro-Hungarian, Russian, and German empires existed up to World War I. As the centuries rolled on, to be sure, European empires came increasingly to resemble national states. In their heterogeneity and their residues of indirect rule through viceroys or the equivalent, nevertheless, they faced distinctive problems of control over their subject populations.

Beginning in the fifteenth century, European powers moved toward the creation of empires far outside of the continent. Portuguese Christians had eliminated the last Moorish kingdom from their end of the peninsula in 1249. For another century and a half the Portuguese confined their maritime attentions to trade in Europe and Africa, but in 1415 their capture of Ceuta on the Moroccan coast launched an expansion that did not cease for two hundred years. By the time of the death of Prince Henry (the so-called Navigator) in 1460, his forces had extended their control, both political and commercial, well down Africa's western coast as well as seizing Madeira and the Azores in the Atlantic. With the assistance of Genoese *condottieri* and entrepreneurs, they began almost at once to make new colonies commercially viable. Before the century's end Vasco da Gama had sailed around Africa to Calicut, thus extending Portuguese influence into the Indian Ocean and the Pacific.

The Portuguese sought deliberately to break Muslim–Venetian control of European access to Asian spices and luxury goods, and to establish their own hegemony in the sea lanes to Asia. Through great energy, exceptional risk-taking, and supreme ruthlessness, they almost succeeded. During the sixteenth century Portuguese carracks and galleons commanded much of the Indian Ocean, and carried close to half of all spices shipped to Europe and the Ottoman Empire (Boxer 1969: 59). In the course of the same century Portuguese settlers began migrating to Brazil; they started to export sugar produced by the labor of impressed Amerindians and, increasingly, slaves imported from Angola, Congo, and Senegambia. The Portuguese crown then received a major share of its income from customs duties on goods from its colonies.

Portugal, however, suffered some severe handicaps. Its domestic supply of men, timber, and other resources for imperial adventure remained perilously thin, so much so that sixteenth-century "Portuguese" ships often bore no native Portuguese but their commanders. From 1580 to 1640 Portugal merged with the Spanish crown, and thus inherited Spain's war with the fearsome Dutch. With its rebellion against Spain in 1640, the small kingdom warred against both the Dutch and the Spanish until 1689. Wars with maritime rivals endangered Portuguese merchants on the high seas. That Portugal remained powerful for so long testifies to extraordinary toughness and ingenuity.

As they attached an immense empire to a fragile home base, Portuguese conquerors established characteristic forms of rule overseas, and transformed their own state. Overseas, Portugal made most of its colonies into military outposts, one of whose chief activities was to generate revenues for the crown. Unlike the Dutch, the English, and the Venetians, Portuguese rulers did not license merchants to organize colonial rule. Unlike the Spanish, they did not tolerate the creation of great autonomous domains in their overseas territories. But they could not stop colonial administrators, priests, and soldiers from trading on their own account, or from accepting payoffs for illegal uses of their official powers. Colonial revenues thus made Lisbon and its king relatively independent of powerholders elsewhere in Portugal, but dependent on frequently corrupt officials. Such a monarchy could only prosper when gold and goods flowed freely from the colonies.

As compared to the neighboring Portuguese, Spaniards were latecomers to overseas conquest. In 1492, Granada, last Muslim stronghold on the Iberian peninsula, fell to Castile. By then, the south-driving Spaniards were already beginning settlement of the Canary Islands. The same year, Queen Isabella authorized the Genoese *condottiere* Christopher Columbus to sail west, via the Canaries, in search of India and Cathay. Within fifteen years Spain had functioning colonies in the Caribbean. A century after Granada's fall, Spaniards ruled – however thinly – almost all of Central and South America except Brazil, and had reached out to conquer the Philippines as well.

About that time, Dutch and English seafarers sailed onto the scene. The two nations' civilian-run East and West India companies, not to mention their freebooters, moved aggressively into Portuguese and Spanish waters in the South Atlantic, the Indian Ocean, and the Pacific. During their eighty-year war of independence against Spain, ironically, Dutch merchants made their greatest profits by trading with the enemy; they brought goods from northern Europe to Iberia, and used old commercial ties to penetrate the trading networks of the Spanish and Portuguese empires. That initiated their construction of a world-wide Dutch empire. In the Atlantic, English merchants attached themselves to Portuguese trade, and became specialists in outwitting royal customs officers. They started as parasites, but soon became the chief organisms in their territories.

Throughout the history of European imperialism, indeed, a new phase usually began with competition between an established dominant in one world region or trade route and a newcomer who attempted either to challenge the hegemon or to outflank him, or both. The early targets of European attack were usually Muslims, but by the fifteenth century Europeans were battling each other for access to the East. Sixteenth-century Portuguese adventurers almost succeeded in reaching around the Venetians who controlled the western end of Europe's land connection with East and South Asia, only to find themselves challenged on the sea by Spain, Holland, and England a century later. The English and Dutch never expelled Portuguese merchants and viceroys from their entire domain, but they ended the supremacy Portugal had enjoyed until 1600. (During the Dutch war of 1647–8, for example, enemy action took 220 vessels from the Portuguese Brazil fleet: Boxer 1969: 221.) The Dutch East India and West India companies governed great empires of their own, gaining the advantage over their competitors "by virtue of their greater control of the market and the internalization of protection costs" (Steensgaard 1974: 11). Over the seventeenth century as a whole, the Dutch became the world's greatest naval and commercial power.

Then the British displaced the Dutch. As Dutch naval strength faltered, British ships came to prevail on most of the world's seas. By the eighteenth century, French corsairs, men-of-war, and merchantmen were likewise venturing to the Americas, Asia, and the Pacific – they made little impact in Africa before the nineteenth century – and further crowding the sea lanes. The eighteenth-century discovery of gold and diamonds in Brazil revived the Portuguese colonial economy, but failed to restore anything like Portugal's sixteenth-century hegemony. France and Britain came late to territorial conquest outside of their own immediate perimeters, but swiftly made up the lag after 1700. By the end of the eighteenth century, Spain, Portugal, the United Provinces, France, and Great Britain all had large overseas empires and world-wide webs of trade; Britain stood above all the rest. Imperial conquest accelerated in the nineteenth century. "Between 1876 and 1915," notes Eric Hobsbawm, "about one-quarter of the globe's land surface was distributed or redistributed as colonies among a half-dozen states" (Hobsbawm 1987: 59). By World War I, Spain, Portugal, and what was then the kingdom of the Netherlands held little more than shreds of their former empires, while the fabric of French and, especially, British dominion stretched across the world.

All these empires combined conquered territories with "factories," recognized trading settlements at the edges of lands governed by indigenous rulers. With exceptions such as Portuguese Macao, no European powers conquered in Japan or China. But the Portuguese, the Spanish, and then the Dutch maintained commercial enclaves in Japan; during the closed years of the Tokugawa shogunate (1640–1854), the Dutch outpost at Deshima was practically Japan's only point of contact with Europe (Boxer 1965: 237). Over time, however, the European pattern shifted toward conquest and partial settlement. Starting in 1652, for example, even the Dutch – who actually colonized very few of the lands in which they gained commercial hegemony – began to conquer, administer, and settle around the Cape of Good Hope; the word *Afrikaner* began to apply to transplanted Europeans early in the eighteenth century (Boxer 1965: 266). In the nineteenth century especially, European states tried to carve up most of the non-European world into mutually exclusive colonial territories.

Empire overseas did not build up state structure to the same extent as land war at home. Nevertheless, the connection between state and empire ran in both directions: the character of the European state governed the form of its expansion outside of Europe, and the nature of the empire significantly affected the metropole's operation. Capital-intensive states such as Venice and the Dutch Republic reached out chiefly by the ruthless pursuit of trading monopolies, but invested little effort in military conquest and colonization. Coercion-intensive states such as the Norse and the Spanish devoted more of their energy to settlement, enslavement of the indigenous (or imported) labor force, and exaction of tribute. The in-between states, such as Britain and France, entered the imperial game relatively late, and excelled at it by combining the capitalist and coercive strategies.

The capitalist strategy added relatively little bulk to the central state, especially when conducted through essentially private organizations such as the Dutch East India Company. These commercial megaliths, however, became political forces to be contended with in their own right; thus privatization pushed the state toward bargaining with its subject population, or at least with the dominant commercial class. The strategy of conquest and settlement, which inevitably called forth durable armies and navies, added to the central state bureaucracy, not to mention the world-wide web of officialdom it called into being. Where it brought in riches – especially in the form of bullion, as in Spain – conquest created an alternative to domestic taxation, and thereby shielded rulers from some of the bargaining that established citizens' rights and set limits on state prerogatives elsewhere.

On both the domestic and overseas fronts, how much state apparatus emerged from the interaction between the creation of a military machine and the development of markets depended on several factors: the bulk of the machine in relation to the population that supported it, the prior commercialization of the economy, and the extent to which the state relied on the wartime mobilization of powerholders who provided their own military force and retained the ability to return it to peacetime uses at the end of war. We might imagine a continuum from an imperial Russia in which a cumbersome state apparatus grew up to wrest military men and resources from a huge but uncommercialized economy to a Dutch Republic which relied heavily on navies, ran its military forces on temporary grants from its city-dominated provinces, easily drew taxes from customs and excise, and never created a substantial central bureaucracy. In between we would place cases such as France and Prussia, where kings had access to important regions of agricultural and commercial capitalism, but had to bargain with powerful landlords for support of their military activity. In the long run, military requirements for men, money, and supplies grew so demanding that rulers bargained with the bulk of the population as well. The next chapter focuses on that bargaining and its variations from one sort of state to another.

4
States and their Citizens

Over the last thousand years, European states have undergone a peculiar evolution: from wasps to locomotives. Long they concentrated on war, leaving most activities to other organizations, just so long as those organizations yielded tribute at appropriate intervals. Tribute-taking states remained fierce but light in weight by comparison with their bulky successors; they stung, but they didn't suck dry. As time went on, states – even the capital-intensive varieties – took on activities, powers and commitments whose very support constrained them. These locomotives ran on the rails of sustenance from the civilian population and maintenance by a civilian staff. Off the rails, the warlike engines could not run at all.

A state's essential minimum activities form a trio:

statemaking: attacking and checking competitors and challengers within the territory claimed by the state;

warmaking: attacking rivals outside the territory already claimed by the state;

protection: attacking and checking rivals of the rulers' principal allies, whether inside or outside the state's claimed territory.

No state lasts long, however, that neglects a crucial fourth activity:

extraction: drawing from its subject population the means of statemaking, warmaking, and protection.

At the minimum, tribute-taking states stayed close to this indispensable set of four activities, intervening in the lives of their nominal subjects chiefly to impose ruling-class power and to extract revenues. Beyond a certain scale, however, all states found themselves venturing into three other risky terrains:

adjudication: authoritative settlement of disputes among members of the subject population;

distribution: intervention in the allocation of goods among members of the subject population;

production: control of the creation and transformation of goods and services by members of the subject population.

The major connections among these activities run roughly as shown in figure 4.1. Warmaking and statemaking reinforced each other, indeed remained practically indistinguishable until states began to form secure, recognized boundaries around substantial contiguous territories. Both led to extraction of resources from the local population. The play of alliances and the attempt to draw resources from relatively powerful or mobile actors promoted the state's involvement in protection, checking the competitors and enemies of selected clients. As extraction and protection expanded, they created demands for adjudication of disputes within the subject population, including the legal regularization of both extraction and protection themselves.

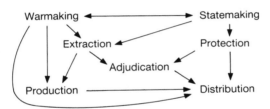

Figure 4.1   Relations among major activities of states.

Over time, the weight and impact of state activities standing lower in the diagram – adjudication, production, and distribution – grew faster than those at the top: warmaking, statemaking, extraction, and protection. The sheer volume most European states invested in warmaking (attacking rivals outside the territory claimed by the state) or statemaking (attacking and checking competitors and challengers within the territory) continued to increase irregularly into the twentieth century; but adjudication, production, and distribution went from trivial to tremendous. Even those non-socialist states that maintained wide private ownership, for example, eventually invested large sums in the production and/or regulation of energy, transportation, communication, food, and arms. As rulers drew more and more resources for war and other coercive enterprises from their local economies, the major classes within those economies successfully demanded more and more state intervention outside the realm of coercion and war. Over the thousand-year span we are surveying here, nevertheless, coercive activities clearly predominated.

Warmaking frequently involved European states in the production of arms, and extraction in the production of goods (e.g. salt, matches, and tobacco) whose monopolies fed state coffers. Later, all states intervened more generally in production as demands from workers and intellectuals for the checking of capitalist excesses became effective; socialist states merely represent the extreme of a general tendency. Extraction, protection, and adjudication intertwined, finally, to draw states into control of distribution – first as a way of assuring state revenues from the flow of goods, then as a response to popular demands for correction of inequities and local shortages. Again socialist states mark but the extreme version of a very general expansion in state activity outside the military realm.

In the course of extracting resources and pacifying the population, every European state eventually created new administrative structure at the local and regional levels as well as on a national scale. The treaty of Cateau-Cambrésis (1559), for example, created the kingdom of Savoy-Piedmont, and placed Emmanuel-Philibert on its throne. Soon the quest for funds drove the new king to innovate: first a profitable forced sale of salt, second a census to determine who was taxable, then a tax based on each community's productive area. The tax forced adjacent communities to delineate their boundaries precisely, which drew them into preparing cadasters and creating officials to administer them (Rambaud and Vincienne 1964: 11). Everywhere extractive efforts not only withdrew valuable resources from their customary uses but also created new forms of political organization.

State activities therefore had profound implications for the interests of the general population, for collective action, and for the rights of citizens. As rulers and agents of states pursued the work of warmaking, statemaking, protection, extraction, adjudication, distribution, and production, they impinged on well-defined interests of people who lived within their range of control; the impact was often negative, since states repeatedly seized for their own use land, capital, goods, and services that had previously served other commitments. Most of the resources that kings and ministers used to build armed might came ultimately from the labor and accumulation of ordinary people, and represented a diversion of valuable means from pursuits to which ordinary people attached much higher priority. Although capitalists sometimes invested gladly in state finances and in the protection that state power gave to their business, and although regional magnates sometimes allied themselves with kings in order to hold off their own enemies, most people who had an investment in the resources that monarchs sought to seize resisted royal demands tenaciously.

The labor, goods, money, and other resources demanded by states were, after all, typically embedded in webs of obligation and committed to ends that households and communities prized. From the short-run perspectives of ordinary people, what we in blithe retrospect call "state formation" included the setting of ruthless tax farmers against poor peasants and artisans, the forced sale for taxes of animals that would have paid for dowries, the imprisoning of local leaders as hostages to the local community's payment of overdue taxes, the hanging of others who dared to protest, the loosing of brutal soldiers on a hapless civilian population, the conscription of young men who were their parents' main hope for comfort in old age, the forced purchase of tainted salt, the elevation of already arrogant local propertyholders into officers of the state, and the imposition of religious conformity in the name of public order and morality. Small wonder that powerless Europeans so often accepted the legend of the "good tsar" who had been misled, or even held captive, by bad advisors.

Both the character and the weight of state activity varied systematically as a function of the economy that prevailed within a state's boundaries. In *coercion-intensive* regions, rulers commonly drew resources for warmaking and other activities in kind, through direct requisition and conscription. Customs and excise yielded small returns in relatively uncommercialized economies, but the institution of head taxes and land taxes created ponderous fiscal machines, and put extensive power into the hands of landlords, village heads, and others who exercised intermediate control over essential resources. In *capital-intensive* regions, the presence of capitalists, commercial exchange, and substantial municipal organizations set serious limits on the state's direct exertion of control over individuals and households, but facilitated the use of relatively efficient and painless taxes on commerce as sources of state revenue. The ready availability of credit, furthermore, allowed rulers to spread the costs of military activity over substantial periods rather than extracting in quick, calamitous bursts. As a result, states in those regions generally created slight, segmented central apparatuses. In regions of *capitalized coercion*, an intermediate situation prevailed: however uneasily, rulers relied on acquiescence from both landlords and merchants, drew revenues from both land and trade, and thus created dual state structures in which nobles confronted – but also finally collaborated with – financiers.

BARGAINING, RIGHTS, AND COLLECTIVE ACTION

State intervention in everyday life incited popular collective action, often in the form of resistance to the state but sometimes in the guise of new claims on the state. As authorities sought to draw resources and acquiescence from the subject population, state authorities, other powerholders, and groups of ordinary people bargained out (however lopsidedly) new agreements concerning the conditions under which the state *could* extract or control, and the kinds of claims that powerholders or ordinary people could make on the state. The bargaining and the claims changed fundamentally with the movement from patrimonialism to brokerage to nationalization to specialization; under patrimonialism, for example, bargaining often occurred in regional rebellions led by magnates who advanced their own claims to independent statehood, while under brokerage, as former patrons sided with the state, magnate-led rebellions gave way to popular insurrections against taxation or conscription.

The actual forms and sequences of state impact on interests, collective action, bargaining, and establishment of rights varied greatly as a function of the relative salience of coercion and capital as the basis of state formation. In coercion-intensive regions such as Poland and Russia, control over land and of labor attached to the land long remained the central object of struggle, while in regions of capital intensity, such as the Low Countries, capital and marketable commodities occupied a more salient position with respect to the bargaining that created state structure and citizens' claims on states. In capital-intensive zones, furthermore, states acted earlier and more effectively to establish bourgeois property rights – to reduce multiple claims on the same property, to enforce contracts, and to strengthen the principal owner's capacity to determine the property's use. Everywhere, nevertheless, the state's creation of military might involved its agents in bargaining with powerholders and with groups of ordinary people. The subject population's class structure therefore helped determine the state's organization: its repressive apparatus, its fiscal administration, its services, its forms of representation.

The translation from class structure to state organization occurred through struggle. The tax rebellions that shook much of western Europe during the seventeenth century sprang from the competing claims of kings, regional powerholders, local communities, and individual households to land, labor, commodities, cattle, tools, credit, and household wealth that could not serve all ends at once. When resistance to taxation aligned the claims of great lords with those of local communities, as it often did in early seventeenth-century France, it threatened the very viability of the crown. But even on a smaller scale, day-to-day individual and collective action against the growing state's extractive efforts posed serious challenges to every ruler.

To the extent that a state's population was segmented and heterogeneous, the likelihood of large-scale rebellion declined, but the difficulty of imposing uniform administrative arrangements increased. In a homogeneous, connected population, an administrative innovation installed and tested in one region had a reasonable chance of working elsewhere, and officials could easily transfer their knowledge from one locality to another. In the period of movement from tribute to tax, from indirect to direct rule, from subordination to assimilation, states generally worked to homogenize their populations and break down their segmentation by imposing common languages, religions, currencies, and legal systems, as well as promoting the construction of connected systems of trade, transportation, and communication. When those standardizing efforts threatened the very identities on which subordinate populations based their everyday social relations, however, they often stirred massive resistance.

Resistance to state demands usually occurred covertly, on a local scale, employing the "weapons of the weak" James Scott has described – sabotage, foot-dragging, concealment, evasion (Scott, 1985). It compounded into mass rebellion chiefly when (1) the state's demands and actions offended citizens' standards of justice or attacked their primary collective identities, (2) the people touched by offensive state actions were already connected by durable social ties, (3) ordinary people had powerful allies inside or outside the state, and (4) the state's recent actions or interactions revealed that it was vulnerable to attack. Under these circumstances, popular rebellion not only was likely to occur, but also had some chance of success.

The 1640s combined all these conditions in a number of European states, and one of the most rebellious decades in European history resulted. The nasty tangle of struggles we now remember as the Thirty Years' War taxed the capacities of most western European states, revealing their vulnerability at the very time when they were demanding unprecedented sacrifices of their subjects. England went through a civil war, France entered the turmoil of the Fronde, Scotland almost shook itself free of England, Catalonia and Portugal broke loose (the former provisionally, the latter definitively) from the control of the composite Spanish crown, while in Naples the fisherman Masaniello led a great popular revolt.

In Catalonia, for example, royal demands for increased war taxes brought the king (or, rather, his minister Olivares) into bitter conflict with the Cortes. In 1640, the crown dispatched 9,000 troops into the province to enforce its claims for payment, reduce the likelihood of organized resistance, and apply a kind of blackmail (since the Catalans had to support the troops and endure their depredations so long as their obligations remained unpaid). The stationing of troops without provincial consent violated established Catalan rights. A broad popular rebellion followed. As it began to spread, the Diputació – loosely speaking, the Cortes' executive committee – placed itself at the revolt's head, and went so far as to call France's Louis XIII to assume sovereignty in Catalonia. Profiting from France's distraction by the Fronde, a Spanish army finally reconquered Barcelona, and hence Catalonia, in 1652. At that point, "Philip IV granted an amnesty and vowed to respect Catalonia's traditional liberties" (Zagorin 1982: II, 37).

When faced with resistance, dispersed or massive, what did rulers do? They bargained. Now, you may object to using the word "bargain" for the sending in of troops to crush a tax rebellion or capture a reluctant taxpayer. Nonetheless, the frequent use of exemplary punishment – hanging a few ringleaders rather than all the rebels, jailing the richest local taxpayer instead of all the delinquents – indicates that the authorities were negotiating with the bulk of the population. In any case, bargaining took many other more acceptable forms: pleading with parliaments, buying off city officials with tax exemptions, confirming guild privileges in return for loans or fees, regularizing the assessment and collection of taxes against the guarantee of their more willing payment, and so on. All this bargaining created or confirmed individual and collective claims on the state, individual and collective rights vis-à-vis the state, and obligations of the state to its citizens. It also created rights – recognized enforceable claims – of states with respect to their citizens. The core of what we now call "citizenship," indeed, consists of multiple bargains hammered out by rulers and ruled in the course of their struggles over the means of state action, especially the making of war.

Bargaining was obviously asymmetrical: at the showdown, cannon versus staves; the state's steady disarmament of the general population compounded the asymmetry. Yet even forceful repression of rebellions against taxation and conscription ordinarily involved both a set of agreements with those who cooperated in the pacification and public affirmation of the peaceful means by which ordinary citizens *could* rightfully seek redress of the state's errors and injustices. Those means commonly included petition, suit, and representation through local assemblies. As workers and bourgeois (or, less often, peasants) organized, they took advantage of the permitted means to press for expanded rights and direct representation. During the age of specialization, states preempted or responded to the growing demands of bourgeois and workers by committing their agents to such programs as social insurance, veterans' pensions, public education, and housing; all of these programs added bureaux, bureaucrats, and budget lines to increasingly civilian states.

Through struggle, negotiation, and sustained interaction with the holders of essential resources, states came to reflect the class structures of their subject populations. The dominant classes had the largest effects, so that states dominated by great landlords developed very different structures from those controlled by capitalists (Moore 1966). But the sheer necessity of dealing with peasants, or artisans, or landless laborers, also marked a state's fiscal organization, controls over trade, police forces, and much more. Specifically negotiated agreements that ended sustained resistance or facilitated popular assent created a significant share of those state institutions.

Again we must imagine a continuum of experiences. At one extreme stand those bargains struck with powerful organizations that existed before the great expansion of state power, and survived the expansion, notably the governing bodies of capitalist municipalities such as Amsterdam. Those bargains generally incorporated the governing bodies into the state, and turned them into representative institutions. On a larger scale, rulers in areas having prosperous cities often treated with councils representing the urban powerholders. Thus the early princes of Catalonia admitted delegates of Barcelona and other Catalan cities into their councils beside nobles and clergy, and thereby established the predecessor of the tricameral Catalan *Corts* (Vilar 1962: I, 439).

At the other extreme stand bargains struck with large blocs of the population, such as all landowners, especially in the form of legislation establishing rules for taxation, conscription, and other extractive activities.

Thus when Britain's prime minister William Pitt sought to pay part of the cost of warring with France by means of Britain's first general income tax (1799), he struck implicit bargains with landholders, capitalists, and wage-earners alike: he engineered a bill permitting redemption of the inequitable old land tax (Watson 1960: 375–6). When peace with France returned (abortively) in 1802 and (definitively) in 1815, Parliament soon took steps to repeal the tax; although Prime Minister Liverpool tried in 1816 to retain the income tax to help pay off Britain's huge accumulation of war debt, Parliament clearly read the bargain as tying the tax to the war emergency (Levi 1988: 140–3).

In between the extremes we find bargains struck with defined groups of powerholders such as church officials, who when defeated and dispossessed commonly acquired state-guaranteed claims to stipends and protection, and who, when effective in their resistance to extraction, often forced the creation or recognition of representative bodies such as church assemblies. England's Henry VIII stripped his country's church of its lands and its ties to Rome, but thereby took on the obligation to provide stipends forever to all priests who accepted his version of Reform.

On the whole, the officials of states that grew up amid the network of trading cities stretching from northern Italy to Flanders and the Baltic found themselves near the first extreme, bargaining with municipal oligarchies that had their way, survived, and became major components of the state; city-empires such as that of Venice mark the extreme case. Agents of states-in-the-making that formed outside the city-state band more often found themselves bargaining with great landlords and their clientele, and creating new representative institutions in the process. In those larger states, nobles often gained confirmations of their privileges and monopolies of higher military offices in return for their collaboration with royal attempts to build national armies. But all along the continuum bargaining over the state's extractive claims produced rights, privileges, and protective institutions that had not previously existed.

THE INSTITUTION OF DIRECT RULE

A widespread movement from indirect to direct rule occurred with the nationalization of military power. It offered a seductive but costly opportunity to ordinary people. After 1750, in the eras of nationalization and specialization, states began moving aggressively from a nearly universal system of indirect rule to a new system of direct rule: unmediated intervention in the lives of local communities, households, and productive enterprises. As rulers shifted from the hiring of mercenaries to the recruitment of warriors from their own national populations, and as they increased taxation to support the great military forces of eighteenth-century warfare, they bargained out access to communities, households, and enterprises, sweeping away autonomous intermediaries in the process.

Throughout the millennium we have been surveying, city-states, autonomous bishoprics, petty principalities, and other microstates ruled in a relatively direct way. Agents who were immediately responsible to the crown and served at the monarch's pleasure collected taxes, administered courts, tended crown property, and maintained day-to-day contact with local communities falling under the crown's jurisdiction. Larger states, however, invariably opted for some form of indirect rule, co-opting local powerholders and confirming their privileges without incorporating them directly into the state apparatus.

Before the seventeenth century, every large European state ruled its subjects through powerful intermediaries who enjoyed significant autonomy, hindered state demands that were not to their own interest, and profited on their own accounts from the delegated exercise of state power. The intermediaries were often privileged members of subordinate populations, and made their way by assuring rulers of tribute and acquiescence from those populations. In southeastern Europe especially, the presence of multiple populations mixed by centuries of conquest and Mediterranean trade combined with the characteristic forms of Muslim rule through semi-autonomous subordinates to produce a vast zone of indirect rule whose traces remain today in the region's cultural heterogeneity and its continuing struggles over the rights of minorities. Crucial intermediaries included clergy, landlords, urban oligarchies, and independent professional warriors, in proportions that varied along the continuum from capital-intensive to coercion-intensive regions. The centrality of these various intermediaries identified alternative systems of indirect rule.

Any system of indirect rule set serious limits on the quantity of resources rulers could extract from the ambient economy. Beyond that limit, intermediaries acquired an interest in impeding extracting, even in allying themselves with ordinary people's resistance to state demands. In the same circumstances, however, rulers developed an interest both in undermining the autonomous powers of intermediaries and in making coalitions with major segments of the subject population. As war demanded greater resources, emphatically including manpower, and as the threat of conquest by the largest states grew more serious, ever more rulers bypassed, suppressed, or co-opted old intermediaries and reached directly into communities and households to seize the wherewithal of war. Thus national standing armies, national states, and direct rule caused each other.

Before then, how much autonomy powerholders enjoyed varied significantly from state to state; after its early phase of conquest and military administration, the Ottoman Empire installed two successive forms of rule in the Balkans, the second even more indirect than the first. Into the seventeenth century, sultans drew tribute from their vassal states but within their own domains divided substantial parts of their lands into *timars*, grants held by warriors so long as they continued to serve in the armed forces. The *timarlis* (grant-holders) drew their own revenues from the land, collected taxes for the sultan, ran the civil administration, and controlled the Christian serfs, but gained no right to alienate the land or pass it on to their children. Sixteenth- and seventeenth-century wars, however, killed off many *timarlis*, and the demand to collect more and more taxes for increasingly expensive warmaking made the grants less attractive to warriors. Sultans turned increasingly to tax farmers, who used their leverage to convert the lands they taxed into their own property. As that happened, other groups demanded and received the right to buy and own lands that paid taxes; *chiftliks*, private lands, displaced *timars* (Roider 1987: 133–4).

Thus the Ottomans inadvertently installed a classic system of indirect rule. That system later turned against both subjects and rulers by virtue of the power it put into the hands of semi-independent warriors. At the peace of Sistova between the Ottoman and Austrian empires (1791), for example,

the janissaries and the irregular military units [in Serbia] found themselves unemployed. They thus turned and preyed on the population. Bands of these men seized villages and their lands and converted the property into their own estates. Others joined rebel *avans* or bandit organizations and plundered peaceful Muslims and Christians alike.

(Jelavich and Jelavich 1977: 27)

The autonomy and predation of the janissaries eventually hindered Ottoman rule so seriously that in 1826 the sultan's troops, at his behest, joined with the crowds of Constantinople in slaughtering the remainder of their corps. The great risks of indirect rule were predation by intermediaries, which incited resistance to the intermediaries by the general population, and resistance by the intermediaries, which incited recalcitrance of whole regions to national role.

Most of the time, however, local rulers governed in a relatively stable fashion, and bought insulation for the local population through the timely payment of tribute to the Ottoman state. Meanwhile, Prussian Junkers served simultaneously as masters of their own great estates, judges, military commanders, and spokesmen of the crown, as the English gentry, nobility, and clergy divided the work of civil administration outside of the capital. Under favorable circumstances, the middlemen thus empowered mitigated the effects of state expansion on the social organization and wealth of their subjects. The nature of their mediation differed significantly between two types of regions: those having an indigenous nobility and those dominated by aliens. Where the nobility shared religion, tongue, and tradition with the peasantry (as in Austria and Bohemia), some possibility of regional solidarity against the crown's demands existed. Where nobles were foreigners (as in the European portion of the Ottoman Empire through much of its history), village headmen and tribal elders frequently linked local people to national authorities. In such regions, the empire's collapse left peasants, merchants, and professionals in direct contact with the state (Berend and Ránki 1977: 29–36).

Whether indigenous or alien, middlemen were usually tyrants within their own zones of control. As the *chiftlik* system displaced the *timars* in Ottoman territory, even the appeal to Muslim courts and officials disappeared as a resource, and absentee landlords frequently pressed their peasants harder than their military predecessors (Roider 1987: 134). When the center's power declined – as it did generally during the nineteenth century – landlords acquired increasing control of local affairs. In nineteenth-century Bosnia and Serbia, Muslim landlords drove their Christian tenants into serfdom (Donia 1981: 4–5). In those circumstances, banditry became rampant in the Balkans. As a result of exploitation by middlemen, an alliance with the distant king or his agents often seemed an attractive alternative to exploitation close at hand; villagers then appealed to royal agents, took their cases against landlords to royal courts, and cheered the curtailment of urban privileges. In the short run, they sometimes gained by these choices. But in the long run, the destruction of intermediate barriers made them more vulnerable to the state's next round of war-generated demands.

The growth of domestically recruited standing armies offered a strong stimulus to direct rule. Although rented troops persisted in some armies through the eighteenth century, rulers in regions of capitalized coercion – especially in France, Prussia, and England – began to move away from wholesale engagement of mercenary armies during the seventeenth. Mercenaries had the severe drawbacks of being unreliable when poorly paid, seeking booty and rapine when not closely supervised, causing widespread trouble when demobilized, and costing a great deal of cash. The effort to maintain substantial armies in peacetime, pioneered by such rulers as Prussia's Friedrich Wilhelm in the seventeenth century, exceeded most states' ability to tax the essential revenues, especially in the face of competition from regional powerholders. These circumstances encouraged rulers to establish durable domestic military administrations, and then to conscript, co-opt, and penetrate. These steps bypassed intermediaries, and led the way from indirect to direct rule.

The domestic recruitment of large standing armies entailed serious costs. While discharged mercenaries had few enforceable claims on any states, veterans of a national force did, especially if they had incurred disabilities in the nation's service. Families of dead or wounded warriors likewise acquired benefits such as preference in the state-run sale of tobacco and matches. The garrisoning of troops within the country involved military officials and their civilian counterparts in food supply, housing, and public order. Eventually the health and education of all young males, which affected their military effectiveness, became governmental concerns. Thus military reorganization entered a wedge for expansion of state activity into what had previously been local and private spheres.

In one of their more self-conscious attempts to engineer state power, rulers frequently sought to homogenize their populations in the course of installing direct rule. From a ruler's point of view, a linguistically, religiously, and ideologically homogeneous population presented the risk of a common front against royal demands; homogenization made a policy of divide and rule more costly. But homogeneity had many compensating advantages: within a homogeneous population, ordinary people were more likely to identify with their rulers, communication could run more efficiently, and an administrative innovation that worked in one segment was likely to work elsewhere as well. People who sensed a common origin, furthermore, were more likely to unite against external threats. Spain, France, and other large states recurrently homogenized by giving religious minorities – especially Muslims and Jews – the choice between conversion and emigration; in 1492, shortly after the completed conquest of Granada, for example, Ferdinand and Isabella gave Spanish Jews just that choice; Portugal followed suit in 1497. As it happened, Jewish exiles from Iberia, the Sephardim, then constituted a trade diaspora elsewhere in Europe, using their existing connections to set up a powerful system of long-distance credit and communication that allowed them to establish near-monopolies in precious stones, sugar, spices, and tobacco at various times in the succeeding centuries (von Greyerz 1989).

The Protestant Reformation gave rulers of smaller states a splendid opportunity to define their nation's distinctness and homogeneity vis-à-vis the great empires, not to mention a chance to co-opt the clergy and their administrative apparatus in the service of royal ends. Sweden set an early example, with large chunks of public administration placed in the hands of Lutheran pastors. (Today's Swedish historians still benefit from the long series of parish registers, complete with information about literacy and changes of residence, those pastors prepared faithfully from the seventeenth century onward.) Over and above any possible influence on beliefs about the state's legitimacy, a shared clergy and a common faith linked to the sovereign provided a powerful instrument of rule.

THE FRENCH REVOLUTION: FROM INDIRECT TO DIRECT RULE

European states began forcing the choice between local and national loyalties during the eighteenth century. Although Enlightenment "reforms" often had the effect of reinforcing direct rule, the most sensational move in that direction was no doubt the work of the French Revolution and Empire. French actions from 1789 to 1815 forwarded the general European transition from indirect to direct rule in two ways: by providing a model of centralized government that other states emulated, and by imposing variants of that model wherever France conquered. Even though many of the period's innovations in French government emerged from desperate improvisations in response to threats of rebellion and bankruptcy, their battle-tested forms endured beyond the Revolution and Empire.

What happened to France's system of rule during the revolutionary years? Before 1789 the French state, like almost all other states, ruled indirectly at the local level, relying especially on priests and nobles for mediation. From the end of the American war, the government's efforts to collect money to cover its war debts crystallized an antigovernmental coalition that initially included the Parlements and other powerholders, but changed toward a more popular composition as the confrontation between the regime and its opponents sharpened (Comninel 1987, Doyle 1986, Egret 1962, Frêche 1974, Stone 1981). The state's visible vulnerability in 1788–9 encouraged any group that had a stifled claim or grievance against the state, its agents, or its allies to articulate its demands and join others in calling for change. The rural revolts – Great Fear, grain seizures, tax rebellions, attacks on landlords, and so on – of spring and summer 1789 occurred disproportionately in regions with large towns, commercialized agriculture, and many roads (Markoff 1985). Their geography reflected a composite but largely bourgeois-led settling of scores.

At the same time, those whose social survival depended most directly on the Old Regime state – nobles, officeholders, and higher clergy are the obvious examples – generally aligned themselves with the king (Dawson 1972: 334–46). Thus a revolutionary situation began to form: two distinct blocs both claimed power and both received support from some significant part of the population. With significant defections of military men from the crown and the formation of militias devoted to the popular cause, the opposition acquired force of its own. The popular bloc, connected and often led by members of the bourgeoisie, started to gain control over parts of the state apparatus.

The lawyers, officials, and other bourgeois who seized the state apparatus in 1789–90 rapidly displaced the old intermediaries: landlords, seigneurial officials, venal officeholders, clergy, and sometimes municipal oligarchies as well. "[I]t was not a rural class of English-style gentlemen," declares Lynn Hunt, "who gained political prominence on either the national or the regional level, but rather thousands of city professionals who seized the opportunity to develop political careers" (Hunt 1984: 155; see also Hunt 1978, Vovelle 1987). At a local level, the so-called Municipal Revolution widely transferred power to enemies of the old rulers; patriot coalitions based in militias, clubs, and revolutionary committees and linked to Parisian activists ousted the old municipalities. Even where the old powerholders managed to survive the Revolution's early turmoil, relations between each locality and the national capital altered abruptly. Village "republics" of the Alps, for example, found their ancient liberties – including ostensibly free consent to taxes – crumbling as outsiders clamped them into the new administrative machine (Rosenberg 1988: 72–89). Then Parisian revolutionaries faced the problem of governing without intermediaries; they experimented with the committees and militias that had appeared in the mobilization of 1789, but found them hard to control from the center. More or less simultaneously they recast the French map into a nested system of departments, districts, cantons, and communes, while sending out *représentants en mission* to forward revolutionary reorganization. They installed direct rule.

Given the unequal spatial distribution of cities, merchants, and capital, furthermore, the imposition of a uniform geographic grid altered the relations between cities' economic and political power, placing insignificant Mende and Niort at the same administrative level as mighty Lyon and Bordeaux (Lepetit 1988: 200–37; Margadant 1988a, 1988b; Ozouf-Marignier 1986; Schulz 1982). As a result, the balance of forces in regional capitals shifted significantly: in the great commercial centers, where merchants, lawyers, and professionals already clustered, departmental officials (who frequently came, in any case, from the same milieux) had no choice but to bargain with the locals. Where the National Assembly carved departments out of relatively uncommercialized rural regions, the Revolution's administrators overshadowed other residents of the new capitals, and could plausibly threaten to use force if they were recalcitrant. But in those regions, they lacked the bourgeois allies who helped their confreres do the Revolution's work elsewhere, and confronted old intermediaries who still commanded significant followings.

In great mercantile centers such as Marseille and Lyon, the political situation was very different. By and large, the Federalist movement, with its protests against Jacobin centralism and its demands for regional autonomy, took root in cities whose commercial positions greatly outpaced their administrative rank. In dealing with these alternative obstacles to direct rule, Parisian revolutionaries improvised three parallel, and sometimes conflicting, systems of rule: the committees and militias; a geographically-defined hierarchy of elected officials and representatives; and roving commissioners from the central government. To collect information and gain support, all three relied extensively on the existing personal networks of lawyers, professionals, and merchants.

As the system began to work, revolutionary leaders strove to routinize their control and contain independent action by local enthusiasts, who often resisted. Using both co-optation and repression, they gradually squeezed out the committees and militias. Mobilization for war put great pressure on the system, incited new resistance, and increased the national leaders' incentives for a tight system of control. Starting in 1792, the central administration (which until then had continued in a form greatly resembling that of the Old Regime) underwent its own revolution: the staff expanded enormously, and a genuine hierarchical bureaucracy took shape. In the process, revolutionaries installed one of the first systems of direct rule ever to take shape in a large state.

That shift entailed changes in systems of taxation, justice, public works, and much more. Consider policing. Outside of the Paris region, France's Old Regime state had almost no specialized police of its own; it dispatched the

Maréchaussée to pursue tax evaders, vagabonds, and other violators of royal will and occasionally authorized the army to quell rebellious subjects, but otherwise relied on local and regional authorities to deploy armed force against civilians. The revolutionaries changed things. With respect to ordinary people, they moved from reactive to proactive policing and information-gathering: instead of simply waiting until a rebellion or collective violation of the law occurred, and then retaliating ferociously but selectively, they began to station agents whose job was to anticipate and prevent threatening popular collective action. During the Revolution's early years, Old Regime police forces generally dissolved as popular committees, national guards, and revolutionary tribunals took over their day-to-day activities. But with the Directory the state concentrated surveillance and apprehension in a single centralized organization. Fouché of Nantes became minister of police in the year VII/1799, and thenceforth ran a ministry whose powers extended throughout France and its conquered territories. By the time of Fouché, France had become one of the world's most closely-policed countries.

Going to war accelerated the move from indirect to direct rule. Almost any state that makes war finds that it cannot pay for the effort from its accumulated reserves and current revenues. Almost all warmaking states borrow extensively, raise taxes, and seize the means of combat – including men – from reluctant citizens who have other uses for their resources. Pre-revolutionary France followed these rules faithfully, to the point of accumulating debts that eventually forced the calling of the Estates General. Nor did the Revolution repeal the rules: once France declared war on Austria in 1792, the state's demands for revenues and manpower excited resistance just as fierce as that which had broken out under the Old Regime. In overcoming that resistance, revolutionaries built yet another set of centralized controls.

The French used their own new system as a template for the reconstruction of other states. As revolutionary and imperial armies conquered, they attempted to build replicas of that system of direct rule elsewhere in Europe. Napoleon's government consolidated the system and turned it into a reliable instrument of rule. The system survived the Revolution and Empire in France and, to some degree, elsewhere; Europe as a whole shifted massively toward centralized direct rule with at least a modicum of representation for the ruled.

Resistance and counter-revolutionary action followed directly from the process by which the new state established direct rule. Remember how much change the revolutionaries introduced in a very short time. They eliminated all previous territorial jurisdictions, consolidated many old parishes into larger communes, abolished the tithe and feudal dues, dissolved corporations and their privileges, constructed a top-to-bottom administrative and electoral system, imposed expanded and standardized taxes through that system, seized the properties of emigrant nobles and of the church, disbanded monastic orders, subjected clergy to the state and imposed upon them an oath to defend the new state church, conscripted young men at an unprecedented rate, and displaced both nobles and priests from the automatic exercise of local leadership. All this occurred between 1789 and 1793.

Subsequent regimes added more ephemeral changes such as the revolutionary calendar and the cult of the Supreme Being, but the early Revolution's overhaul of the state endured into the nineteenth century, and set the pattern for many other European states. The greatest reversals concerned the throttling of local militias and revolutionary committees, the restoration or compensation of some confiscated properties, and Napoleon's Concordat with the Catholic Church. All in all, these changes constituted a dramatic, rapid substitution of uniform, centralized, direct rule for a system of government mediated by local and regional notables. What is more, the new state hierarchy consisted largely of lawyers, physicians, notaries, merchants, and other bourgeois.

Like their pre-revolutionary counterparts, these fundamental changes attacked many existing interests, and opened opportunities to groups that had previously had little access to state-sanctioned power – especially the village and small-town bourgeoisie. As a result, they precipitated both resistance and struggles for power. Artois (the department of Pas-de-Calais) underwent a moderate version of the transition (Jessenne 1987). Before the Revolution, Artesian nobles and churchmen held a little over half of all land as against a third for peasants. Between 60 and 80 percent of all farms had fewer than 5 hectares (which implies that a similar large majority of farm operators worked part-time for others), and a quarter of household heads worked primarily as agricultural wage-laborers. Taxes, tithes, rents, and feudal dues took a relatively low 30 percent of the income from leased land in Artois, and a fifth of rural land went on sale with the revolutionary seizure of church and noble properties. Agricultural capitalism, in short, was well advanced by 1770.

In such a region, large leaseholders (*fermiers*) dominated local politics, but only within limits set by their noble and ecclesiastical landlords. The Revolution, by sweeping away the privileges of those patrons, threatened the leaseholders' power. They survived the challenge, however, as a class, if not as a particular set of individuals: many officeholders lost their posts during the struggles of the early Revolution, especially when the community was already at odds with its lord. Yet their replacements came disproportionately from the same class of comfortable leaseholders. The struggle of wage-laborers and smallholders against the *coqs de village* that Georges Lefebvre discovered in the adjacent Nord was less intense, or less effective, in the Pas-de-Calais. Although the larger farmers, viewed with suspicion by national authorities, lost some of their grip on public office during the Terror and again under the Directory, they regained it later, and continued to rule their roosts through the middle of the nineteenth century. By that time, nobles and ecclesiastics had lost much of their capacity to contain local powerholders, but manufacturers, merchants, and other capitalists had taken their places. The displacement of the old intermediaries opened the way to a new alliance between large farmers and bourgeoisie.

Under the lead of Paris, the transition to direct rule went relatively smoothly in Artois. Elsewhere, intense struggle accompanied the change. The career of Claude Javogues, agent of the Revolution in his native department of the Loire, reveals that struggle, and the political process that incited it (Lucas 1973). Javogues was a huge, violent, hard-drinking roustabout whose close kin were lawyers, notaries, and merchants in Forez, a region not far to the west of Lyon. The family was on the ascendant in the eighteenth century, and in 1789 Claude himself was a well-connected thirty-year-old *avocat* at Montbrison. The Convention dispatched this raging bourgeois bull to the Loire in July 1793 and recalled him in February 1794. During those six months, Javogues relied heavily upon his existing connections, concentrated on repression of the Revolution's enemies, acted to a large degree on the theory that priests, nobles, and rich landlords were the enemies, neglected and bungled administrative matters such as the organization of food supply, and left behind him a reputation for arbitrariness and cruelty.

Yet Javogues and his co-workers did, in fact, reorganize local life. In following his action in the Loire, we encounter clubs, surveillance committees, revolutionary armed forces, commissars, courts, and *représentants en mission*. We see an almost unbelievable attempt to extend the direct administrative purview of the central government to everyday individual life. We recognize the importance of popular mobilization against the Revolution's enemies – real or imagined – as a force that displaced the old intermediaries. We therefore gain insight into the conflict between two objectives of the Terror: extirpation of the Revolution's opponents and forging of instruments to do the work of the Revolution. We discover again the great importance of control over food as an administrative challenge, as a point of political contention, and as an incentive to popular action.

Contrary to the old image of a unitary people welcoming the arrival of long-awaited reform, local histories of the Revolution make clear that France's revolutionaries established their power through struggle, and frequently over stubborn popular resistance. Most of the resistance, it is true, took the form of evasion, cheating, and sabotage rather than outright rebellion. Where the fault lines ran deep, however, resistance consolidated into counter-revolution: the formation of effective alternative authorities to those put in place by the Revolution. Counter-revolution occurred not where everyone opposed the Revolution, but where irreconcilable differences divided well-defined blocs of supporters and opponents.

France's South and West, through similar processes, produced the largest zones of sustained counter-revolution (Lebrun and Dupuy 1987, Nicolas 1985, Lewis and Lucas 1983). The geography of executions under the Terror provides a reasonable picture of counter-revolutionary activity. The departments having more than 200 executions included: Loire Inférieure (3,548), Seine (2,639), Maine-et-Loire (1,886), Rhône (1,880), Vendée (1,616), Ille-et-Vilaine (509), Mayenne (495), Vaucluse (442), Bouches-du-Rhône (409), Pas-de-Calais (392), Var (309), Gironde (299), and Sarthe (225). These departments accounted for 89 percent of all executions under the Terror (Greer 1935: 147). Except for the Seine and the Pas-de-Calais, they concentrated in the South, the Southwest and, especially, the West. In the South and Southwest, Languedoc, Provence, Gascony, and the Lyonnais hosted military insurrections against the Revolution, insurrections whose geography corresponded closely to support for Federalism (Forrest 1975; Hood 1971, 1979, Lewis 1978; Lyons 1980; Scott 1973). Federalist movements began in the spring of 1793, when the Jacobin expansion of the foreign war – including the declaration of war on Spain – incited resistance to taxation and conscription, which in turn led to a tightening of revolutionary surveillance and discipline. The autonomist movement peaked in commercial cities that had enjoyed extensive liberties under the Old Regime, notably Marseille, Bordeaux, Lyon, and Caen. In those cities and their hinterlands, France fell into bloody civil war.

In the West, guerrilla raids against republican strongholds and personnel unsettled Brittany, Maine, and Normandy from 1791 to 1799, while open armed rebellion flared south of the Loire in parts of Brittany, Anjou, and Poitou beginning in the fall of 1792 and likewise continuing intermittently until Napoleon pacified the region in 1799 (Bois 1981, Le Goff and Sutherland 1984, Martin 1987). The western counter-revolution reached its high point in the spring of 1793, when the Republic's call for troops precipitated armed resistance through much of the West. That phase saw massacres of "patriots" and "aristocrats" (as the proponents and opponents of the Revolution came to be called), invasion and temporary occupation of such major cities as Angers, and pitched battles between armies of Blues and Whites (as the armed elements of the two parties were known).

The West's counter-revolution grew directly from the efforts of revolutionary officials to install a particular kind of direct rule in the region: a rule that practically eliminated nobles and priests from their positions as partly autonomous intermediaries, that brought the state's demands for taxes, manpower, and deference to the level of individual communities, neighborhoods, and households, that gave the region's bourgeois political power they had never before wielded. In seeking to extend the state's rule to every locality, and to dislodge all enemies of that rule, French revolutionaries started a process that did not cease for twenty-five years. In some ways, it has not yet ceased today.

In these regards, for all its counter-revolutionary ferocity, the West conformed to France's general experience. Everywhere in France, bourgeois – not owners of large industrial establishments, for the most part, but merchants, lawyers, notaries, and others who made their livings from the possession and manipulation of capital – were gaining strength during the eighteenth century. Throughout France, the mobilization of 1789 brought disproportionate numbers of bourgeois into political action. As the revolutionaries of Paris and their provincial allies displaced nobles and priests from their critical positions as agents of indirect rule, the existing networks of bourgeois served as alternative connections between the state and thousands of communities across the land. For a while, those connections rested on a vast popular mobilization through clubs, militias, and committees. Gradually, however, revolutionary leaders contained or even suppressed their turbulent partners. With trial, error, and struggle, the ruling bourgeoisie worked out a system of rule that reached directly into local communities, and passed chiefly through administrators who served under the scrutiny and budgetary control of their superiors.

This process of state expansion encountered three huge obstacles. First, many people saw the opening up of opportunities to forward their own interests and settle old scores in the crisis of 1789. They either managed to capitalize on the opportunity or found their hopes blocked by competition from other actors; both categories lacked incentives to support further revolutionary changes. Second, the immense effort of warring with most other European powers strained the state's capacity at least as gravely as had the wars of Old Regime kings. Third, in some regions the political bases of the newly-empowered bourgeois were too fragile to support the work of cajoling, containing, inspiring, threatening, extracting, and mobilizing that revolutionary agents carried on everywhere; resistance to demands for taxes, conscripts, and compliance with moralizing legislation occurred widely in France, but where preexisting rivalries placed a well-connected bloc in opposition to the revolutionary bourgeoisie, civil war frequently developed. In these senses, the revolutionary transition from indirect to direct rule embodied a bourgeois revolution and engendered a series of anti-bourgeois counter-revolutions.

Outside of France, finally, the imposition of French-style administrative hierarchies almost everywhere the revolutionary and imperial armies conquered, pushed the experiment yet another step, installing direct rule (mediated, it is true, by viceroys and military commanders) in half of Europe. In mobilizing against the French, many German states likewise undertook extensive programs of centralization, nationalization, and penetration (Walker 1971: 185–216). If Napoleon's armies eventually lost and France's puppet states eventually collapsed, the administrative reorganization left a great impact on such countries-to-be as Belgium and Italy. The age of direct rule had begun.

STATE EXPANSION, DIRECT RULE, AND NATIONALISM

The most dramatic expansion of nonmilitary state activity began in the age of military specialization after 1850 or so. In that period, which extends to the recent past, military organization moved from a dominant, partly autonomous segment of state structure to a more subordinated position as the largest of several differentiated departments under control of a predominantly civilian administration. (That subordination was, of course, greater in peace than in war, greater in Holland than in Spain.) The nationalization of military forces during the previous century had already drawn most European states into bargaining with their subject populations over the yielding of conscripts, war materials, and taxes; immense citizen armies like those of the Napoleonic Wars entailed an unprecedented invasion of everyday social relations by the predatory state.

In the process of installing direct rule, European states shifted from what we might call reactive to proactive repression, especially with respect to potential enemies outside the national elite. Up to the eighteenth century, agents of European states spent little time trying to anticipate popular demands on the state, rebellious movements, risky collective action, or the spread of new organizations; their spies, when they had them, concentrated on the rich and powerful. When a rebellion or "sedition" occurred, governors brought in armed force as fast as they could, punishing in as visible and minatory a manner as they could devise. They reacted, but not by establishing continuous monitoring of potential subversives. With the installation of direct rule came the creation of systems of surveillance and reporting that made local and regional administrators responsible for prediction and prevention of movements that would threaten state power or the welfare of its chief clients. National police forces penetrated local communities (see Thibon 1987). Political and criminal police made common cause in preparing dossiers, listening posts, routine reports, and periodic surveys of any persons, organizations, or events that were likely to trouble "public order." The long disarmament of the civilian population culminated in tight containment of militants and malcontents.

In similar ways, European states began to monitor industrial conflict and working conditions, install and regulate national systems of education, organize aid to the poor and disabled, build and maintain communication lines, impose tariffs for the benefit of home industries, and the thousand other activities Europeans now take for granted as attributes of state power. The state's sphere expanded far beyond its military core, and its citizens began to make claims on it for a very wide range of protection, adjudication, production, and distribution. As national legislatures extended their own ranges well beyond the approval of taxation, they became the targets of claims from all well-organized groups whose interests the state did or could affect. Direct rule and mass national politics grew up together, and reinforced each other mightily.

As direct rule expanded throughout Europe, the welfare, culture, and daily routines of ordinary Europeans came to depend as never before on which state they happened to reside in. Internally, states undertook to impose national languages, national educational systems, national military service, and much more. Externally, they began to control movement across frontiers, to use tariffs and customs as instruments of economic policy, and to treat foreigners as distinctive kinds of people deserving limited rights and close surveillance. As states invested not only in war and public services but also in economic infrastructure, their economies came to have distinctive characteristics, which once again differentiated the experiences of living in adjacent states.

To that degree, life homogenized within states and heterogenized among states. National symbols crystallized, national languages standardized, national labor markets organized. War itself became a homogenizing experience, as soldiers and sailors represented the entire nation and the civilian population endured common privations and responsibilities. Among other consequences, demographic characteristics began to resemble each other within the same state and to differ ever more widely among states (Watkins 1989).

The later stages of European state formation produced both of the disparate phenomena we group together under the label "nationalism." The word refers to the mobilization of populations that do not have their own state around a claim to political independence; thus we speak of Palestinian, Armenian, Welsh, or French-Canadian nationalism. It also, regrettably, refers to the mobilization of the population of an existing state around a strong identification with that state; thus, in the 1982 Malvinas/Falklands War, we speak of clashing British and Argentinian nationalisms. Nationalism in the first sense ran throughout European history, whenever and wherever rulers of a given religion or language conquered people of another religion or language. Nationalism in the sense of heightened commitment to a state's international strategy appeared rarely before the nineteenth century, and then chiefly in the heat of war. The homogenization of the population and the imposition of direct rule both encouraged this second variety of nationalism.

Both nationalisms multiplied during the nineteenth century, so much so that it might be better to invent a different term for their equivalents before 1800. As regions of fragmented sovereignty such as Germany and Italy consolidated into substantial national states and the whole map of Europe crystallized into 25 or 30 mutually exclusive territories, the two nationalisms incited each other. Great movements of conquest have typically aroused both nationalisms, as citizens of existing states saw their independence threatened and members of stateless but coherent populations saw possibilities both for extinction and for new autonomy. As Napoleon and the French reached out into Europe, national-state nationalism swelled on the French side and on the side of the states France menaced; by the time Napoleon lost, however, his imperial administrations had created the bases for new nationalisms of both types – Russian, Prussian, and British, to be sure, but Polish, German, and Italian as well – through much of Europe.

During the twentieth century, the two kinds of nationalism have increasingly intertwined, with one nationalism provoking the other – the attempt of rulers to commit their subjects to the national cause generating resistance on the part of unassimilated minorities, the demand of unrepresented minorities for political autonomy fostering commitment to the existing state on the part of those who benefit most from its existence. After World War II, as decolonizing powers started to map the entire remainder of the world into bounded, recognized, mutually exclusive states, the connection between the two nationalisms grew ever tighter, for the successful claim of one relatively distinct people to its own state usually spelled the rejection of at least one other people's claim to a state; as the door closes, more peoples try to escape through it. At the same time, through implicit international compact, the boundaries of existing states have become less subject to alteration through warfare or statecraft. More and more, the only way minority nationalisms can achieve their goal is through the subdivision of existing states. In recent years, such composite states as Lebanon and the Soviet Union have felt acutely the pressure for subdivision. Under that pressure, the Soviet Union exploded.

UNINTENDED BURDENS

Struggle over the means of war produced state structures that no one had planned to create, or even particularly desired. Because no ruler or ruling coalition had absolute power and because classes outside the ruling coalition always held day-to-day control over a significant share of the resources rulers drew on for war, no state escaped the creation of some organizational burdens rulers would have preferred to avoid. A second, parallel process also generated unintended burdens for the state: as rulers created organizations either to make war or to draw the requisites of war from the subject population – not only armies and navies but also tax offices, customs services, treasuries, regional administrations, and armed forces to forward their work among the civilian population – they discovered that the organizations themselves developed interests, rights, perquisites, needs, and demands requiring attention on their own. Speaking of Brandenburg-Prussia, Hans Rosenberg says that the bureaucracy

acquired an *esprit de corps* and developed into a force formidable enough to recast the system of government in its own image. It restrained the autocratic authority of the monarch. It ceased to be responsible to the dynastic interest. It captured control of the central administration and of public policy.

(Rosenberg 1958: vii-viii)

In similar ways, bureaucracies developed their own interests and power bases throughout Europe.

Response to the new interests brought more organization into being: niches for military veterans, orders of nobility for state officials, training schools, courts and lawyers adjudicating official privileges, providers of food, housing, and other necessities for the state's agents. From the sixteenth century onward, many states undertook their own production of materials that were crucial to either the conduct of war or the collection of revenue; at one time or another, many states manufactured weapons, gunpowder, salt, tobacco products, and matches for the one purpose or the other.

A third process likewise added to the state's burdens. Classes outside the state found they could turn institutions that originated with a narrow range of activities into solutions for problems that interested them seriously, even when the problems interested state officials very little. In order to build the coalitions required to get their own work done, officials accepted the broadening of institutions. Courts originally convened to enforce the king's writ with respect to arms and taxes became vehicles for the settlement of private disputes, army regiments became convenient places to lodge the nobility's incompetent younger sons, registry offices set up to receive fees for the certification of documents became sites of negotiation over inheritances.

The history of state intervention in food supplies illustrates how these three processes created unintended burdens for the state. Since urban food supplies remained risky for centuries, municipal officers bore the major responsibility for overseeing markets, seeking extra supplies in times of shortage, and making sure that poor people could get enough to keep them alive. Palermo's authorities, for example, faced an especially serious problem because their native nobles disdained commerce, which remained largely in the hands of foreign merchants. During seventeenth-century threats of famine:

citizens of Palermo had to carry identity cards in order to exclude aliens from the bread queues. Those who had lawsuits at Palermo received special permission to enter the town, but only if they brought their own food; everyone else was liable to be excluded by a rigid watch and ward at the city gate. The making of sweet pastries was sometimes forbidden altogether, or only stale bread was sold so as to diminish consumption. Special police used to ferret out stocks of wheat concealed in the countryside, and Spaniards were preferred for this office since Sicilians had too many friends to favour and enemies to injure.

(Mack Smith 1968a: 221)

Although these regulations applied to citizens, they laid onerous burdens of enforcement on authorities. Where municipal officers did not meet their responsibilities, they faced the possibility of rebellions based on coalitions of their own enemies with the urban poor. On the whole rebellions did not occur when people were hungriest, but when people saw that officials were failing to apply the standard controls, tolerating profiteering or, worst of all, authorizing shipments of precious local grain to other places.

In most of Europe, cities adopted elaborate rules forbidding wholesale purchases of grain outside the public market, withholding of locally-stored grain from the market, and charging a price for bread that was greatly out of line with the going price for the staple grain. States that built substantial armies, administrative staffs, and capital cities thereby multiplied the number of people who did not produce their own food, and added to the demand for grain outside of the usual regional markets. Regional and national officials of the state found themselves spending large proportions of their time assuring and regulating the food supply.

Beholden to landlords who did not welcome state interference in their operations, European states concentrated their controls on distribution, not production. States such as Prussia and Russia, which ceded enormous powers to landlords and reinforced landlords' domination of peasants in return for noble provision of military and administrative service, thereby affected the character of agriculture profoundly, but only indirectly. State-led redistribution of church lands, as in France, Italy, and Spain, impinged significantly on agriculture, but did not cause the states to supervise production as such. Not until the twentieth century, when some socialist regimes took over agricultural production and most capitalist regimes intervened in production by manipulating credit, prices, and markets, did states involve themselves heavily in that end of the food supply. Except for wartime rationing and occasional interdictions motivated by fiscal or political programs, states steered clear of consumption as well. But in the sphere of distribution, European states all found themselves dealing seriously with food.

Following decisively different timetables in different parts of Europe, the sixteenth to nineteenth centuries saw the interdependent expansion of international markets, rise of the wholesale food merchant, and increase in the number of wage-earners who depended on the market for food. At this point, the managers of states were balancing the demands of farmers, food merchants, municipal officials, their own dependents, and the urban poor – all of whom caused the state trouble when it harmed their particular interests. State and national officials developed the theory and practice of Police, in which the detection and apprehension of criminals played a minor part. Before the nineteenth-century proliferation of professional police forces as we know them, the word Police referred to public management, especially at the local level; regulation of the food supply was its single largest component. The great treatise of Nicolas de la Mare, *Traité de la Police*, first published in 1705, sums up that broad but food-centered conception of the state's police powers.

To be sure, state approaches to food supply varied with the character of the state and its dominant classes. As Prussia built a standing army that was very large for the size of its base population, it also created stores and supply systems for the army, as well as encouragements for grain to flow into provinces where the army was concentrated; that system, like almost everything else in the Prussian state, depended on the cooperation of landlords and on the subordination of the peasantry. Despite intermittent national legislation on the subject, England generally left practical control over food supply in the hands of its local magistrates, and only intervened actively in the shipment of grain into and out of the whole country; the repeal of the Corn Laws in 1846 marked the end of the long period in which the state restricted the importation of grain when prices were not very high, hence the period in which the state protected grain-growing landowners and their farmers against foreign competition. In Spain, the administrative effort to feed landlocked Madrid froze the food supply through much of Castile, and probably slowed the development of large-scale markets over the whole Iberian peninsula (Ringrose 1983).

Increasing state action caused a large expansion in the bulk of the national political apparatus devoted to regulation of flows of food, even when the avowed objective of state policy was to "free" the grain trade. That policy, increasingly adopted in the eighteenth and nineteenth centuries, consisted essentially of reinforcing the right of large merchants to ship food to where it would fetch the highest price. Eventually municipalities, urged on by state legislation, dismantled the old controls. In the long run, agricultural productivity rose and distribution improved sufficiently to reduce the vulnerability of cities, armies, and poor people to sudden food shortages. But along the way states created staffs that specialized in food, in surveillance and intervention to assure the flow of supplies to those whose action the state prized or feared. Indirectly, the pursuit of military power led to intervention in subsistence. Similarly, attempts to acquire men, uniforms, arms, lodgings and, above all, money to sustain military activity drew state officials into creating administrative structures they then had to supervise and sustain.

The forms of mass representation that European rulers bargained out with their subjects-become-citizens during the nineteenth century involved states in whole new arenas of activity, especially with respect to production and distribution. Characteristic bourgeois political programs – elections, parliaments, wide access to office, civil rights – became realities. Once citizens had enforceable claims on the state backed by popular elections and parliamentary legislation, the better organized among them demanded state action on employment, on foreign trade, on education, and eventually much more. States intervened in capital–labor relations by defining acceptable strikes and labor unions, by monitoring both of them, and by negotiating or imposing settlements to conflicts. On the whole, states that industrialized late committed more of the governmental apparatus – banks, courts, and public administrations – to the promotion of industry than did those that led the way (Berend and Ránki 1982: 59–72).

Table 4.1 shows how much state expenditures altered. Over these years, the Norwegian state's personnel expanded as well: in 1875, the central government employed about 12,000 civilians, about 2 percent of the labor force; in 1920, 54,000 (5 percent); in 1970, 157,000 (10 percent: Flora 1983: I, 228; see also Gran 1988b: 185). In Norway and elsewhere in Europe, central administration, justice, economic intervention, and, especially, social services all grew as an

Table 4.1   State expenditure as a percentage of GDP in Norway, 1875–1975

Year	Total government	military	Administration, justice	Economy, environment	Social services
1875	3.2	1.1	1.0	0.4	0.3
1900	5.7	1.6	1.2	1.0	1.2
1925	6.5	0.9	0.7	0.8	1.8
1950	16.8	3.3	1.4	3.9	7.4
1975	24.2	3.2	2.3	6.8	9.5

Source: Flora 1983: I, 418–19

outcome of political bargaining over the state's protection of its clients and citizens.

The increase in social services occurred across Europe. Table 4.2 takes Austria, France, the United Kingdom, the Netherlands, and Germany as exemplars, simply because Peter Flora has assembled comparable data on them. States that moved to centrally planned economies, such as the Soviet Union, surely saw even larger increases in the proportion of national income devoted to social services. Everywhere, especially after World War II, the state intervened in health, in education, in family life and finances.

Table 4.2   State expenditure on social services as a percentage of GDP, 1900–75

Year[a]	Austria	France	UK	Netherlands	Denmark	"Germany"
1900			0.7		1.0	
1920	2.0	2.8	4.1	3.2	2.7	7.5
1940	2.3	5.1	5.3	4.4	4.8	11.1
1960	7.3	8.9	9.6	8.7	7.6	14.9
1975	10.8	9.2	15.0	17.2	24.6	20.8

[a] Dates are approximate
Source: Flora 1983: I, 348–9

As the availability of the figures itself suggests, all these interventions produced monitoring and reporting, so much so that the period from about 1870 to 1914 became a golden age of state-sponsored statistics on strikes, employment, economic production, and much more. Thus the state's managers became responsible for the national economy and the condition of workers to a degree unimaginable a century earlier. If the extent and timing of these changes varied dramatically from a resistant Russia to a volatile Great Britain, almost all nineteenth-century states moved in the same general direction.

MILITARIZATION = CIVILIANIZATION

The state-transforming processes we have surveyed produced a surprising result: civilianization of government. The result is surprising because the expansion of military force drove the processes of state formation. Schematically, the transformation occurred in the now-familiar four stages of patrimonialism, brokerage, nationalization, and specialization: first, a period in which major powerholders themselves were active military men, recruiting and commanding their own armies and navies; then the heyday of military entrepreneurs and mercenary troops in the hire of civilian powerholders; followed by the incorporation of the military structure into the state with the creation of standing armies; and finally, the shift to mass conscription, organized reserves, and well-paid volunteer armies drawn essentially from the state's own citizenry, which led in turn to systems of veterans' benefits, legislative oversight, and claims of potential or former soldiers to political representation.

We see the transition from patrimonialism to brokerage in the rise of the Italian *condottieri*. The shift from brokerage to nationalization begins with the Thirty Years' War, which brought the apogee and self-destruction of such great military entrepreneurs as Wallenstein and Tilly – no relation of mine, so far as I know. One sign of that shift appears in the elimination of Prussian colonels from the clothing business, from which they once made handsome profits, in 1713–14 (Redlich 1965: II, 107). France's *levée en masse* of 1793 and thereafter signals the shift from nationalization toward specialization. Elsewhere in Europe it became quite general after 1850. By the end of the process civilian bureaucracies and legislatures contained the military, legal obligations for military service extended with relative equality across social classes, the ideology of military professionalism restrained the involvement of generals and admirals in civilian politics, and the possibility of direct military rule or coup d'état declined greatly.

After 1850, during the age of specialization, civilianization of government accelerated. In absolute terms, military activity continued to grow in expense and importance. But three trends checked its relative importance. First, limited by the competing demands of the civilian economy, peacetime military personnel stabilized as a proportion of the total population while other government employment continued to expand. Second, expenditure on non-military activities grew even faster than military expenditure. Third, civilian production eventually grew quickly enough to outstrip military expansion, with the result that military expenditures declined as a share of national income. Non-military activity and expenditure captured a larger and larger part of governmental attention.

In the same states whose social expenditure we examined earlier, military personnel fluctuated as a percentage of the male population aged 20–44 (see

Table 4.3   Military personnel as a percentage of the male population aged 20–44, 1850–1970[a]

Year[a]	Austria	France	UK	Netherlands	Denmark	"Germany"
1850	14.5	6.5	4.3	5.4	10.3	4.7
1875	8.4	7.4	4.5	6.4	6.4	5.9
1900	6.9	8.8	6.6	3.6	2.8	6.3
1925	2.5	6.7	4.3	1.2	2.3	1.0
1950	?	8.4	7.6	12.7	2.3	?
1970	4.2	5.8	4.2	5.3	5.3	4.5

[a] Boundaries and identities of these states varied significantly with the fortunes of war
Source: Flora 1983: I, 251–3

table 4.3). With important variations due to wartime deaths and war-related mobilizations, the western European states of 1970 were generally maintaining troops at around 5 percent of the male population aged 20–44. In 1984, the percentage of the *total* population in military service varied as follows (Sivard 1988: 43–4):

less than 0.5 percent: Iceland (0.0), Luxembourg (0.2), Ireland (0.4), Malta (0.3), Switzerland (0.3);

0.5 to 0.9 percent: Denmark (0.6), West Germany (0.8), Italy (0.9), Netherlands (0.7), Norway (0.9), Spain (0.9), United Kingdom (0.6), Poland (0.9), Rumania (0.8), Austria (0.7), Sweden (0.8);

1.0 to 1.4 percent: Belgium (1.1), France (1.0), Portugal (1.0), Czechoslovakia (1.3), East Germany (1.0), Hungary (1.0), USSR (1.4), Albania (1.4), Finland (1.1), Yugoslavia (1.0);

1.5 percent or more: Greece (2.0), Turkey (1.6), Bulgaria (1.6).

A few essentially demilitarized states now have less than 0.5 percent of their population under arms, and a few militarized ones run above 1.4 percent, but the bulk of European states lie in between. All of these shares – even those of semi-belligerent Greece and Turkey – run far below the 8 percent of its population Sweden placed in its military at its peak toward 1710. With high proportions of their able-bodied populations already at work and low proportions in agriculture, furthermore, European states now face severe limits to the number of additional troops they can mobilize in wartime without major reorientations of their economies.

Meanwhile, non-military activities were ballooning so fast that military expenditure declined as a share of most state budgets, despite the great expansion of those budgets. Taking the same countries as before, we find the decreasing trends in percentage of budget devoted to military expenditure shown in table 4.4. In every state, the long-term trend led to a declining proportion of expenditure on military activity.

Table 4.4   Military expenditure as a percentage of state budget 1850–1975

Year[a]	Austria	France	UK	Netherlands	Denmark	"Germany"
1850		27.4				
1875		23.2			37.8	34.0
1900		37.7	74.2	26.4	28.9	22.9
1925	7.7	27.8	19.1	15.1	14.2	4.0
1950		20.7	24.0	18.3	15.6	13.5
1975	4.9	17.9	14.7	11.3	7.4	6.4

[a] Dates are very approximate
Source: Flora 1983: I, 355–449

Eventually, indeed, national income rose faster than military expenditure. In 1984, the proportion of Gross National Product devoted to military expenditure varied in a pattern similar to that of men under arms (Sivard 1988: 43–4):

less than 2 percent: Iceland (0.0), Luxembourg (0.8), Rumania (1.4), Austria (1.2), Finland (1.5), Ireland (1.8), Malta (0.9);

from 2 to 3.9 percent: Belgium (3.1), Denmark (2.4), West Germany (3.3), Italy (2.7), Netherlands (3.2), Norway (2.9), Portugal (3.5), Spain (2.4), Hungary (2.2), Poland (2.5), Sweden (3.1), Switzerland (2.2), Yugoslavia (3.7);

from 4 to 5.9 percent: France (4.1), Turkey (4.5), United Kingdom (5.4), Bulgaria (4.0), Czechoslovakia (4.0), East Germany (4.9), Albania (4.4).

6 percent or more: Greece (7.2), USSR (11.5);

The standoff between the United States and the Soviet Union helped create this distribution of expenditures. In 1984, the United States was spending 6.4 percent of its own enormous GNP on military activity to match the 11.5 percent the Soviet Union was squeezing from its significantly smaller economy. Nevertheless, the general European trend ran downward: smaller proportions of the population under arms, smaller shares of state budgets devoted to the military, smaller percentages of national income spent on soldiers and weapons. These changes resulted from, and reinforced, the organizational containment of military men. At each step from patrimonialism to brokerage, from brokerage to nationalization, and from nationalization to specialization, then, new and significant barriers arose to limit the autonomous power of military men.

Deviations from the idealized sequence confirm its logic. Spain and Portugal escaped the civilianization of government by drawing on colonial revenues for a major share of military expenditures, continuing to recruit officers from the Spanish aristocracy and foot soldiers from the poorest classes, and maintaining military officers as the crown's representatives in provinces and colonies (Ballbé 1983: 25–36; Sales 1974, 1986). All these factors minimized the sort of bargaining for warmaking resources with the subject population that elsewhere built up rights and restraints. Spain and Portugal may also have caught themselves in the "territorial trap" – the conquest of so much dependent territory, relative to their means of extraction, that administrative costs ate up their gains from imperial control (Thompson and Zuk 1986). Spain and Portugal thus anticipated, in some regards, the situations of many contemporary Third World states in which military men hold power.

Behind the differentiation of civilian from military organization, and the subordination of the military to the civilian, lay a fundamental geographic problem. Under most circumstances, the spatial distribution of state activity that serves military purposes well differs sharply from the spatial distribution that serves the production of revenues. So long as a state is operating through conquest and tribute in a contiguous territory, the discrepancy need not be large; occupying soldiers can then serve as monitors, administrators, and tax collectors. Beyond that point, however, four interests pull in different directions: the placement of military forces between their likely sites of activity and their major sources of supplies; the distribution of state officials who specialize in surveillance and control of the civilian population in a pattern that compromises between spatial completeness and correspondence to the population distribution; the apportioning of state revenue-collecting activities to the geography of trade, wealth, and income, and finally, the distribution of state activities resulting from bargaining over revenues according to the spatial structures of the parties to the bargains.

Obviously the resulting geography of state activity varies with its relation to all four of these forces; navies concentrate in deep-water locations along a state's periphery, while post offices distribute in close correspondence to the population as a whole and central administrative offices cling to each other. The bigger the military establishment, the greater its orientation to war outside the state's own territory, and the more extensive the apparatus of extraction and control that grows up to support it, the greater is the discrepancy between their geographies, and the more distant the ideal military geography from one that gives the armed forces substantial day-to-day control over the civilian population.

The geographic discrepancy encourages the creation of separate organizations for each activity, including the division of armed force into armies and police forces. The distribution of police forces comes to approximate the geography of the civilian population, while the distribution of troops isolates them from civilians and places them where international strategy dictates. Indeed, the French model divides land forces into three parts: soldiers grouped into garrisons located for administrative and tactical convenience; gendarmes (remaining under military control, and mobilizable into the military in wartime) spread across the communications lines and thinly-settled segments of the territory; and police stationed in the country's larger agglomerations. Soldiers then patrol the frontiers, protect the sites of national power, intervene overseas, but rarely take part in control of crime or civilian conflicts.

Except for highways, gendarmes deal chiefly with those portions of the territory in which private property occupies most of the space, and therefore spend most of their time patrolling communication lines and responding to calls from civilians. Urban police, in contrast, crisscross territories dominated by public space and having valuable property within reach of that public space; they correspondingly spend more of their effort reaching out to control and apprehend without calls from civilians. Ultimately, any such geographic division separates the military from political power and makes it dependent for survival on civilians whose preoccupations include fiscal soundness, administrative efficiency, public order, and the keeping of political bargains as well as (perhaps even instead of) military efficacy. This complex logic strongly affected the spatial differentiation of European states.

To be sure, the discrepancy was more than geographic. As we have seen, the people who ran the state's civilian half had little choice but to establish working relations with capitalists, and to bargain with the rest of the population over the yielding of resources for an expanding range of state activities. As they pursued revenue and acquiescence, officials built organizations that grew quite distinct from the military, and for most purposes became increasingly independent of it. In Europe as a whole, these processes did not prevent steadily increasing military expenditure or ever more destructive wars, but they did contain domestic military power to a degree that would have astonished a European observer of AD 990 or 1490.

5
Lineages of the National State

G. William Skinner portrays the social geography of late imperial China as the intersection of two sets of central-place hierarchies (Skinner 1977: 275–352; see also Wakeman 1985, Whitney 1970). The first, constructed largely from the bottom up, emerged from exchange; its overlapping units consisted of larger and larger market areas centered on towns and cities of increasing size. The second, imposed mainly from the top down, resulted from imperial control; its nested units comprised a hierarchy of administrative jurisdictions. Down to the level of the *hsien*, or county, every city had a place in both the commercial and the administrative hierarchy. Below that level, even the mighty Chinese Empire ruled indirectly via its gentry. In the top-down system, we find the spatial logic of coercion. In the bottom-up system, the spatial logic of capital. We have seen two similar hierarchies at work repeatedly in the unequal encounter between European states and cities.

In some Chinese regions, imperial control was relatively weak and commercial activity relatively strong; there, cities generally occupied higher ranks in the order of markets than in the imperial order. Elsewhere (especially at the empire's periphery, where regions were typically more valuable to the center for security than for revenue), imperial control placed a city higher than did commercial activity. Skinner sketches some critical correlates of a city's relative position in the two hierarchies; for example, imperial administrators assigned to cities occupying relatively high positions in the market hierarchy accomplished more of their work by dealing with "parapolitical" networks of merchants and other prospering notables than did their colleagues in less well-favored areas, while the regions including those major market cities financed more than their share of candidates for the imperial examinations that led to careers in the bureaucracy. Many other consequences flowed from that interplay of top-down and bottom-up systems.

How did China differ from Europe? In a pamphlet published in 1637, Jesuit Giuldo Aldeni reported that his Chinese friends often asked of Europe "If there are so many kings, how can you avoid wars?" He reported answering, naively or disingenuously, "The kings of Europe are all connected by marriage, and therefore live on good terms with one another. If there is a war, the Pope intervenes; he sends out envoys to warn the belligerents to stop fighting" (Bünger 1987: 320). This in the middle of the frightful Thirty Years' War, which eventually drew the vast majority of European states into the bloodletting. The difference is critical: although China had once lived through an era of Warring States that had much in common with the international anarchy of Europe, and if insurrections and invasions from the frontiers recurrently threatened imperial control, most of the time a single center dominated much of Chinese space, a zone that was unimaginably large by European standards. Empire was long China's normal condition; when one empire declined, another seized its place. During the eighteenth century, furthermore, while direct rule from a single center was beginning to take hold in Europe, Qing emperors were imposing an even more far-reaching direct rule throughout their domains; in 1726 Emperor Yongzheng went so far as to replace the chiefs of ethnic minorities in southwest China with administrators of his own regime (Bai 1988: 197). In Europe, fragmentation into multiple competing states has prevailed over all of the last millennium.

Although Russian tsars eventually commanded a huge expanse of Asia, Europe itself never hosted an empire of the scale of China's at its prime. After the fragmentation of Rome's domains, nonetheless, many rulers attempted to build empires in Europe, or to extend them into Europe. A succession of Muslim empires reached into Spain and the Balkans, but got no farther. Byzantine, Bulgarian, Serbian, and Ottoman empires sometimes straddled the Balkans and the Middle East, while Mongols and other Asian invaders left an imperial heritage in Russia. In Europe's heartlands, Charlemagne pieced together a fissiparous empire, Normans made several attempts at empire-building, and both a Holy Roman empire (*de jure*) and a Habsburg empire (*de facto*) made their presence felt. Yet these imperial efforts all fell far short of grasping the entire continent. After Rome no large section of Europe felt the rule of another empire on a Roman, much less a Chinese, scale.

Nevertheless Europe experienced in its own more segmented way the interplay of the two processes Skinner detects in China: the bottom-up building of regional hierarchies based on trade and manufacturing, the top-down imposition of political control. Europe's urban networks represented the hierarchy of capital; they comprised the higher levels of commercial connections that reached into towns and villages, linked by *colporteurs* (etymologically, those who carried goods on their shoulders), peddlers (etymologically, those who walked their goods from place to place), and other more substantial merchants who made capital accumulation through local and regional trade their business. As an English king or a Burgundian duke reached into the countryside for taxes and soldiers, he found well-established commercial connections he had played little part in creating, and could not completely control. Indeed, Europe's bottom-up hierarchies long remained more complete, connected, and extensive than its top-down structures of political control. That was a major reason for the failure of the many post-Roman attempts to build empires spanning the continent.

R. Bin Wong's comparison of struggles over food in Europe and China suggests some important Skinnerian parallels between the experiences of the two continents (Wong 1983; Wong and Perdue 1983). Despite significant differences in structure, people in both regions seem to have been especially likely to seize food forcefully in times of shortage and/or high prices where and when the gap was widening between the extent of food marketing and the degree of governmental control over food supply. Poor people who depended on local markets for their food substituted themselves for authorities who could or would no longer enforce the locality's claims to food stored, marketed, or shipped within its perimeter. Eighteenth- and nineteenth-century China experienced a decline in imperial control as markets held their own or even expanded, and local people blocked shipments, bullied merchants, or seized stored grain to enforce their claims to the supply.

Eighteenth- and nineteenth-century Europe, for its part, saw marketing of food expand even faster than the local strength of governments: its local people seized grain to enforce claims that *their* officials would no longer respect (Bohstedt 1983, Charlesworth 1983, Tilly 1971). No one has done a sufficiently broad geography of grain seizures in Europe to determine whether they followed an appropriately Skinnerian pattern. Given the marked tendency of grain seizures to ring major cities and ports, however, such a pattern is quite plausible. China's banditry, rebellion, and other forms of collective conflict also showed marked regional differences that bear at least a rough correspondence to the joint distribution of imperial and mercantile activity. From that fact, we might reasonably search for similar geographic inequalities within Europe. Popular collective action might well display a Skinnerian logic.

The patterns of political covariation Skinner describes also have European counterparts: the administrative capitals in regions of scanty commerce in which a viceroy held power through direct military control but could produce little revenue for the king, the lower-ranking royal officials surrounded by prosperous landlords and merchants with whom they had no choice but to negotiate. Consider the contrast between eastern Prussia, where the state's administrative apparatus overwhelmed merchants in favor of great landlords, and western Prussia, where a similar apparatus almost dissolved in the region's commercial activity. Gabriel Ardant pointed out thirty years ago that the "fit" between fiscal system and regional economy determines the cost and effectiveness of attempts to tax (Ardant 1965). In an area with little market activity, a land tax based on cstimated value and levied in cash is likely to cost a great deal to collect, strike the population very inequitably, miss a good deal of potential revenue, and incite widespread resistance. In a highly commercialized area, in contrast, a flat head tax generates less revenue at higher cost than a comparable tax designed to fit the loci of capital and the paths of commerce.

On the other hand (as Ardant did not observe), with high levels of commercial activity, merchants often hold considerable political power, and therefore are in a position to prevent the creation of a state that will seize their assets and cramp their transactions. In Europe, as we have seen, the extent of commercial activity strongly affected the viability of the various tactics used to build state strength. Outside of Gdansk, which prospered with the quickening of Baltic trade, Polish merchants were unable to break the grip of great landlords. (Ironically, the power of Polish landlords also cramped Poland's elected king, and thereby made him an attractive suzerain for Prussian cities that were trying to escape the more demanding tutelage of the Teutonic Knights.) But the merchants of Amsterdam, Dubrovnik, Venice, and Genoa, high points in the commercial hierarchy, could dictate the terms on which any state would operate in their territories. Thus Skinner's model of China sheds light on the geography of state formation in Europe.

In fact, earlier chapters have laid out a model of Europe a Skinnerian can easily recognize. It has three elements:

1   a set of social relations characterized by exchange and capital accumulation in which concentration produces cities and inequality rests on exploitation;

2   another set of social relations characterized by coercion in which concentration produces states and inequality rests on domination;

3   a set of activities carried on by states which involve their agents in acquiring resources from others.

The networks defined by the two sets of social relations articulate unevenly: at some locations dense concentrations of coercion meet equally dense concentrations of capital, at others dense coercion encounters sparse capital, and so on. Similar state activities carried on at different locations therefore work differently, and have different organizational consequences. That sums up, very abstractly, the main message of this whole book so far.

STATES AND CITIES REEXAMINED

Recall what a state is: a distinct organization that controls the principal concentrated means of coercion within a well-defined territory, and in some respects exercises priority over all other organizations operating within the same territory. (A *national* state, then, extends the territory in question to multiple contiguous regions, and maintains a relatively centralized, differentiated, and autonomous structure of its own.) Armed men form states by accumulating and concentrating their means of coercion within a given territory, by creating an organization that is at least partially distinct from those that govern production and reproduction in the territory, by seizing, co-opting, or liquidating other concentrations of coercion within the same territory, by defining boundaries, and by exercising jurisdiction within those boundaries. They create national states by extending the same processes to new adjacent territories and by elaborating a centralized, differentiated, and autonomous organization as they go.

The formation and transformation of state organization occur largely as consequences of efforts to conquer, and to maintain control over the people and property in the territory. Although statemakers always have models of conquest and control in mind, and frequently follow them self-consciously, they rarely plan out the step-by-step construction of the state that these activities bring into being. Nevertheless, their activity inevitably creates top-down hierarchies of coercive control.

As rulers form and transform states, they and their agents consume large quantities of resources, especially resources that lend themselves to military applications: men, arms, transport, food. Those resources are, for the most part, already embedded in other organizations and social relations: households, manors, churches, villages, feudal obligations, connections among neighbors. The ruler's problem is to extract the essential resources from those organizations and social relations, while ensuring that someone will reproduce and yield similar resources in the future. Two factors shape the process by which states acquire resources, and strongly affect the organization that results from the process: the character of the bottom-up hierarchy of capital, and the place within that hierarchy of any location from which a state's agents try to extract resources.

The range of cities a would-be statemaker faced in Europe was very large. Resorting to yet another two-dimensional diagram (figure 5.1), we might array cities by the extent to which their activities articulated with those of their hinterlands (from a superficial to a profound connection) and by their market position (from a purely local or regional market to an international center of trade, processing, and capital accumulation). Thus thirteenth-century Florence, whose merchants and rentiers exercised extensive control over land, production, and trade in its *contado*, qualified as more of a metropolis than Genoa, an international link having weaker ties to its own hinterland. Fifteenth-century Madrid, rather closed in upon itself and its section of Castile, looked more like a regional market than Lisbon, whose dominance extended both inside and outside of Portugal.

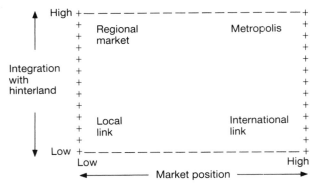

Figure 5.1   Types of cities.

The distinctions matter because they significantly affected the prospects for the formation of different kinds of states. The higher a city's market position, the more likely that anyone building up concentrated force had to negotiate with the capitalists based there, or even be one of them. The greater its economic articulation with its hinterland, the less likely that a separate group of landlords would serve as the city's counterweight or enemy in any process of state formation. In the early stages of European state formation, a city that dominated its own hinterland and occupied an international market position had a strong probability of constituting its own autonomous state, whether a city-state like Milan or a city-empire like Venice.

Under the conditions prevailing in Europe before 1800 or so, in regions where cities proliferated, international trade was intense. Some of the cities occupied central positions in international markets, and capital accumulated and concentrated. In those circumstances, no one created or altered a state except in close collaboration with the local capitalists. Flanders, the Rhineland, and the Po Valley illustrate the principle dramatically. Conditions differed where cities were sparse; there, international trade played a small part in economic life, few cities (if any) occupied high positions in international markets, and capital neither accumulated nor concentrated at a rapid rate. In such regions, states commonly formed without either the collaboration or the effective opposition of local capitalists. There, coercion reigned. Poland and Hungary stand as exemplars. In between, the presence of at least one major center of capital accumulation in a region otherwise dominated by landlords made possible an intermediate path to the state, a path in which holders of capital and of coercion struggled, but ultimately bargained out a *modus vivendi*. Aragon and England provide cases in point.

These differences followed a well-defined geographic pattern in Europe. Although seacoast regions had more than their share of cities, ports outside of the Mediterranean generally had shallow hinterlands, and backed on larger regions controlled by landlords. The broad urban column that reached roughly northwest from the Italian peninsula to southern England dominated the map of fragmented sovereignty, the zone of capitalist strength in state formation; as commerce on the Atlantic coast, the North Sea, and the Baltic gained importance, the column acted as a kind of percolator, pumping merchandise, capital, and urban population up from the Mediterranean and the various Easts to which it connected. Big, powerful national states formed chiefly at the edges of the urban column, where cities and their capital were accessible but not overwhelming. Farther out, states occupied even larger territories, but until fairly late exercised only episodic control over the people and activities within them.

These contrasting circumstances marked out different paths of change in states. To make discussion feasible, let us again schematize (see figure 5.2), reducing many paths to just three. The diagram argues that when men began to concentrate coercion in various parts of Europe the relative presence or absence of concentrated capital predicted (and to some degree caused) different trajectories of change in state structure; although all regions of Europe eventually converged toward the large national state, states actually diverged over a long period; for several centuries, coercive, capitalist, and capitalized-coercion states moved further apart in structure and action. For all its crudity, the diagram allows some useful distinctions. Within the Nordic countries, for example, we might sketch the alternative paths as in figure 5.3. In order to take the scheme seriously, to be sure, we would have to recognize that at various times Finland, Sweden, Norway, and Denmark all belonged to empires and federations dominated by others, that the boundaries of the states and dependencies designated by those names fluctuated significantly as a result of conquest and negotiation, that before the middle of the seventeenth century Denmark operated a classic coalition between powerful landlord nobles and a

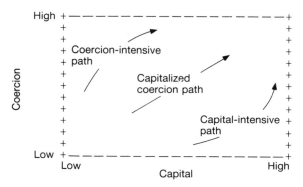

Figure 5.2   Relative concentration of capital and coercion as determinants of states' paths of growth.

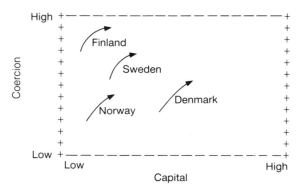

Figure 5.3   Paths of state formation in Scandinavia.

landlord king, and that over the entire time since AD 900 Finland has enjoyed only a few decades of existence independent of neighboring powers. With those qualifications, the diagram provides an opportunity to sketch how Denmark began the millennium as a relatively uncommercialized conquering power, then capitalized on growing trade between western Europe and the Baltic to become significantly more prosperous than its neighbors, while Finland remained a commercial backwater, governed by force, much longer.

The Nordic countries created their own variant of coercive state formation. Before the seventeenth century, they comprised one of Europe's most profoundly rural regions. Many towns came into being as fortified outposts of royal power rather than as significant commercial centers. Despite the early importance of Bergen, Copenhagen, and other commercial centers as outposts for trade, in 1500 no city in the region had as many as 10,000 inhabitants (de Vries 1984: 270). German merchants long dominated Scandinavian trade, to the extent that city councils and urban geography alike often split into distinct German and local sections.

Scandinavian trade became a near-monopoly of the Hanse. The Hanse cities resolutely excluded Italian bankers and refused to create banks and credit institutions of their own. Instead they relied on bilaterally balanced trade, often in kind (Kindleberger 1984: 44). Only with the quickening of Baltic trade during the sixteenth century did significant concentrations of capital and urban population start to appear in Norway, Sweden, Finland, or Denmark. Even then, the Dutch merchants who succeeded the Germans managed much of the trade, capital, and shipping. Yet the region's warriors left their mark on many parts of Europe.

In the centuries around AD 900 Vikings and their cousins conquered widely outside of the North, and often set up states dominated by warrior-landlords. They were generally unable, however, to follow the same course in their homelands. There the salience of forestry and fishing, the thinness of settlement, the openness of frontiers, and the rarity of external invasions combined to assure the survival of smallholders and to set limits on the ability of warriors to become great landlords. In seeking to secure military service, Swedish kings made grants that actually multiplied small landowners. Up to the seventeenth century, they drew most of their troops by means of variants of the same system: nobles (and later rich peasants) qualified for tax exemption by fitting out cavalrymen for poorly-paid royal service, while commoners shared the responsibility for supplying infantrymen as well as providing land to them and their families. Except for mercenaries stationed in war zones and frontier provinces, the arrangements sustained themselves without large cash outlays by the crown.

Sweden and Denmark maintained major military forces for several centuries. Under Gustav Vasa (1521–60) and his successors, Sweden built up formidable military power at the cost of subjecting large parts of the economy to demands of the state. The Scandinavian Union of Denmark, Sweden, and Norway (1397–1523) formed largely as a means of asserting royal power against the commercial dominance of German merchants and the Hanseatic League. Among other moves, Vasa dispossessed the clergy and created a Protestant church subordinated to the state. Like his Russian contemporaries, Gustav Vasa also forwarded the view "that all land belonged to the crown and those non-nobles enjoying temporary possession of it could only expect continued tenure while they fulfilled their fiscal obligations to the government" (Shennan 1974: 63). The state's search for cash to pay for war in a largely subsistence economy motivated an expansion of mining and manufacturing, an elaboration of the fiscal apparatus, the beginning of a substantial national debt, a bypassing of older representative assemblies, and an increasing involvement of the clergy (now Protestant and national) in record-keeping for the crown (Lindegren 1985, Nilsson 1988).

More commercial Denmark financed its warmaking from the income of crown lands up through the Thirty Years' War. Indeed, until 1660 no commoner could own land in Denmark. The war beween Sweden and Denmark in the 1640s combined with economic depression to precipitate a struggle over revenues between the Danish aristocracy and the elected king. In a coup d'état, the crown established a hereditary monarchy and greatly reduced noble power. But that meant reduced cooperation from the nobility. As a result Denmark made a decisive shift to taxation, including the lucrative tolls of the Sound. "Whereas 67% of Danish state revenues in 1608 consisted of income from crown lands, a half century later such revenues amounted to only 10%" (Rystad 1983: 15). To liquidate its war-induced debts, indeed, the monarchy sold off the bulk of its lands between 1660 and 1675 (Ladewig Petersen 1983: 47). Thus the expense of seventeenth-century warmaking produced major governmental changes in both Denmark and Sweden.

Sweden (like Denmark) relied largely on mercenaries during the Thirty

Years' War, but shifted back toward a conscripted national force as its troop requirements rose during the later seventeenth century. Charles XI (1672–97) engineered his own coup d'état by wresting from magnates crown lands his predecessors had been selling off to pay for their warmaking, and then allocating much of the land to part-time soldiers who thus owed military service for their means of subsistence. By 1708 Sweden and Finland (then a Swedish province) were fielding 111,000 troops from a total population of about two million (Roberts 1979: 45). The Swedish monarchy was constantly short of funds, but was able to pay for war without bankruptcy by exporting copper and iron, by building its own large arms industry on its rich base of minerals, and by exacting enormous payments from the territories it won. That system of tribute worked well enough so long as conquest continued, but collapsed at the advent of peace and stable rule.

With the assassination of Charles XII (1718), Sweden abandoned its drive for imperial power. By that time, however, the creation of a large military force on the basis of a small population, a relatively unmonetized economy, and an exiguous bourgeoisie had produced a very substantial state apparatus in which civil bureaucrats and clergy did a great deal of work for the crown. Norway (which lived under Danish, and then Swedish, rule until 1905) and Finland (which was a province of Sweden until 1809 and then a Russian grand duchy until 1917) underwent similar evolutions despite their dependent positions and greater peripherality with respect to European markets. Denmark, commanding the traffic of the Sound with the substantial tolls that traffic generated, putting a much larger part of its military effort into the navy than its neighbors, and building commercialized agriculture in trade with Germans to the south, created a larger bourgeoisie and a smaller state apparatus.

Although Swedish landless laborers increased greatly in number with the consolidation of holdings after 1750 (Winberg 1978), they never fell under the control of big landholders. Instead, the state bureaucracy extended its monitoring directly to peasants and laborers, who retained considerable bargaining power; in Sweden, indeed, peasants maintained representation through a separate Estate from those of the clergy, nobility, and bourgeoisie. The resulting states organized around coercion and gave little scope to capital, but lacked the great territorial lords of their neighbors to the south.

In comparison with the rest of Europe, then, the Nordic areas all clustered along the coercion-intensive path to statehood. At the other extreme, the commercial city-states and city-empires of Italy followed a distinctly different path to the state, relying on high concentrations of capital, but concentrating coercion less decisively and more temporarily than their North European cousins. That is the main point: trajectories of change in European states differed dramatically, and produced contrasting kinds of state. Those that followed the capitalized-coercion path eventually became dominant in Europe, and other states converged on their characteristics. But before that late consolidation of the European state system, many other kinds of state formed and performed quite effectively.

Let me recall the crucial points. Interacting with each other and jointly involved in international wars, rulers in different parts of Europe pursued similar activities: they sought to create and use warmaking capacity to their own advantages. But each one did so under the highly variable conditions set by the combination of coercion and capital that prevailed in his own territory. Alternative combinations meant different class configurations, different potential allies and enemies, different organizational residues of state activity, different forms of resistance to state activity, different strategies for the extraction of resources, and therefore different levels of efficiency in resource extraction. Because each interaction produced new organizational residues and social relations, the path followed by a state up to a certain point in time limited the strategies open to its rulers beyond that point. For that reason, even states occupying identical locations with respect to coercion and capital at different points in time behaved somewhat differently. Nevertheless, the great distinctions separated coercion-intensive, capital-intensive, and capitalized-coercion trajectories of state formation.

COERCIVE TRAJECTORIES

Take the path that led through high coercion. In the European portion of what is now the USSR, trade routes were thin and capital lacking. In AD 990, the chief center of commerce and manufacturing was Kiev, which served as a northern offshoot of the great commercial band connecting Byzantium with India, China, and the rest of the civilized world; Kiev also lay on the lesser north–south trade route linking the Baltic to Byzantium. In the year 988, tradition says, Prince Vladimir of Kiev had cemented the Byzantine connection by accepting baptism into its branch of Christianity. Princes of Kiev, descendants of Vikings who had moved south to conquer, exercised weak sovereignty over the rulers of other Russian city-states and regional dukedoms. At a local level, much of the land remained under the control of peasant communes; as in the rest of eastern Europe, landlords were able to coerce income from peasants in the form of dues, fines, use fees, and part-time labor on their estates, but could only intervene with difficulty in households' and communities' management of their own plots. The thinness of settlement made it relatively easy for cultivators to flee oppressive masters and seek refuge in the lands of other lords. Great landlords also suffered repeated raids and conquests from the mobile peoples of the steppe. On a larger scale, nevertheless, relatively autonomous armed landlords dominated most of the territory.

To the west, in AD 990, a Polish state was aggrandizing by conquest of territories nominally belonging to the Holy Roman Empire. It was also expanding eastward; in 1069 its grand duke drove his armies to Kiev and put one of his kinsmen on the Russian throne. To the northwest, Viking states made periodic attempts to extend their frontiers into the lands claimed by Russia and Poland. A bellicose Bulgarian state flexed its muscles to Russia's southwest. In the same region, kings of Bohemia and Hungary (the latter newly crowned) were likewise marking out their own zones of control. Around Europe's western rim – notably in the British Isles, the Iberian peninsula, and Italy – the armed invaders that rolled continually out of Scandinavia and the Middle East commonly seized land and created states based on agriculture; however thinly, they settled on the land. Almost all of Europe's eastern third, in contrast, was forming into tribute-taking states that claimed priority in large territories but governed them only loosely, if at all.

In the East, nomadic conquerors simultaneously threatened the hegemony of any substantial state and maintained a strong investment in the continued existence of agrarian states they could exploit. When their numbers were large and their force too great for them to fix themselves as parasites on existing states, some of them gradually settled and formed their own exploitative states. In all these ways, they shaped the east European pattern of state formation for a thousand years after AD 500. One after another, they roared out of the steppe: Bulgars, Magyars, Petchenegs, Mongols, Turks, and many lesser peoples.

Invasions from the southeast continued well past the Millennium, reaching their peak in the 1230s, when Mongols sacked Kiev and established hegemony in its domains. At that point, Mongols were on their way to ruling most of Eurasia, from Russia to China. In much of their domain, to be sure, that "rule" consisted of little more than the requirement of formal submission, the exaction of tribute, the fighting off of rival claimants, and the conduct of occasional military raids on insufficiently cooperative subjects. For two centuries, nevertheless, Russian princes paid tribute and homage to the Golden Horde, who set their capital on the lower Volga. Indeed, the Horde's khans commonly forced sons of ruling Russian princes to inhabit the Mongol capital, and thus to serve as hostages to their fathers' performances (Dewey 1988: 254).

From the fifteenth century onward the frequency and intensity of attacks from the southeast seems to have declined as the central Mongol empire collapsed and the steppe's armed horsemen turned their attention to the vulnerable, and much richer, states along their southern flank. When Tatars sacked Moscow in 1571, they unknowingly marked the end of major incursions into Russia. During the seventeenth century, Zunghar Mongols actually collaborated with the Russians in the conquest of Siberia. Very likely the combination of devastating disease (especially plague) on the Eurasian steppe and the European opening of sea routes that offered viable alternatives to the ancient caravan road from China and India to Europe diminished the threat from the steppe to creators of Russian states (McNeill 1976: 195–6).

By 1400, Europe from the Vistula to the Urals was consolidating into large states, including Lithuania, the republic of Novgorod, and the realm of the Golden Horde. To the northwest, the Prussia of the Teutonic Knights and a Denmark temporarily including Sweden and Norway dominated the Baltic. During the first half of the sixteenth century, the vast grand duchies of Lithuania and Moscow divided the area above the band of Muslim kingdoms that extended from the east along the north shore of the Black Sea all the way to Hungary, Greece, and the Adriatic. (In 1569, Lithuania would unite with Poland, to its west, placing a huge, if thinly-governed, state between Russia and the rest of Europe.) The sixteenth-century establishment of an Arctic sea route from England and Holland to Archangel fortified the European connections of the growing Russian state.

Conquests of Peter the Great (1689–1725) and Catherine the Great (1762–96) brought Russia's boundaries definitively to the Black Sea and provisionally to Estonia, Latvia, and Karelia. Both rulers intensified the involvement of Russia in the culture and politics of western Europe. The end of the Napoleonic Wars left European Russia within something like its present borders, adjacent to Prussia, Poland, Hungary, and the Ottoman Empire. The Ottoman state, itself an outgrowth of conquest from the east, covered the Balkans and reached west to touch the thin strip of Austrian territory bordering the Adriatic. Between the sixteenth and eighteenth centuries, Europe's entire eastern frontier consolidated into states that claimed control over large expanses of land. At the same time, the Russian state and economy shifted their orientations from southeast to northwest. As compared with the tribute-collecting states of the thirteenth and fourteenth centuries these states exercised significant control over their borders and substantial power over the populations within them.

Poland remained for centuries the exception that proved the rule, the country in which the nominal ruler could never rule the great landlords, and could rarely get them to join in a sustained, coordinated military effort. During the 1760s, when the Polish state still occupied a territory larger than that of France, the national army mustered only 16,000 men, while Polish nobles had some 30,000 men under arms. This at a time when adjacent Russia, Austria, and Prussia stood by with armies of 200 to 500 thousand men (Ratajczyk 1987: 167). As mass armies formed, failure to match your great neighbors, or to ally with at least one of them, invited conquest. In the later eighteenth century Russia, Austria, and Prussia swallowed adjacent sections of Poland, eventually leaving none behind.

Poland again fell prey to Prussia, Austria, and Russia in the nineteenth century, but otherwise Russia's European borders remained relatively stable until World War I, whose settlement placed a series of small republics, plus a substantial Poland, to the west of the newly-formed Soviet Union. World War II brought some of those republics back into the USSR's state territory, and the rest of them into its orbit. To discuss the formation of the "Russian" state is thus to follow a titanic series of changes in hegemony and territory.

Before the twentieth century, none of that territory contained a great concentration of cities, and little of it even reached into the continent's regions of intense trade. After 1300, indeed, with the contraction of the old commercial belt that ran from China to the Balkans (and therefore of its northward extension to the Baltic), and with predatory Mongols blocking access to the Mediterranean and the Black Sea, the once-thriving network of cities including Kiev, Smolensk, Moscow, and Novgorod thinned out. The sixteenth-century revival of trade multiplied towns, but did not bring into being anything resembling the urban density of western and Mediterranean Europe. The Russian state took shape in a capital-poor environment.

The environment was also coercion-rich. For five centuries after AD 990 the various states that grew up in that part of Europe operated through conquest, fed on tribute, and ruled (the word exaggerates) chiefly through regional magnates who had their own bases of power. Under Mongol hegemony, the largely independent princes of the North parceled out their sovereignty to landlords who fused economic and political control of the peasants in their jurisdictions. During the sixteenth century, as the Mongol states collapsed, Russian conquests to the south and east brought into being a system of land and labor grants to warriors, forced labor by peasants, restrictions on their right to move, and rising taxation for war; the durable traits of Russian serfdom began to appear.

Up to that point, Russian emperors were trying to rule a vast territory with insufficient force. They governed quite indirectly, through a church and a nobility that held tremendous powers and retained the ability to check royal demands. Muscovite tsars Ivan III (the Great, 1462–1505) and Ivan IV (the Terrible, 1533–84) began to establish more direct rule by sapping the power of independent landlords; in their place they created an army and a bureaucracy attached to the crown through the imperial land grants their chief officers enjoyed. "Ivan [the Great] and his successors," reports Jerome Blum,

> were intent upon building up the military forces they needed to conquer their brother princes, to crush the oligarchic ambitions of their own boyars, to stave off foreign invasions, and to expand their realm. They needed an army that was as dependent as possible upon them, and upon whose loyalty, therefore, they could themselves depend. But they lacked the money to buy the men and the allegiance they required. So they decided to use land.
>
> (Blum 1964: 170–1)

That was the quintessential coercion-intensive strategy. Since most of the essential land belonged to armed, semi-independent landlords, the tsars' reorganization precipitated bloody battles with the nobility. The tsars won. In the process, landlords who enjoyed imperial favor gained a signal advantage over their rebellious neighbors: they could count on the government's armed force to fix an otherwise footloose peasantry on their lands. Thus the logic of warmaking and statemaking in a region of little capital led rulers to buy officeholders with expropriated land. Eventually Russia's rulers established the principle that only servants of the state could own land; although exceptions and violations abounded, the principle provided yet another incentive for the multiplication of offices, and for collaboration between officials and landholders in the exploitation of the peasantry.

The placing of small estates in the hands of profit-seeking officeholders increased the pressure on peasants in the northwest. Combined with the opening of new territories to the south and east, that pressure induced a depopulation of the old areas of settled agriculture, which only increased the incentive to fix peasants in place by local practice and imperial decree; the so-called Assembly Code of 1649 codified a system of serfdom that had been developing for two centuries. In addition, slave labor, especially in the newer areas of settlement, continued to expand during the sixteenth and seventeenth centuries. During the eighteenth century, in seeking to extract revenue from slaves as well as serfs, the tsars practically eliminated the legal distinction between them. After an abortive attempt to tax individual peasants, Peter the Great made landlords responsible for the soul tax, an act that reinforced the interdependence of crown and landlords, not to mention the state-backed power that landlords wielded over their hapless serfs. Peter decreed in 1700 that any freed slave or serf must report immediately for military service, and if rejected for service bind himself to another master. Peter likewise created a distinctive nobility, neatly graded by rank of service to the tsar. To a degree unimaginable in western Europe, Russia acquired a social hierarchy defined, supported, and dominated by the state.

From top to bottom, the emerging structure of social relations depended on coercion. As the Russian state began seriously to engage in war with its heavily armed western neighbors, the effort to extract essential revenues from an uncommercialized economy multiplied the state structure. At the same time, the conquest of lands lying between Muscovy and the Ottoman Empire expanded the military apparatus, exported the Russian mode of serfdom and landholding, and built up the imperial bureaucracy to its full, ponderous form. Peter the Great began the great effort to eliminate separatisms, to subject all segments of the empire – and their revenues – to Muscovite regulations and central administration:

Accompanying Peter's campaign to weed out Ukrainian separatism was a policy of extracting the maximum in economic and human resources from the Hetmanate. Regulations on trade routes, state monopolies, tariffs on foreign goods, and import-export taxes were introduced for the first time ... Peter also began a massive conscription of Cossacks, not for war but for imperial public works – the building of canals, fortifications, and, especially, Peter's favorite project, the new capital of St. Petersburg.

(Kohut 1988: 71; see also Raeff 1983)

Catherine the Great completed the incorporation of the Ukraine by abolishing the semi-autonomous Hetmanate outright. The same bureaucracy then reached all parts of the empire. The challenge of war with Napoleonic France, which transformed state structure through much of Europe, fortified the Russian state, magnified its budget, taxation, and staff, expanded its military, and locked into place a deeply coercive state.

In broadly similar ways, Russian, Polish, Hungarian, Serbian, and Brandenburger states formed on the basis of strong alliances between warmaking princes and armed landlords, large concessions of governmental power to nobles and gentry, joint exploitation of the peasantry, and restricted scope for merchant capital. Repeatedly, leaders of conquering forces who lacked capital offered their followers booty and land, only to face the problem of containing the great warrior-landlords they thereby created. Mongols stood out as exceptions because they rarely settled down to run their own lands, and usually continued to live on tribute exacted by the perpetual threat of devastating invasion.

Although the relative weight of crown and nobility (and therefore the extent to which warfare created durable state structure) varied significantly from state to state, all these states stood out from their European neighbors by heavy reliance on brute coercion. When, in the sixteenth century, large volumes of eastern European grain began to flow westward, the existing structure of control permitted great landlords to profit directly from those shipments; they used state power to contain merchants and coerce peasant producers, building a new serfdom in the process. In that balance of power, even extensive commercialization did not build cities, an independent capitalist class, or a state more greatly resembling those of urban Europe.

The experience of Sicily curiously parallels that of eastern European powers. Sicily was for centuries a breadbasket, a rich source of grain for all the Mediterranean. Yet its Arab and Norman rulers clamped on the island a system of alliance with militarily-active landlords that left little scope for cities and capitalists. King Frederick II, who came to power in 1208, subordinated cities to his glorious state. "Frederick's subjection of the towns," reports Dennis Mack Smith,

helped to ensure that there was never any class of merchants or civic officials independent and vigorous enough to offset the landowning aristocracy; and this lack of challenge to the aristocracy was to be a fundamental factor in the political, cultural and economic decline of Sicily. Whenever strong government failed, it was the nobles and not the local cities which filled the vacuum of power. It was therefore foreign towns – Pisa, Genoa, Venice, Amalfi, Lucca – which dominated Sicilian commerce.

(Mack Smith 1968a: 56)

That external control over commerce continued for six centuries, with the result that an agriculturally rich Sicily remained capital-poor and subject to coercive control.

We begin to see a pattern of uniformity and variation among coercion-intensive paths of state formation. All Europe's areas of high coercion began with some combination of two conditions: (1) a major effort to expel a tribute-taking power, (2) few cities and little concentrated capital. The expulsion of tribute takers was relatively unimportant in the Nordic countries, the extent of cities and capital greater in the Iberian peninsula and Sicily than in eastern and northern Europe. But everywhere the combination encouraged a strategy of conquest in which territorial lords simultaneously leagued together against common enemies and fought each other for priority within their own territory, with the leading lord ceding control over land and labor to his fellows in exchange for military assistance. On the whole, that strategy left little space for an autonomous bourgeoisie, hence for accumulation and concentration of capital outside the state.

There the differences began. In some areas (Poland and Hungary are the obvious examples) warrior nobles retained great power, including the ability to install and depose kings. In others (Sweden and Russia are cases in point) a single power managed to establish priority by constructing a state bureaucracy that gave nobles and clergy great privileges with respect to the commoner population, but committed them to service of the state. In still others (Sicily and Castile come to mind), a nobility whose richer and more powerful members resided in the capital on incomes drawn from distant estates and state revenues coexisted with state officials who reached far into the provinces and relied on priests and local nobles for assistance in working the royal will. The big division, then, separated the first variant from the other two – marked off states in which rival armed landlords long held the upper hand from those in which one of them early established supremacy over all the others. In all of them, states grew up starved for capital, bartered state-guaranteed privileges for national armed force, and relied heavily on coercion to assure compliance with royal demands.

CAPITALIST TRAJECTORIES

What a contrast with the states of Flanders or northern Italy! Consider the upper Adriatic, the arc of coastline from Ravenna to Trieste. For centuries, Venice dominated the region both economically and politically. But to the south rival powers struggled for control of the coastal area. Ravenna, for example, having been the residence of Roman and Goth emperors, passed the Millennium as a republic, only came under Venetian control during the fourteenth and fifteenth centuries, and from then until the Risorgimento belonged to the pope's domains. To the west, a region of multiple city-states yielded to Venice's fourteenth-century conquests, giving the Venetian city-empire a common frontier with a Lombardy that was first an independent state, then a possession successively of Spain, Austria, and unified Italy. To the north, the Holy Roman Empire and its successor states always loomed large, and sometimes held the coast. To the east, empire after empire surged and pushed toward the Adriatic. In the year 990, the Byzantine Empire exercised nominal control in Dalmatia and the Venetian region, while a shadowy "Roman" empire based in central Europe claimed sovereignty in the adjacent sections of Italy.

To simplify a very complicated story, let us concentrate on Venice, and simply note the city's interactions with all those competing powers. We shall look for: the interaction between substantial, increasing concentrations of capital and weak, fragmented concentrations of coercion; the profound influence of capitalists over any attempt to create autonomous coercive power; the emergence of a sleek, efficient, rapacious, protection-oriented seafaring state; the eventual hemming-in of that state by larger land-based powers; in short, the quintessence of capital-intensive state formation.

The Lombard invasion of Italy (AD 568) had transformed a scattering of boatmen and saltmakers into a set of refugee settlements with strong ties to mainland Italy. Venice remained a nominal part of the Byzantine Empire while Lombards and then Franks seized much of the nearby territory. Up to AD 990, as the Byzantine Empire reached its high point, Venice served chiefly as a transfer station for goods dispatched to northern Italy by traders within the Byzantine system; the city sent its own merchants to Pavia and other inland markets, exchanging salt, fish, and precious goods from the East for grain and other necessities. As they turned seaward, however, Venetian merchants added slaves and lumber to their wares. They also extended the city's commercial and political influence to much of the Adriatic.

In the Mediterranean of that time, the limits of shipbuilding and navigation meant that ships hugged shores, followed a relatively small number of routes defined by winds, currents, and shoals, put in frequently for water and other supplies, evaded corsairs with difficulty once they encountered them, and when they traveled long distances could only afford to carry valuable goods (Pryor 1988). No state became a great maritime power without having extensive privileges in many ports away from its home territory. States that did control many ports gained from them a triple return: access to long trade routes, trade in those ports, and use of the ports as bases for corsairs to prey on the commerce of other powers. For a time, Venice met these conditions and became the Mediterranean's greatest seapower. It contributed mightily to the Christian states' capture of major sea lanes from Muslim control, which began in the tenth century and did not recede until the Turkish advances of the fourteenth. Only the consolidation of Ottoman power during the fifteenth and sixteenth centuries seriously compromised Western domination of Mediterranean sea-lanes (Pryor 1988: 172–8).

During the eleventh century, Venice's fleet began both to carry its trade into the Mediterranean and to fight off rivals for control of the Adriatic – Dalmatians, Hungarians, Saracens, and Normans. Venetian forces annexed Dalmatia in the year 990, but lost it to an expanding Hungarian state around 1100; for five centuries thereafter, they dominated Dalmatia's commercial activity, but waxed and waned in its political control as a function of expansion and contraction of territorial states to the east. For their collaboration with the Byzantine emperor in wars against his enemies, they received exceptional trading privileges in the empire, including their own quarter in Constantinople (1082). Like Hanse merchants in Scandinavia and North Germany, Venetian traders came to manage much of Byzantium's long-distance commerce. During the twelfth century, they expanded their scope to the whole eastern Mediterranean, profitably mixing trade, piracy, conquest, and participation in crusades. Since crusading itself combined trade, piracy, and conquest, the activities complemented each other. By 1102, Venice had its own merchant quarter in Sidon; by 1123 it had established a base in Tyre as well.

In 1203 and 1204 Venice received the payoff on its combined strategy, as a crafty doge diverted a crusade to Constantinople and delivered a death blow to the Byzantine Empire. The bronze horses of San Marco, seized in Constantinople, still stand as monuments to that *tour de force*. Venice ended up in control of large pieces (legally, three eighths) of the late empire. The city then granted fiefs in the Greek islands to members of its great families, on condition that they keep the trade routes open.

Through all the conquest, Venetian commercial interests reigned supreme. The city's leading families were merchants and bankers, the city's governing council represented the leading families, the doge came from that same patriciate, the city's military forces drew on its own population, and its military and diplomatic policies promoted the establishment of commercial monopolies, protection for its merchants, and channeling of trade through Venice rather than the creation of a territorial empire. Once they consolidated their superior position, Venetian authorities became reluctant to tolerate piracy and license privateers, since both would menace their investment in peaceful commerce.

The city's maritime dominance, in its turn, opened new opportunities for profit in transporting goods and people safely. Venetian shippers grew rich by carrying crusaders, and then pilgrims, to the Holy Land. Freight charges on the transport of crusaders to Constantinople in 1203, "came to about twice the annual income of the king of England" (Scammell 1981: 108). For all their service of crusaders and pilgrims, furthermore, Venetian rulers did not hesitate to deal with the enemies of Christendom. After Tripoli (1289) and Acre (1291) fell to the Ottoman Turks, for example, Venice immediately negotiated a treaty with the Ottomans for retention of their old trading rights.

Within the Adriatic, rival cities were unable to hold their own against Venice without the aid of territorial powers. Trieste and Ragusa, for example, were likewise trading cities that enjoyed a certain independence, but they could not check Venice without outside help. Venice conquered Trieste in 1203, and held the port in uneasy thrall for more than a century. During Trieste's unsuccessful rebellion of 1368, Duke Leopold of Austria, an old enemy of Venice who coveted an opening onto the Adriatic, sent a relieving force. In 1382, Trieste succeeded in placing itself under Leopold's overlordship; Trieste then remained Austrian (indeed, remained Austria's principal port) until the twentieth century.

Ragusa/Dubrovnik followed a broadly similar strategy. Ragusa lived under nominal Venetian overlordship until 1358, but maintained relative independence before then by cultivating good relations with the neighboring kingdoms of Serbia and Bosnia, in whose trade its merchants played a dominant role. An expanding Hungary expelled Venice from Dalmatia in the 1350s, and granted Ragusa a nearly independent position at the periphery of its empire. As Ottoman Turks won the Balkans in the 1460s, the merchant-patricians of Ragusa managed to negotiate similar arrangements with the new Muslim rulers. Shielded from Italian conquest by its successive protectors and guaranteed great autonomy within Slavic and Ottoman empires by its commercial position, Ragusa operated as an essentially independent city-state until the Napoleonic invasion of 1808.

Although the Italian cities whose supply lines Venice dominated and the Dalmatian cities over whom Venice exercised direct control struggled continually to check Venetian hegemony, Venice competed for seapower most directly with Genoa, a similar ocean-going city-state. During the later thirteenth century, Genoa expanded through the western Mediterranean and out past Gibraltar along the Atlantic coast in the same way that Venice penetrated the eastern Mediterranean and the Black Sea; but Genoa reached more effectively east than Venice reached west; the two powers clashed especially at the meeting points of their maritime zones. Genoese control of the Black Sea during the later thirteenth century blocked Venetian access to the lucrative trade with that which passed from Trebizond to China through Mongol-held territory. Once Venetian forces blockaded and captured the Genoese fleet in Chioggia's lagoon (1380), however, Venice held priority in the east.

After the Millennium, as Venice's place in the trade of the Adriatic and eastern Mediterranean grew ever larger, the city's population bounded to one of Europe's greatest: 80,000 or more in 1200, 120,000 or so in 1300. Although the Black Death (introduced into Italy by Genoese galleys returning from Caffa) killed over half the city's population in 1347, 1348, and 1349, the number of inhabitants swung around 120,000 for centuries thereafter, in fact until now. From the thirteenth century onward, manufacturing and commerce displaced seafaring as the city's dominant activities. But Venice remained a critical link in maritime trade, and a great power in maritime politics. Its empire extended, for example, to Cyprus until 1573 and to Crete until 1669. The city's forces warred to maintain access to commercial opportunities, and warred to hold off such rivals as Genoa. More than anything else, its rulers gained reputations from the ability to wage canny and successful sea wars at relatively low cost to the city's merchants, bankers, and manufacturers.

The nature of Venetian trade facilitated creation of an exceptionally supple and predatory state. Unlike the Dutch, who gained their riches transporting bulky products such as grain, salt, and wine, Venetians concentrated on high-priced luxuries: spices, silks, slaves. What is more, they frequently carried great quantities of bullion. Efficiency, monopoly, and military protection from marauders therefore became crucial to their success. "[T]hough other imperial powers might devote much of their energies and resources to the defence of some particular monopoly," remarks G. V. Scammell, "with none, except Venice, did its running and protection become in effect the whole purpose of their being, with the state providing the ships for its operation and a navy and empire for its safeguard" (Scammell 1981: 116). Such a state made as little war as possible, but made that war ruthlessly.

Doges, especially, bore responsibility for warfare. The first doges had been servitors of the Byzantine Empire. As Venice established its independence from the empire, doges had acted increasingly like elected but thenceforth sovereign princes, acting without formal consultation of the community and designating their successors from within their own dynasties. With the city's growth after AD 990, however, Venice moved increasingly to formal oligarchy. A general assembly in which the great families played a preponderant role elected the doge. He had to consult a council that, in theory, represented the Commune formed by all the settlements of the lagoons and, in practice, spoke for the great families in the central settlement. As is so often the case, a formal council took shape when a would-be sovereign faced a group of well-defined and disparate interests without whose support he could not govern. Over time, the great council became more and more exclusive; in 1297, membership became essentially hereditary. In 1300 and 1310, the council fought off popular rebellions against the exclusion of non-patricians from its deliberations. From that point on, members of the oligarchy struggled for preeminence within the city, but never relinquished collective control over its destiny.

Rather than a single governing council, indeed, successive struggles over power produced a shifting hierarchy of councils, from the doge's own advisors to the general assembly of all inhabitants, the latter now reduced to ratifying the decisions of their betters. On the other hand, Venice secreted no bureaucracy; elected committees and officials' personal retainers did the bulk of governmental work. By 1200, the doge had become rather the oligarchy's executive officer than an autocrat chosen by popular acclamation. As a result, the interests of merchant capitalists dominated the policy – domestic and foreign – of the Venetian state.

If commercial interests guided Venice, the state in turn regulated its citizens' commercial activity. "The Venetian travelling to the Levant on business," remarks Daniel Waley,

> was likely to go in a state-built galley, commanded by a captain chosen by the state, within a convoy organised by the state, and when he reached Alexandria or Acre he might well be ordered to join other Venetians in a joint, state-organised purchase of cotton or pepper. The advantage of the last system was that prices would be kept lower if Venetians were not competing against each other. The convoy system for longer voyages goes back at least to the twelfth century. By the thirteenth the routine arrangements allowed for two convoys of galleys a year to the eastern Mediterranean and by the beginning of the fourteenth there were also annual sailings to England and Flanders, to north Africa ("Barbary") and to Aigues-Mortes (near the mouth of the Rhone). The arsenal, the state shipbuilding yard, dates back to the early thirteenth century and the materials used there were usually purchased directly by the Venetian republic.
>
> (Waley 1969: 96)

The state, executive committee of the bourgeoisie, took its responsibilities seriously.

Yet the Venetian state was never bulky. The fiscal system lent itself to slim government. In 1184, for example, Venice established a monopoly over the production and sale of salt from Chioggia's lagoon; although such a monopoly encouraged petty smuggling and fraud, it also produced substantial revenues without extensive manpower. From the thirteenth century onward, the commune established a funded debt. The Monte Vecchio and the other Monti succeeding it, the securities representing that debt, came to be a favorite investment in Venice and elsewhere. The city borrowed to finance wars, then relied on customs and excise to pay for them. The great ritual and charitable confraternities, the Scuole Grandi, loaned substantial sums to the state (Pullan 1971: 138). Since it could borrow from its own merchants and tax the flows through an extensively commercialized economy, the state created little new organization for its finances.

The fourteenth century involved Venice more emphatically in land warfare, and built up the state structure correspondingly. As the city-states of northern Italy began to expand their territories, they threatened both Venice's sources of industrial supplies on the mainland and its merchants' access to vital trade routes across the Alps. Venetians began two fateful games: conquest on the mainland, and shifting alliances with other north Italian powers. By the end of the century, as transalpine powers started serious incursions into northern Italy, Venice was organizing coalitions against France, and joining with such powers as the king of Castile and the German emperor. A set of permanent ambassadors fanned out to the major courts of Europe. The advance of the

Turks around the eastern Mediterranean, and even into Italy, simultaneously drew the city into increased naval warfare.

The expanded scale of warfare caused changes in the city's organization for war. For the first time, Venice entrusted warfare to outsiders, *condottieri*, who employed mercenaries in large numbers. The government balanced *condottiere* influence by sending out patrician commissioners, *provveditori*, who had widespread power over supplies, pay, and sometimes military strategy itself (Hale 1979). Not long after, the city resorted to conscription in its subject territories and in Venice itself, where the guilds of artisans and shopkeepers received quotas of oarsmen for war galleys. During the fifteenth century, Venice began to force convicts and captives to man its galleys; in the process, the galleys shifted from the trireme, which required three skilled rowers, each with his own oar, on every bench, to the ship with one large oar per bench, on which even unskilled, reluctant, and shackled prisoners could lean their weight. The day of an all-volunteer force had long since passed.

The swelling of warfare and the shift away from citizen-soldiers placed new financial burdens on the city. By the later fourteenth century, Venice was levying forced loans, income taxes, and direct property taxes to pay its war-induced debts. Nevertheless, these exceptional efforts did not build up a bulky or permanent bureaucracy; in a highly commercialized economy, elected officials and a small professional corps of clerks and secretaries administered the city's accounts without a large staff. The state parceled out many responsibilities to the citizenry, as when they required the Scuole Grandi to raise portions of a war fleet on their own (Pullan 1971: 147–56; Lane 1973b: 163). Nor did financial obligations overwhelm the city's fiscal apparatus. At the start of the seventeenth century, while other European states were painfully accumulating war debts, Venice actually managed temporarily to liquidate its entire long-term indebtedness (Lane 1973a: 326).

Well before 1600, the city passed its apogee of commercial power. From the fifteenth century onward, a concatenation of changes reduced Venice to a second-rank actor on the international scene: Turkey's exclusion of Venice from Black Sea and eastern Mediterranean ports, the near-surrounding of Venetian territory by Habsburg, Bourbon, and Turkish empires, Venice's declining access to timber, its consequently dwindling shipbuilding industry, its diminishing ability to control Dalmatia, and Mediterranean competition-cum-piracy of Atlantic maritime powers such as Holland and England. By circumnavigating Africa and penetrating the Indian Ocean's trade routes, Portuguese merchants broke the Venetian stranglehold on the spice trade. At the end of the sixteenth century, Portuguese vessels were carrying from a quarter to a half of all the spices and drugs that Europeans brought from the Far East (Steensgard 1981: 131). Portuguese dominance did not last long, however; within a century the efficiently-organized Dutch and British East India Companies had displaced their Iberian rivals (Steensgard 1974).

The arrival of the large, armed sailing ship on the Mediterranean scene cracked the long hegemony of the Venetian galley. Thereafter Venice remained bustling and independent, increasingly engaged in manufacturing and in administration of its mainland territory, but no longer the Mediterranean's leading force. Even within the Adriatic, once practically the city's private lake, sixteenth-century Venetian vessels were unable to contain the rival merchants of Ragusa or to check the depredations of pirates. In the eighteenth century, they gave up trying to exclude foreign warships from their gulf. By then, not only Ragusa but also Trieste and Ancona competed actively for Adriatic trade.

Venice settled for a general policy of military and diplomatic neutrality, an important commercial niche, an increasing reliance on mainland territories as an economic base, and a republican public life dominated by the old oligarchy. "In the hard choice between political independence and commercial success," concludes Alberto Tenenti about the seventeenth century, "in her uncertainty about her own fate, the proud determination of Venice still shone forth above all her mistaken and her shabby actions. Instead of choosing, like her neighbor Ragusa, a life with no risks and no history, the old city-state refused to give way to the predominance of any power, be it Turkish or Papal, Spanish or Habsburg" (Tenenti 1967: xvii–xviii).

Yet that choice finally failed: in 1797, Napoleon's invasion brought the eighteenth-century settlement to an end. Venice and its mainland territories became properties first of Austria, then of a Napoleonic kingdom of Italy, then again of Austria. In 1848, a group of insurgents led by Daniele Manin briefly held power, but Austria soon brought its revolutionary subjects into line. Finally, in 1866, Prussia's defeat of Austria freed Venice to join the new Italian national state.

Venice followed a unique historical trajectory. Yet the city's history had something in common with Genoa, Ragusa, Milan, Florence, and even Holland, Catalonia, or the Hanse. During the fourteenth century, after all, Barcelona sent traders up and down the Mediterranean, and ruled Thebes, Athens, and Piraeus. The Dutch Republic, a frequently turbulent federation of trading centers, remained one of Europe's dominant states for more than a century. City-states, city-empires, and urban federations all held their own for centuries as commercial and political powers, gave high priority to commercial objectives, created effective state structures without large bureaucracies, invented relatively efficient ways of paying for war and other state expenditures, and built institutions representing their commercial oligarchies into the very organization of their states.

Capital-intensive state formation differed from coercion-intensive and capitalized-coercion paths of change in three fundamental regards. (1) The influence of commercial oligarchies promoted the development of states organized around the protection and expansion of commercial enterprise – especially, in European experience, maritime enterprise. (2) The institutions created by the bourgeoisie for the defense of their own interests actually became sometime instruments of state administration; Venice, Genoa, and the Dutch Republic achieved a remarkable fusion of municipal and national government. (3) The availability of capital and capitalists permitted these states to borrow, tax, purchase, and wage war effectively without creating bulky, durable national administrations. Until the sheer scale of war with nationally recruited armies and navies overwhelmed their efficient but compact military power, capital-intensive states prospered in a warlike world. Not long after the Medici, with the aid of papal armies, returned to rule his native Florence, Niccolò Machiavelli wrote that

if any one should wish to establish a republic in a country where there are many gentlemen, he will not succeed until he has destroyed them all; and whoever desires to establish a kingdom or principality where liberty and equality prevail, will equally fail, unless he withdraws from that general equality a number of the boldest and most ambitious spirits, and makes gentlemen of them, not merely in name but in fact, by giving to them castles and possessions, as well as money and subjects; so that surrounded by these he may be able to maintain his power, and that by his support they may satisfy their ambition, and the others may be constrained to submit to that yoke to which force alone has been able to subject them.

(Discourses, I, 55; I owe this apt reference to Richard Frank)

More than anything else, gentlemen – that is, aristocratic landlords – shouldered coercion-intensive states, while capitalists – that is, merchants, bankers, and manufacturers – dominated their capital-intensive rivals. The differences in their experiences depended on when they formed, how much territory they attempted to control, the extent to which agriculture and manufacturing became significant parts of their economic bases, and in what kinds of commodities they specialized.

These factors depended, in their turn, on the geographic and geopolitical locations of the core cities in each state. The presence of large agricultural hinterlands, when it occurred, promoted the formation of larger territorial states. Port cities serving primarily as markets for long-distance trade more frequently created city-states or city-empires on the basis of small home territories. Adjacency to substantial empires and national states favored either absorption into those states or entry into the same struggle for control of territory. These variations, nevertheless, operated within limits set by the powerful presence of capital and capitalists.

TRAJECTORIES OF CAPITALIZED COERCION

Not all of the upper Adriatic, obviously, illustrates the capitalist path through state formation equally well. Austria eventually managed to claim a significant section of the shore, including Trieste, and to subordinate it to a state that had strong coercive interests elsewhere. Byzantine, Serbian, Hungarian, and Ottoman empires all struggled with Venice for control of Dalmatia, and the Ottomans won – at least for several centuries. Nevertheless, the upper Adriatic's history contrasts sharply with that of European Russia. In the Adriatic, abundant capital facilitated the building of armed force, especially maritime force, but provided an incentive and a means for capitalists' resistance to the creation of large states that could subordinate their interests to those of a dynasty. In Russia, the rarity of concentrated capital (especially after the fourteenth-century contraction of trade connections with Asia and the Byzantine Empire) and the presence of warrior-landlords predisposed all the states that formed toward coercive means. There the big question was whether magnates would continue to hold fragmented sovereignty in their many hands, or a single ruler would somehow establish firm priority over all the rest. Once the Russian state opted for the centralized construction of armed force, its efforts brought into being a ponderous state in which landlords retained great discretion within their own territories, but lost it vis-à-vis the tsar.

The fate of peasants – the bulk of the population almost everywhere in Europe before the eighteenth century – differed dramatically between coercion-intensive and capital-intensive regions. In most areas of coercion-intensive state formation, rulers created states in close collaboration with large landlords who retained extensive military and civilian powers. Russia, Poland, Hungary, and Brandenburg-Prussia exemplify the process, which had some parallels in Sicily and Castile. In such states, the expansion of trade in the sixteenth century encouraged and enabled landlords, backed by state power, to enserf peasants from whom they had previously drawn ample rents; most commonly, they required poorly-remunerated labor service on the landlord's demesne from cultivator households who drew their own subsistence from small farms to which they were attached by law. In other coercion-intensive regions (especially Scandinavia) where landlords never acquired the economic and political power of their eastern European counterparts, rulers of the sixteenth century and later instituted direct controls over the peasantry with the help of clergy and other bureaucrats, thus guaranteeing the long survival of subsistence-oriented peasants.

In capital-intensive areas, such as the Netherlands and some of Switzerland, the peasantry underwent bifurcation. In the presence of urban markets and aggressive capitalists, agriculture commercialized early and frequently combined with rural industry. As a result, a minority of peasants grew rich on cash crops and the labor of their neighbors. The majority became poor wage-laborers, many of whom doubled in domestic manufacturing or peddling when demand was on the upswing. In the company of omnipresent merchants, the minority and the majority produced a rural economy that supplied its cities easily, lent itself to efficient taxation, and fell under the control of cities that were regional centers of trade. Contrasting peasant experiences were both cause and effect of the very different trajectories of state formation in capital-intensive and coercion-intensive regions.

In between the capitalist and coercive extremes lay the paths of capitalized coercion, those instances where the concentrations of coercion and of capital occurred in greater equality and tighter connection with each other. The British Isles – Ireland, Scotland, England, and Wales – illustrate the path. They also show how much the placement of any experience within the coercion–capital diagram depends on the temporal and geographic limits we place on the experience. Seen from Denmark in the year 990, the British Isles look like a peripheral zone of conquest and tribute within a substantial empire centered on Scandinavia. Seen from Ireland over the period since then, state formation in the British Isles has a much more coercive cast than when seen from southeastern England. Seen from Scotland over the years 1500 to 1700, state formation looks like the competition and interaction of three rather separate states having different economic bases – English, Irish, and Scottish. Let it be clear, then, that we are examining the whole region during the thousand years following AD 900. Over the whole millennium the central drama was the expansion of an English state initially formed in conquest but soon counter-balanced by a great port and a commercialized economy.

In the year 990, Ireland was locked in struggle among multiple Celtic kingdoms and the coastal dominions of Norsemen. Although multiple Nordic conquerors divided the islands of the North Sea, mainland Scotland and Wales were more or less unified under the leadership of warrior-kings. A Dane, Canute, was in the process of wresting a weakly-connected England from Anglo-Saxon King Ethelred, who had already paid tribute to the Danes for a decade. Not only paid tribute, but suffered continual depredation. In its entry for 997, the Laud Chronicle reports that:

In this year the [Danish] host went around Devonshire into the mouth of the Severn, and there harried, both in Cornwall, Wales, and Devon, and landed at Watchet; they wrought great havoc by burning and killing people and went back round Land's End to the south side, and entered the estuary of the Tamar, and so up it until they came to Lydford. There they burned and slew everything they met, and burnt to the ground Ordwul's abbey church at Tavistock, carrying off an indescribable amount of plunder with them to the ships.

(Garmonsway 1953: 131)

As other Scandinavians sailed out to Iceland, Greenland, and America, Canute and his raiders brought England temporarily into a tribute-taking empire that stretched to Denmark and Norway. The new domains were valuable: at that point, Dublin had perhaps 4,000 inhabitants, York 10,000, Norwich 4,000, and London 25,000, far larger than any Scandinavian town. York served as an important link to Scandinavia, and London to the rest of the world. While not exactly criss-crossed with urban networks, the islands connected well with the cities of continental Europe.

Only sixty years later, Normans (descendants of earlier Viking warriors who had settled in Gaul) organized one more invasion of Britain. Their conquest of England followed the characteristic pattern of distributing land in fief to soldiers become regional agents (and potential rivals) of the crown. It slowed Scandinavian incursions and started the process by which the rulers of England expanded their domains both within and beyond Britain. Over the next two centuries, Norman-English and Scottish arms practically eliminated Danes and Norwegians from control of territory in the British Isles.

As the play of alliance and inheritance increased "English" holdings in what was to become France, the rulers of England began warring with their Norman cousins. During the twelfth century, they also attempted to extend their rule to Wales, Scotland, and Ireland. With his marriage to Eleanor of Aquitaine in 1152, Henry II had strong claims to rule England, Normandy, Maine, Brittany, Anjou, Aquitaine, and much of Wales; during the following years, he extended those claims to Scotland and portions of Ireland. As he ran that empire, he built up a relatively effective royal judicial structure. Yet from 1173 onward his sons began to contest his power in alliance with many barons and, at times, the queen.

In the process of making war and intervening in dynastic rivalries, the barons on whom English kings relied for their wars acquired enough power to fight the king as well as each other, exacting chartered concessions – most dramatically in Magna Carta – from the monarch. The Great Charter of 1215 committed the king to cease squeezing feudal obligations for the wherewithal to conduct wars, to stop hiring mercenaries when barons would not fight, and to impose the major taxes only with the consent of the great council, representative of the magnates. The council started to wield durable power, reinforced especially by its place in the approval of new taxation. Later kings confirmed the charter repeatedly. Nevertheless, the continuing efforts of English monarchs to create armed force produced a durable central structure: royal treasury, courts, and domain.

Edward I (1272–1307), for example, extended compulsory knighthood to all holders of lands worth twenty pounds a year, required all knights to serve in royal militias, established taxation for the payment of foot soldiers, imposed the first regular customs dues on wool and hides, built up a permanent central staff who took over some of the activities previously performed by barons and the king's personal retainers, and regularized the separate assemblies of barons, knights of the shire, burgesses, and clergy that granted him money. (In 1294, preparing for another campaign in France, Edward went so far as to sextuple the export duty on wool and demand half the clergy's income in taxes: Miller 1975: 11–12.) The creation of central state structure continued during the fourteenth century: not only did royal courts extend their jurisdiction throughout the land, but justices of the peace began to wield local power as commissioned agents of the crown.

Not that stability prevailed at the center. After all, Edward II died, murdered, in prison (1327), Edward III expired practically powerless (1377), and a deposed Richard II died – perhaps murdered as well – in prison (1400). The houses of Lancaster and York fought thirty years of civil war (the Wars of the Roses, 1455–85) over the right to the crown; the wars ended with Richard III slain by the forces of Henry Tudor, who thereupon became Henry VII. Armed struggles over royal power and royal succession continued for three centuries, until the Glorious Revolution of 1688 set the House of Orange on the throne.

At the same time, English kings tried repeatedly to capture territory in Ireland, Wales, Scotland, and France. Edward I reduced Wales to subjugation as well as nominally subordinating Ireland and Scotland to the English crown. Welshmen only mounted one more serious rising, that of Owen Glendower (1400–9). Both Irish and Scots, however, resisted English rule tenaciously, and often found support from French kings who were happy to see their English rivals distracted by military activity within the British Isles. In the course of resistance both created parliaments having some parallels to their English counterpart. Both also experienced bloody internal struggles over royal succession and over the relative powers of kings and barons. While Ireland remained a fractious colony, Scotland became an independent European power in its own right. Not until the seventeenth century did Ireland and Scotland succumb to relatively stable English control.

The long, and ultimately losing, effort of English kings to hold their French possessions kept the state at war through most of the years from 1337 to 1453. The financial demands of that effort (later called the Hundred Years' War) consolidated the position of Parliament, and regularized the division between its two houses. For well over a century thereafter, wars against Scotland and France (and sometimes both together) involved Parliament in royal fund-raising, and established its right to consent to taxation.

The lower house, eventually to be called the Commons, assembled representatives of the boroughs and the counties, who were largely merchants on the one hand and landlords on the other. A long, if uneasy, alliance between merchants and landlords began in the thirteenth century, as British wool first fed continental textile manufactures and then became the basis for spinning and weaving in Britain. Britain began the slow but fateful shift from exporting wool to manufacturing and exporting woolens. From that point on, English merchants established themselves in Flanders, and began to spread out through the rest of Europe. During the fifteenth century, the English likewise proved themselves formidable men of the sea; east coast sailors, for example, reopened the continent's trade with Iceland around 1412 (Scammell 1981: 460). The Intercursus Magnus, a commercial treaty of 1496, established England as a recognized partner in Flemish international trade. Although foreign merchants and vessels dominated England's trade for another half-century, by 1600 the

English were competing with Spaniards, Portuguese, and Dutchmen throughout the world.

In the same period, British seafarers such as the Bristol men who sailed with John Cabot (himself, as it happens, a Venetian) began joining Dutchmen, Italians, Spaniards, and Portuguese in exploring distant parts of the world, and in laying the bases for a world-wide trading empire. By 1577 Sir Francis Drake was circumnavigating the globe. The crown participated in these adventures to the extent that they promised additions to governmental revenues or military power (Andrews 1984: 14–15). British landlords, aided by legally sanctioned enclosures of open fields and common lands, involved themselves heavily in the marketing of wool and grain; the House of Commons came increasingly to represent a tight alliance of merchants and cash-cropping landowners. The country's growing commercial strength facilitated a growth in state power; it enabled Henry VII (1484–1509) and the later Tudors to check the Scots and challenge the French, expand the state's warmaking powers, extend taxation, and reduce the great lords' private armies.

Henry VIII's secession from Rome, seizure of church revenues, and expropriation of monasteries (1534–9) enhanced royal revenues and aligned the cooperating clergy with royal interests. Tudor aggrandizement also incited repeated regional rebellions, including the great Pilgrimage of Grace (1536). Nevertheless the Tudors eventually curbed the great aristocrats, with their private armies and claims to autonomous power (Stone 1965: 199–270). The country's nearly ceaseless commercialization, proletarianization, and economic expansion provided an economic base for state activity, and the state's reliance on customs and excise made extraction of resources from that base more efficient – but only when magnates, crown, and Parliament could bargain out an agreement to cooperate.

During the sixteenth century, Scotland drew ever closer to France; when the young Mary Queen of Scots became queen of France as well (1559), the two kingdoms approached merger. But a Protestant rebellion then contained Mary's power in Scotland, where she ruled unsteadily for six years before inciting another insurrection and fleeing to protective detention by Elizabeth in England; her beheading in 1586 ended the threat of a French Scotland and of a Catholic queen of England. At Elizabeth's death, however, Mary's son James, who had been James VI of Scotland since 1567, succeeded to the crown of England as James I. The French connection had almost dissolved.

Under James I (1603–25) and the later Stuarts, struggles within England over royal revenues for continental wars precipitated great constitutional divisions, attempts of kings to rule (and, especially, to tax) without Parliament, and eventually a civil war entailing execution of Charles I. In a sign of the times, Charles alienated the last block of crown lands to the City of London in 1627, receiving for it a cancellation of past debts and a further loan; from that point onward his credit failed, and his demands for loans and taxes only sharpened conflict with Parliament and its financiers. By 1640 he was seizing the gold and silver left in the Tower of London for safekeeping, and bargaining with the goldsmiths and merchants who owned it for a loan secured by customs revenues (Kindleberger 1984: 51). Charles' attempt to raise and control an army to put down rebellion in Ireland and resistance in Scotland did him in. During the Commonwealth and Protectorate (1649–60), varying fragments of the army and of Parliament ruled the country while trying to bring Ireland and Scotland back under state control and to battle against Spain and Holland as well. The Restoration, initiated by an army-inspired Parliamentary invitation to Charles II, confirmed the power of Parliament within the British state, especially when it came to revenues and expenditures. The tight interdependence of royal affairs and continental wars continued with the Stuart restoration, as England continued to fight Holland on the seas. The 1688 revolution brought a dramatic reversal of alliances; it carried Dutch Protestant William of Orange and his wife Mary, daughter of the duke of York, to the throne, as France's Louis XIV supported the exiled Stuarts. At that point Britain reverted to its historic rivalry with France, and borrowed Dutch institutions in the process. The state founded the Bank of England in 1694 as a vehicle for financing the war with France that had begun in 1688 (Kindleberger 1984: 52–3). With the end of revolution and the renewal of British military involvement on the Continent, a new era began. Britain started to form a substantial standing army, an effective central bureaucracy took shape, and the tax-granting House of Commons gained power vis-à-vis the king and his ministers (Brewer 1989).

Once again repeated rebellions in Scotland and Ireland – often involving rival claimants to the English crown, not to mention the fine hand of France – strained the state's warmaking powers. Wars and dynastic struggles combined to produce great transformations of the state, including a stable union of England with Scotland (1707), the definitive seating of the German house of Hanover (later renamed Windsor) on the throne (1714–15), and the establishment of a *modus vivendi* between the monarchy and a powerful Parliament representing the country's landed and commercial interests. A rebellion on behalf of the Stuart claimant to the throne (1715) failed utterly, as did a second rebellion in 1745, which marked the last serious threat to royal succession in Great Britain. British military power kept on growing: "By 1714, the British Navy was the largest in Europe, and it employed more workers than any other industry in the country" (Plumb 1967: 119).

As compared with its continental neighbors, the British state governed by means of a relatively small central apparatus, supplemented by a vast system of patronage and local powerholding in which Lords Lieutenant, sheriffs, mayors, constables and justices of the peace did the crown's work without serving as its full-time employees; before the Napoleonic Wars, only customs and excise had substantial numbers of regularly appointed officials. Until then, Britain did not maintain a standing army, and relied especially on wartime mobilization of naval power for its armed force. Except in Ireland, the army played a relatively small part, and militias a relatively large part, in control of Britain's domestic population. In Ireland, the British government continued to deploy armed force and experiment with new means of policing throughout its time of hegemony; indeed, Britain generally used Ireland as a proving ground for techniques of policing the state later introduced in England, Wales, and Scotland (Palmer 1988).

Great Britain kept on making war in Europe and striving for empire in the rest of the world; the end of the Seven Years' War against France (1763) left Britain the world's greatest colonial power. The loss of American colonies (1776–83) did not threaten state power in the way that previous defeats had. Repeated mobilizations for war with France, especially between 1793 and 1815, greatly expanded taxation, national debt, and state intervention in the economy, while causing a subtle but definitive shift in influence from the king and his ministers to Parliament. During those wars (1801), Great Britain incorporated Ireland (not definitively, but for more than a century) into a United Kingdom. By the early nineteenth century that United Kingdom had become the very model of a parliamentary monarchy dominated by landlords, financiers, and merchants.

Imperial expansion continued through the rapid industrialization and urbanization of the nineteenth century. Within Britain the state made a decisive shift toward direct intervention in local affairs: while in previous centuries king and parliament had frequently enacted legislation to govern the sale of food, the control of collective action, the treatment of the poor, or the rights and obligations of workers, they had almost always relied on local authorities for initiative and enforcement. While Britain maintained local authorities to a larger degree than many of its continental neighbors, during the nineteenth century national officials involved themselves as never before in policing, education, factory inspection, industrial conflict, housing, public health, and a wide range of other affairs. Incrementally but decisively, the British state moved toward direct rule.

Despite occasional mobilization of national sentiment, Wales and Scotland had long since ceased threatening the breakup of the British state. But Britain never succeeded in integrating, or even cowing, most of Ireland. Irish resistance and rebellion peaked in the aftermath of World War I; through several steps all but the more heavily Protestant and anglicized northeast corner (Ulster) became an independent state, first within the British Commonwealth, then finally outside it. The struggle in and over Ulster has not ended.

Although in retrospect Great Britain often serves as a model of political stability, a close look at state formation in the British Isles shows how continuously powerful parties battled for control of the state, and how often the transition from one regime to the next occurred in violence. Ireland's experience demonstrates the capacity of the region to create a relatively weak state along a coercion-intensive path. Nevertheless the British state came to dominate much of the world during the eighteenth and nineteenth centuries, and remains a world power today. The history of that state is not simply a compromise (or even a synthesis) between the histories of Venice and Russia, of coercion-intensive and capital-intensive countries.

The English, then British, state built on a conjunction of capital and coercion that from very early on gave any monarch access to immense means of warmaking, but only at the price of large concessions to the country's merchants and bankers. The uneasy alliance between landlords and merchants constrained royal autonomy, but fortified state power. Commercialized agriculture, far-ranging trade, imperial conquest, and war against rival European powers complemented each other, promoting an investment in naval power and a readiness to mobilize land forces for action overseas. The commercialization of both urban and rural economies meant that taxation and borrowing for war went more easily, and with less state apparatus, than in many other European countries. Adam Smith put it in terms of a simple comparison between England and France. "In England," he remarked, "the seat of government being in the greatest mercantile city in the world, the merchants are generally the people who advance money to government . . . In France, the seat of government not being in a great mercantile city, merchants do not make so great a proportion of the people who advance money to government" (Smith 1910 [1778]: II, 401). At that point England stood closer to the capital-intensive path of state formation than did France. England wrought a remarkable combination of easy access to capital and heavy reliance on landlords for day-to-day government of the realm. Although pre-revolutionary France relied similarly on nobles and priests for much of its local government, the effort to wring the means of war from a less capitalized and commercialized economy built up a significantly bulkier central state apparatus than in England.

Yet if we consider Venice or Moscow we immediately see great resemblances between capital–coercion relations in Britain and France. We are accustomed to contrasting the trajectories of Britain, France, Prussia, and Spain as the chief alternative types of state formation. Within the whole European range, however, the four have common properties that distinguish them clearly from the capital-intensive and coercion-intensive paths. In all four cases ambitious monarchs tried, with varying success, to crush or circumvent representative assemblies such as provincial Estates during the sixteenth- and seventeenth-century buildup of military power; in France and Prussia, the Estates succumbed, in Spain the Cortes staggered on, and in Britain Parliament survived as the bulwark of ruling-class power. In all four cases the coincidence of coercive centers with centers of capital facilitated – at least for a while – the creation of massive military force in a time when large, expensive, well-armed armies and navies gave those national states that were able to create them the overwhelming advantage in the search for hegemony and empire.

Why didn't Venice or Russia become England? The question is not absurd; it follows from the recognition that European states in general moved toward greater concentrations of capital and coercion, converging on the national state. Part of the answer is: they did. The Russian and Italian states that entered World War I had far more of the traits of national states than had their predecessors of a century of two before. But the more profound answer is that their previous histories haunted them. Venice created a state that bent to the interests of a mercantile patriciate, and that patriciate found its advantage in seeking out the interstices of the European commercial system rather than by collaborating in any effort to build up massive, durable military power. Russia created a state led by a supposed autocrat, but totally dependent on the cooperation of landlords whose own interests dictated a withholding of peasant labor and its products from the state's ends, and on a bureaucracy that could easily consume any surplus the state generated. Different kinds of revolution – a Risorgimento and a Bolshevik seizure of power – drew Venetians and Muscovites into new states that came increasingly to resemble the great national states of western Europe. But even the successor states bore marks of their previous identities.

G. William Skinner's schematic portrait of China, set into motion, thus provides keen insight into European experience. It helps us recognize how the construction of armed force and its organizational consequences varied from one section of Europe to another as a function of the relative weight of capital and coercion, of the "bottom-up" and "top-down" systems of exploitation and domination, of cities and states. Although all states devoted major efforts to war and preparation for war, beyond that commonality their predominant activities varied according to their positions in the networks of capital and coercion and their prior histories. Even similar activities, furthermore, laid down different organizational residues depending on where and when they occurred. Increasingly, however, relations to other states determined the structure and activity of any particular state. Because of their advantages in translating national resources into success in international war, large national states superseded tribute-taking empires, federations, city-states, and all their other competitors as the predominant European political entities, and as the models for state formation. Those states finally defined the character of the European state system and spearheaded its extension to the entire world.

6

The European State System

Ottoman naval might drove Venice from the eastern Mediterranean, and hastened the city-empire's descent as a major military power. When warlike Turks started moving into Europe from the Asian steppe they were landbound nomads like many of their bellicose neighbors. But once they reached the Black Sea and the Mediterranean they quickly learned to build ships and to sail. What is more, during the fifteenth century they started using gunpowder on a scale Europeans had not previously seen. They struck terror into European hearts because they won both hard-fought victories at sea and brutal conquests on land. No one, it seemed, would be safe from these fierce marauders. By the fifteenth century, their advances into the Mediterranean and the Balkans menaced Italy and Austria as well.

The Ottoman seizure of Constantinople (1453) clearly threatened Venetian interests, but Venice bought time by making a commercial treaty with the Turks. The time purchased was short: Turkey and Venice soon went to war, with dire results for Venice. The loss of Negroponte, chief Venetian base in the northern Aegean (1470) initiated the city's exit from the Ottoman zone. From that time, Venice conducted intermittent defensive warfare against the Ottoman Empire, while the Turks carried on raids into the Italian mainland, for fifty years.

The Venetian–Turkish war of 1499–1503 forced Venice down one more step of the international ladder. Although sometime enemy Hungary joined Venice against the Ottoman Empire in 1500, the city's mariners failed to defeat the Turks. Instead, a Turkish navy led by Kemal Re'is gave a drubbing to the largest fleet Venice had ever assembled, in the "deplorable battle of Zonchio" (Lane 1973a: 242). Venice lost Modon, Koron, and Lepanto, important

Mediterranean outposts, in battle. At the peace the Venetians surrendered their claims to a number of Greek and Albanian cities.

Other European powers saw the settlement of that war as a critical event, and joined in the writing of the treaty. For at the same time as Venice had been losing outposts in the eastern Mediterranean, the republic had been conquering important territories in northern Italy, where Spain and France intervened in the 1490s. Southern Europe's political boundaries were shifting with exceptional speed. "The peace of Buda (August, 1503) included Turkey, Moldavia, Ragusa, Venice, the Papacy, Bohemia–Hungary, Poland–Lithuania, Rhodes, Spain, Portugal, and England, and ranks as the first great international settlement of modern times" (Pitcher 1972: 98–9). The holding of that great peace conference has an additional meaning: in the face of Ottoman expansion, and in the aftermath of French and Spanish warmaking in Italy, Europeans were beginning to fashion a distinctive and connected system of states.

States form a *system* to the extent that they interact with each other regularly, and to the degree that their interaction affects the behavior of each state. In AD 990, nothing like a European state system existed. By AD 1990, a system that once was primarily European had exploded to include almost the entire earth. In between, Europe passed through a few centuries during which most European states maintained fairly strong connections – hostile, friendly, neutral or, more likely, mixed and variable – with most other European states but with few others outside the continent. In their collective power and connectedness those states stood out from the rest of the world. The dominant political fact of the last thousand years is the formation and extension of a European state system consisting largely of national states rather than empires, city-states, or other variants of coercive power.

The world headed toward its present peculiar condition from a very different set of circumstances. A thousand years ago, people throughout the earth lived either under loose-knit empires or in situations of fragmented sovereignty. Although empires such as the Mayan and Chinese had achieved a fair degree of centralization, even they ruled quite indirectly outside their cores, taking tribute and entrusting government to regional powerholders who enjoyed considerable autonomy. Movements of conquest, battles at the margins of state territories and raids for tribute, booty, and captives often occurred, but declared wars with formal alliances and massed armies were rare events anywhere.

As of 990, Europe's own space fragmented into four or five relatively distinct clusters of states. The conquest regimes of eastern Europe raided continually into each other's zones of control, while maintaining some connections with the Scandinavians to their north, the Byzantines to their south, and the armed peoples of the steppe to their east. A better-defined and more tightly-connected set of states, predominantly Muslim, ringed the Mediterranean and covered most of Iberia. In the relatively urban band from central Italy to Flanders, hundreds of semi-autonomous powers overlapped with the claimed jurisdictions of the papacy and Holy Roman Empire. A Saxon realm touched the northeastern edge of that band. In a somewhat separate sphere of influence to the north, a Danish empire reached out to the British Isles.

These partly separate clusters of states were soon to acquire stronger mutual connections, as well as a sharper distinction from the states of Asia and Africa. They began to connect through the expansion of trade northward from the Mediterranean, the continuous movement of nomadic troops from the steppe, the struggle for territory between Christians and Muslims, and widespread raiding by seaborne warriors from the north. Norman descendants of the Vikings who had been pillaging northern and western Europe for several centuries, for example, were not only to consolidate their own kingdom in the midst of what we now call France, but also to conquer England and Sicily.

The history of Sicily illustrates how large conquests knit Europe together. The island had lain under the domination of one non-Italian power after another from the fall of the Roman Empire: first Byzantium, then (starting in AD 827) a series of Muslim states. After two centuries of Muslim rule, Norman adventurers seized the island during the later eleventh century. Their successors became kings of Sicily and married into transalpine royal families. On Christmas Day 1194 Holy Roman Emperor Henry VI (strong in the combined rights of inheritance and conquest) awarded himself the crown. Thereafter, members of German, French, or Spanish royal houses governed Sicily until Napoleon arrived. For a thousand years, Sicily served as a crossroads for movements of conquest that reached the Mediterranean.

International connections also cut across the city-states of northern Italy. They often articulated, furthermore, with domestic politics. Thirteenth-century Florence, for instance, divided bitterly over allegiance to the pope or the emperor. The struggle continued until the victorious Black (anti-imperial) party managed to exile the rival Whites, including Dante Alighieri. In 1311, the Blacks obliterated from the streets of Florence the many representations of the imperial eagle (Schevill 1963: 187). That did not, however, end Florence's international involvements. During the thirteenth and fourteenth centuries, Florence devoted an important part of its public life to receiving the princes and ambassadors of all Europe (Trexler 1980: 279–330). Meanwhile, Venice and Genoa conquered up and down the Mediterranean. Well before 1500, in short, Italian states engaged themselves actively in European politics. In Italy, especially, we can see the elements of a European state system, more or less deliberately separated from the Muslim powers of the south and east, that was forming during the thirteenth and fourteenth centuries.

Move forward to 1490. Five hundred years ago, Europeans were busy creating a pair of arrangements that were then unique: first, a system of interconnected states linked by treaties, embassies, marriages, and extensive communication; second, declared wars fought by large, disciplined military forces and ended by formal peace settlements. They were entering a period in which the major realignments of boundaries and sovereigns throughout the continent occurred at the ends of wars, under the terms of agreements joined by multiple states. Older styles of warfare survived in piracy and banditry, in the last phases of Mongol intervention, in the irregular battles of Muslims and Christians across the Balkans, and in European adventurers' voyages to Africa, Asia, the Americas, and the rest of the world. But in Europe something resembling the state system we know today was taking shape. The participants, moreover, were increasingly not city-states, leagues, or empires, but national states: relatively autonomous, centralized, and differentiated organizations exerting close control over the population within several sharply-bounded contiguous regions.

Historical starting points are always illusory, because in a continuous historical process some earlier element always links to any supposed beginning. Nevertheless, we can reasonably date the establishment of regular diplomatic missions within Europe to the fifteenth-century practise of Italian states. The French and Spanish invasions of Italy generalized the practise:

By the early 1490s Milan had resident representatives in Spain, in England, in France, and at the imperial court. Ferdinand of Aragon had blazed the trail with a resident in Rome by the 1480s, later one in Venice, and in England by 1495. His representation to the Hapsburgs (*sic*) was by 1495 the double one of an ambassador at the imperial court and another in the Netherlands. The Emperor Maximilian's network, built up before the end of 1496, collapsed through lack of money, as it did again in 1504. The papacy eventually succumbed to this trend. Resident nuncios, who in a sense were the direct descendants of the tax collectors, were sent to Spain, France, England, Venice and the Emperor by the end of Alexander VI's pontificate (1503).

(Russell 1986: 68)

With the institution of embassies came extended information-gathering, widened alliances, multilateral negotiations over royal marriages, greater investment of each individual state in the recognition of other states, and a generalization of war.

We can reasonably date a comprehensive European state system from the French and Spanish invasions of Italy, which greatly expanded the scale of European warmaking, and opened the age of mass mercenary armies. The Peace of Cateau-Cambrésis (1559) ended the Habsburg–Valois wars. It confirmed the virtual exclusion of France from Italy, the primacy of Spain there, and the expulsion of England from Calais. In addition to the cessation of hostilities, ambassadors at that conference negotiated a remarkable range of European affairs, including the fates of such powers as Savoy and Scotland, and the marriage of King Philip of Spain to Princess Elisabeth of France. Statecraft, backed by war, was flowering.

Not all European states nested neatly into the emerging system. During the sixteenth century, the Nordic countries still formed a region apart, although quickened trade between the Low Countries and the Baltic was beginning to knit Denmark and Sweden into western European connections. Poland–Lithuania was distant, and Russia, from a western European perspective, half-mythical: Sebastian Münster's *Kosmographie* of 1550 located the "Muscovites" on the Baltic (Platzhoff 1928: 30–1). Yet the Habsburgs had established diplomatic relations with the grand duke of Moscow during the fifteenth century, and through its repercussions on powers farther west the continuing Russian expansion connected the Muscovites with Europe.

The diplomatic and dynastic connections of Sweden under Johan III (1568–92) demonstrate that even peripheral states reached far into the system. As the Livonian empire of the Teutonic Knights disintegrated, Sweden, Poland, Denmark, and Russia all tried to claim their pieces of the wreck. In his campaigns, Johan seized Reval, Estonia, and other lands along what came to be a lengthy Swedish–Russian border; despite great rivalry among them, he also managed to join Poland and Denmark in holding Russia back. As he warred, Johan also scored diplomatic successes. Johan's wife Katarina Jagellonica was a Polish princess and the daughter of a Sforza from Milan. The Polish link made possible the election of their son Sigismund as king of Poland. When Johan died, Sigismund became king of Sweden as well – at least until his uncle Karl deposed him. Another son of Johan, Gustavus Adolphus, later built peripheral Sweden into one of Europe's great powers. By the early seventeenth century the European state system spanned from Sweden to the Ottoman Empire, from Portugal to Russia.

THE ENDS OF WARS

The increasingly connected European state system shifted to the rhythm of major wars. Jack Levy has prepared a valuable catalog of European great powers and their wars since the end of the fifteenth century. Let us arbitrarily take all wars in Levy's list during which great powers suffered at least 100,000 battle deaths. They include:

War	Great Power Battle Deaths	Principal Settlement
Thirty Years' (1618–48)	2,071,000	Treaty of Westphalia
Franco-Spanish (1648–59)	108,000	Treaty of Pyrenees
Ottoman (1657–64)	109,000	Truce of Vasvar
Franco-Dutch (1672–8)	342,000	Treaty of Nimwegen
Ottoman (1682–99)	384,000	Treaty of Karlowitz
League of Augsburg (1688–97)	680,000	Treaty of Ryswick
Spanish Succession (1701–13)	1,251,000	Treaty of Utrecht
Austrian Succession (1739–48)	359,000	Treaty of Aix-la-Chapelle

War	Great Power Battle Deaths	Principal Settlement
Seven Years' (1755–63)	992,000	Treaties of Paris, Hubertusburg
Ottoman (1787–92)	192,000	Treaty of Jassy
French Revolutionary (1792–1802)	663,000	Treaty of Amiens
Napoleonic (1803–15)	1,869,000	Congress of Vienna
Crimean (1853–6)	217,000	Congress of Paris
Franco-Prussian (1870–1)	180,000	Treaty of Frankfurt
Russo-Turkish (1877–8)	120,000	Treaty of San Stefano, Congress of Berlin
World War I (1914–18)	7,734,300	Treaties of Brest-Litovsk, Versailles, St Germain, Neuilly, Trianon
Sino-Japanese (1937–41)	250,000	none: merged into World War II
World War II (1939–45)	12,948,300	no general settlement
Korean (1950–3)	954,960	armistice: no settlement

Casualty figures for great power battle deaths only are, of course, misleading: considering the enormous decline of European population, only some of which could have resulted from outmigration, total deaths directly attributable to the Thirty Years' War, including civilians and the troops of all powers, may well have topped five million, instead of the two million sustained by the great powers.

The roughly 750,000 Chinese losses in the 1937–41 death struggle with Japan disappear from the count because China did not then qualify as a great power. The Vietnam war misses the cutoff (mine, I hasten to add, not Levy's) because the United States lost "only" 56,000 troops as compared to the estimated 650,000 battle deaths among Vietnamese forces. Nevertheless, the catalog gives an idea of the enlarging scale of war, and the increasing generality of peace settlements up to World War I. It also suggests that with World War II the internationalization of conflicts burst the four-hundred-year-old system of peace settlements by general congresses. Since that time, the standoff between the Soviet Union and the USA has greatly complicated the completion of any general peace settlement.

The cruel Thirty Years' War locked the European state system in place. Actually a complex web of wars, the struggle that began as a Holy Roman Emperor's attempt to put down the Protestants of Bohemia eventually involved most of Europe's powers. The Ottoman Empire, the Italian states, England, and the states of eastern Europe were the principal absentees. The Ottomans were preoccupied with their Persian struggles, and England had major divisions of its own to deal with. At the end, the chief alignment pitted Spain and the Holy

Roman Empire against France and Sweden. Another way to put it is: Habsburgs against the rest of Europe.

It took seven years of negotiations, beginning in 1641, even to assure a peace conference – or, rather, two of them, one at Münster (mainly for Protestant powers) and the other at Osnabrück (for Catholics). Fighting continued through those seven years. Threatened with their making separate peaces, Emperor Ferdinand conceded to individual imperial states the right to attend the conference, and to treat it as an imperial diet. The Dutch Republic, which finally wrested recognition of its independence from Spain in January 1648, likewise participated. Venice and the papacy, although not belligerents, played the parts of chairs and mediators.

Altogether, the Treaty of Westphalia (1648) brought together 145 representatives from most parts of the European state system. They not only bargained out terms for ending the war but also settled a number of outstanding diplomatic issues, such as whether to recognize the Swiss Confederation and the Dutch Republic as sovereign states. By placing the mouth of the Scheldt in Dutch territory, they assured the blockage of overseas traffic to Antwerp, and thus confirmed the commercial advantage of the Dutch Republic over the Spanish Netherlands. The treaty froze the existing divisions between Protestant and Catholic states by threatening to depose any monarch who changed religion. In the process, France gained Alsace and other territories, Sweden acquired (among other lands) Western Pomerania, and important realignments occurred within the Holy Roman Empire.

In an empire, one state exercises sovereignty over at least one other distinct state (Doyle 1986: 30). A century before the Treaty of Westphalia, empires of one sort or another had dominated Europe. The settlement of the Thirty Years' War, however, definitively blocked consolidation of a Habsburg empire, sounded the death knell of the Habsburg-dominated Holy Roman Empire, and made it unlikely that any other empire – except perhaps the Russian or Ottoman – would expand within the continent. After the peace settlement's precedent, individual German states carried on diplomacy for themselves, instead of accepting the emperor as their spokesman. Thus the end of the Thirty Years' War consolidated the European system of national states.

At the same moment as empires were losing out *within* Europe, to be sure, Europe's major states were creating empires *beyond* Europe, in the Americas, Africa, Asia, and the Pacific. The construction of external empires provided some of the means and some of the impetus for the fashioning of relatively powerful, centralized, and homogenized national states within the continent. European powers fought each other in those imperial zones. During the long war following the Dutch revolt, the Dutch battled Spain in America, Africa, and Asia as well as in Europe; Dutch mariners practically expelled Portugal (until 1640 subject to the Spanish monarchy) from Asia and Africa (Parker 1975: 57–8). But in 1648 those external empires were not yet subject to negotiation.

Subsequent peace settlements followed the pattern of 1648, with one critical difference: non-European empires entered the picture. Although victory and defeat in the war that was ending continued to determine the bargaining positions of states as negotiations began, boundaries and rulers shifted most decisively at the moment of settlement. In fact, states often gave up territories they had conquered in exchange for others they found more desirable. At the Treaty of Breda (1667), which ended one of the era's multiple Anglo-Dutch wars, all the important transfers of territory occurred in the Americas. The Dutch, among other things, gave up New Amsterdam (now New York) for Suriname, an exchange that (at least in retrospect) marks the advantage Britain was then winning over Holland.

The War of the League of Augsburg (1688–97) set Louis XIV against that league, which included the Holy Roman Empire, Sweden, Spain, Bavaria, Saxony, the Palatinate and, later, Savoy; Holland and England allied themselves with the league without joining it. France, England, Spain, and Holland ended the war by means of the Treaty of Ryswick. In addition to territorial adjustments, recognitions, and guarantees of security, the settlement included another Anglo-Dutch colonial agreement, and a score for France: Holland returned Pondicherry (India) to France's East India Company in return for trading rights. From that point on, non-European territories figured more and more prominently in European peace settlements.

By the early eighteenth century, wars among Europe's great powers regularly included overseas combat, and their settlements often included realignments of overseas empires. The War of the Spanish Succession began in 1701 when Louis XIV sought to press the advantage given him by the accession of his grandson, the duke of Anjou, to the Spanish throne; among other moves, wily King Louis immediately dispatched troops to occupy Spanish-held fortresses in Flanders. During the war, France and Britain fought in America and India as well as on the high seas. The war ended in the Treaty of Utrecht (1713), which established Britain as the leading colonial power and confirmed the declining relative position of Spain within Europe. In that treaty, among other outcomes, Britain received Newfoundland, Nova Scotia, the Hudson's Bay Territory, Gibraltar, and Minorca, access to Spanish colonial ports, rights to supply slaves to Spanish colonies, and recognition of its Protestant succession. Savoy annexed Sicily and other Italian territory at Spain's expense; Prussia gained recognition as a kingdom; France, while a loser in many respects, not only regained Lille but also had a Bourbon recognized as king of Spain; and in the closely related treaties of Rastatt and Baden (1714) the Austrian Habsburgs acquired control of what had been the Spanish Netherlands.

The Seven Years' War (1756–63) and the War of the American Revolution (1778–84) again pitted France against Britain in America; as a result of the first, France ceded mainland Canada, while in the second Britain lost thirteen prosperous North American colonies. With the independence of the United

States, European politics spilled over into the creation of new members for the state system, members entirely outside of Europe.

The Congress of Vienna (1815), ending the Napoleonic Wars, brought together representatives of all Europe's powers, not to mention many of its would-be powers. The Congress rewrote much of Europe's map, restoring only a few prewar boundaries and creating such entirely new entities as the kingdom of the Netherlands, the Germanic Confederation, and the Lombardo-Venetian Kingdom. But it also added Ceylon, the Cape of Good Hope, Tobago, St Lucia, Mauritius, and Malta to Britain's empire. In that settlement and in the negotiations following World War I, the great powers came as close as they ever have to the deliberate collective mapping of the entire state system, right down to the boundaries, rulers, and constitutions of individual states.

Through the nineteenth century and up to World War I, war settlements continued to engage many members of the state system, and to mark the major realignments in its membership. It may stretch the point to include the establishment of a separate Belgium (whose secession from the Netherlands occurred immediately after the French revolution of 1830, and survived thanks to direct armed intervention by the French) as a delayed portion of the Napoleonic Wars' settlement. But the French annexation of Savoy and Nice and the creation of a kingdom of Italy sprang from the 1859 war of France and Piedmont against Austria. The formation of both a dual Austro-Hungarian monarchy and a North German Confederation (immediate predecessor of the empire, itself a fairly direct outcome of the Franco-Prussian War), furthermore, issued from the Austro-Prussian war of 1866. In southeastern Europe, the Crimean, Austro-German, and multiple Russo-Turkish wars each precipitated a further disintegration of Ottoman control and the formation of new national states under strong international influence: Greece, Serbia, Rumania, Bulgaria, Montenegro. The Crimean War's settlement (1856), moreover, recast the Ottoman Empire as Turkey, a new state in something resembling the European format.

The settlements of World War I brought the last more or less general, simultaneous, and consensual redrawing of Europe's map. New or renewed states of Czechoslovakia, Hungary, Poland, and Yugoslavia gained independence, Germany lost substantial territory to France, Poland, and other adjacent powers, Rumania gained Transylvania as consequence of a late switch to the Allied side, the remainder of the Ottoman Empire fell into fragments, and the League of Nations claimed its place as an arbiter of state system membership and behavior. The multiple treaties of 1919 and 1920 included such temporizations as the French control, without sovereignty, of the Saar, and suffered from the American rejection of the League. The cracks in World War I's settlement, indeed, forecast the fissures that opened up at the end of World War II. By that time the world-wide reach of the formerly European state system, and the emergence of such geographically and politically eccentric powers as Japan and the United States put great stress on a set of relations that had worked more or less well for four centuries.

MEMBERS OF THE SYSTEM

Who were the great powers? We might compare two recent efforts to identify them. George Modelski and William Thompson have used naval power to compile the roster of "global powers" from 1494 to the present. A "global power," according to their definition, had at least 5 percent of the total naval expenditures or 10 percent of the total warships of the global powers and carried its naval activity outside of its own region into the oceans. Similarly, Jack Levy has assembled a catalog of the world's great powers and of major wars involving them from 1495 to 1975. As great powers, he singled out those states anywhere on earth that, in his estimation, had high military capabilities relative to others, pursued continental or global interests, defended those interests by means of a wide range of instrumentalities, including force and threats of force, received recognition from the most powerful states as major actors, and exercised exceptional formal rights in international relations (Levy 1983: 16–18). Among likely European candidates, Levy judged his criteria to exclude the Holy Roman Empire, Venice, the Swiss Confederation, Portugal, Poland, and Denmark throughout the period from 1495 to 1975.

The two rosters include:

State	Levy	Modelski–Thompson
Portugal	—	1494–1580
France	1495–	1494–1945
England/Great Britain	1495–	1494–1945
"Austria"[a]	1495–1519, 1556–1918	—
Spain	1495–1519	1494–1808
Ottoman Empire	1495–1699	—
United Habsburgs	1519–56	—
Netherlands	1609–1713	1579–1810
Sweden	1617–1721	—
Russia/Soviet Union	1721–	1714–
Prussia/Germany/West Germany	1740–	1871–1945
Italy	1861–1943	—
United States	1898–	1816–
Japan	1905–45	1875–1945
China	1949–	—

[a] Includes Austrian Habsburgs, Austria, and Austria-Hungary

The demanding Modelski–Thompson criterion excludes a number of great powers that relied primarily on armies rather than navies. Some of these assignments, furthermore, are contestable. No doubt a national state called France has existed more or less continuously since 1495. Nor is it absurd to see some continuity in the mutable entity successively called England, Great Britain, and the United Kingdom. But in what sense Prussia, the German Confederation, the German Empire, the Weimar Republic, the Third Reich and the Federal Republic of Germany are successive manifestations of a single entity called Germany is open to question.

Again, various agglomerations of Habsburg lands appear at four different places in the catalog: as Austrian Habsburgs, Spain, the United Habsburgs, and the Netherlands. Spain and the Habsburgs, furthermore, certainly did not disappear from the European scene with the abdication of Charles V in 1556, as Levy's chronology indicates; the Spanish Armada was still a formidable force in 1588. Yet the entity "Spain" is problematic, considering that during the war-torn years of the 1630s Philip IV, nominally head of all the various Iberian kingdoms, was unable to persuade Catalonia, Valencia, and several of his other domains to join the war effort Castile was then leading. And what of Portugal? Levy does not mention Portugal. Modelski and Thompson identify Portugal as a global power (the elite of great powers) between 1494 and 1580, when Portugal was independent of the Spanish crown. Even during the following sixty years of Spanish hegemony, Portugal operated as a distinct power. In terms of international relations, in short, it is hard to speak of Spain in the singular before the eighteenth century. The lists therefore simplify radically. Still, they provide a defensible first approximation of an important succession in priorities among European powers.

The two lists display a very strong bias toward Europe. Until the arrival of the United States (1816 for Modelski–Thompson, 1898 for Levy), the set consists exclusively of powers having a major base in Europe. From this information a reader would find it hard to imagine, for example, that in 1495 China had about a million men under arms, or that the Mali, Songhai, Persian, Mughal, Aztec, and Inca empires were thriving outside of Europe. Nor can we assume that the European network was incomparably richer and therefore worthier of attention than the others. During the seventeenth century as much as half the silver mined in the Americas may have ended up in China, traded for silks, porcelains, and other precious goods (Wakeman 1985: 2–3). At that point, per capita income in Europe was not obviously superior to that in China. Before the later eighteenth century, in short, it was not clear that European powers led the world economically.

A eurocentric list nevertheless has a military justification; not long after 1495, Europeans (including the now semi-European Ottomans) had so far extended their military control that their system had become the great power system of the entire world. By the 1540s, for example, the Ottoman Empire was entering regularly into alliances with European powers such as France. By virtue of its threat to Italy and the Habsburg lands it was applying considerable leverage to the alignments and strategies of the other major players.

By the end of the fifteenth century, then, the European state system had acquired a clear structure and membership. It was on its way, furthermore, to dominating the world. The Levy and Modelski–Thompson compilations identify great powers, but not lesser members of the system. As a first approximation of the entire system's limits around 1500, we might take Eduard Fueter's breakdown in the first volume of the von Below and Meinicke *Politische Geschichte* (Fueter 1919). Understandably, Fueter pivots his classification of states on involvement in the wars precipitated by the French and Spanish invasions of Italy:

major states that took part directly in the Italian struggles

France
Spain
the Habsburg power
  Burgundy
  Austria
  Germany
Venice

minor states that took part directly

Milan
Florence
Papal states
Naples and Sicily
Genoa
Savoy
other small Italian states: Ancona, Ferrara, Urbino, Mantua, Monaco etc.
Switzerland

major states that did not take part directly

Ottoman Empire
England

minor states that did not take part directly

Hungary
North African corsair states
Poland
Scotland
Denmark, then Denmark and Sweden
Portugal
Persia
Navarre

Fueter's inventory of the state system differs from its chief alternative, a catalog of states and rulers by Spuler (Spuler 1977, vol. 2) in consolidating all members of the Holy Roman Empire (Baden, Brandenburg, Cologne, Hanover, Hesse-Cassel, Mainz and dozens more) into a single state, in lumping together the far-flung Habsburg domains, in neglecting the Ottoman Empire's European tributary states (e.g. Bosnia, Moldavia, and Wallachia), in slighting the semi-independent states of eastern Europe (e.g. Lithuania), and in placing Persia on the list of participants.

Fueter defended the treatment of the multiple states of the Holy Roman Empire as a single "Germany" on the ground that members of the Empire could only carry on diplomatic relations with external powers through their elected emperor. But he conceded that the Reformation, in which many German territorial lords found Protestantism an attractive alternative to the emperor's Catholicism, accentuated the Empire's fractionation (Fueter 1919: 123–36). Similarly, he lumped together Castile, Aragon, and the territories they controlled on the ground that their common monarch spoke for all of them (Fueter 1919: 79–103). He included Persia in the system because European states sometimes allied with the Persians against the Ottomans, and the North African pirates because they carried on running warfare with Mediterranean seafarers.

If we compare Fueter's rollcall of the European state system from 1492 to 1559 with the later two volumes in the same series by Walter Platzhoff (1559–1660) and Max Immich (1660–1789), the membership of the system shows the following changes (Platzhoff 1928, Immich 1905):

State	1492–1559	1559–1660	1660–1789
Austria	+	+	+
Brandenburg-Prussia	−	?	+
Burgundy	+	−	−
Denmark	+	+	+
England	+	+	+
Florence	+	?	−
France	+	+	+
Genoa	+	+	?
Germany/H.R. Empire	+	+	+
Hungary	+	?	?
Livonia	−	+	−
Milan	+	−	−
Naples-Sicily	+	−	−
Navarre	+	−	−
Netherlands	−	+	+
North African corsairs	+	−	−
Ottoman Empire	+	+	+

State	1492–1559	1559–1660	1660–1789
Papacy	+	+	+
Persia	+	−	−
Poland	+	+	+
Portugal	+	+	+
Russia	−	+	+
Savoy	+	+	+
Scotland	+	+	−
small Italian states	+	+	+
Spain	+	+	+
Sweden	+	+	+
Swiss federation	+	+	+
Venice	+	+	+

? = not listed, but mentioned in text as separate state

Since in 1500 Russia and Livonia were actually present, although weakly connected with the rest of Europe, the only genuine newcomers are the Netherlands, formed in revolt against the Habsburgs, and Brandenburg-Prussia, forged in centuries of war. The insistence of these German authors on keeping "Germany" together, even after the disintegration of the Holy Roman Empire, hides the independent importance of such states as Bavaria and Saxony. Despite Fueter's separate listing, the duchy of Burgundy had fallen to France in 1477, and the Burgundian dynasty of the Netherlands had given way to the Habsburgs in 1482. With the qualifications that the Holy Roman and Habsburg empires fell to pieces and an independent Netherlands became a major power, then, the main movement from 1495 to 1789 ran toward agglomeration: as Milan, Naples, Navarre, and Sicily disappear into France and Spain, as Hungary dissolves into the Ottoman Empire and as Scotland blends into Great Britain, we see the consolidation of European states at work.

How did these states connect with each other? Historians and political scientists have often treated the European state system as a simple hierarchy, with either one hegemonic power or two competing powers at the summit (Gilpin 1988, Modelski and Thompson 1988, Levy 1988, Thompson 1988). Whole theories of hegemonic war have built on the supposition that states struggled for the top position. In fact, no single state has ever dominated the system in the way such a model requires; at the peak of France's power toward 1812, Britain and Russia remained anything but subordinate. As Britain flourished during the nineteenth century, France, Germany, Russia, and the United States disputed British power at every turn.

The flaw in the single hierarchy model is obvious and critical: the exercise of power always depends on location; he who deploys immense power in his immediate vicinity finds his power dwindling as he moves away from his base. Venice, as we have seen, once exerted enormous influence in the Adriatic –

indeed, stood for a time as Europe's greatest single power – yet made almost no difference at all in the Baltic. A far better conception of the European state system treats it as a geographically dispersed network in which some states are more central and influential than others, but hierarchies differ from one location in the system to another.

Again Jack Levy's compilation helps us. Levy defines a major war as one involving an average of 1,000 or more battle deaths per year. He excludes civil, colonial and imperial wars. By his criteria, the world experienced 119 major wars involving at least one great power between 1495 and 1975. The participants in those wars (including those that did not qualify as great powers) set a rough boundary to membership in the state system of the last half-millennium. Who, then, were the members? Levy does not say, but a look at the full set of participants in wars during the first twenty years of his inventory (1495–1514) gives an interesting idea (Levy does not enumerate all the belligerents, but standard histories easily yield their identities):

War of the League of Venice (1495–7): France, Venice, Holy Roman Empire, Papacy, Milan, Spain, Naples

Polish-Turkish War (1497–8): Ottoman Empire, Poland, Krim Tatars, Russia, Moldavia

Venetian-Turkish War (1499–1503): Ottoman Empire, Venice, Hungary

First Milanese War (1499–1500): France, Milan

Neapolitan War (1501–4): France, Spain, Papacy, Naples

War of the League of Cambrai (1508–9): France, Spain, Austrian Habsburgs, Papacy, Milan, Venice

War of the Holy League (1511–14): France, England, Spain, Austrian Habsburgs, Papacy, Venice, Milan, Swiss cantons

Austro-Turkish War (1512–19): Austrian Habsburgs, Hungary, Ottoman Empire

Scottish War (1513–15): England, Scotland

The implied list of members resembles Fueter's enumeration for 1492–1559, but is narrower. From Fueter's participants in the state system, Levy's inventory of wars omits Denmark, Florence, Genoa, Savoy, the North African corsairs, Persia, and the smaller Italian city-states, because they involved themselves no more than marginally in great power wars during those two decades. Florence, for example, actually declared for the French side in the War of the Holy League – and suffered for it at the peace settlement; but between 1495 and 1514 Florentines were so concerned with their internal divisions and the rebellions of such dependencies as Pisa that they stayed out of the larger-scale combats swirling about them. Off in the east, on the other hand, the wars identify Russia, Moldavia, and the Krim Tatars, through their battles with the Ottomans, as part of the European state system.

Figure 6.1 graphs the joint involvement of the various states in these wars. It simplifies a complex set of relations by disregarding who fought whom, by lumping together the Austrian Habsburgs and the Holy Roman Empire they dominated, and by distinguishing only among (1) no joint involvement, (2) joint involvement in a single war, and (3) joint involvement in two or more of the wars. Since participation of at least one great power qualified a war for Levy's list, the graph necessarily exaggerates the centrality of those powers in the wars of 1495 to 1515. Yet a plausible picture of the European state system emerges: Russia, Poland, the Krim (Crimean) Tatars, Moldavia, and the Ottoman Empire form a distinct set (the restriction of the catalog to wars involving great powers eliminates repeated struggles between Poland and Russia and between Poland and Livonia during the two decades, but their inclusion would merely accentuate the distinctness of the eastern–southeastern set). The Ottomans war with the closest European powers, Hungary hangs between Venice and the Ottoman Empire, England and (especially) Scotland stand at the periphery of international relations, while Aragon, France, the Austrian Habsburgs, Venice, the papacy, Milan, and Naples interact constantly. Note the centrality of Milan, Venice, and the papacy (not, by Levy's standards, great powers) in European affairs, the position of Venice as (in William McNeill's phrase) the "hinge of Europe," the looming presence of the Ottoman Empire, and the weak involvement of northern Europe as a whole.

If we stride forward a century and a half, we discover a very different state

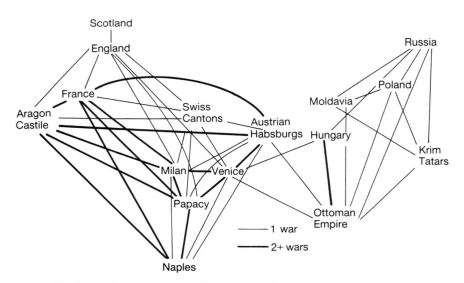

Figure 6.1   Joint involvement of European states in great power wars, 1496–1514.

system. Levy's catalog of wars involving great powers that were raging in any year from 1655 to 1674 includes these:

Spanish-Portuguese (1642–68): Spain, Portugal

Turkish-Venetian (1645–69): Ottoman Empire, Venice, France

Franco-Spanish (1648–59): France, Spain, England

Scottish (1650–1): Scotland, England

Anglo-Dutch (1652–5): England, Netherlands

Northern (1654–60): Austrian Habsburgs, Netherlands, Sweden, Poland, Brandenburg, Russia, Denmark

English-Spanish (1656–9): England, Spain

Dutch-Portuguese (1657–61): Netherlands, Portugal

Ottoman (1657–64): Ottomans, France, Austrian Habsburgs

Sweden-Bremen (1665–6): Sweden, Bremen

Anglo-Dutch (1665–7): England, Netherlands, France, Denmark

Devolutionary (1667–8): France, Spain, Austrian Habsburgs

Dutch (1672–8): France, Netherlands, England, Spain, Austrian Habsburgs, Sweden, Brandenburg

Turkish-Polish (1672–6): Ottoman Empire, Poland

Figure 6.2 summarizes the joint involvements. As compared with the earlier diagram, it reveals a European state system that had become more tightly knit,

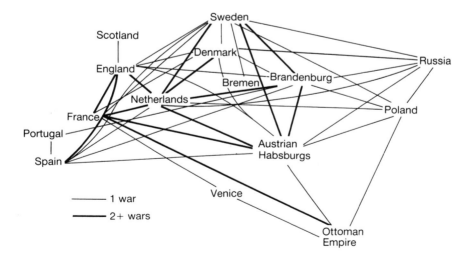

Figure 6.2   Joint involvement of European states in great power wars, 1656–74.

had shifted decisively northward, and had thereby lost its Italian focus. As of 1655–75, France and Spain retained their importance, England and the Austrian Habsburgs had become more central, and Sweden, the Netherlands and Brandenburg had appeared as important actors. Although the relative power and centrality of the participants altered considerably during the next two centuries, the map for the later seventeenth century shows us something like the structure that prevailed into our own time. The main thing it does not show is the expanding involvement of most of these states in the world outside Europe.

Diagrams for later periods become impossible to read; first they connect every European state with almost every other European state, then they reach with link after link to the world outside of Europe. For the twenty years from 1790 to 1809, Levy's great power wars include the *Russo-Swedish* (1788–90): Russia, Sweden, Denmark; *French Revolutionary* (1792–1802): France, Great Britain, Spain, Austria, Holland, Russia, Prussia, Sardinia, Saxony, Hanover, Oldenbourg, Hesse-Cassel, Baden, Württemberg, Bavaria, Piedmont, Parma, Modena, Mantua, the papacy, Malta, Venice, Genoa, Switzerland, Egypt, Ottoman Empire, Portugal, Naples, Tuscany; *Napoleonic* (1803–15): France, United Kingdom, Spain, Austria, Russia, Prussia, Sweden, Bavaria, Württemberg, Hesse, Nassau, Naples, Baden, Darmstadt, Berg, Brunswick, Nürnberg, Ottoman Empire, Moldavia, Wallachia; *Russo-Turkish* (1806–12): United Kingdom, Russia, Ottoman Empire; *Russo-Swedish* (1808–9): Russia, Sweden, Denmark.

Except for the somewhat separate triangle connecting Russia, Sweden, and Denmark, we might as well treat the period as one continuous war drawing in all European states; the corresponding network shows almost every European state including the Ottoman Empire coinvolved with every other one, and Egypt drawn into the system by Napoleon's invasion. If we were to extend the period to 1812, we would find the recently-formed United States entering the system as well. Despite these outliers and despite the pursuit of these wars in many colonial territories, the wars of the period were essentially European.

The restriction of great power wars to European states soon ended. Changes in the system since 1815 are clear and dramatic. Between the Franco-Prussian War of 1870–1 and the end of World War I, three critical transformations appeared in the European state system: the fragmented states of Germany and Italy consolidated into substantial, relatively unitary national states; the Ottoman and Habsburg empires fractured into a limited number of distinct national states, and multiple European states struggled with each other and with indigenous peoples for colonial empires in Africa, Asia, and the Pacific. In this period treaties among European powers – for example, the Triple Alliance of Germany, Austria, and Italy – typically included provisions concerning the defense of overseas interests against other European states. Those clashing interests often issued in war, overt or covert.

During the two decades from 1880 to 1899 major wars (those causing at least 1,000 battle deaths per year) included the *British-Afghan* (1878–80: UK and Afghans), *Pacific* (1879–83: Chile, Bolivia, and Peru), *Franco-Indochinese* (1882–4: France and Indochinese), *Mahdist* (1882–5: UK, Egypt and Sudanese), *Sino-French* (1884–5: France and China), *Central American* (1885: El Salvador, Guatemala), *Serbo-Bulgarian* (1885: Serbia and Bulgaria), *Franco-Madagascan* (1894–5: France and Madagascans), *Cuban* (1894–8: Spain and Cubans), *Sino-Japanese* (1894–5: China and Japan), *Italo-Ethiopian* (1895–6: Italy, Ethiopians), *First Philippine* (1896–8: Spain and Philippines), *Greco-Turkish* (1897: Ottoman Empire, Greece), *Spanish-American* (1898: Spain and USA), *Second Philippine* (1899–1902: USA and Philippines), and *Boer* (1899–1902: UK and Boers; Small and Singer 1982: 85–99). Levy classifies none of these as a great power war, and only the Sino-French as a war involving the great power system. All the others pitted either minor powers or a major power and colonized people against each other. All but two (the Serbo-Bulgarian and Greco-Turkish wars, which took place at the edges of a disintegrating Ottoman Empire) began in battlegrounds far outside Europe.

The settlements of World War I (more or less conclusive) and World War II (still unsettled) produced further critical changes in the European state system, including the wave of decolonizations since 1945. From World War I onward, indeed, it becomes increasingly difficult to separate the European system from the world system of states that was forming rapidly. Belligerents during World War I included not only almost all European states, but also Turkey, Japan, Panama, Cuba, Bolivia, Siam, Liberia, China, Peru, Uruguay, Brazil, Ecuador, Guatemala, Nicaragua, Costa Rica, Haiti, and Honduras. European colonies in Africa, Asia, and the Pacific contributed troops as well.

In recent decades, war has become even more international. During the last twenty years of Levy's compilation (1956–75) Small and Singer enumerate twelve interstate wars causing at least 1,000 battle deaths per year:

Russo-Hungarian (1956): USSR, Hungary

Sinai (1956): France, United Kingdom, Israel, Egypt

Sino-Indian (1962): China, India

Vietnamese (1965–75): North Vietnam, South Vietnam, Thailand, USA, Kampuchea, Korea, Australia, Philippines

Second Kashmir (1965): Pakistan, India

Six Day (1967): Israel, Eygpt/UAR, Jordan, Syria

Israeli-Egyptian (1969–70): Israel, Egypt/UAR

Football (1969): El Salvador, Honduras

Bangladesh (1971): India, Pakistan

Yom Kippur (1973): Israel, Egypt/UAR, Iraq, Syria, Jordan, Saudi Arabia

Turko-Cypriot (1974): Turkey, Cyprus

Vietnamese-Cambodian (1975–): Vietnam, Kampuchea

Of this set, the only wars directly involving great powers, by Levy's criteria, were the Russian invasion of Hungary (1956), the Sinai war (1956), the Sino-Indian war (1962), and the war in Vietnam (1965–73). Only one of the four took place in Europe. In Hungary one of the world's dominant powers put down rebellion in a satellite state. In Sinai, France and Britain intervened quickly after Israel invaded Egyptian territory and Egypt, retaliating, entered the Suez Canal zone and sank ships to block the canal. A United Nations peacekeeping force stabilized the territory, and after two months Israel withdrew its forces from the Sinai peninsula, except for the Gaza Strip and Sharm el Sheikh. On the Chinese Indian border, Chinese troops invaded highland territories after India attempted to occupy a high ridge in a disputed zone. The Chinese stopped in their tracks and then began withdrawing.

The Vietnamese conflict far surpassed the others in duration and casualties; over its ten brutal years, it produced some 1.2 million battle deaths, plus countless civilian casualties (Small and Singer 1982: 93). There the former colonial overlord, France, had withdrawn, leaving behind a war between two halves of a divided state. After two years of clandestine involvement, the world's greatest power, the United States, then intervened openly with devastating – but finally ineffectual – force. US troops later invaded the neighboring state of Cambodia, and bombed its cities. A rising great power, China, watched closely from just across the border, as the Soviet Union sent in supplies for the north, as Australia, New Zealand, South Korea, the Philippines, and Thailand aided the American effort in the south, and as the whole conflict boiled over into a Laotian civil war. The Cambodian–Vietnamese war likewise grew from struggles that began during the American intervention in Vietnam.

The Vietnam War dramatizes what had happened to the state system. Wars among or by the great powers had become relatively infrequent but immensely destructive. An increasing share of all major wars occurred within constituted states, as one or more of the great powers intervened directly or indirectly on behalf of local parties to a civil war. With the important exception of separatist demands, the contest rarely concerned the territory to be occupied by a given state; instead, the combatants fought over what groups were to control the existing state within its established boundaries. State persecution, liquidation, or expulsion of ethnic minorities began to generate refugees on a scale unprecedented in world history. Yet the displacement of the European concert by bipolar Soviet–American hegemony destroyed the practice of general peace settlements.

This set of changes, if it persists, constitutes a remarkable break with the past. It alters the stakes of war: no longer can a state's rulers hope to gain (or fear to lose) substantial territory through belligerence. Israel's territorial wars with its neighbors would have surprised no European of the eighteenth century, but in the period since 1945 they have become anomalies. Wars increasingly concern who is to rule in each state, which states will control the policies of other states, and what transfers of resources, people, and goods among states will occur.

THE CREATION OF A STATE-LINKED WORLD

During the last five hundred years, then, three striking things have occurred. First, almost all of Europe has formed into national states with well-defined boundaries and mutual relations. Second, the European system has spread to virtually the entire world. Third, other states, acting in concert, have exerted a growing influence over the organization and territory of new states. The three changes link closely, since Europe's leading states actively spread the system by colonization, conquest, and penetration of non-European states. The creation first of a League of Nations, then of a United Nations, simply ratified and rationalized the organization of all the earth's people into a single state system.

Note the meaning of these changes. On the average state formation moved from a relatively "internal" to a strongly "external" process. War has weighed heavily on the formation of states throughout the history we have been surveying; to that extent the process has always been external. Nonetheless the further we go back in time the more we see rulers and would-be rulers struggle to tame the populations within the territories they nominally control, fight off armed rivals within those territories, conquer adjacent lands and peoples, and build up their own monopolies of force. Thus we see them inadvertently constructing states whose structures bear the marks of the struggles and bargains that brought them into being. Conversely, as we move forward in time we witness the increasing salience of concerts among states for the fate of any particular state – at least until World War II (see Chapman 1988, Cronin 1988, Cumings 1988, Dower 1988, Eden 1988, Geyer 1988, Gran 1988a, Levine 1988, Rice 1988, Stein 1988).

Belgium's appearance as a separate state illustrates the significance of external influences in Europe (Clark 1984, Zolberg 1978). Never really a distinct and unified state before 1831, Belgium formed in approximately the section of the Low Countries that Spain, and then the Austrian Habsburgs, retained after the revolt of the Netherlands. France conquered and incorporated those territories in 1795, and held them until the war settlement of 1815; twenty years of French administration transformed the region's economy, and made it one of Europe's prime industrial centers. The post-Napoleonic settlement assigned the region to a newly-formed kingdom of the Netherlands seated at the Hague. Soon a coalition of industrialists, liberals, francophones, and Catholics (the categories overlapped, but were by no means identical) were pressing for regional rights.

In October 1830 the activists of that coalition, inspired by the July Revolution in neighboring France, formed a revolutionary provisional government, and the threat of French retaliation stayed the Dutch government from reacting with force. In November, the British convened a conference of European powers, which the following month declared the dissolution of the kingdom of the Netherlands into its two component parts. Under the close surveillance of France and Britain the newly baptized Belgians then went about recruiting a king and drafting a liberal constitution. When the London conference proposed a long-term settlement that was relatively unfavorable to Holland, Holland's King William sent in an army, defeated improvised Belgian troops, and incited a French invasion; the British later joined in the effort to expel Dutch forces from what was now to be Belgian territory. In 1839, King William finally accepted a settlement that not only recognized Belgium but also launched an independent (if territorially diminished) duchy of Luxembourg as a distinct state. From beginning to end, the entrance of Belgium into the European state system passed through a channel dug by its powerful neighbours.

Over the last three centuries, compacts of powerful states have increasingly narrowed the limits within which any national struggle for power occurred. They have done so through imposition of international war settlements, organization of colonies, diffusion of standard models for armies, bureaucracies, and other elements of the state apparatus, creation of international organizations charged with tending the state system, collective guarantee of national borders, and intervention to maintain domestic order. That narrowing restricted the alternative paths of state formation. Throughout the world state formation converged on the more or less deliberate construction of national states – not empires, not city-states, not federations, but national states – according to models offered, subsidized, and enforced by the great powers.

Not that would-be rulers or their patrons simply ordered up a whole state like a prefabricated house. When a European power installed courts, fiscal systems, police, armies, or schools in one of its colonies it usually followed European precepts. When independent Third World states turned to great powers for help in organizing markets, manufacturing, or military might the great powers commonly persuaded them to organize the European way. When such international institutions as the World Bank loaned money to struggling non-European states they regularly stipulated that those states undertake "reforms" bringing them into line with European and American practices. When, finally, poor countries looked around for places to educate their bureaucrats, technicians, and military officers they often sent them to train in Europe or one of its extensions. Once the national state dominated Europe and parts of the world settled chiefly by Europeans, it served as the template for state formation everywhere.

Why national states? National states won out in the world as a whole because they first won out in Europe, whose states then acted to reproduce themselves. They won out in Europe because the most powerful states – France and Spain before all others – adopted forms of warfare that temporarily crushed their neighbors, and whose support generated as by-products centralization, differentiation, and autonomy of the state apparatus. Those states took that step in the late fifteenth century both because they had recently completed the expulsion of rival powers from their territories and because they had access to capitalists who could help them finance wars fought by means of expensive fortifications, artillery and, above all, mercenary soldiers.

Let me not exaggerate: maritime states such as the Dutch Republic and Venice competed effectively with major land powers for another century; control of coasts remained crucial for supplying the interior, their fleets helped protect them from invasion, and overseas empires were growing in importance. Some relatively uncommercialized states, such as Sweden and Brandenburg, managed to build competitive military forces through an enormous coercive penetration of their territories. But eventually only those countries that combined significant sources of capital with substantial populations yielding large domestic military forces did well in the new European style of warfare. Those countries were, or became, national states.

National states would no doubt have prevailed in Europe even if France and Spain had been less aggressive at the end of the fifteenth century. During the sixteenth and seventeenth centuries many other European states attempted conquest within Europe for a time: Sweden, Brandenburg, and Russia come immediately to mind. In addition, the Dutch Republic, Portugal and Great Britain began competing for overseas empires, with many of the same effects on relations between states and citizens. European states held political control over about 7 percent of the earth's land in 1500, 35 percent in 1800, and 84 percent in 1914 (Headrick 1981: 3). That expansion in itself facilitated the multiplication of national states throughout the world. If another combination of states had dominated the struggles, their character would have affected the path and outcomes of European state formation significantly. Still, the expansion of capital and the reorganization of war in the sixteenth century jointly favored the increasing dominance of national states.

HOW WARS BEGAN

A system wrought by war shaped the conditions under which its members went to war. The conditions under which states went to war changed significantly – and more than once – during the long period we are examining. With significant modulations as a function of a state's chief rivals, the character of its dominant classes, and the sort of protective activity undertaken on its dominant classes' behalf, conditions changed as a function of a now-familiar constant logic that continued to operate under shifting circumstances: rulers normally tried to establish both a secure area within which they could enjoy the returns from coercion and a fortified buffer zone to protect the secure area. When the effort worked well, the buffer zone became a secure area, which encouraged the wielder of coercion to acquire a new buffer zone surrounding the old. So long as adjacent powers were pursuing the same logic, war resulted. In Europe, once the Roman Empire collapsed, thousands of warlords engaged in the same exercise. Hence unceasing and widespread, if chiefly regional, warfare. The later enlargement of state territories, the substitution of compact national states for multiple territories and the securing of borders through international agreements greatly reduced the length of vulnerable borders, but did not eliminate the war-promoting logic.

Other conditions, however, altered drastically. During the era of *patrimonialism* (up to 1400 in much of Europe), the groups that controlled substantial coercive means were typically either kin groups, neighbors, sworn communities of warriors, or combinations of the three. Ducal lineages exemplify the first, crusading orders the second, and feudal aristocracies their combination. Groups that controlled substantial coercive means generally sought to maximize the tribute they could extract from surrounding populations, by force if necessary, and to assure the future availability of tribute for their offspring and followers. By intermarrying, creating a noble caste, and (encouraged by a Catholic church that benefited from donations of land and revenues) establishing widely shared rules of inheritance, the ruling classes laid the groundwork for dynastic politics in which marriages cemented alliances among states and successions became the object of international attention. At the same time peasant communities, urban militias, groups of brigands, and other groups having no claims to state authority often warred on their own. As a result, wars tended to occur when a powerholder showed signs of weakness vis-à-vis his neighbor, when a disputable succession occurred, and when a new conqueror heaved onto the scene.

For the first half of our millennium, indeed, it is hardly worth asking *when* states warred, since most states were warring most of the time. True, massed armies drew chiefly on militias and feudal levies, which means that campaigns ordinarily went on during only a few months of each year. When an international war began, nevertheless, it usually ran for many campaigns. The decades from about 1150 to 1300 broke the nearly annual rhythm of war in England and France, but even then Scandinavia, Russia, Italy, the Mediterranean, and Iberia all saw incessant warfare. In a period of intensely fragmented sovereignty, furthermore, the differences among soldiers, bandits, pirates, rebels, and lords doing their duty blurred into a continuum of coercive action. Between great campaigns, local battles multiplied. Before 1500, the more meaningful questions are not when states warred, but who fought whom, how often, and how vigorously.

From the sixteenth century onward, the situation changed fundamentally. Consolidation of the state system, segregation of military from civilian life, and disarmament of the civilian population sharpened the distinction between war and peace. War became more intense and destructive, more continuous once it began, but a much rarer event. The twentieth century, in that respect, merely caps a long-term trend.

In the time of *brokerage* (roughly 1400 to 1700 in important parts of the continent), dynastic ambitions still dominated state policy, but the bulk of the state apparatus and the scale of war efforts meant that the interests of the major classes supporting the state seriously limited the possibilities for war; only with their consent and collaboration could monarchs assemble the means to fight. The interests of landlords weighed heavily in coercion-intensive states, the interests of capitalists in capital-intensive states.

Under the regime of brokerage, wars still followed dynastic opportunity, the weakness of adjacent states, and the arrival of conquerors such as the Tatars or the Turks, but several things changed. The dominant classes' commercial opportunities and threats became more frequently occasions for war, states whose economic bases were expanding became much more able to seize opportunities and head off threats, alliances among states entered the definitions of those opportunities and threats, such alliances frequently formed to contain the expansion of the currently most powerful state, expanding states fought more often to enlarge their contiguous territories rather than to accrete new tribute-paying units regardless of their location, and large-scale rebellions incited by rulers' attempts to extract the means of war or to impose a national religion provided more frequent opportunities for intervention by neighboring states. Meanwhile the gradual disarmament of the civilian population reduced the involvement of non-governmental groups as combatants – but not, alas, as victims – in wars. To some extent, the defense of coreligionists displaced dynastic inheritance as the ground of intervention by one state in the affairs of another.

As European states moved into the phase of *nationalization* (especially between 1700 and 1850, with wide variation from one kind of state to another), dynasties lost much of their ability to make war on their own behalf, and something we vaguely call "national interest" came to dominate states' involvement or non-involvement in wars. National interest synthesized the interests of the dominant classes, but compounded them with a much stronger drive to control contiguous territories and populations within Europe, as well as a fiercer competition for land outside of Europe.

Under nationalization, three critical changes affected the conditions for war: the current condition of the entire state system – notably the extent to which a balance of power currently obtained – began to make a major difference in the likelihood and location of war (Levy 1988); increasingly, pairs of states that were approaching equality of power went to war, especially if they occupied adjacent territories (Organski and Kugler 1980, Moul 1988, Houweling and Siccama 1988); total (rather than per capita) national income began limiting the military capacity of states as never before, with the result that large commercial and industrial states began to prevail within the state system. The era of war on the basis of rational expectations of gain and rational minimization of loss came upon Europe and its extensions. At the same time, third parties intervened much more frequently in nationalist rebellions against composite monarchies, as when France, Britain, and Russia joined the Greeks in their 1827 revolt against the Ottoman Empire. As grounds for intervention, common nationality displaced both dynastic inheritance and shared religion.

During the subsequent period of *specialization*, the conditions for war altered relatively little, except that competition for empire – direct or indirect – far from the national territory played a larger part than ever. After 1945, the standoff between the Soviet Union and the United States almost eliminated war among European states within Europe, but made the points of contact among Soviet, American, and Chinese power outside of Europe critical locations for the pursuit of national interest.

With the nationalization and specialization of armed force, international war developed a reciprocal relationship to revolution, rebellion, and civil war. During the centuries in which dynasties usually controlled states, a weakening in the ruling kin group – for example, the death of a king with an infant heir or none at all – signaled to rivals outside the state an opportunity to attack. When rebellion occurred first, it invited outsiders to intervene on behalf of the challengers. As religious divisions became fundamental matters of state (which means especially between 1520 and 1650), the incentives to intervene became even more compelling. Both the effort of a ruler to extract greatly increased means of war from a reluctant population and the weakening of a state through losses in war sometimes incited rebellions and civil wars. If the rebel coalition won its battle with the rulers, displaced them, and undertook a social transformation, a full-scale revolution resulted.

All of Europe's great revolutions, and many of its lesser ones, began with the strains imposed by war. The English Revolution began with the efforts of Charles I to bypass Parliament in acquiring revenues for war on the continent and in Scotland and Ireland. The debt accumulated by the French monarchy during the Seven Years' War and the War of American Independence precipitated the struggles of the French Revolution. Russian losses in World War I discredited tsarist rule, encouraged military defections, and made the state's vulnerability patent; the revolutions of 1917 followed.

State formation also affected the rhythms and character of popular collective action short of revolution. During the phases of brokerage and nationalization, episodic but massively increasing demands for money and men repeatedly stimulated resistance at the level of the village or the region. Local people ran out the tax collector, attacked the house of the tax farmer, hid their young men from recruiters, petitioned the king for relief, asked patrons to intercede for them, and fought efforts to inventory their wealth. They aimed especially at local people who were linked to the state, either as state officials or as agents of indirect rule. With the later stages of nationalization and the movement to specialization, popular collective action itself nationalized and became more autonomous; as the national state's policies and demands came to bear more and more directly on their fates, workers, peasants, and other ordinary people banded together to make claims on the state – claims for redress, certainly, but also claims for rights they had never previously enjoyed at a national scale (Tilly, Tilly, and Tilly 1975, Tilly 1986). The political party, the special-interest association, the national social movement, and all the rest of popular politics took shape. Thus war drove not only the state system and the formation of individual states, but also the distribution of power over the state. Even with the last few centuries' civilianization of Western governments, war has remained the defining activity of national states.

SIX SALIENT QUESTIONS

As a way of gauging how far we have come, let us return to the questions that began this inquiry. This time, let us reverse the order, taking the more detailed questions, and leading up to the general problem.

What accounts for the roughly concentric pattern of state formation in Europe as a whole? We now see that the question misstates the initial situation in some regards. In AD 990, almost all of Europe lived in fragmented sovereignty. Yet the character and degree of fragmentation varied. In different segments of the outer circle, large landlords and nomadic raiders deployed coercion in relative autonomy, although in most cases one of them bore some such title as duke, khan, or king, received deference and tribute from the others, and had claims on the intermittent military service of the rest.

Europe's gross geographic variation in paths of state formation reflected the differential distribution of coercion and capital. In the outer circle, typified by Russia and Hungary, the rarity of concentrated capital, the consequent weakness of cities and capitalists, the strength of armed landlords, and the struggle with powerful invaders such as the Mongols gave the advantage to rulers who could squeeze military force from landlords and peasants without raising large amounts of cash. States following the coercion-intensive path co-opted landlords and clergy, subordinated the peasantry, built extensive bureaucracies, and stifled their bourgeoisies.

In the inner zone, typified by Venice and the Netherlands, the concentration of capital and predominance of capitalists simultaneously facilitated the creation of military force and inhibited the seizure of states by specialists in coercion. For centuries the maritime states of the zone enjoyed great economic and political power. Finally, however, they found themselves hedged in or conquered by large land-based states that drew large armies from their own populations.

In between lay those states – notably France, Britain, and the later Prussia – that combined substantial sources of domestic capital with landlord–cultivator relations facilitating the creation of massive armed force. Their superior ability to sustain armies from their own resources eventually made them dominant over other sorts of states. The activity of building armies, furthermore, turned them early into national states.

The Iberian peninsula provides an interesting composite of all three experiences: a Catalonia, dominated by Barcelona, that acted much like a city-state so long as Mediterranean trade flourished, a Castile building military might on a warrior nobility and a subjugated peasantry but drawing on foreign riches to hire mercenaries, a Portugal sharply divided between Lisbon and its profoundly rural hinterland, other combinations yet in Valencia, Andalusia, Navarre, and elsewhere. But then all states were more composite than my simple typology demands: Britain with its England, Wales, Scotland, Ireland, and overseas possessions; Prussia with its eventual stretch from rural Pomerania to citified Rhineland, the Ottoman Empire with its span sometimes reaching from Persia to Hungary via the trading Mediterranean islands, the various Habsburg empires and their successors, scattered over most of Europe's climes and economies. The distinction between coercion-intensive, capital-intensive, and capitalized-coercion paths of state formation captures a significant part of the geographic and temporal variation, but not all of it.

Why, despite obvious interests to the contrary, did rulers frequently accept the establishment of institutions representing the major classes within the populations that fell subject to the state's jurisdiction? Monarchs were playing the same game – the game of war and competition for territory – under vastly different conditions. The more expensive and demanding war became, the more they had to bargain for its wherewithal. The bargaining produced or fortified representative institutions in the form of Estates, Cortes, and eventually national legislatures. Bargaining ranged from co-optation with privilege to massive armed repression, but it left behind compacts between sovereign and subjects. Although rulers of states such as France and Prussia managed to circumvent most of the old representative institutions for several centuries, those representative institutions or their successors eventually acquired more power vis-à-vis the crown as regular taxation, credit, and payment for the national debt became essential to the continued production of armed force.

Why did European states vary so much with respect to the incorporation of urban oligarchies and institutions into national state structure? On the whole, urban institutions became durable elements of national state structure where – and to the degree that – concentrated capital prevailed. That happened for two reasons: first because strong clusters of capitalists long had the incentive and the means to block any attempt by non-capitalist landlords at accumulating coercive power in their vicinities; second, because as the scale and expense of war expanded rulers who had access to credit and a commercialized, easily taxable, economy gained great advantages in the conduct of war, a fact which gave considerable bargaining power to major trading cities and their commercial oligarchies.

At one extreme, the weakness of capital in Poland facilitated mastery of landlords over the state, to such a degree that kings never acquired effective priority over their nominal subjects. With the partial exception of Gdansk, Polish nobles squeezed their cities dry. At the other extreme, the strength of capital in the Dutch Republic practically reduced the national government to a federation of city-states. Nevertheless, the immense commercial power of those federated city-states gave them the means of forming navies and hiring armies with great rapidity. In state-capital regions, rulers subordinated cities to the state and used them as instruments of rule, but also employed their capital and capitalists in the production of armed force; states did not generally incorporate urban institutions and oligarchies into the national structure as such, but bargained out forms of representation that gave them considerable power.

Why did political and commercial power slide from the city-states and city-empires of the Mediterranean to the substantial states and relatively subordinated cities of the Atlantic? Our review of the millennium from 990 to 1990 puts that important shift into perspective, and raises doubts about the neat succession of single hegemony from, say, Venice to Portugal to Britain. Perhaps we can award the palm to Great Britain for part of the nineteenth century (and thus help explain the relative absence of major European wars between 1815 and 1914). But before then at least two powerful states were always contending for dominance in Europe; none of them ever made it. On the commercial side, the expansion that became evident in the later fifteenth century impinged on a wide range of European urban areas; it supported a Renaissance whose center remained the city-states of northern Italy, but whose ramifications reached Germany, Flanders, and France, as well as a Reformation whose initial focus was the cities of southern and central Germany. Venice, Genoa, Ragusa, and other Mediterranean city-states, furthermore, continued to prosper, if not to prevail, into the eighteenth century.

Yet the centers of commercial and political gravity certainly moved northwest after the fifteenth century. First the overland and coast-hugging commercial exchanges of Europe with the cities of the East shriveled as a consequence of nomadic invasions, disease, and eventually the European establishment of high-seas itineraries to Asia around Africa. Then the mutually-reinforcing Atlantic and Baltic trades enriched Castile, Portugal, France, England, and the Netherlands more than the rest of Europe. All those states drew on their new wealth to build military power, and used their military to seek out new wealth. The ability to make large armies, big ships, long voyages, and overseas conquests gave them great advantages over Mediterranean city-states whose own waterways were limited by Muslim powers.

Why did city-states, city-empires, federations, and religious organizations lose their importance as prevailing kinds of state in Europe? Throughout the history of European states, warmaking and protection led to extractive activity, which entailed bargaining with those who held the means of war and protection. That bargaining sometimes led to further involvement of states in production, distribution, and adjudication. It always created some form of state structure, variable according to the economy and configuration of classes within which it occurred.

In their own ways and places, city-states, city-empires, federations, and religious organizations all thrived in Europe until the sixteenth century; indeed, empires of one kind or another still predominated in Europe at Charles V's abdication in 1557. Then national states began to gain priority. They did so for two related reasons: first, commercialization and capital accumulation in larger states such as England and France reduced the warmaking advantages of the small mercantile states and second, war expanded in scale and cost, partly as a function of the increased ability of the larger states to milk their economies, or their colonies, to pay for armed force. They won at war. The efforts of the smaller states to defend themselves either transformed, absorbed, or combined them into national states.

Why did war shift from conquest for tribute and struggle among armed tribute-takers to sustained battles among massed armies and navies? Remember the transitions from patrimonialism to brokerage to nationalization to specialization. What drove those transitions? Successful tribute-takers found themselves in indirect control of extensive lands and populations, whose administration and exploitation – especially in time of war with other major powers – created durable state structure. Those populous states that managed to incorporate substantial capital and capitalists into their preparations for war first built armies and navies through brokerage, and then incorporated the armed forces into state structure through nationalization, followed by specialization. At each stage, they had the means of acquiring and deploying the most effective military technology on a much larger scale than their neighbors. Since war pays off on effectiveness rather than efficiency, they gave smaller neighbors hard choices: mount the same sort of military effort at great cost, accept conquest, or find a safe subordinate niche. National states drove out the other forms of war.

To sum up: *What accounts for the great variation over time and space in the kinds of states that have prevailed in Europe since AD 990, and why did European states eventually converge on different variants of the national state? Why were the directions of change so similar and the paths so different?* European states started in very different positions as a function of the distribution of concentrated capital and coercion. They changed as the intersections of capital and coercion altered. But military competition eventually drove them all in the same general direction. It underlay both the creation and the ultimate predominance of the national state. In the process, Europeans created a state system that dominated the entire world. We live within that state system today. Yet the world outside of Europe resembles Europe no more than superficially. Something has changed in the extension of the European state system to the rest of the earth – including the relationship between military activity and state formation. Knowledge of the European experience helps identify some worrisome peculiarities of the contemporary world. The next (and final) chapter worries about those peculiarities.

7
Soldiers and States in 1992

POLITICAL MISDEVELOPMENT

As recently as twenty years ago, many scholars thought that Third World states would recapitulate the Western experience of state formation. The idea of "political development," now largely abandoned, epitomized the conception of a standard track along which states could roll toward the terminus of full participation and effectiveness – the model of participation and effectiveness being, of course, one or another of the existing Western states. The confidence of political developmentalists shattered with the emergence of clear alternative models such as China, Japan, Korea, and Cuba, the embarrassing failure of existing development schemes to anticipate the actual experiences of Third World states, resistance by Third World leaders and scholars to the condescension of Western academic advice, turns to *Realpolitik* in the great powers' treatment of Third World states, and disputes among Western scholars themselves as to the proper reading of past experience (see Evans and Stephens 1989). Along with "modernization," "educational development," and other well-meaning but obfuscatory slogans, political development is fast disappearing from the analytical lexicon.

As misconceived as the old analyses now seem, it was not utterly stupid to suppose that non-Western states would undergo some of the same experiences as their Western counterparts and end up looking much more like them. As recent colonies of various Western powers, a majority of newly independent states began their careers with formal organizations traced on Western lines and incorporating significant parts of the colonial apparatus. Western-educated state leaders sought self-consciously to install administrations, parliaments, parties, armies, and public services of Western inspiration.

What is more, they said so; Third World leaders declared that they would modernize their countries, develop them politically. Major Western powers assisted them actively, lending experts, models, training programs, and funds. So long as Japan was reeling from its losses in World War II and China was consumed with its internal struggles, no other models were obviously available. The choices seemed to run from Soviet-type socialism to American-style capitalism, with no viable paths of state formation beyond either extreme. The entire range recapitulated one version or another of European–American experience. Speaking of Southeast Asia in 1960, Lucian Pye declared that:

the dominant theme of Southeast Asia is the effort of the leaders of these new countries to create modern nation-states out of their transitional societies. These leaders have committed their peoples to the task of establishing representative institutions of government and developing more productive modes of economic life. Although enthusiasm for these goals has not been lacking, it is difficult to estimate their chances of being realized, for it is still hard to discern even the outlines of the political and social systems that are evolving in Southeast Asia. The possibility of failure is great, and leaders and citizens can be troubled with self-doubts. Already the tendency toward more authoritarian practices is widespread: for example, armies are coming to play roles that were originally reserved for democratic politicians.

(Pye 1960: 65–6)

Note the language: it speaks of constructing something whose characteristics are well known in a situation that is poorly understood, and menacing to the enterprise. The "something" to construct was an effective national state on a Western design. To be sure, Pye saw the possibility that something quite different might emerge in Southeast Asia, even that Southeast Asian leaders might press for something different. Most leaders of newly independent states actually declared that they sought a third way, at least vaguely socialist, somewhere between the American Scylla and the Russian Charybdis. But the existing Western states defined the range of choice. With varying degrees of dogmatism and perspicacity, political developmentalists said exactly that.

Even historically sophisticated analysts such as Cyril Black promulgated models featuring successive stages of political development. Black distinguished no fewer than seven different concrete paths of modernization, those illustrated by the United Kingdom, the United States, Belgium, Uruguay, Russia, Algeria, and Liberia, in that order (Black 1966: 90–4). But he argued that all his varied instances passed through four stages: a challenge of modernity, a consolidation of modernizing leadership, an economic and social transformation, and then the integration of society. Previous history, in his analysis, affected exactly how any particular society faced these challenges. But eventually all the European cases he examined arrived at something like societal integration after crossing the three previous thresholds in the same order.

The plausible collective reasoning had a great flaw. It supposed that a single standard process of state formation existed, that each state passed through the same internal process more or less separately, that Western experience exemplified the process, that contemporary Western states had generally reached the end of the process, and that the problem was one of social engineering on a very large scale. The effort to put those suppositions to the test in the construction of "modern" African, Asian, Latin American, or Middle Eastern states immediately raised doubts. Major powerholders resisted or distorted the transformation of existing governmental organization, officials used state power for their own ends, political parties became vehicles of ethnic blocs or patron–client chains, state-led enterprises collapsed, charismatic leaders suppressed Western-style electoral politics, and many more features of Third World states challenged the Western models.

Western models? In fact, the standard treatments of "political development" also misconstrued the Western experience on which they ostensibly drew. On the whole, they presented it as a conscious problem-solving process that passed through a series of standard internally-generated stages and finally produced mature, stable states. For A.F.K. Organski (1965: 7), the stages were:

1   the politics of primitive unification;

2   the politics of industrialization;

3   the politics of national welfare;

4   the politics of abundance.

Organski's characteristic scheme compressed a great deal of Third World experience into its first stage, but then delineated a path that clearly led toward the existing European world and its extensions.

Similarly, a great many political analysts thought that the transition to modernity passed from one condition of equilibrium – traditional society, or something of the sort – to another, superior, modern equilibrium. In between, according to this line of argument, lay the turbulence of rapid social change. Because social change was occurring much more rapidly in the twentieth century than before, new states were experiencing greater stresses than their European predecessors. Thus Third World states ran the risk of simultaneous foreign and domestic conflict, each stimulating the other (see Wilkenfeld 1973). Eventually, however, they would learn to contain conflict and achieve stable government of a modern kind. So, at least, taught much of the literature on political development.

Since the 1960s, a clearer reading of Western experience has made the inadequacy of those suppositions obvious. This book has borrowed greedily from the subsequent fund of knowledge, and has reinvested the accumulation in a reinterpretation of Western states' history. In earlier chapters, we have seen how widely the trajectories of European state formation varied as a function of the geography of coercion and capital, the organization of major powerholders, and pressure from other states. We have examined how a long series of unequal struggles among rulers, other powerholders, and ordinary people created specific state institutions and claims on the state. We have noticed how much the eventual organizational convergence of European states resulted from competition among them, both within Europe and in the rest of the world. We have witnessed the profound impact of war, and preparation for war, on other features of state structure. All these observations lead to the conclusions – vague but helpful – that Third World state formation should be distinctively different, and that the changed relations between coercion and capital should provide clues as to the nature of that difference.

In what ways should contemporary experience differ from that of the European past? After centuries of divergences among capital-intensive, coercion-intensive, and capitalized-coercion paths of state formation, European states began to converge a few centuries ago; war and mutual influence caused the convergence. Although shared colonial experience imposed common properties on many Third World states, however, no great homogenization has so far occurred among them. On the contrary. Any student of European state formation can hardly help noticing the variety of today's Third World states. Variety marks any category that includes both immense, ancient China and tiny, brand-new Vanuatu, both wealthy Singapore and dirt-poor Chad; we are unlikely to generalize successfully about such a heterogeneous set of experiences. Not all the states of the Third World, furthermore, are "new" states, by any stretch of the imagination. China and Japan stand among the world's oldest continuously existing states, Siam/Thailand is centuries old, and most Latin American states acquired formal independence during the Napoleonic Wars. They stand with states formed since 1945 chiefly in their recent acquisition of full membership in the state system that European struggles created and defined.

Look more closely, however: exactly what is heterogeneous about Third World states? Not so much their organizational structures as relations between citizens and states. Formal organizational characteristics of the world's states have, in fact, converged dramatically over the last century or so; the adoption of one Western model or another has become a virtual prerequisite for recognition by prior members of the state system. The present 160-odd recognized states cover a much narrower organizational range than the 200-odd European states of 1500, which included city-states, city-empires, federations, kingdoms, territorial empires, and more. Except for relatively centralized federations and quite attenuated kingdoms, those once-abundant political forms have all but disappeared. After 1500, both the pressures of large-scale warmaking and the negotiations of large-scale peacemaking drove all European states toward a new organizational form: the national state. The drift from "internal" to "external" state formation which prevailed in Europe has continued into our own time, and imposed a common definition on states in very diverse parts of the world. Contemporary state structures, in the narrow sense, resemble each other in featuring courts, legislatures, central bureaucracies, field administrations, standing armies, specialized police forces, and a panoply of public services; even the differences among socialist, capitalist, and mixed economies fail to override these common properties.

Yet such formally similar organizations do not work at all in the same manner. The differences lie in both the internal operation of superficially indistinguishable courts, legislatures, bureaux, or schools and the relations between governmental agencies and citizens. In the European experience, states took forms that mediated between the exigencies of external war and the claims of the subject population; to some degree, each state's organization adapted to local social and economic conditions. As existing national states sculptured newcomers in their own image, local adaptation occurred instead in relations between citizens and states. These days the difference between coercion-intensive, capital-intensive, and capitalized-coercion settings affects the formal structure of states much less than it used to, but affects relations between citizens and states even more. In that regard, the contemporary world remains extremely diverse.

Does the Third World exist? Certainly Latin American, Middle Eastern, and East Asian states differ greatly with respect both to internal organization and to position within the world system of states. The justification for beginning with such a crude, composite category rests on the fact that states in lower-income regions of the world have long endured under the formal control of Europe and its extensions, have commonly adopted European or American models of formal organization, find themselves caught in superpower struggles over which they can exert little control, and constitute an uneasy but recurrent pool for alliances with newcomers to the state system (Ayoob 1989). In extending to the non-European world, the state system did not simply remain the same; the entrance of scores of independent states from Asia, Africa, and Latin America transformed the system in ways that a comparison with previous European experience can illuminate.

We still have something to gain, then, from the comparison of contemporary Third World experience with that of national states for which a long record is already available. At a minimum, that comparison will help us take two useful steps: (1) to discard ideas about state formation that have already proven themselves faulty before wasting time applying them to contemporary experience; (2) to sharpen our sense of what is distinctive, and what familiar, in the processes of state formation, transformation, and deformation now occurring in the poorer parts of the world.

Reflecting on European experience, what might we expect to find happening in the contemporary world? Given the diversity of state formation within Europe, we have no reason to anticipate a single trajectory of change. But we might reasonably extrapolate from Europe to:

- significant influence of the relative distributions of coercion and capital on the paths of state formation;

- distinctively different directions of change in the presence and absence of significant clusters of cities;
- strong effects of war and preparation for war on the creation and alteration of state structure;
- mediation of those effects through (a) fiscal structure and (b) the sources of arms and military personnel;
- civilianization of state power through the creation of central bureaucracies, increasing reliance on credit and taxation for the purchase of military means, and bargaining with the subject population over those means;
- continuation of the trend from "internal" to "external" determination of the organizational forms of states.

In a world so different from that in which most European states took shape, to be sure, these remain no more than orienting hypotheses. Yet they improve considerably on the old notion that Third World states would somehow recapitulate the idealized experience of the most effective Western national states.

THE IMPACT AND HERITAGE OF WORLD WAR II

What, then, distinguishes state formation in the contemporary world from its counterparts in the past? Although twentieth-century war takes a deadlier toll than ever, war has changed significantly in character. Large-scale civil wars, often aided and abetted by great powers, have become much more common in the world since 1945 than they were in European experience. The threat of nuclear arms and other technical menaces has compounded the likely costs of a major war. The formation of a bipolar state system on a nearly global scale affected the politics, and the military prospects, of most states. On the principle that the number of relations among states increases geometrically as the number of states increases arithmetically, the sheer proliferation of connected but nominally independent states greatly complicated the state system.

World War II transformed the state system and the states within it. As citizens of belligerent states, as inhabitants of battle zones, or both, most of the world's people felt the war's impact. The war broke all records for killing, for destruction of property, and for displacement of populations. By dropping atomic bombs on Hiroshima and Nagasaki, the United States introduced into warfare the first weapons in history with the potential to annihilate all humanity in a few days.

We can reasonably place the start of World War II in 1938 (when Japan and Russia began to fight while Germany annexed Poland and dismembered Czechoslovakia) or in 1939 (when Germany invaded Poland and then the rest of Czechoslovakia). In either case, Japan's surrender in 1945 marks a relatively neat end to the war. Perhaps fifteen million deaths in battle and another twenty-five million as a direct result of war made World War II by far the most destructive belligerency in human history. Powers sustaining at least a thousand battle deaths included Bulgaria, the United Kingdom, Australia, Canada, Ethiopia, Poland, USA, USSR, Belgium, Brazil, China, Yugoslavia, the Netherlands, Rumania, Italy, New Zealand, France, South Africa, Greece, Norway, Mongolia, Japan, Germany, Hungary, and Finland (Small and Singer 1982: 91). The war left Japan, important parts of China, and much of Europe devastated.

As the war ended, two states towered over all the rest: the USA and the USSR. The United States had suffered relatively light losses (408 thousand battle deaths as compared, for instance, with Germany's 3.5 million) during World War II but had mobilized enormous industrial capacity after a debilitating depression. It is not surprising that the United States, an industrial colossus grown even more muscular in war, seized a dominant position in the world system of states. The rise of the Soviet Union is the greater puzzle. The USSR had endured terrible privations in the war (7.5 million battle deaths, perhaps 20 million in total fatalities, and 60 percent of industrial capacity lost) but had built up a formidable state organization in the process (Rice 1988). No doubt that enhanced state capacity, and the extension of Soviet control to other eastern European states, helps account for the other pole of the bipolar world. Almost immediately the former allies turned to an enmity that blocked a general peace settlement for the first time in four centuries. As a result, losers of the war such as Japan and Germany long endured the victors' military occupation, and only slowly regained membership in the state system. In fact, the victors and the vanquished only settled the war piecemeal, in occupations, provisional international agreements, partial treaties, and *de facto* recognitions. The war's complexity and scale, plus its bipolar outcome, overwhelmed the capacity of the international system to produce the sort of general settlement that had ended major European wars since 1503.

The postwar process of state formation distinguished itself from its predecessors especially in the wholesale transformation of Western colonies into formally independent states. The situation favored European withdrawal: the USSR had no colonies in the major areas of European colonization, and the United States had few, while the European powers were preoccupied with recovery from the ravages of war. At a dizzying pace, dependencies demanded and won recognition as autonomous entities. In 1960 alone the Belgian Congo (now Zaïre), Benin, Cameroon, the Central African Republic, Chad, the Congo, Cyprus, Gabon, Côte d'Ivoire, Madagascar, Mali, Niger, Nigeria, Senegal, Somalia, Togo and Upper Volta (now Burkina Faso) all joined the United Nations shortly after receiving recognition as independent states.

At the same time the Soviet Union and, especially, the United States, extended the networks of their military bases, military assistance programs, and intelligence facilities throughout the world (Eden 1988). In East Asia, for example, the United States substituted its own military power for that of a demilitarized Japan, reorganized and ran the South Korean military, and subsidized China's KMT forces both in their losing mainland battles and in their retreat to control of Taiwan (Cumings 1988, Dower 1988, Levine 1988). Between 1945 and 1984, furthermore, the United States pumped $13 billion of military-economic aid into South Korea and another $5.6 billion into Taiwan, as compared with a total for all Africa of $6.89 billion and all Latin America of $14.8 billion (Cumings 1984: 24).

For the most part, European powers relinquished their overlordships with remarkably little travail. With the exception of the Algerian struggle for independence and the early stages of the Indochinese conflicts, the bitterest battles occurred where more than one group claimed the right to rule the new state, where a segment of the liberated population demanded its own state, and where the division among the claimants incited extensive great power intervention; China, Palestine, Malaya, Kenya, Cyprus, Aden, Borneo, Korea, Vietnam, the Philippines, Ruanda, Angola, and Mozambique provide the obvious examples. The United Nations undertook to register and manage the entry of new members into the international system of states.

For the period since 1945, we can therefore take the membership of the United Nations at any point in time as an approximation of the world's state system. The approximation is imperfect: Switzerland, South Korea, North Korea, Taiwan, Monaco, Tuvalu, and a few other units behave like states but do not belong, while the Byelorussian and Ukrainian republics (until the recent stirrings of nationalism, wholly owned subsidiaries of the USSR) belong as concessions to the power the Soviet Union wielded at the end of World War II. But in general, the organization includes the world's important states, and has absorbed new states as they have achieved a measure of autonomy in international affairs.

Figure 7.1 presents the geographic distribution of UN members from the organization's founding in 1945 to 1988. The story is obvious: the UN started out with a large majority of states from Europe and the Americas – the old European state system and its extensions, minus the major losers of World War II and plus a few important states outside of the West. The numbers of states from Europe and the Americas increased modestly as European peace settlements fell into place and as Caribbean states began acquiring independence and international recognition. But after 1955 Asian states entered the UN at a faster rate than those of the West. From 1960 onward African states dominated the new entries.

The new entrants, on the average, were following coercion-intensive paths to statehood. The departing colonial powers left little accumulated capital behind them, but bequeathed to their successor states military forces drawn from and modeled on the repressive forces they had previously established to maintain

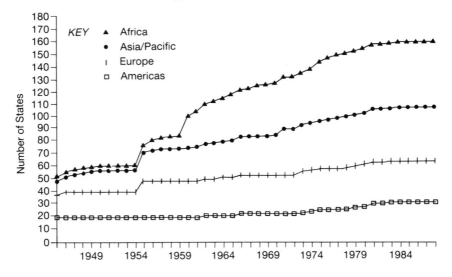

Figure 7.1   Membership of United Nations by geographic region, 1945–88.

their own local administrations. Relatively well equipped and trained armed forces then specialized in control of civilian populations and in combat against insurgents rather than interstate war. Once Europeans dismantled their own governmental apparatus, the armed forces, the churches, and Western corporations were frequently the most effective organizations operating in the state's territory. The armed forces, furthermore, had some distinctive characteristics: their senior ranks filled rapidly with men who had previously occupied subordinate positions in colonial armies. Often, continuing a pattern of recruitment established by colonial powers, they drew disproportionately on one linguistic, religious, and/or regional population, and therefore became the instrument or the site of sharp ethnic rivalries. Up to 1966, for example, the Nigerian army held itself aloof from manifest division by region or ethnicity. But with the military coup d'état of January 1966, fissures began to show. In July, a coalition of officers from the north led another coup, and acted quickly to expel Ibos (who came especially from Nigeria's Eastern Region) from the army and power. Soon (May 1967) the east, as Biafra, broke into open rebellion, and one of Africa's bloodiest civil wars began (Luckham 1971: 17–82).

Except where charismatic national leaders deliberately held them in check, Third World armies commonly resisted civilian control. Senior officers frequently felt, and said, that they knew better than mere politicians what the country's destiny required, and how to maintain order on the way to fulfilling that destiny. To the extent that their states generated revenues by selling commodities on the international market, bought arms overseas, and received military aid from great powers, furthermore, the armed forces enjoyed insulation from reliance on taxation and conscription authorized by civilian governments.

How far the military of exporting countries were able to maintain autonomy, however, depended on the alliances they formed (or failed to form) with major elements of the ruling class, and on the success of the export program. In Bolivia, the encapsulation of tin tycoons, who lived handsomely on export income and established few strong ties within the country, made them vulnerable to military seizure of state power and of tin revenues (Gallo 1985). In Taiwan, a quintessential police state under Jiang Jie-Shi (Chiang Kai-Shek), the great success of the industrial export program eventually diverted the military from their preparations to invade the Chinese mainland, reduced their control over policy and day-to-day governmental operations, and surrounded them with powerful civilian officials (Amsden 1985).

What is more, the character of war changed significantly after 1945. Despite the near-disappearance of wars among Western powers, lethal combat actually became more frequent in the world as a whole. Table 7.1 shows the trend since 1893, expressed as thousands of battle deaths in wars involving at least a thousand battle deaths in a given year. The totals fluctuate sharply from one period to the next. Yet the figures show several trends clearly: the concentration of deaths in the periods of general war, the stabilization or decline of "extrasystemic" wars as more and more states entered the international state system, the irregularly increasing prominence of civil wars as the origin of deaths in battle. The number of new civil wars rose from about ten thousand battle deaths per year at the century's start to a hundred thousand deaths per year between 1937 and 1947, then fluctuated around the hundred-thousand mark over the next three decades.

With the twentieth century, battle deaths underestimated more and more the damage done by war. The bombing and shelling of civilian settlements

Table 7.1   Battle deaths in wars involving at least a thousand battle deaths in a given year, 1893–1980

Period	Interstate	Extrasystematic	Civil	Total	Percent civil
		Locus of war			
1893–1903	30	96	112	238	47.1
1904–1914	8,860	0	270	9,130	3.0
1915–1925	161	83	506	750	67.5
1926–1936	213	0	955	1,168	81.8
1937–1947	16,292	100	1,161	17,553	6.6
1948–1958	1,913	59	372	2,344	15.9
1959–1969	1,250	0	1,830	3,080	59.4
1970–1980	78	73	820	921	89.0

Source: Small and Singer 1982: 134, 263

destroyed increasing numbers of non-combatants, not to mention their means of livelihood. During and after wars, states began to displace or even expel populations as never before. And the deliberate attempt to kill entire populations – genocide and politicide – has turned from the rare, appalling aberration that it once seemed to a standard technique of government. Between 1945 and 1987, deliberate mass killing of civilians by agents of states probably caused from 7 million to 16 million deaths throughout the world, more than died in the direct engagements of international and civil wars (Harff and Gurr 1988).

Civil wars that occurred after 1945 sometimes arose from general struggles among classes for state power. More often they sprang from the claims of particular religious, linguistic, and territorial groups for autonomy or for control of an existing state. In this limited sense, nationalism has become more salient in wars as the world as a whole has settled into a complete map of stable, mutually-exclusive state territories; the powerholders of excluded nationalities see their chances slipping away from them.

At the same time, great powers have intervened increasingly in civil wars, seeking alignment and cooperation of those who control the state by assuring that the sympathetic faction wins. During the 1970s, substantial civil wars began in Angola, Burundi, Cambodia, Guatemala, Iran, Jordan, Lebanon, Nicaragua, Pakistan, the Philippines, Rhodesia, and Sri Lanka; in only one of them (Guatemala) did outside powers refrain from intervening in a substantial way (Dunér 1985: 140). When 1980 ended, wars were raging in the Philippines, Angola, Guatemala, Afghanistan, El Salvador, Nicaragua, Cambodia, Mozambique, and Peru. In most of these cases, the United States, the Soviet Union, or South Africa was at least marginally involved. Although the 1980s offered some respite by comparison with previous decades, the destructiveness of the Iran–Iraq war (perhaps a million battle deaths) and the continuation of other struggles into the decade makes it unlikely that the completion of the next interval in 1991 will establish a downward trend.

Available weaponry promised new levels of destructiveness, as the proliferation of nuclear arms threatened the whole world with extinction. At the moment, the USA, Russia, the United Kingdom, France, China, and India definitely have their own nuclear weapons. In addition to them, West Germany, Israel, Brazil, Argentina, Pakistan, and Japan are processing plutonium, which brings them at least within striking distance of nuclear military capacity. The other ostensibly non-nuclear states that did not sign the 1968 nuclear non-proliferation treaty – and therefore remain active candidates for nuclear capacity – include Spain, Israel, Chile, Cuba, and South Africa. About 10 percent of the world's recognized states, including its greatest powers, then, either deploy nuclear arms or retain the right to do so. War will not become more benign as time goes on. (A. J. P. Taylor ends his otherwise chatty *How Wars End* with a chilling reminder of the nuclear threat: "However, do not worry. The Third World War will be the last": Taylor 1985: 118.) In the meantime, non-nuclear wars proliferate.

The continued rise of war couples with a fixation of international boundaries. With a few significant exceptions, military conquest across borders has ended, states have ceased fighting each other over disputed territory, and border forces have shifted their efforts from defense against direct attack toward control of infiltration. Armies (and, for that matter, navies and air forces) concentrate increasingly on repression of civilian populations, combat of insurgents, and seizures of power. As a consequence, governments become more unstable as their borders become more secure. Because those who control states define whole populations as their enemies, wars generate refugees at a huge rate (conventional estimates set the number of refugees in the world at 8 million toward 1970 and 10.5 million toward 1980: Zolberg 1981: 21).

If the end of World War II began a new era for worldwide war and peace, the 1960s brought the largest transition so far within that era. During the early 1960s, decolonization and entry of new states into the international system accelerated, civil wars greatly increased in destructiveness and in their share of all wars, military power consolidated in Latin America, Asia, and the Middle East, and military struggles for control of African states multiplied rapidly. The Cuban missile crisis confirmed the rough strategic equality of the United States and Soviet Union, as well as stabilizing their claims to mutually exclusive zones of influence around their own frontiers. Above all else, military men became increasingly involved in struggles for state power. Let us therefore focus on the place of military power in Third World states.

THE ASCENT OF MILITARY MEN

Although writing on the Third World's military was always more tentative and divided than analyses of political or economic development, there too Western analysts commonly adopted an implicit model of the "mature" polity. In such a polity, they supposed, impeccably professional military men occupied a significant but clearly subordinate place; the model followed directly from the experience of most European states during the last few centuries of state formation. The analyst's job was then to chart the path that would or could lead from the present condition of the military in Indonesia or the Congo to the condition appropriate for stable democracy. That job entailed the further task of accounting for deviations from the favored path – in particular, the puzzling way in which many colonial territories gained formal independence blessed with ostensibly democratic and representative governments, yet quickly moved to military rule.

Most analysts thought, with Edward Shils, that "Military rule is one of the several practicable and apparently stable alternatives when parliamentary, democratic regimes falter. The inherited and the newly engendered obstacles over which these regimes have been stumbling are more determinative than the aspirations of the military elites of these states, although the latter are not unimportant" (Shils in Johnson 1962: 9). Thus political development and military development merged into the same problem. Both ideas have now dissolved in skepticism, contradiction, and despair.

In Third World regions such as Africa and South Asia, a student of Western history cannot help noticing apparent disjunctions between the existence of Western-looking twentieth-century armies, on the one hand, and the prevalence of military politics reminiscent of the Renaissance, between the apparatus of representative government and the arbitrary use of state power against citizens, between the installation of apparently conventional bureaucracies and the widespread use of governmental organization for individual gain. These disjunctions are more visible in states that have recently escaped from colonial rule than in the rest of the Third World. Contrary to the apparent teaching of European history, the growth of big government, arbitrary rule, and militarization now seem to be going hand in hand.

Thirty years ago, Samuel Huntington argued that civilian control over the military occurred through two different processes, one unstable and one stable. The unstable process was a power struggle in which one civilian group or another subordinated the military to a governmental institution, a constitution, or a particular social class; Huntington gave it the odd name of "subjective" control. "Objective" control, in his eyes, resulted from maximizing military professionalism and recognizing an independent military sphere outside of politics. "Historically," said Huntington, "the demand for objective control has come from the military profession, the demand for subjective control from the multifarious civilian groups anxious to maximize their power in military affairs" (Huntington 1957: 84–5). Paradoxically, civilians who sought to increase their own power by interfering in military professionalization thereby promoted military seizure of power. A pro-military ideology, low military political power, and high military professionalism, by this argument, promote civilian control, while anti-military ideology, high military political power and low military professionalism promote military control.

The insertion of military political power into the explanation of military control introduces an element of circularity into the argument, but we can break the circle by checking the factors Huntington considers to promote political power: personal affiliation of the military with other powerful groups, resources placed directly under the control of the officer corps, hierarchical interpenetration of the officer corps with civilian power structures, prestige and popularity of the officer corps and its leaders. Thus we would expect an officer corps to have relatively little political power if it recruited chiefly from outside the ruling classes, had few non-military resources at its disposal, held few non-military offices, and had little popular following.

Huntington wrote in a time of optimism about the professionalization of Third World armies and the strengthening of civilian control. Five years after Huntington, the Spanish-Mexican writer Victor Alba continued the note of optimism in his declaration that Latin American militarism:

> has arrived at the penultimate phase in its history. In its final stage it will disappear. That epoch may be near. Encouraged by the increased possibilities of legislative and diplomatic action and the growing concern of international organizations, powerful elements in Latin America have made the obliteration of militarism their major preoccupation.
>
> (Alba in Johnson 1962: 165–6)

The millennium, however, has dragged its feet. Despite dramatic containment of the military in Brazil and Argentina, the end of Chile's Pinochet regime, and the collapse of Alfredo Stroessner's personalistic rule in Paraguay, nine of the 24 larger Latin American and Caribbean states still accord extensive power and autonomy to their armed forces. Behind the scenes, furthermore, the militaries of South America still constitute a political force to reckon with.

Treated as a prediction made thirty years ago, Huntington's analysis indicates that in so far as pro-military ideologies have arisen, military political power has declined, and military professionalism has increased in different parts of the world, civilian control should have become more effective. If, on the other hand, military control has actually become more widespread, then we should find that anti-military ideologies have gained, military political power has risen, and military professionalism has declined. Something in those predictions looks wrong: military control has increased in the world's states over the last thirty years, but while military political power, by Huntington's standards, has surely expanded, anti-military ideology does not seem to have become more prevalent, and military professionalism has almost certainly grown. To clarify what has happened, we should look at the place of militarizing states in the world's system of states.

TODAY'S MILITARY IN HISTORICAL PERSPECTIVE

Starting in the sixteenth century and ending only very recently, Western states incorporated the rest of the world into their system through colonization, elaboration of commercial ties, and direct negotiation. Most recent entrants joined the system as independent actors through decolonization, and therefore arrived with administrative structures, fiscal systems, and armed forces designed on Western lines; titles, perquisites, and uniforms of the former colonies reflect those national influences. Yet reproducing a table of organization provides no guarantee that the new state will behave like the old. Nowhere is that clearer than in the behavior of the Third World's military. The armies of poor countries resemble those of rich countries in many regards. But on the whole they intervene in domestic political life far more directly and frequently, and with more obviously damaging consequences for rights of citizens. Why should that be?

Think back to the central paradox of European state formation: that the pursuit of war and military capacity, after having created national states as a sort of by-product, led to a civilianization of government and domestic politics. That happened, I have argued, for five main reasons: because the effort to build and sustain military forces led agents of states to build bulky extractive apparatuses staffed by civilians, and those extractive apparatuses came to contain and constrain the military forces; because agents of states bargained with civilian groups that controlled the resources required for effective warmaking, and in bargaining gave the civilian groups enforceable claims on the state that further constrained the military; because the expansion of state capacity in wartime gave those states that had not suffered great losses in war expanded capacity at the ends of wars, and agents of those states took advantage of the situation by taking on new activities, or continuing activities they had started as emergency measures; because participants in the war effort, including military personnel, acquired claims on the state that they deferred during the war in response to repression or mutual consent but which they reactivated at demobilization; and finally because wartime borrowing led to great increases in national debts, which in turn generated service bureaucracies and encouraged greater state intervention in national economies.

In a cartoon history of Europe, the story would appear in four panels. In the first panel, the king wears armor and carries a sword, recruiting and commanding his own army and navy, which maintain personal loyalty to his service. In the second, the king bears glorified military garb, but contracts with a *condottiere* for the hire of mercenaries to fight his battles. In the third panel, the king, fitted out in a grand costume utterly unsuitable for fighting wars, consults with generals and ministers of war who find their places in a complex, civilian-dominated structure. In the last scene we see a king (who may now be a president or prime minister in disguise) sporting a business suit and negotiating not only with his staff but also with duly constituted representatives of major civilian interests and of the population at large. (The four panels bear the familiar subtitles Patrimonialism, Brokerage, Nationalization, and Specialization.) To be sure, the comic-book version of civilianization describes different national experiences with varying verisimilitude; it fits German experience better than Dutch or Russian. But it will do as a schematic summary of civilianization in European states.

Another general feature of European state formation deserves our attention. Relations with other states played a significant part in the formation of any particular state, if only because wars and war settlements significantly affected the state's structure and boundaries. Nevertheless, the organizational structures of the first national states to form took shape mainly as a consequence of struggles between would-be rulers and the people they were trying to rule. As the European state system solidified, however, whole sets of states began to decide the outcomes of wars, and therefore the organizational structures of states that emerged from the wars. Thus Napoleon's forces drastically reorganized states as they conquered, and the Congress of Vienna redrew the map to include a previously nonexistent kingdom of the Netherlands plus a greatly-reshaped Prussia, Sardinia, Bavaria, Baden, and Austria. Europe moved from relatively "internal" to relatively "external" processes of state formation.

That shift toward the external continued into the twentieth century. Only a glance at twentieth-century processes of state formation reveals that they are triply external: many new national states formed as colonial possessions of other states, especially European states; many built their governing institutions under the influence of another, much greater, power; and concerts of nations – the United Nations being their latest embodiment – have ratified and to some extent sustained their existence as separate members of the international state system. One consequence is a decreasing flexibility of state boundaries in the twentieth century. Except as a part of a general peace settlement negotiated by many states, it becomes decreasingly likely that conquest will lead to a major redrawing of any state's perimeter. These days Guatemala claims all of Belize and Venezuela claims some of Guyana, but other states of the Americas will not tolerate a territorial grab in either case. Although wars, guerrilla and otherwise, continue to occur quite frequently, many states face no serious external military threat. That means many armies have little prospect of going to war. They specialize in internal control.

Third World militaries have drawn specifically on European or American models, aid, and training to a far larger degree than European states intervened in the formation of each other's armies. In Latin America, for example, before World War II France and Germany trained many of the officers of Argentina, Bolivia, Brazil, Chile, and Peru. After the war, the United States took over the task (Nunn 1971). This external intervention gave Latin American militaries exceptional maneuverability vis-à-vis their potential rivals and chosen enemies.

In Europe, the external imposition of state forms occurred without obvious impact on the stability of regimes. Most of the states formed out of the ruins of the Ottoman and Austro-Hungarian empires had, it is true, unsteadier holds on stable democracy than their northern neighbors, and one might argue a connection between late national state formation and vulnerability to fascism in Germany and Italy. But in northern Europe, the late independence of Finland, Norway, and the Baltic republics did not stop them from establishing relatively durable regimes (see Alapuro 1988).

In the world since 1945, however, the relationship between external imposition and instability seems to have increased. Where the ability of rulers to draw revenues from commodity exports or from great-power military aid has allowed them to bypass bargaining with their subject populations, large state edifices have grown up in the absence of significant consent or support from citizens. Lacking strong ties between particular state institutions and major social classes within the population, those states have become more vulnerable to forcible seizures of power and abrupt changes in the form of government. Among the world's poorer states that were already independent in 1955, for example, higher shares of government expenditure in Gross National Product (arguably an outcome of external influence) predicted more frequent regime changes during the next two decades, just as more frequent regime changes between 1950 and 1960 predict higher shares of government expenditure in the subsequent fifteen years (Thomas and Meyer 1980). These circumstances invite military buildup, and military bids for power.

Most likely the relationship between external influence and political instability is curvilinear, with instability highest at intermediate and/or changing levels of external control. That between external influence and military control, on the other hand, is quite direct. The extreme form of external influence is military occupation; as long as it lasts, the occupied regime tends to stay in place. World War II differed from previous general wars by not ending in a general settlement; it left military occupations in Germany, Austria, Japan, Korea, and elsewhere to drag on for years. During the postwar years, the great Western powers – incomparably, the USSR and the USA – maintained unprecedented numbers of troops abroad. In 1987, 29 states officially stationed troops within some other state's territory. The USA had 250,000 troops in West Germany, 54,000 in Japan and 43,000 in South Korea, while the Soviet Union deployed 380,000 in East Germany, 110,000 in Afghanistan, 65,000 in Hungary, and 60,000 in Czechoslovakia. The Soviet Union led the occupiers:

> USSR: 730,090 troops abroad
> USA: 492,500
> Vietnam: 190,000
> United Kingdom: 89,500
> France: 84,450
> Cuba: 29,250

The surprises are Vietnam (with an estimated 140,000 troops in Cambodia and another 50,000 in Laos) and Cuba (with 27,000 in Angola and other forces scattered in Congo, Nicaragua, and Yemen: Sivard 1988: 12–13). Although dominant states sometimes sent troops in to forestall or reverse transfers of power, on the whole their presence greatly reduced the odds for further changes of regime.

MILITARY BUILDUP

The military investments of the world's states are increasing apace. After the demobilization following World War II, military expenditure has risen dramatically on a per capita basis, especially in the Third World. Between 1960 and 1987, with corrections for inflation, per capita military spending increased by almost 150 percent, while GNP per capita rose about 60 percent (Sivard 1988: 6). In the world's richer countries, however, military budgets actually declined from about 6.9 percent of GNP in 1960 to about 5.5 percent in 1984; in poorer countries, the percentage has risen from 3.6 to 5.6 percent; the poor world is now spending a larger share of its meager income on arms and armies than the rich world spends of its much more ample income. ("Rich countries" include Australia, Austria, Belgium, Bulgaria, Canada, Czechoslovakia, Denmark, East Germany, Finland, France, Hungary, Iceland, Ireland, Israel, Italy, Japan, Luxemburg, the Netherlands, New Zealand, Norway, Poland, Rumania, Spain, Sweden, Switzerland, the former USSR, the United Kingdom, the United States, and West Germany. "Poor countries" include all other states.)

World regions vary considerably in their devotion to military expenditure. Table 7.2 provides details. In per capita expenditures for 1984, the world's leading spenders were North America, the Warsaw Pact countries and the Middle East, while in proportion of GNP spent on the military the Middle East left the rest of the world far behind. The champions in this dubious contest were Iraq, with an estimated 38.5 percent of GNP devoted to military activity, Oman, with 27.9 percent, Israel, with 24.4 percent, Saudi Arabia, with 22 percent, North and South Yemen, with 16.9 and 15.1 percent, Syria, with 14.9

Table 7.2   Military expenditure and military power in world regions, 1972–86

Region	Military expenditure per capita (US$)			Military expense as percent of GNP			Percent of states under military control		
	1972	*1978*	*1984*	*1972*	*1978*	*1984*	*1978*	*1983*	*1986*
North America	346	468	935	6.3	4.9	6.1	0.0	0.0	0.0
Latin America	12	22	31	1.9	1.5	1.6	54.2	54.2	37.5
NATO Europe	108	237	280	3.8	3.6	3.8	7.1	7.1	7.1
Warsaw Pact	204	311	631	9.0	8.2	9.6	0.0	14.3	14.3
Other Europe	56	121	181	2.8	2.3	2.4	0.0	0.0	0.0
Middle East	55	250	441	12.2	12.2	17.9	25.0	37.5	37.5
South Asia	4	5	9	4.0	2.8	3.5	50.0	50.0	50.0
Far East	12	30	34	3.3	2.7	2.8	62.5	62.5	56.2
Oceania	98	156	276	3.1	2.4	3.0	0.0	0.0	0.0
Africa	7	22	30	3.0	3.6	3.9	52.3	51.1	64.4
World	58	97	161	5.4	4.5	5.6	38.3	40.1	40.8

Source: Ruth Leger Sivard, *World Military and Social Expenditures*, 1974, 1981, 1983 and 1988 editions

percent, and Iran, with 14.6 percent; only at that point does the list break out of the Middle East to reach Angola, the USSR, Mongolia, Libya, Nicaragua, and Ethiopia. Examining 60 Third World countries in 1960, 1970, and 1980, Su-Hoon Lee found that the strongest predictors of rising military expenditure were, first, involvement in interstate wars and, second, dependence on foreign trade (Lee 1988: 95–111). The finding underscores the vulnerable positions of Middle Eastern states, where oil and warfare cross.

Similarly, armed forces have remained fairly constant in number throughout the rich parts of the world since 1960 even if expenditure per soldier, sailor or airman has skyrocketed, while in poorer countries troops have roughly doubled in number since 1960 (Sivard 1986: 32). In 1960, 0.61 percent of the world's population served in the military; by 1984, the figure had declined slightly to 0.57. In poor countries, however, the proportion had risen from 0.39 to 0.45; the richer countries still have higher proportions of troops under arms, but those proportions are dropping while the poorer countries creep up. Between 1964 and 1984, for example, Guyana's military forces (excluding police) rose from 0.1 to 1.8 percent of the entire population (calculated from Danns 1986: 113–14); similar expansions occurred elsewhere as former colonies moved from the rudimentary forces of order left by the departing imperial powers to their own full-fledged armies, militias, and navies. In the 1980s, the Middle East led the world in proportion of military to civilian population, followed by the Warsaw Pact countries and North America. The individual champions included Vietnam (2.1 percent), Iran (2.4), Syria (2.7), Iraq (3.5), and Israel (4.3); 4.3 percent meant one person in twenty-three, including women, men, and children. Such a level approached the intense militarization of Sweden in the early seventeenth century.

The world pattern of arms flows, moreover, has shifted significantly over the last quarter-century. The sheer volume of exports has expanded rapidly, multiplying from about $2.5 billion in 1960 to $37.3 billion in 1983 (Sivard 1986: 32). Spurred by great power military aid, arms are flowing increasingly to the Third World. From a system in which major shipments of arms went chiefly from one part of the Western world to another has evolved a system in which rich countries export to poor countries. In 1965, the poorer parts of the world were receiving about 55 percent of all international arms shipments; by 1983, the proportion was 77 percent. (True, Brazil and Israel were then beginning to compete actively in the world arms market, and Argentina was beginning to build a serious arms industry of its own, but none of them had yet challenged the arms-sale dominance of the United States, the Soviet Union, France, or Britain.) At that point, Middle Eastern countries were importing some $106 worth of arms per capita each year, as compared with $19 in Oceania, and $11 in NATO Europe. In fact, Middle Eastern states, many of which could pay with oil, were receiving about half of all arms shipped to the Third World.

Yet the Middle East was not alone in buying war. Richard Tanter sums up for the rest of Asia:

There is no other part of the earth which has experienced greater suffering from organized violence: of the 10.7 million people throughout the world who died from war-related causes between 1960 and 1982, almost half were Asian. Even after the end of the second Indochina war in 1975, armaments are still flowing into the region, and at levels as high as, or usually higher than before. Moreover, military governments in Asia have become the norm rather than the exception, and they have achieved a greater penetration of the social fabric than in earlier times. The weapon systems imported into the region from the industrialized producers and the increasing number of domestically produced sophisticated weapons are of ever greater destructive capability.

(Tanter 1984: 161)

Between 1972 and 1981, among all Asian states outside the Middle East, only Burma's military expenditure, in constant dollars, declined; military spending increased by at least half, in constant dollars, in the two Koreas, Taiwan, Indonesia, Malaysia, the Philippines, Thailand, Afghanistan, Sri Lanka and Bangladesh. In Asia and elsewhere, the scale of military activity is increasing along almost every dimension.

SOLDIERS IN POWER

With growing military establishments, is the process of civilianization that European experience might lead us to expect continuing? We have some indications that it is not. Suppose we call "military control" the presence of any of these: key political leadership by military officers, existence of martial law, extrajudicial authority exercised by security forces, lack of central political control over the armed forces, or occupation by foreign military forces (Sivard 1986: 24; for a more sophisticated set of criteria, but also one that is harder to apply empirically, see Stepan 1988, 93–127). The absence of all of these elements constitutes civilian control of the state; civilianization occurs when any of these happens:

decline in political leadership by military officers;

end of martial law;

curbing of security forces' extrajudicial authority;

increase of centralized control over armed forces;

end of occupation by foreign military forces.

In the Middle East, Iran, Iraq, Jordan, Lebanon, Syria and the Arab Republic of Yemen meet the test of military control; in Latin America, Chile, Colombia, El Salvador, Guatemala, Haiti, Honduras, Nicaragua, Panama, Paraguay; in Europe, Turkey and perhaps Poland alone. As the lists show, the criteria include a number of states that do not have military government in the strict sense of the term, and rest on debatable judgments about the power and autonomy of the armed forces. In Guatemala, for example, an elected civilian government has nominally ruled since 1985. At the Indian center of Nebaj, however, a religious worker told Stephen Kinzer: "There is a mayor here, there are councilors, and there is a legal apparatus. But there is never any doubt that the army has precedence. No one who is elected here has authority over anyone in uniform. Elections have no impact here" (Kinzer 1989: 34). Most of the Latin American instances fall into this gray zone: formal democracy, military power. If we tightened the standards, however, the trends and regional distributions of military states would not change substantially.

The term "military control," to be sure, applies to many different kinds of regimes. Thomas Callaghy denies that Zaïre, despite being led by General Mobutu, lives under military rule. He claims that differences between military and civilian heads of state matter little as compared to the common properties of the "authoritarian, organic-statist administrative state drawing heavily on a centralist and corporatist colonial tradition that is held together, often loosely and in an unstable fashion, by strong personalistic rulership" that is becoming a major African type (Callaghy 1984: 45). Yet he concedes that military men have exceptional opportunities to seize power in Africa. "These distinctly early modern, weakly institutionalized military forces," he reports, "are, however, *relatively* powerful in the African context of early modern states and societies" (Callaghy 1984: 44). Thus in Africa as elsewhere in the Third World military expansion seems to promote rather than deter military rule. The process is not proceeding as it did in Europe.

By the standards I laid down earlier, about 40 percent of the world's states lived under military control in the 1980s, and the proportion was slowly rising. Variations from region to region were dramatic: in Latin America about 38 percent of all governments are military, and this proportion declining (after a rapid rise in the 1960s and early 1970s); 38 percent in the Middle East, up from 25 percent in the 1970s; a stable 50 percent in South Asia, a mildly fluctuating 60 percent in the Far East, 64 percent and rising in Africa. Military control, of one variety or another, had become the standard form of government in much of the Third World, notably in South Asia, East Asia, and Africa. The proportion of states under military control in a region correlated with the recency of decolonization in that region. Many recent states had known little but military rule since they gained, or regained, their sovereignty. As of 1990 Ghanaians had lived under military control for 18 of their 30 years of independence, and had experienced four major coups in the process.

Not all military states, however, are new states. Most Latin American states, including those governed by soldiers, have existed as formally independent units since the early nineteenth century; in fact, they antedate the majority of European states. Again, old Thailand provides a textbook case of military rule.

Siam, as it then was called, stood out in the 1930s for its military government. The military overthrew the monarchy in 1932, and have run the state most of the time since then. Of the 50 years from 1932 to 1982, military officers served as prime ministers for 41; during that time Siam/Thailand went through nine successful coups and seven more abortive ones; the coups and coup attempts concentrate disproportionately in the period since 1945 (Chinwanno 1985: 114–15). With generous assistance from the United States, the Thai military have built up their strength in the name of anti-communism. Between 1972 and 1982 the armed forces increased from about 30,000 to about 233,000 – a sevenfold expansion – not including an estimated 500,000 reserves and 600,000 paramilitary forces (Chinwanno 1985: 115). The forces run numerous rural development programs and promote the formation of paramilitary groups to combat Communist guerrillas.

Once the Thais were unusual. But by now, many other states have caught up with Thailand. Using criteria similar to Ruth Sivard's, Talukder Maniruzzaman (1987: 221–2) has calculated for 61 Third World states the proportion of all years of independence between 1946 and 1984 during which they had military government. The leaders run as follows:

80–100 percent: China/Taiwan, Thailand, El Salvador, Nicaragua, Algeria, Egypt, Zaïre, Burundi, Syria

60–79 percent: Paraguay, Sudan, Upper Volta, Argentina, Benin, Central African Republic, Togo, Equatorial Guinea, Guatemala, Iraq, People's Republic of Congo, Mali, Burma, Republic of Korea, Brazil, Somalia, Bangladesh, Yemen Arab Republic

40–59 percent: Nigeria, Pakistan, Peru, Ghana, Indonesia, Grenada, Honduras, Madagascar, Bolivia, Panama, Dominican Republic, Libya, Kampuchea, Suriname, Niger

Maniruzzaman has omitted such cases as Haiti, where the Duvalier family not only assumed military titles but also used public and private armies to terrorize the civilian population; he therefore underestimates the prevalence of military control. The average Third World state has spent more than half its years of independence since 1946 in the hands of soldiers.

As military control rose, the frequency of coups d'état rose in the Third World. Figure 7.2 conveys the main messages: an increase from eight or ten attempted military coups, about half of them successful, somewhere in the world during the 1940s to about double the number, and similar success rates, during the 1970s. Unlike civil wars, coups usually occurred without manifest involvement of outside powers. Over the forty years, foreign powers intervened to promote about 7 percent of all coup attempts, and to deter another 4 percent (David 1987: 1–2). The figures mean, of course, that almost 90 percent of the world's coups occurred *without* substantial foreign intervention.

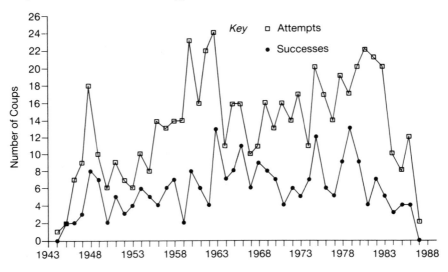

Figure 7.2   Military coups, 1944–87.

Coups multiplied in part because independent states multiplied. Figure 7.3, which compares the numbers of attempted and successful coups to the number of UN members year by year, shows that the per-state frequencies ran higher before the entry of numerous Asian and African states in the 1960s than

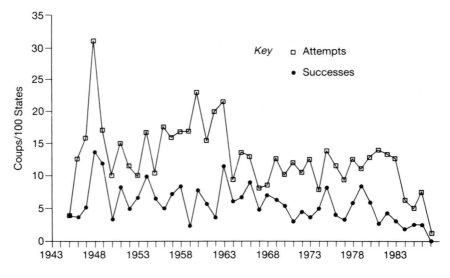

Figure 7.3   Coups per 100 states, 1944–87.

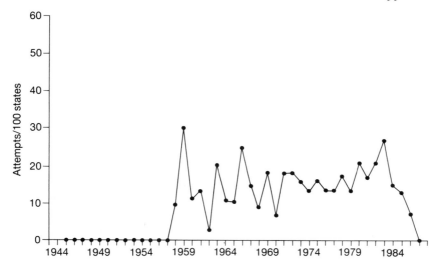

Figure 7.4   Coup attempts per 100 states, Africa 1944–87.

afterward. Figures 7.4 to 7.6 specify what was happening: in Latin America, the Middle East, and Asia, coups swung wildly around an average of one each year for every three states until about 1964, then settled down to one each year per five or ten states after that. In Africa, however, coups rose in frequency from none whatsoever during the period of continued European control to higher

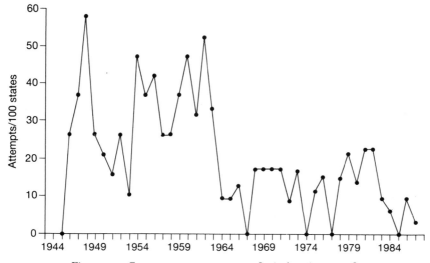

Figure 7.5   Coup attempts per 100 states, Latin America 1944–87.

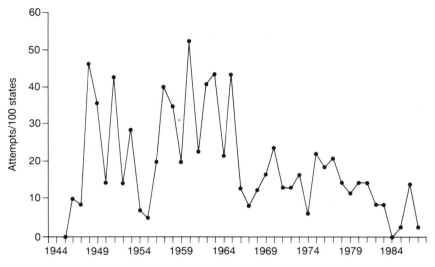

Figure 7.6   Coup attempts per 100 states, Asia and Middle East 1944–87.

frequencies of coups per state than elsewhere in the Third World from 1959 onward. This does not mean, however, that the rising frequency of coups is a statistical mirage. On the contrary: it means that the states entering the United Nations after 1960 were disproportionately vulnerable to military coups.

Unsurprisingly, the geography of coups corresponds to the geography of military rule. From 1980 through 1987, the world's coup attempts occurred in Spain, North Yemen, South Yemen, Egypt, Bahrein, Syria, Lebanon, Libya, Bangladesh, Thailand, Indonesia, the Philippines, North Korea, Bolivia, Suriname, Argentina, Haiti, Guatemala, Panama, Grenada, Sudan, Mauritania, Equatorial Guinea, Liberia, Gambia, Central African Republic, Seychelles, Ghana, Zimbabwe, Chad, Somalia, Kenya, Upper Volta, Tanzania, Togo, Swaziland, Cameroons, Niger, Lesotho, Nigeria, Guinea-Bissau, the Comores, Guinea, and Uganda; military insurgents actually seized power in South Yemen, Bangladesh, the Philippines, Argentina, Suriname, Guatemala, Bolivia, Grenada, Panama, Haiti, Central African Republic, Ghana, Chad, Upper Volta, Nigeria, and Guinea – a disproportionate concentration of coups, and especially of attempts, in Africa.

Whether the apparent fall-off in attempts and successes after 1980 represents a definitive change still remains to be seen. So far the net effect of changes since World War II has been a massive increase in the share of the world's independent states controlled more or less directly by military men. Maniruzzaman's counts show that returns from military to civilian rule were fewer than military coups in every interval from 1946 to 1981, and that they balanced at six each in 1982–4. In Latin America, a shift to civilian control of states seems to be following the decline in the frequency of military coups (itself the result of the installation of relatively stable military regimes) that began in the 1960s. Latin America has gone through three stages since World War II: a period of constant struggles for state power, resulting in a net increase in militarization (1945 to early 1960s); a period of relatively stable military rule (1960s to late 1970s); and a period of partial reduction in military power (since 1980). Given repeated premature announcements of civilianization in Latin America, we can have no confidence that the reversal since 1980 will continue (Rouquié 1987: 2–3). States in Asia, Africa, and the Middle East, in any case, appear to have settled into more stable forms of military rule; so far the decline in coup frequencies does not bespeak liberation from military control.

Third World states have, then, militarized extensively since World War II; with the exception of Latin America, we have no strong signs that the trend is reversing, and a process of civilianization setting in. If so, the world has something to worry about: not only because it means our old ideas about the "maturing" of national states with experience are wrong, not only because of the risk that a war in the Third World will involve nuclear arms or lead to a great power confrontation, but also because military control and state violence against citizens go hand in hand.

Consider official violence against citizens, in the form of torture, brutality, kidnappings, and political killings. In the Third World as a whole, according to Ruth Sivard's ratings, half of all military-controlled states "frequently" employed violence against their citizens, while only a fifth of non-military states did so. The differences are stronger in Latin America, the Middle East, and the Far East than in South Asia and Africa. Similarly, restrictions on the right to vote are significantly more common in military than in non-military Third World states. The relationship, furthermore, looks like cause and effect: when the military gain power, civil and human rights fail. Anyone who values political representation and the protection of citizens against abuses of state power should worry about world-wide militarization.

HOW DID THE MILITARY GAIN POWER?

If, after centuries of civilianization in the European state system, the states that have joined the system recently are moving toward military rule, what might explain the shift? Let us be clear: given the variety of Third World states, no single explanation will account in detail for the rise of military power in each country. For sub-Saharan Africa, Samuel Decalo denies that the strength and coherence of the military has anything to do with their great propensity to bid for national power; on the contrary, he argues, "many African armies [consist of] a coterie of distinct armed camps owing primarily clientelistic allegiance to a handful of mutually competitive officers of different ranks seething with a variety of corporate, ethnic and personal grievances" (Decalo 1976: 14–15), with internal competition driving them to attempt coups, while Maxwell Owusu (1989) inserts Ghana's post-independence coups in a long tradition of populist rebellions against unworthy chiefs. Ruth Collier points out, however, that the African military seized power more often in states where one faction imposed one-party rule on others, or a multi-party system representing numerous ethnicities appeared at independence than where one-party dominance grew up through electoral successes prior to independence (Collier 1982: 95–117). The coexistence of multiple patron–client chains and ethnic fragmentation apparently makes African states vulnerable to military power, but within the limits set by national coalitions and parties.

In any case, such an explanation holds less weight in much of South Asia, Latin America, and the Middle East. Concerning Latin America, according to J. Samuel Fitch:

A growing consensus has emerged regarding the preconditions for military coups. Coups occur when military officers believe a crisis situation exists. Public disorders and public opinion hostile to the government, threats to the military's institutional interests, violations of the constitution by civilian presidents, evident inability of the incumbent administration to manage a serious economic crisis, or a significant "Communist threat" will increase the military's sense of crisis. Personal ambitions and personal ties may influence individual officers, but the decision to stage a military coup is generally an institutional decision, reflecting the collective evaluation of government performance within the upper ranks of the armed forces as a whole.

(Fitch 1986: 27–8)

On a world scale, then, we can only hope to identify conditions that made military power easier or more probable before turning to the particular histories of states and regions for the examination of precise paths to military hegemony. Three main possibilities come to mind.

First, civilian-dominated institutions might be failing with sufficient frequency in the Third World that the military take over by default. Twenty-five years ago, Western political analysts who noticed the increased intervention of armies in Third World civilian politics leaned toward that explanation.

Second, the disproportionate support that outside powers give to Third World military organizations might be lending those organizations extra strength vis-à-vis their competitors within their own states. Radical critics of American military assistance programs often articulate that explanation.

Third, the process of negotiation and containment of the military that occurred widely in the West may not be occurring, because states acquire their military means from great powers outside the state, in return for commodities or political subordination. Or all three could be happening at once.

We lack reliable evidence on which of the three is occurring. A careful analysis of military intervention in politics within 35 African states between 1960 and 1982 indicates that these factors promoted intervention:

domination of the army by a single ethnic group;

high military expenditure combined with frequent sanctions against government opponents;

absence of political pluralism;

low electoral turnout before independence;

low proportion of the population in agriculture;

rapid increase in the population of the capital city;

slow increase in industrial jobs and in GNP;

low proportion of exports to GNP;

decreasingly diversified commodity exports.

(Johnson, Slater and McGowan 1984: 635)

Despite the miscellaneous character that infects many such statistical searches for causes, the list sounds some recurrent themes. More than anything else, it portrays a combination of military autonomy and economic crisis as favorable to military involvement. The authors themselves conclude that "social mobilization" favors military intervention and "political participation" works against it. "It would appear," they remark, "that in states where influentials have internalized the rules of the capitalist world economy and thereby coped relatively well with the very harsh international economic environment of the last 10 years, these states have lessened their peripherality to a degree, strengthened their civilian structures somewhat, and experienced less military interventionism than states whose influentials have not coped as well" (Johnson, Slater and McGowan 1984: 636). Although each of these factors deserves discussion in its own right, none of them sheds much light on the historical process by which states become more or less vulnerable to military takeovers.

Let us be clear. Characteristic schisms within states vary fundamentally from one world region to another, and the actual alliances between ambitious military men and groups within the civilian population vary accordingly. Ethnic cleavages matter a great deal in contemporary African and South Asian states, but much less so within contemporary Latin American states. Religious divisions, within and outside Islam, enter most major conflicts in the Middle East. Where military rule already prevails, furthermore, competition within the armed forces themselves frequently produces bids for state power. Argentina's attempted coup of 15 April 1987 and thereafter represented one segment of the army's resistance to prosecution for human rights violations under the preceding military dictatorship (Bigo et al. 1988: 56–7), Fiji's coup of 14 May 1987 occurred "expressly to protect the special interests of Fiji's indigenous Fijian community" against the electoral power of the islands' Indian near-majority (Kelly 1988: 399), and Burundi's coup of 3 September 1987 pitted one army faction against another (Bigo et al. 1988: 65). At this level, every military regime and every attempted military seizure of state power depends on local social structure and previous history. If we can't explain the courses of particular military regimes without particular histories, however, we can still reasonably ask whether some world-wide changes since 1945 have made military bids for power more feasible and attractive throughout the world, and therefore help explain the world-wide increase in military regimes.

So far we don't know if any of the three hypothetical processes – failure of civilian institutions, external support for the military, minimization of negotiations between state and citizens – is really occurring in the contemporary world. We should be finding out. But contrasts between the recent experiences of Third World states and the conditions that civilized Europe suggest an important speculation about what *might* be happening in Africa, the Middle East, and much of Asia. Here is the speculation: the creation of a bipolar, then incipiently tripolar world system of states since World War II intensified the competition among great powers for the allegiance of Third World states, and the tendency to leave no part of the Third World neutral. That competition induced the great powers, especially the United States and the Soviet Union, to provide arms, military training, and military advice to many states.

In return, the great powers, or major interests within them, received commodities such as oil, political support in the world arena and, sometimes, profits from the sale of arms. In those states, military organizations grew in size, strength, and efficacy while other organizations stood still or withered. The relative viability of military organizations made them attractive to ambitious but impecunious young men, so the military diverted talent from business, education, and civilian public administration. The military thus found it easier and easier to seize control of the state, and civilian rulers found it more and more difficult to check them. One form or another of pretorianism – oligarchical, radical, or mass, to use Samuel Huntington's labels – emerged. Militarization prevailed.

Is the speculation credible? The experience of countries for which we have detailed postwar political histories give it some support. Extreme cases include Taiwan and the two Koreas, where the massive support of foreign powers for the local military produced steely control of the national economies, until the very success of economic expansion began to undermine military hegemony (Amsden 1985, Cumings 1984, 1988, Deyo, Haggard and Koo 1987, Hamilton 1986). In South Korea, for example, Park Chung-Hee, a former officer in the Japanese occupation army, seized power in 1961. Park deliberately set out to establish a Japanese-style "rich country and powerful military" (Launius 1985: 2). He was able to do so for two main reasons: because Korea had lived from 1907 to 1945 as a tightly-controlled Japanese colony, whose Korean officials had easily moved into positions of power within the new regime, and because the American occupying army – which remains in Korea today – backed the plan, and participated in the containment of opposing workers and students.

The revolutionary redistribution of land that occurred when North Korea occupied South Korea during the summer of 1950 had liquidated landlords as another possible source of opposition to military hegemony (Cumings 1989: 12). Although South Korea has gone through several brief periods of nominal democracy under American auspices, the 1961 coup d'état put the military definitely in the saddle. Under military control and American sponsorship, South Korea built a low-wage, export-oriented economy aimed especially at Japanese and American markets. In similar ways, although with less economic success, the Soviet Union long maintained a military presence and supervision in such satellites as the German Democratic Republic, Hungary, and Czechoslovakia.

Except possibly for Panama, Cuba, and Honduras, direct foreign control of the national military, and thus of the state, does not approach East Asian extremes in Latin America. Latin American states have sustained their own strong tradition of military intervention in politics since they wrenched themselves independent of Spain and Portugal almost two centuries ago. Durable political regimes, however, became more prevalent during the 1960s and 1970s. They took two rather different forms: the personalistic, clientelistic rule of a Stroessner in Paraguay or a Somoza in Nicaragua, and the "institutional" control by the military that prevailed in post-Péron Argentina and post-Vargas Brazil.

For some time before the 1960s the United States had held many Caribbean and Central American states in "military tutelage," feeling free to send the US Marines to maintain or restore regimes it preferred (Rouquié 1987: 117–28). Up to that point, however, neither American capital nor American military aid extended very deeply into the rest of Latin America. The very frequent South American coups d'état attracted little direct US intervention. With the Cuban revolution and incipient Soviet–Cuban cooperation, the Kennedy administration began to redefine its Latin American policy; beginning in 1962, American military aid

became more intensive and better institutionalized than before. American military planning became more structured and the relations between the Latin American armies and that of the metropole grew closer. The U.S. Army had military missions of varying importance in nineteen countries of the subcontinent and their presence was often an integral part of the agreements for the sale or loan of military equipment.

(Rouquié 1987: 132)

American military aid to Latin America rose from about $40 million per year in 1953–63 to about $125 million per year in 1964–7 (Rouquié 1987: 131). That presence helped reduce the frequency of military seizures of power in Latin America by reinforcing those military regimes that already held power. Not until the end of the 1970s, when the United States began to withdraw its support for resident militaries, did a minor trend toward civilianization set in.

Brazil is an obvious case in point. Although the military had hovered over civilian politics from the army's overthrow of the Brazilian Empire in 1889, it did not seize direct, durable control over the state until the "April Revolution" of 1964. But then military-dominated regimes opened Brazil to American capital, American military aid, and Brazilian-American cooperation in the Cold War. Military control continued to 1985. In 1982 regional elections, opposition leaders took key provincial governorships, and in 1984 a moderate opponent of military power, Tancredo Neves, won the Brazilian presidency. Demilitarization began, but with significant compensating gains for the military: an expanding domestic arms industry, and an increase in the national military budget. The United States did not intervene directly in Brazilian civilianization, but its increased concern for human rights and its decreased readiness to prop up declining militaries surely helped set the stage.

Neighboring Suriname arrived at military rule within five years of its independence from the Netherlands, but its soldiers declared themselves socialists (Sedoc-Dahlberg 1986). From independence in 1975 to the military coup of 1980, Suriname's three major political parties represented its dominant ethnic groups: Hindustani, Creole, and Javanese. But when a force of 600 troops led by sergeants seized control of the state after a series of labor disputes within the army, the new government began receiving substantial aid from Cuba, and aligning its politics with Cuba's. At the same time the military expanded their numbers, organizing a People's Militia of some 3,000 troops for internal control, and maintaining about 1.4 percent of the entire population under arms, more than three times the world average for low-income states. Brazilian leaders, alarmed by the presence of a leftist state on their flank, began an arrangement in 1983 by which "Suriname would sell rice and alumina to Brazil in exchange for arms shipments sufficient to allow Suriname's army to double in size," (Sedoc-Dahlberg 1986: 97), and Suriname would also moderate its social policies. The combination of aid from Cuba and Brazil served to increase the military's room for maneuver within Suriname, allowing them to rule without a broad social base.

Libya followed yet another path to military rule (Anderson 1986: 251–69). Italian imperialism made a single territory of hostile and distinctly different Tripolitania and Cyrenaica. Sanusi leader Idris, who became king at independence in 1951, drew support chiefly from Cyrenaica; his cooperation in the Allied effort to oust Italy from North Africa gave him a decisive political advantage over his Tripolitanian rivals. No well-defined national state emerged in independent Libya. Instead, overlapping extended families governed through patronage. Oil revenues enriched them, allowed the construction of a measure of infrastructure, and permitted the king and his satraps to rule without building a substantial central bureaucracy. The small Royal Libyan Army formed from units that had fought with the British in World War II, but were overshadowed by provincial security forces drawn from tribal populations and by the presence of American and British military bases. Despite the Anglo-American presence, captain Mu'ammar al-Qadhdhafi led a successful coup d'état in 1969. Indeed, control over oil revenues made it possible for Qadhdhafi to expel the British and Americans, root out most of the old rulers, Islamize and Arabize the state, undertake a program of assistance to nascent revolutionary regimes elsewhere, and yet to continue his predecessor's avoidance of bulky central structure. The transformed state gingerly began a courtship with the Soviet Union and a campaign of opposition to American power. A kind of nationalism, then, bolstered a fragile state and justified military rule.

In South Korea, an American occupation directly shaped the postwar state. In Brazil, changing American orientations toward Latin American militaries conditioned political shifts but by no means governed the history of military power. Libya moved to a military regime despite an American military presence. Conditions and consequences of military power obviously vary significantly from one part of the Third World to another. Great power competition and intervention play no more than supporting parts in any particular coup and in the maintenance of any particular military regime. But alterations in relations of Third World states to great powers and to each other seem to have contributed importantly to changes in the overall rhythms of military control in the world as a whole. To that extent, the state system as such has made a difference.

If great power confrontation and intervention in national militaries has the influence this analysis gives it, one path toward civilianization seems clear. It has two branches: either a reduction in the great power competition to build up the military strength of the Third World states or an insulation of the target states from that competition. It involves the promotion of bargaining between the state's civilian institutions and the bulk of its citizens. The creation of regular systems of taxation, equitably administered and responsive to the citizenry, would probably speed the process. So would the opening of viable career alternatives to military service. It is possible, as Alfred Stepan (1988: 84–5) argues, that Brazil's mounting of a major arms export industry will have the paradoxical effect of reducing the autonomy of its generals, and thus speeding a kind of democracy through the accretion of civilian bureaucracies, vested interests, and bargains with the civilian population; more generally (and, one might hope, less belligerently), the growth of government involvement in expanding production of goods and services is likely to promote civilianization. Not by any means a recapitulation of the European experience; these days, presumably, we can escape some of the cruelty of that experience. But yet a set of opportunities that a sober reflection on European state formation makes a bit less obscure.

ENVOI

To be sure, my treatment of these themes has peculiar overtones. It returns, despite all my earlier protestations, to a form of intellectual colonialism, to the presumption that if European states worked their ways to civilianization of public life, so could and should today's Third World states – if only they or their patrons would let the European process unfold. It neglects the geopolitical variation among regions that makes such a difference to military–civil relations: the constant threat of direct American military intervention in Central America or the Caribbean, the centrality of oil to many Middle Eastern economies, the wide reach of South Africa within the states to its north, the industrial expansion of Japan, South Korea, and Taiwan as a factor in the politics of their neighbors. It forgets ethnic fragmentation and strife as promoters of military power. My attempt to place contemporary militarization in historical perspective runs the risk of shining so bright a beam that it actually obscures its subject's subtleties, wipes out its actual pattern of light and shade. My defense is simple: we need to be aware that the rise of military power in Third World states is not simply a natural phase of state formation, one that previous experience tells us will pass gradually as states mature.

In any case, contemporary militarization is not the only important subject on which the study of European state formation sheds light. The process deserves attention for its own sake, simply because the formation of a European system of national states profoundly affected the lives of all Westerners, and of most non-Westerners as well. This book has, I hope, shown the great contingency of European state formation, indeed of the national state's ultimate triumph over other forms of political organization. Only the great sixteenth-century expansion in the scale and expense of international wars (which was, to be sure, an outcome of rivalries among European states as well as their interaction with Turks and Chinese) gave national states a definitive advantage over the empires, city-states, and federations that prevailed in Europe up to that time.

Nor did Europeans follow a single path to the national state. As a function of the relative predominance of concentrated capital and concentrated coercion in different parts of the continent, three partly distinct patterns of transformation – coercion-intensive, capital-intensive, and capitalized-coercion – marked out deeply different experiences for rulers, landlords, capitalists, workers, and peasants alike. Along the way, most states that once existed disappeared, and the rest underwent fundamental changes in form and action. In regions and periods where capitalists held the upper hand, states commonly fragmented, resisted centralization, and gave a large scope to formal institutions representing their dominant classes. Before the eighteenth- and nineteenth-century growth of huge citizen armies, such states mobilized easily for warfare (especially naval warfare), yet created relatively little durable state structure as they did so.

Landlord-dominated regions, in contrast, more often produced bulky, centralized states as the sheer effort of squeezing the means of war from uncommercialized economies created extensive administrations and far-reaching compacts between rulers and their landed allies. At the extreme, as in the case of Poland over four or five centuries, the weight of landlords swamped royal power and promoted immobility or collapse.

In between the capital-intensive and coercion-intensive paths of state formation, a more even balance of capital and coercion guaranteed class struggle, but in a few cases such as France and Great Britain opened the way to formation of a national state having the capacity to create and sustain massive armed force. Those few survivors set the standard of war for all other states, playing disproportionate parts in the imposition of the European state system, and the European variety of national state, on the rest of the world. Since World War II, the once-European system of national states has claimed control over the entire earth. Because the system originated in Europe, the close examination of European history helps us understand the origins, character, and limits of the contemporary world system.

All the more reason to scrutinize changes that are rushing European states into a new era as I write in the spring of 1992. The inconceivable has happened. Since 1988, the Soviet Union has first withdrawn its military from its deep, if indirect, confrontation with the United States in Afghanistan, then splintered into its component republics, some of which have begun to splinter in their turn. Russia and Ukraine (now separate states within a shaky federation) have made warlike noises at each other over possession of nuclear weapons, the Crimea, and the Black Sea fleet. Yugoslavia has split into Serbia and a semi-circle of fleeing non-Serbian republics. The German Democratic Republic has dissolved into its larger, richer, German neighbor and erstwhile enemy. Other east and central European states have repudiated their socialist regimes after varying degrees of struggle, and fissures have opened up between Czech and Slovak segments of recently desocialized Czechoslovakia. The prospects for military rule have risen in a number of states within the former Soviet zone of influence.

That is not all. With the dying Soviet Union's blessing, the United States has led a number of European states into a devastating attack on Iraq in response to Iraq's invasion of Kuwait. Meanwhile, the European Community has moved several steps closer to economic unification, as adjacent states – including a number of recently socialist states – have begun to compete eagerly for some form of inclusion in the EC. In scope, rapidity, and interdependence, these shifts resemble the momentous alterations in the European state system that have typically stemmed from the settlements of previous general wars, as in 1815–18, 1918–21, or 1945–8. It is as if the Cold War was more than a metaphor.

How, if at all, do these changes connect? No doubt the central nexus joins three structures: the American state, the Soviet state, and the European Community. On grossly unequal economic bases, Americans and Soviets had for forty years organized their foreign policies around military and political competition with each other. The two sides' interventions in Afghanistan (the Americans' through support of guerrilla oppositions to the Soviet-backed regime, the Soviets' through financial aid and direct military involvement) had demonstrated the American capacity to block a Soviet victory, if not to install a pro-American regime, while draining Soviet finances, manpower, morale, and military prestige.

Coming to power in 1985, Mikhail Gorbachev not only started to organize withdrawal from Afghanistan. He extended the Soviet Union's demilitarization, furthermore, to general policies of ceasing forceful repression against dissident movements within the Warsaw Pact zone as well as of shifting the Soviet economy from military toward civilian production. Although the policies deeply threatened the Soviet Union's military, intelligence, and party establishments, they made access to the European Community both thinkable and attractive to most segments of the former Soviet bloc. At the same time, they rapidly and visibly weakened the authority of Soviet collaborators in Poland, Czechoslovakia, Estonia, Latvia, Lithuania, and other regions along the USSR's western frontier. When Gorbachev refrained from military intervention against challengers to its satellite regimes in that zone, oppositions mobilized quickly.

Demands for autonomy or independence multiplied in other states and subdivisions of states the first departures would otherwise leave behind. Leaders of both constituent republics and connected ethnic groups within the USSR appealed effectively to outside states, citing the magic principle of national self-determination. Thus Estonia, Lithuania, and Latvia escaped quickly from the still-extant Soviet Union. Later Slovenia, Croatia, and Bosnia-Herzegovina gained similar support for their exits from Yugoslavia.

Within his own shaken country, Gorbachev faced opposition not only from the military, intelligence, and party establishments he was undermining, but also from two other crucial clusters. The first contained competing groups of nationalists and pseudonationalists in the USSR's various administrative subdivisions – Georgia, Ossetia, Moldavia, Nagorno-Karabakh, even Leningrad. The second included a loose network of economic and political reformers who eventually grouped around Boris Yeltsin, the former Moscow party boss. The proliferation of opinion surveys and the holding of contested elections for a newly-created Congress of People's Deputies gave the reformers comfort and connection. In August 1991 an attempted coup by members of the old establishments lost to military defections and concerted opposition by reformers including Yeltsin; in the wake of that coup, however, Gorbachev left office, Yeltsin became effective national leader as chief of the Russian federation, the USSR broke into nominally confederated republics, and the

Baltic states departed definitively. Not only was the Cold War over, one of its superpowers had crumbled into dust.

In the longer run, if this chapter's reasoning runs true, the decline of Cold War hostilities should reduce the pressure to align non-European countries with a great power bloc, to arm them in exchange for commodities and political loyalty, to establish or maintain military regimes, and to intervene in civil wars throughout the world. It should also accelerate the dissolution of the state system Europeans created during the ages of patrimonialism, brokerage, and nationalization, then imposed on almost the entire world during the 19th and 20th centuries. If so, the world has an unparalleled opportunity for peaceful reconstruction.

How long will the system last? We see some signs that the era of formally autonomous states is passing: the stalemate of the United Nations, the displacement of rapidly shifting alliances by durable military–economic blocs, the formation of market-linked ensembles such as the EEC and EFTA, the internationalization of capital, the rise of corporations whose capital is everywhere and nowhere, demands for autonomy and nationality within existing states that could eventually reduce them to crumbs of the former cake, the shift toward internal concerns by the United States and the Soviet Union, the activation of nationalities within the former USSR, the achievement of substantial world power by an essentially demilitarized state – Japan – the promise or threat that China will extend its enormous organizational, demographic, and ideological power into the rest of the world. The state system Europeans fashioned has not always existed. It will not endure forever.

Its obituary will be hard to write. On one side, we see the pacification of European civil life and the fashioning of more or less representative political institutions, both by-products of a state formation driven by the pursuit of military might. On the other side, we notice the rising destructiveness of war, the pervasive intervention of states in individual lives, the creation of incomparable instruments of class control. Destroy the state, and create Lebanon. Fortify it, and create Korea. Until other forms displace the national state, neither alternative will do. The only real answer is to turn the immense power of national states away from war and toward the creation of justice, personal security, and democracy. My inquiry has not shown how to accomplish that gigantic task. It has, however, shown why the task is urgent.

References

Abel, Wilhelm, 1966 *Agrarkrisen und Agrarkonjunktur. Eine Geschichte der Land- und Ernährungswirtschaft Mitteleuropas seit dem hohen Mittelalter*. Hamburg and Berlin: Paul Parey.
—— 1974 *Massenarmut und Hungerkrisen im vorindustriellen Europa*. Hamburg and Berlin: Paul Parey.
Aberg, Alf, 1973 "The Swedish Army, from Lutzen to Narva" in Michael Roberts, ed., *Sweden's Age of Greatness, 1632–1718*. New York: St Martin's.
Abu-Lughod, Janet, 1987 "Did the West Rise or Did the East Fall? Some Reflections from the Thirteenth Century World System," Working Paper 50, Center for Studies of Social Change, New School for Social Research.
—— 1989 *Before European Hegemony*. New York: Oxford University Press.
Adelman, Jonathan R., 1985 *Revolution, Armies, and War: A Political History*. Boulder, Colorado: Lynne Rienner.
Adelmann, Gerhard, 1979 "Die ländlichen Textilgewerbe des Rheinlandes vor der Industrialisierung," *Rheinische Vierteljahrsblätter* 43: 260–88.
Ågren, Kurt et al., 1973 *Aristocrats, Farmers, Proletarians. Essays in Swedish Demographic History*. Uppsala: Almqvist and Wiksell. Studia Historica Upsaliensia, 47.
Aguero, Felipe, 1984 "Social Effects: Military Autonomy in Developing Countries," *Alternatives* 10: 75–92.
Alapuro, Risto, 1976 "Regional Variation in Political Mobilization. On the Incorporation of the Agrarian Population into the State of Finland, 1907–1932," *Scandinavian Journal of History* 1: 215–42.
—— 1985 "Interstate Relationships and Political Mobilization in the Nordic Countries: A Perspective," in Risto Alapuro et al., eds, *Small States in Comparative Perspective. Essays for Erik Allardt*. Oslo: Norwegian University Press.
—— 1988 *State and Revolution in Finland*. Berkeley, California: University of California Press.
Alestalo, Matti and Stein Kuhnle, 1984 "The Scandinavian Route. Economic,

Social and Political Developments in Denmark, Finland, Norway, and Sweden," Research Report no. 31, Research Group for Comparative Sociology, University of Helsinki.

Ames, Edward and Richard T. Rapp, 1977 "The Birth and Death of Taxes: A Hypothesis," *Journal of Economic History* 37: 161–78.

Amsden, Alice H., 1985 "The State and Taiwan's Economic Development," in Peter Evans, Dietrich Rueschemeyer and Theda Skocpol, eds, *Bringing the State Back In.* Cambridge: Cambridge University Press.

Anderson, Lisa, 1986 *The State and Social Transformation in Tunisia and Libya, 1830–1980.* Princeton, New Jersey: Princeton University Press.

Anderson, M. S., 1988 *War and Society in Europe of the Old Regime 1618–1789.* London: Fontana.

Anderson, Perry, 1974 *Lineages of the Absolutist State.* London: NLB.

Andrén, Anders, 1989 "States and Towns in the Middle Ages: The Scandinavian Experience," forthcoming in *Theory and Society.*

Andrews, Kenneth R., 1984 *Trade, Plunder and Settlement. Maritime Enterprise and the Genesis of the British Empire, 1480–1630.* Cambridge: Cambridge University Press.

Antoine, Michel, 1970 *Le Conseil du Roi sous le règne de Louis XV.* Geneva: Droz.

Apter, David and Nagayo Sawa, 1984 *Against the State. Politics and Social Protest in Japan.* Cambridge: Harvard University Press.

Ardant, Gabriel, 1965 *Théorie sociologique de l'impôt.* Paris: SEVPEN. 2 vols.

—— 1975 "Financial Policy and Economic Infrastructure of Modern States and Nations," in Charles Tilly, ed., *The Formation of National States in Western Europe.* Princeton, New Jersey: Princeton University Press.

Arrighi, Giovanni, 1985 ed., *Semiperipheral Development. The Politics of Southern Europe in the Twentieth Century.* Beverly Hills, California: Sage.

Artéus, Gunnar, 1982 *Krigsmakt och Samhälle i Frihetstidens Sverige.* Stockholm: Militärhistoriska Förlaget.

—— 1986 *Till Militärstatens Förhistoria. Krig, professionalisering och social förändring under Vasasönernas regering.* Stockholm: Probus.

Attman, Artur, 1986 *American Bullion in the European World Trade, 1600–1800.* Göteberg: Kungl. Vetenskaps- och Vitterhets-Samhället.

Aubert, Jacques and Raphaël Petit, 1981 *La police en France. Service public.* Paris: Berger-Levrault.

—— et al., 1979 *L'Etat et la police en France (1789–1914).* Geneva: Droz.

Aydelot, Philippe, Louis Bergeron and Marcel Roncayolo, 1981 *Industrialisation et croissance urbaine dans la France du XIXe siècle.* Paris: Centre de Recherches Historiques, Ecole des Hautes Etudes en Sciences Sociales.

Ayoob, Mohammed, 1989 "The Third World in the System of States: Acute Schizophrenia or Growing Pains?" *International Studies Quarterly* 33: 67–79.

Bade, Klaus J., 1982 "Transnationale Migration und Arbeitsmarkt im Kaiserreich. Vom Agrarstaat mit stärker Industrie zum Industriestaat mit stärker agrarischen Basis," in Toni Pierenkemper and Richard Tilly, eds, *Historisch Arbeitsmarktforschung.*

Entstehung, Entwicklung und Probleme der Vermarktung von Arbeitskraft. Göttingen: Vandenhoeck and Ruprecht.

Badie, Bertrand, 1980 *Le développement politique.* Paris: Economica. 2nd edn.

—— and Pierre Birnbaum, 1979 *Sociologie de l'Etat.* Paris: Grasset.

Bai, Shouyi, 1988 ed., *Précis d'histoire de Chine.* Beijing: Foreign Language Publishing House.

Bairoch, Paul, 1977 *Taille des villes, conditions de vie et développement économique.* Paris: Editions de l'Ecole des Hautes Etudes en Sciences Sociales.

—— 1985 *De Jéricho à Mexico. Villes et économie dans l'histoire.* Paris: Gallimard.

Baker, Brenda J. and George G. Armelagos, 1988 "The Origin and Antiquity of Syphilis," *Current Anthropology* 29: 703–37.

Ballbé, Manuel, 1983 *Ordén público y militarismo en la España constitucional (1812–1983).* Madrid: Alianza Editorial.

Barfield, Thomas J., 1989 *The Perilous Frontier. Nomadic Empires and China.* Oxford: Basil Blackwell.

Barnett, Corelli, 1974 *Britain and Her Army, 1509–1970. A Military, Political and Social Survey.* Harmondsworth: Penguin. First published in 1970.

Batchelder, Ronald W. and Herman Freudenberger, 1983 "On the Rational Origins of the Modern Centralized State," *Explorations in Economic History* 20: 1–13.

Bates, Robert H., 1988 "Lessons from History, or the Perfidy of English Exceptionalism and the Significance of Historical France," *World Politics* 40: 499–516.

Baxter, Douglas Clark, 1976 *Servants of the Sword: Intendants of the Army, 1630–70.* Urbana, Illinois: University of Illinois Press.

Baynham, Simon, 1986 ed., *Military Power and Politics in Black Africa.* New York: St Martins.

Bean, Richard, 1973 "War and the Birth of the Nation State," *Journal of Economic History* 33: 203–21.

Becker, Marvin B., 1966 "Economic Change and the Emerging Florentine Territorial State," *Studies in the Renaissance* 13: 7–39.

—— 1988 *Civility and Society in Western Europe, 1300–1600.* Bloomington, Indiana: Indiana University Press.

Beer, Francis A., 1974 *How Much War in History: Definitions, Estimates, Extrapolations and Trends.* Beverly Hills, California: Sage Publications. Sage Professional Papers, International Studies Series, 02–030.

Beer, Samuel H., 1974 *Modern Political Development.* New York: Random House.

Beik, William H., 1985 *Absolutism and Society in Seventeenth-Century France.* Cambridge: Cambridge University Press.

Bendix, Reinhard, 1977 *Nation-Building and Citizenship: Studies of Our Changing Social Order.* Berkeley, California: University of California Press. Revised edn.

Berend, Iván, 1988 "The Place of Hungary in Europe: On the Identity Concept of the Intelligentsia between the Two World Wars," paper presented to the Conference on Models of Development and Theories of Modernization in Eastern Europe Between the World Wars, Ráckeve, Hungary.

—— 1982 *The European Periphery and Industrialization 1780–1914*. Budapest: Akademiai Kiado.

—— and György Ránki, 1977 *East Central Europe in the 19th and 20th Centuries*. Budapest: Akademiai Kiado.

Berg, Maxine, Pat Hudson and Michael Sonenscher, 1983 eds, *Manufacturer in Town and Country before the Factory*. Cambridge: Cambridge University Press.

Best, Geoffrey, 1982 *War and Society in Revolutionary Europe, 1770–1870*. London: Fontana.

Bethell, Leslie and Ian Roxborough, 1988 "Latin America between the Second World War and the Cold War: Some Reflections on the 1945–8 Conjuncture," *Journal of Latin American Studies* 20: 167–89.

Bigo, Didier, 1988 *Pouvoir et obéissance en Centrafrique*. Paris: Karthala.

—— Gaëtan de Capele, Daniel Hermant and Nicolas Regaud, 1988 "Les conflits intermittents: Les coups d'état, les litiges frontaliers," *Etudes Polémologiques* 46: 53–75.

Binney, J. E. D., 1958 *British Public Finance and Administration 1774–92*. Oxford: Clarendon Press.

Birnbaum, Pierre, 1988 *States and Collective Action: The European Experience*. Cambridge: Cambridge University Press.

Bisson, Thomas N., 1966 "The Military Origins of Medieval Representation," *American Historical Review*. 71: 1199–218.

Black, Cyril, 1966 *The Dynamics of Modernization*. New York: Harper and Row.

Black, Jeremy, 1987 ed., *The Origins of War in Early Modern Europe*. Edinburgh: John Donald.

Blechman, Barry and Stephen S. Kaplan, 1978 *Force without War. U.S. Armed Forces as a Political Instrument*. Washington DC: Brookings Institution.

Blickle, Peter, 1988 Unruhen in der ständischen Gesellschaft, 1300–1800. Munich: Oldenbourg. *Enzyklopädie Deutscher Geschichte*, vol. I.

Blockmans, Wim P., 1978 "A Typology of Representative Institutions in Late Medieval Europe," *Journal of Medieval History* 4: 189–215.

—— 1988a "Alternatives to Monarchical Centralisation: The Great Tradition of Revolt in Flanders and Brabant," in Helmut Koenigsberger, ed., *Republiken und Republikanismus im Europa der Frühen Neuzeit*. Munich: Oldenbourg.

—— 1988b "La répression de révoltes urbaines comme méthode de centralisation dans les Pays-Bas bourguignons," in *Rencontres de Milan (1er au 3 octobre 1987): Milan et les États bourguignons: deux ensembles politiques princiers entre Moyen Age et Renaissance (XIVe–XVIe s.)*. Louvain: Centre Européen d'Études Bourguignonnes (XIVe–XVIe s.).

—— 1988c "Patronage, Brokerage and Corruption as Symptoms of Incipient State Formation in the Burgundian-Habsburg Netherlands," in Antoni Maczak, ed., *Klientelsysteme im Europa der Frühen Neuzeit*. Munich: Oldenbourg.

—— 1988d "Princes conquérants et bourgeois calculateurs. Le poids des réseaux urbains dans la formation des états," in Neithard Bulst and Jean-Philippe Genet, eds, *La ville, la bourgeoisie et la genèse de l'état moderne*. Paris: Editions du Centre National de la Recherche Scientifique.

232   *References*

Blok, Anton, 1974 *The Mafia of a Sicilian Village, 1860–1960. A Study of Violent Peasant Entrepreneurs.* New York: Harper and Row.

Blom, Grethe Authén, 1977 ed., *Urbaniseringsprosessen i norden.* Oslo: Universitetsforlaget. 3 vols.

Blum, Jerome, 1964 *Lord and Peasant in Russia from the Ninth to the Nineteenth Century.* New York: Atheneum.

——— 1978 *The End of the Old Order in Rural Europe.* Princeton, New Jersey: Princeton University Press.

Boelcke, Willi A., 1967 "Wandlungen der dorflichen Sozialstruktur Während Mittelalter und Neuzeit," in Heinz Haushofer and Willi A. Boelcke, eds, *Wege und Forschungen der Agrargeschichte.* Frankfurt a/Main: DLG Verlag.

Böhme, Klaus-Richard, 1983 "Schwedische Finanzbürokratie und Kriegsführung 1611 bis 1721," in Goran Rystad, ed., *Europe and Scandinavia: Aspects of the Process of Integration in the 17th Century.* Lund: Esselte Studium.

Bohstedt, John, 1983 *Riots and Community Politics in England and Wales, 1790–1810.* Cambridge: Harvard University Press.

Bois, Paul, 1981 "Aperçu sur les causes des insurrections de l'Ouest à l'époque révolutionnaire," in J.-C. Martin, ed., *Vendée-Chouannerie.* Nantes: Reflets du Passé.

Boli-Bennett, John, 1979 "The Ideology of Expanding State Authority in National Constitutions, 1870–1970," in John W. Meyer and Michael T. Hannan, ed., *National Development and the World System. Educational, Economic, and Political Change, 1950–1970.* Chicago: University of Chicago Press.

——— 1980 "Global Integration and the Universal Increase of State Dominance, 1910–1970," in Albert Bergesen, ed., *Studies of the Modern World System.* New York: Academic Press.

Bond, Brian, 1983 *War and Society in Europe, 1870–1970.* Leicester: Leicester University Press.

Bosher, J. F., 1970 *French Finances, 1770–1795. From Business to Bureaucracy.* Cambridge: Cambridge University Press.

Bossenga, Gail, 1988a "City and State: An Urban Perspective on the Origins of the French Revolution," in Keith Michael Baker, ed., *The French Revolution and the Creation of Modern Political Culture. 1. The Political Culture of the Old Regime.* Oxford: Pergamon.

——— 1988b "La Révolution française et les corporations: Trois exemples lillois," *Annales; Economies, Sociétés, Civilisations* 43: 405–26.

Boswell, Terry, 1989 "Colonial Empires and the Capitalist World-Economy: A Time Series Analysis of Colonization, 1640–1960," *American Sociological Review* 54: 180–96.

Boxer, C. R., 1965 *The Dutch Seaborne Empire: 1600–1800.* New York: Knopf.

——— 1969 *The Portuguese Seaborne Empire: 1415–1825.* New York: Knopf.

Boyd, Andrew, 1987 *An Atlas of World Affairs.* London: Methuen. 8th edn.

Brady, Jr, Thomas A., 1985 *Turning Swiss. Cities and Empire, 1450–1550.* Cambridge: Cambridge University Press.

Braudel, Fernand, 1979 *Civilisation matérielle, économie, et capitalisme, XVe–XVIIIe siècles*. Paris: Armand Colin. 3 vols.

Braun, Rudolf, 1960 *Industrialisierung und Volksleben*. Zurich: Rentsch.

—— 1975 "Taxation, Sociopolitical Structure, and State-Building: Great Britain and Brandenburg-Prussia," in Charles Tilly, ed., *The Formation of National States in Western Europe*. Princeton, New Jersey: Princeton University Press.

—— 1978 "Early Industrialization and Demographic Change in the Canton of Zurich," in Charles Tilly, ed., *Historical Studies of Changing Fertility*. Princeton, New Jersey: Princeton University Press.

Brenner, Robert, 1976 "Agrarian Class Structure and Economic Development in Pre-Industrial Europe," *Past and Present* 70: 30–75.

—— 1977 "The Origins of Capitalist Development: A Critique of Neo-Smithian Marxism," *New Left Review* 104: 25–92.

—— 1985 "The Agrarian Roots of European Capitalism," in T. H. Aston and C. H. E. Philpin, eds, *The Brenner Debate. Agrarian Class Structure and Economic Development in Pre-Industrial Europe*. Cambridge: Cambridge University Press.

Brewer, John, 1989 *The Sinews of Power. War, Money and the English State, 1688–1783*. New York: Knopf.

Brewer, John D. et al., 1988 *The Police, Public Order and the State. Policing in Great Britain, Northern Ireland, the Irish Republic, the USA, Israel, South Africa and China*. New York: St Martins.

Brower, Daniel, 1977 "L'Urbanisation russe à la fin du XIXe siècle," *Annales; Economies, Sociétés, Civilisations* 32: 70–86.

Bueno de Mesquita, Bruce, 1981 *The War Trap*. New Haven, Connecticut: Yale University Press.

—— 1988 "The Contribution of Expected Utility Theory to the Study of International Conflict," *Journal of Interdisciplinary History* 18: 629–52.

Bulst, Neithard and Jean-Philippe Genet, 1988 eds, *La ville, la bourgeoisie et la genèse de l'Etat moderne (XIIe–XVIIIe siècles)*. Paris: Editions du Centre National de la Recherche Scientifique.

Bünger Karl, 1987 "Concluding Remarks on Two Aspects of the Chinese Unitary State as Compared with the European State System," in Stuart Schram, ed., *Foundations and Limits of State Power in China*. Published for European Science Foundation by School of Oriental and African Studies, University of London, and The Chinese University Press, Chinese University of Hong Kong.

Burke, Peter, 1986 "City-States" in John A. Hall, ed., *States in History*. Oxford: Basil Blackwell.

—— 1988 "Republics of Merchants in Early Modern Europe," in Jean Baechler, John A. Hall and Michael Mann, eds, *Europe and the Rise of Capitalism*. Oxford: Basil Blackwell.

Busch, Otto, 1962 *Militarsystem und Sozialleben im alten Preussen 1713–1807: Die Anfänge der sozialen Militarisierung der preussisch-deutschen Gesellschaft*. Berlin: de Gruyter.

Callaghy, Thomas M., 1984 *The State-Society Struggle. Zaïre in Comparative Perspective*. New York: Columbia University Press.

Calvert, Peter, 1970 *A Study of Revolution*. Oxford: Clarendon Press.

Cameron, Iain A., 1977 "The Police of Eighteenth-Century France," *European Studies Review* 7: 47–75.

Cammack, Paul, 1988 "Dependency and the Politics of Development," in P. F. Leeson and M. M. Minogue, eds, *Perspectives on Development. Cross-disciplinary Themes in Development Studies*. Manchester: Manchester University Press.

Canak, William L., 1984 "The Peripheral State Debate: State Capitalist and Bureaucratic-Authoritarian Regimes in Latin America," *Latin American Research Review* 19: 3–36.

Carsten, F. L., 1954 *The Origins of Prussia*. Oxford: Clarendon Press.

Carter, F. W., 1972 *Dubrovnik (Ragusa), A Classic City State*. London: Seminar Press.

Carver, Michael, 1980 *War since 1945*. London: Weidenfeld and Nicolson.

Centre de la Méditerranée Moderne et Contemporaine, 1969 *Villes de l'Europe méditerranéenne et de l'Europe occidentale du Moyen Age au XIXe siècle*. Saint-Brieuc: Les Belles Lettres. Annales de la Faculté des Lettres et Sciences Humaines de Nice, nos. 9–10.

Chandler, Tertius and Gerald Fox, 1974 *3000 Years of Urban Growth*. New York: Academic Press.

Chapman, Herrick, 1988 "The French State in the Era of the Second World War: A Look at the Recent Scholarship," Working Paper 63, Center for Studies of Social Change, New School for Social Research.

Charlesworth, Andrew, 1983 ed., *An Atlas of Rural Protest in Britain, 1548–1900*. London: Croom Helm.

Chase-Dunn, Chris, 1989 *Global Formation: Structures of the World-Economy*. Oxford: Basil Blackwell.

Chesnais, Jean-Claude, 1981 *Histoire de la violence en Occident de 1800 à nos jours*. Paris: Robert Laffont.

Chevalier, Bernard, 1982 *Les bonnes villes de France du XIVe au XVIe siècle*. Paris: Aubier Montaigne.

Chinwanno, Chulacheeb, 1985 "Militarization in Thai Society," in Peter Wallensteen, Johan Galtung and Carlos Portales, eds, *Global Militarization*. Boulder, Colorado: Westview.

Chisolm, Michael, 1962 *Rural Settlement and Land Use*. London: Hutchinson University Library.

Chittolini, Giorgio, 1989 "Cities, 'City-States' and Regional States in North-Central Italy," forthcoming in *Theory and Society*.

Chorley, Katherine, 1943 *Armies and the Art of Revolution*. London: Faber and Faber.

Choucri, Nazli and Robert C. North, 1975 *Nations in Conflict*. San Francisco: Freeman.

Church, Clive H. 1981 *Revolution and Red Tape. The French Ministerial Bureaucracy 1770–1850*. Oxford: Clarendon Press.

Cipolla, Carlo, 1965 *Guns, Sails, and Empires: Technological Innovation and the Early Phases of European Expansion, 1400–1700*. New York: Pantheon.

—— 1976 *Before the Industrial Revolution. European Society and Economy, 1000–1700*. New York: Norton.

Claessen, Henri J. M., 1984 "The Internal Dynamics of the Early State," *Current Anthropology* 25: 365–79.

—— 1985 "From the Franks to France – The Evolution of a Political Organization," in Henri J. M. Claessen, Pieter van de Velde and M. Estellie Smith, eds, *Development and Decline. The Evolution of Sociopolitical Organization*. Massachusetts: Bergin and Garvey.

—— 1988 "Changing Legitimacy," in Ronald Cohen and Judith D. Toland, eds, *State Formation and Political Legitimacy*. New Brunswick: Transaction. Political Anthropology, vol. VI.

Clark, Sir George, 1969 "The Social Foundations of States," in F. L. Carsten, ed., *The New Cambridge Modern History, vol. 5: The Ascendancy of France, 1648–88*, Cambridge: Cambridge University Press.

Clark, Gordon L. and Michael Dear, 1984 *State Apparatus. Structures and Language of Legitimacy*. Boston, Massachusetts: Allen & Unwin.

Clark, Samuel, 1984 "Nobility, Bourgeoisie and the Industrial Revolution in Belgium," *Past and Present* 105: 140–75.

Clausewitz, Carl von, 1968 (Anatol Rapoport, ed.) *On War*. Harmondsworth: Penguin. First published in 1832.

Clayton, Anthony, 1988 *France, Soldiers and Africa*. London: Brassey's Defence Publishers.

Coale, Ansley J. and Susan Cotts Watkins, 1986 eds, *The Decline of Fertility in Europe*. Princeton, New Jersey: Princeton University Press.

Cobb, Richard, 1970 *The Police and the People*. London: Oxford University Press.

Cohn, Jr, Samuel Kline, 1980 *The Laboring Classes in Renaissance Florence*. New York: Academic Press.

Cohen, Youssef, Brian R. Brown and A. F. K. Organski, 1981 "The Paradoxical Nature of State Making: The Violent Creation of Order," *American Political Science Review* 75: 901–10.

Collier, David, 1979 ed., *The New Authoritarianism in Latin America*. Princeton, New Jersey: Princeton University Press.

Collier, Ruth B., 1982 *Regimes in Tropical Africa. Changing Forms of Supremacy, 1945–1975*. Berkeley, California: University of California Press.

Collins, James B., 1988 *Fiscal Limits of Absolutism. Direct Taxation in Early Seventeenth-Century France*. Berkeley, California: University of California Press.

Comninel, George C., 1987 *Rethinking the French Revolution. Marxism and the Revisionist Challenge*. London: Verso.

Connelly, Owen, 1965 *Napoleon's Satellite Kingdoms*. New York: Free Press.

Contamine, Philippe, 1984 *War in the Middle Ages*. Oxford: Basil Blackwell. French version published in 1980.

Cornette, Joël, 1988 "Le 'point d'Archimède'. Le renouveau de la recherche sur l'Etat des Finances," *Revue d'Histoire Moderne et Contemporaine* 35: 614–29.

Cornwall, Julian, 1977 *Revolt of the Peasantry 1549*. London: Routledge and Kegan Paul.

Corrigan, Philip, 1980 *Capitalism, State Formation and Marxist Theory. Historical Investigations*. London: Quartet Books.

—— and Derek Sayer, 1985 *The Great Arch. English State Formation as Cultural Revolution*. Oxford: Basil Blackwell.

Corvisier, André, 1976 *Armées et sociétés en Europe de 1494 à 1789*. Paris: Presses Universitaires de France.

Cox, Robert W., 1987 *Production, Power, and World Order. Social Forces in the Making of History*. New York: Columbia University Press.

Cozzi, Gaetano and Michael Knapton, 1986 *La Repubblica di Venezia nell'età moderna. Dalla guera di Chioggia al 1517*. Turin: UTET.

Cronin, James E., 1988 "The British State and the Second World War," Working Paper 64, Center for Studies of Social Change, New School for Social Research.

Crosby, Alfred W., 1986 *Ecological Imperialism. The Biological Expansion of Europe, 900–1900*. Cambridge: Cambridge University Press.

Cumings, Bruce, 1984 "The Origins and Development of the Northeast Asian Political Economy: Industrial Sectors, Product Cycle, and Political Consequences," *International Organization* 38: 1–40.

—— 1988 "Korea and the War Settlement in Northeast Asia," Working Paper 65, Center for Studies of Social Change, New School for Social Research.

—— 1989 "The Abortive Abertura: South Korea in the Light of Latin American Experience," *New Left Review* 173: 5–32.

Curtin, Philip D., 1984 *Cross-Cultural Trade in World History*. Cambridge: Cambridge University Press.

Cusack, Thomas R. and Wolf-Dieter Eberwein, 1982 "Prelude to War: Incidence, Escalation and Intervention in International Disputes, 1900–1976," *International Interactions* 9: 9–28.

Dann, Otto, 1983 "Die Region als Gegenstand der Geschichtswissenschaft," *Archiv für Sozialgeschichte* 23: 652–61.

—— and John Dinwiddy, 1988 *Nationalism in the Age of the French Revolution*. London: Hambledon.

Danns, George K., 1986 "The Role of the Military in the National Security of Guyana," in Alma H. Young and Dion E. Phillips, eds, *Militarization in the Non-Hispanic Caribbean*. Boulder, Colorado: Lynne Rienner.

David, Steven R., 1987 *Third World Coups d'Etat and International Security*. Baltimore, Maryland: Johns Hopkins University Press.

Dawson, Philip, 1972 *Provincial Magistrates and Revolutionary Politics in France, 1789–1795*. Cambridge: Harvard University Press.

Decalo, Samuel, 1976 *Coups and Army Rule in Africa. Studies in Military Style*. New Haven, Connecticut: Yale University Press.

Dekker, Rudolf, 1982 *Holland in beroering. Oproeren in de 17de en 18de eeuw.* Baarn: Amboeken.

Dent, Julian, 1973 *Crisis in Finance: Crown, Financiers, and Society in Seventeenth-Century France.* Newton Abbot: David and Charles.

Dessert, Daniel, 1984 *Argent, pouvoir, et société au Grand Siècle.* Paris: Fayard.

Dewey, Horace, 1988 "Russia's Debt to the Mongols in Suretyship and Collective Responsibility," *Comparative Studies in Society and History* 30: 249–70.

Deyo, Frederic, Stephan Haggard, and Hagen Koo, 1987 "Labor in the Political Economy of East Asian Industrialization," *Bulletin of Concerned Asian Scholars* 19: 42–53.

Deyon, Pierre, 1979a "L'Enjeu des discussions autour du concept de 'proto-industrialisation'," *Revue du Nord* 61: 9–15.

—— 1979b "La diffusion rurale des industries textile en Flandre française à la fin de l'Ancien Régime et au début du XIXe siècle," *Revue du Nord* 61: 83–95.

—— 1981 "Un modèle à l'épreuve, le développement industriel de Roubaix de 1762 à la fin du XIXème siècle," *Revue du Nord* 63: 59–66.

Dickson, P. G. M., 1967 *The Financial Revolution in England. A Study in the Development of Public Credit, 1688–1756.* London: Macmillan.

Diehl, Paul F. and Gary Goertz, 1988 "Territorial Changes and Militarized Conflict," *Journal of Conflict Resolution* 32: 103–22.

Dijk, H. van, 1980 *Wealth and Property in the Netherlands in Modern Times.* Rotterdam: Centrum voor Maatschappijgeschiedenis.

Dix, Robert, 1983 "The Varieties of Revolution," *Comparative Politics* 15: 281–93.

Dobb, Maurice, 1963 *Studies in the Development of Capitalism.* London: Routledge and Kegan Paul. Rev. edn.

Dodgshon, Robert A., 1987 *The European Past. Social Evolution and Spatial Order.* London: Macmillan.

Dohaerd, Renée et al., 1983 *Histoire de Flandre des origines à nos jours.* Brussels: Renaissance du Livre.

Donia, Robert J., 1981 *Islam under the Double Eagle: The Muslims of Bosnia and Hercegovina, 1878–1914.* New York: Columbia University Press for Eastern European Monographs, Boulder, Colorado.

Dower, John W., 1988 "Japan: Legacies of a Lost War," Working Paper 66, Center for Studies of Social Change, New School for Social Research.

Downing, Brian M., 1988 "Constitutionalism, Warfare, and Political Change in Early Modern Europe," *Theory and Society* 17: 7–56.

Doyle, Michael W., 1986 *Empires.* Ithaca, New York: Cornell University Press.

Doyle, William, 1986 *The Ancien Regime.* Atlantic Highlands, New Jersey: Humanities Press International.

Duchacek, Ivo D., 1986 *The Territorial Dimension of Politics. Within, Among, and Across Nations.* Boulder, Colorado: Westview.

Duffy, Michael, 1980 ed., *The Military Revolution and the State, 1500–1800.* Exeter: University of Exeter. Exeter Studies in History, 1.

Dunér, Bertil, 1985 *Military Intervention in Civil Wars: the 1970s.* Aldershot: Gower.

Dunford, Michael and Diane Perrons, 1983 *The Arena of Capital.* New York: St Martin's.

Dunn, John, 1972 *Modern Revolutions. An Introduction to the Analysis of a Political Phenomenon.* Cambridge: Cambridge University Press.

DuPlessis, Robert S. and Martha C. Howell, 1982 "Reconsidering Early Modern Urban Economy: The Cases of Leiden and Lille," *Past and Present* 94: 49–84.

Durandin, Catherine, 1989 *Révolution à la Française ou à la Russe. Polonais, Roumains et Russes au XIXe siècle.* Paris: Presses Universitaires de France.

Eckhardt, William, 1988 "Civilian Deaths in Wartime," forthcoming in *Bulletin of Peace Proposals,* 20 (1989).

Eden, Lynn, 1988 "World War II and American Politics," Working Paper 68, Center for Studies of Social Change, New School for Social Research.

Egret, Jean, 1962 *La pré-Révolution française.* Paris: Presses Universitaires de France.

Eisenstadt, S. N., 1963 *The Political Systems of Empires. The Rise and Fall of the Historical Bureaucratic Societies.* Glencoe, New York: Free Press.

Elias, Norbert, 1982 *Power and Civility.* New York: Pantheon. The Civilizing Process, vol. 2.

Elliott, J. H., 1963 *Imperial Spain, 1469–1716.* London: Arnold.

—— 1970 *The Old World and the New, 1492–1650.* Cambridge: Cambridge University Press.

Elton, G. R., 1975 "Taxation for War and Peace in Early-Tudor England," in J. M. Winter, ed., *War and Economic Development: Essays in Memory of David Joslin.* Cambridge: Cambridge University Press.

Evans, Eric J., 1983 *The Forging of the Modern State. Early Industrial Britain, 1783–1870.* London: Longman.

Evans, Peter and John D. Stephens, 1989 "Studying Development since the Sixties: The Emergence of a New Comparative Political Economy," *Theory and Society* 17: 713–46.

Faber, J. A. et al., 1965 "Population Changes and Economic Developments in the Netherlands: A Historical Survey," *A. A. G. Bijdragen* 12: 47–114.

Fernandez Albaladejo, Pablo, 1989 "Cities and the State in Spain," forthcoming in *Theory and Society.*

Fijnaut, Cyrille, 1980a "Les origines de l'appareil policier moderne en Europe de l'Ouest continentale," *Déviance et Société* 4: 19–41.

—— 1980b "Die 'politische Funktion' der Polizei. Zur Geschichte der Polizei als zentralen Faktor in der Entwicklung und Stabilisierung politischer Machtstrukturen in West-Europa," *Kriminologisches Journal* 12: 301–9.

Finer, Samuel E., 1975 "State- and Nation-Building in Europe: The Role of the Military," in Charles Tilly, ed., *The Formation of National States in Western Europe.* Princeton, New Jersey: Princeton University Press.

—— 1982 "The Morphology of Military Regimes," in Roman Kolkowicz and Andrzej Korbonski, eds, *Soldiers, Peasants, and Bureaucrats: Civil-Military Relations in Communist and Modernizing Regimes.* London: Routledge and Kegan Paul.

Fischer, Dietrich, 1985 "Defense without Threat: Switzerland's Security Policy," in Peter Wallensteen, Johan Galtung and Carlos Portales, eds, *Global Militarization*. Boulder, Colorado: Westview.

Fitch, J. Samuel, 1986 "Armies and Politics in Latin America: 1975–1985," in Abraham F. Lowenthal and J. Samuel Fitch, eds, *Armies and Politics in Latin America*. New York: Holmes & Meier.

Flora, Peter et al., 1983, 1987 eds, *State, Economy, and Society in Western Europe 1815–1975. A Data Handbook*. Frankfurt: Campus Verlag. 2 vols.

Fontenay, Michel, 1988a "Corsaires de la foi ou rentiers du sol? Les chevaliers de Malte dans le 'corso' méditerranéen au XVIIe siècle," *Revue d'Histoire Moderne et Contemporaine* 35: 361–84.

—— 1988b "La place de la course dans l'économie portuaire: L'exemple de Malte et des ports barbaresques," *Annales; Economies, Sociétés, Civilisations* 43: 1321–47.

Forrest, Alan, 1975 *Society and Politics in Revolutionary Bordeaux*. London: Oxford University Press.

Fourastié, Jean, 1966 "Observazioni sui prezzi salariali dei cereali e la produttività del lavoro agricolo in Europa dal XV al XX secolo," *Rivista Storica Italiana* 78: 422–30.

Frank, André Gunder, 1978 *World Accumulation, 1492–1789*. New York: Monthly Review Press.

Frankfort, Henri et al., 1946 *The Intellectual Adventure of Ancient Man. An Essay on Speculative Thought in the Ancient Near East*. Chicago: University of Chicago Press.

Frêche, Georges, 1974 *Toulouse et la région Midi-Pyrénées au siècle des Lumières (vers 1670–1789)*. Paris: Cujas.

Freedman, Paul, 1988 "Cowardice, Heroism and the Legendary Origins of Catalonia," *Past and Present* 121: 3–28.

Fremdling, Rainer and Richard Tilly, 1979 eds, *Industrialisierung und Raum. Studien zur regionale Differenzierung im Deutschland des 19. Jahrhunderts*. Stuttgart: Klett-Cotta.

Friedmann, David, 1977 "A Theory of the Size and Shape of Nations," *Journal of Political Economy* 85: 59–78.

Fueter, Edward, 1919 *Geschichte des europäischen Staatensystems von 1492–1559*. Munich: Oldenbourg.

Gallo, Carmenza, 1985 "The State in an Enclave Economy: Political Instability in Bolivia from 1900 to 1950," unpublished doctoral dissertation in sociology, Boston University.

Garcin, Jean-Claude, 1988 "The Mamluk Military System and the Blocking of Medieval Moslem Society," in Jean Baechler, John A. Hall and Michael Mann, eds, *Europe and the Rise of Capitalism*. Oxford: Basil Blackwell.

Garmonsway, G. N., 1953 tr. and ed., *The Anglo-Saxon Chronicle*. London: J. M. Dent.

Genet, Jean-Philippe and Michel Le Mené, 1987 eds, *Genèse de l'état moderne. Prélèvement et Redistribution*. Paris: Editions du Centre National de la Recherche Scientifique.

Gerth, H. H. and C. Wright Mills, 1946 eds, *From Max Weber: Essays in Sociology*. New York: Oxford University Press.

Geyer, Michael, 1988 "Society, State, and Military Apparatus in Germany, 1945–1955," Working Paper 67, Center for Studies of Social Change, New School for Social Research.

Giddens, Anthony, 1985 *The Nation-State and Violence*. Berkeley, California: University of California Press.

Gillis, John, 1970 "Political Decay and the European Revolutions, 1789–1848," *World Politics* 22: 344–70.

Gilpin, Robert, 1981 *War and Change in World Politics*. Cambridge: Cambridge University Press.

—— 1988 "The Theory of Hegemonic War," *Journal of Interdisciplinary History* 18: 591–614.

Gledhill, John, Barbara Bender and Mogens Trolle Larsen, 1988 eds, *State and Society. The Emergence and Development of Social Hierarchy and Political Centralization*. London: Unwin Hyman.

Gokalp, Iskander and Semih Vaner, 1985 "De l'empire à la république: regards sur la Turquie," *Cahiers du Groupe d'Etudes sur la Turquie Contemporaine* 1: 92–102.

Goldstein, Joshua S., 1988 *Long Cycles. Prosperity and War in the Modern Age*. New Haven, Connecticut: Yale University Press.

Goldstone, Jack A., 1986 "Introduction: The Comparative and Historical Study of Revolutions," in Jack A. Goldstone, ed., *Revolutions. Theoretical, Comparative, and Historical Studies*. San Diego, California: Harcourt Brace Jovanovich.

Gooch, John 1980 *Armies in Europe*. London: Routledge and Kegan Paul.

Gran, Thorvald, 1988a "War Settlement in Norway," Working Paper 61, Center for Studies of Social Change, New School for Social Research.

—— 1988b "A Critique of State Autonomy in Norway," unpublished doctoral dissertation in public administration and organization theory, University of Bergen.

Greene, Thomas H., 1974 *Comparative Revolutionary Movements*. Englewood Cliffs, New Jersey: Prentice-Hall.

Greer, Donald, 1935 *The Incidence of the Terror during the French Revolution*. Cambridge: Harvard University Press.

Grew, Raymond, 1978 ed., *Crises of Political Development in Europe and the United States*. Princeton, New Jersey: Princeton University Press.

—— 1984 "The Nineteenth-Century European State," in Charles Bright and Susan Harding, eds, *Statemaking and Social Movements*. Ann Arbor, Michigan: University of Michigan Press.

Greyerz, Kaspar von, 1989 "Portuguese *conversos* on the Upper Rhine and the *converso* community of sixteenth-century Europe," *Social History* 14: 59–82.

Guénée, Bernard, 1985 *States and Rulers in Later Medieval Europe*. Oxford: Basil Blackwell.

Gugler, Josef, 1982 "The Urban Character of Contemporary Revolutions," *Studies in Comparative International Development* 17: 60–73.

Guillerm, Alain, 1985 *La pierre et le vent. Fortifications et marine en Occident*. Paris: Arthaud.

Guilmartin, Jr, John F., 1988 "Ideology and Conflict: The Wars of the Ottoman Empire, 1453–1606," *Journal of Interdisciplinary History* 18: 721–48.

Gurr, Ted Robert, 1981 "Historical Trends in Violent Crime: A Critical Review of the Evidence," *Crime and Justice: An Annual Review of Research* 3: 295–353.

—— 1986 "Persisting Patterns of Repression and Rebellion: Foundations for a General Theory of Political Coercion," in Margaret P. Karns, ed., *Persistent Patterns and Emergent Structures in a Waning Century*. New York: Praeger Special Studies for the International Studies Association.

—— and Desmond S. King, 1987 *The State and the City*. London: Macmillan.

Gutmann, Myron P., 1980 *War and Rural Life in the Early Modern Low Countries*. Princeton, New Jersey: Princeton University Press.

—— 1988 "The Origins of the Thirty Years' War," *Journal of Interdisciplinary History* 18: 749–70.

Hagen, William W., 1988 "Capitalism and the Countryside in Early Modern Europe: Interpretations, Models, Debates," *Agricultural History* 62: 13–47.

Haimson, Leopold and Charles Tilly, 1989 eds, *Strikes, Wars, and Revolutions in an International Perspective*. Cambridge: Cambridge University Press.

Hair, P. E. H., 1971 "Deaths from Violence in Britain: A Tentative Secular Survey," *Population Studies* 25: 5–24.

Hale, J. R., 1967 "International Relations in the West: Diplomacy and War," in G. R. Potter, ed., *The New Cambridge Modern History. Vol. 1: The Renaissance, 1493–1520*. Cambridge: Cambridge University Press.

—— 1968a "Armies, Navies, and the Art of War," in G. R. Elton, ed., *New Cambridge Modern History, vol. 2: The Reformation 1520–1559*. Cambridge: Cambridge University Press.

—— 1968b "Armies, Navies, and the Art of War" (*sic*), in R. B. Wernham, ed., *New Cambridge Modern History, vol. 3: The Counter-Reformation and Price Revolution, 1559–1610*. Cambridge: Cambridge University Press.

—— 1979 "Renaissance Armies and Political Control: The Venetian Proveditorial System 1509–1529," *Journal of Italian History* 2: 11–31.

—— 1983 *Renaissance War Studies*. London: Hambledon Press.

—— 1985 *War and Society in Renaissance Europe, 1450–1620*. New York: St Martin's.

Halicz, Emanuel, 1987 "The Polish Armed Forces and War, 1764–1864," in Stephen Fischer-Galati and Béla K. Király, eds, *Essays on War and Society in East Central Europe, 1740–1920*. Boulder, Colorado: Social Science Monographs.

Hall, Peter and Dennis Hay, 1980 *Growth Centers in the European Urban System*. London: Heinemann.

Hamilton, Clive, 1986 *Capitalist Industrialization in Korea*. Boulder, Colorado: Westview.

Hamilton, Earl J., 1950 "Origin and Growth of the National Debt in France and England," in *Studi in onore di Gino Luzzato, vol. 2*. Milan: Giuffrè.

Harding, Robert R., 1978 *Anatomy of a Power Elite: The Provincial Governors of Early Modern France*. New Haven, Connecticut: Yale University Press.

Harff, Barabara and Ted Robert Gurr, 1988 "Toward Empirical Theory of Genocides and Politicides: Identification and Measurement of Cases since 1945," *International Studies Quarterly* 32: 359–71.

Hart, Marjolein 't, 1984 "In Quest for Funds: State and Taxation in Eighteenth-Century England and France," paper presented to the Workshop on the Politics of Taxation, European Consortium for Political Research, Salzburg.

—— 1985 "Hoe de staat zijn raison d'être verloor. Staat en revolutie in Frankrijk 1775–1789," *Mens en Maatschapij* 1985: 5–25.

—— 1986 "Taxation and the Formation of the Dutch State, 17th Century," paper presented to the Vlaams-Nederlandse Sociologendagen, Amsterdam.

—— 1987 "Salt Tax and Salt Trade in the Low Countries," in Jean-Claude Hocquet, *Le Roi, le Marchand et le Sel*. Villeneuve d'Ascq: Presses Universitaires de Lille.

—— 1989a "Credit and Power. State Making in Seventeenth Century Netherlands," unpublished doctoral dissertation in history, University of Leiden.

—— 1989b "Cities and Statemaking in the Dutch Republic, 1580–1680," forthcoming in *Theory and Society*.

Haskins, Charles Homer, 1915 *The Normans in European History*. Boston, Massachussetts: Houghton Mifflin.

Headrick, Daniel R., 1981 *The Tools of Empire. Technology and European Imperialism in the Nineteenth Century*, New York: Oxford University Press.

Hechter, Michael and William Brustein, 1980 "Regional Modes of Production and Patterns of State Formation in Europe," *American Journal of Sociology* 85: 1061–94.

Henning, Friedrich-Wilhelm, 1977 "Der Beginn der modernen Welt im agrarischen Bereich," in Reinhart Koselleck, ed., *Studien zum Beginn der modernen Welt*. Stuttgart: Klett-Cotta.

Heper, Metin, 1985 "The State and Public Bureaucracy: A Comparative and Historical Perspective," *Comparative Studies in Society and History* 27: 86–110.

Hermant, Daniel, 1987 ed., "Les coups d'État," *Etudes Polémologiques* 41: entire issue.

Hernández, Francesc and Francesc Mercadé, 1986 eds, *Estructuras Sociales y Cuestión Nacional en España*. Barcelona: Ariel.

Hespanha, António Manuel, 1986 "Centro e Periferia nas Estruturas Administrativas do Antigo Regime," *Ler História* 8: 35–60.

—— 1989 "Cities and the State in Portugal," forthcoming in *Theory and Society*.

Hinrichs, Ernst, Eberhard Schmitt and Rudolf Vierhaus, 1978 eds, *Vom Ancien Régime zur Französischen Revolution. Forschungen und Perspektiven*. Göttingen: Vandenhoeck and Ruprecht.

Hirst, Derek, 1986 *Authority and Conflict. England, 1603–1658*. Cambridge: Harvard University Press.

Hitchins, Keith, 1988 "Rumanian Peasantism: The Third Way," paper presented to the Conference on Models of Development and Theories of Modernization in Eastern Europe Between the World Wars, Ráckeve, Hungary.

Hobsbawm, E. J., 1987 *The Age of Empire 1875–1914*. New York: Pantheon.

Hocquet, Jean-Claude, 1982 *Le sel et la fortune de Venise*. Lille: Université de Lille III. 2 vols.

Hohenberg, Paul and Frederick Krantz, 1975 eds, *Transition du féodalisme à la société industrielle: l'échec de l'Italie de la Renaissance et des Pays-Bas du XVIIe siècle*. Montreal: Centre Interuniversitaire d'Etudes Européennes.

——and Lynn Hollen Lees, 1985 *The Making of Urban Europe, 1000–1850*. Cambridge: Harvard University Press.

Holsti, K. J., 1985 *The Dividing Discipline. Hegemony and Diversity in International Theory*. Boston, Massachusetts: Allen & Unwin.

Holton, R. J., 1986 *Cities, Capitalism and Civilization*. London: Allen & Unwin.

Hood, James N., 1971 "Protestant–Catholic Relations and the Roots of the First Popular Counterrevolutionary Movement in France," *Journal of Modern History* 43: 245–75.

——1979 "Revival and Mutation of Old Rivalries in Revolutionary France," *Past and Present* 82: 82–115.

Horowitz, Donald L., 1980 *Coup Theories and Officers' Motives. Sri Lanka in Comparative Perspective*. Princeton, New Jersey: Princeton University Press.

Houweling, Henk and Jan G. Siccama, 1988 "Power Transitions as a Cause of War," *Journal of Conflict Resolution* 32: 87–102.

Howard, Michael, 1976 *War in European History*. Oxford: Oxford University Press.

Hunt, Lynn, 1978 *Revolution and Urban Politics in Provincial France. Troyes and Reims, 1786–1790*. Stanford: Stanford University Press.

——1984 *Politics, Culture, and Class in the French Revolution*. Berkeley, California: University of California Press.

Huntington, Samuel P., 1957 *The Soldier and the State. The Theory and Politics of Civil–Military Relations*. New York: Vintage.

——1968 *Political Order in Changing Societies*. New Haven, Connecticut: Yale University Press.

——and Jorge I. Dominguez, 1975 "Political Development" in Fred I. Greenstein and Nelson W. Polsby, eds, *Handbook of Political Science*. Reading, Massachusetts: Addison-Wesley. Vol. III, 1–114.

Hutchful, Eboe, 1984 "Trends in Africa," *Alternatives* 10: 115–38.

Immich, Max, 1905 *Geschichte des europaïschen Staatensystems von 1660 bis 1789*. Munich and Berlin: Oldenbourg.

Ingrao, Charles W., 1987 *The Hessian Mercenary State. Ideas, Institutions, and Reform under Frederick II, 1760–1785*. Cambridge: Cambridge University Press.

Israel, Jonathan I., 1982 *The Dutch Republic and the Hispanic World*. Oxford: Clarendon Press.

Jackman, Robert W., 1976 "Politicians in Uniform: Military Governments and Social Change in the Third World," *American Political Science Review* 70: 1078–97.

—— 1978 "The Predictability of Coups d'Etat: A Model with African Data," *American Political Science Review* 72: 1262–75.

Janos, Andrew, 1988 "The Rise and Fall of Civil Society. The Politics of Backwardness on the European Peripheries, 1780–1945," paper presented to the Conference on Models of Development and Theories of Modernization in Eastern Europe Between the World Wars, Ráckeve, Hungary.

Janowitz, Morris, 1964 *The Military in the Political Development of New Nations.* Chicago, Illinois: University of Chicago Press.

—— and Jacques Van Doorn, 1971 eds, *On Military Intervention.* Rotterdam: Rotterdam University Press.

Jelavich, Charles and Barbara, 1977 *The Establishment of the Balkan National States, 1804–1920.* Seattle, Washington: University of Washington Press.

Jervis, Robert, 1988a "Realism, Game Theory, and Cooperation," *World Politics* 40: 317–49.

—— 1988b "The Political Effects of Nuclear Weapons," *International Security* 13: 80–90.

Jespersen, Leon, 1985 "The *Machtstaat* in Seventeenth-century Denmark," *Scandinavian Journal of History* 10: 271–304.

Jessenne, Jean-Pierre, 1987 *Pouvoir au village et Révolution. Artois 1760–1848.* Lille: Presses Universitaires de Lille.

Johnson, John J., 1962 ed., *The Role of the Military in Underdeveloped Countries.* Princeton, New Jersey: Princeton University Press.

Johnson, Thomas H., Robert O. Slater and Pat McGowan, 1984 "Explaining African Military Coups d'Etat, 1960–1982," *American Political Science Review* 78: 622–40.

Johnston, R. J., 1982 *Geography and the State.* New York: St Martin's.

Jones, Colin, 1980 "The Military Revolution and the Professionalization of the French Army Under the Ancien Regime," in Michael Duffy, ed., *The Military Revolution and the State, 1500–1800.* Exeter: University of Exeter. Exeter Studies in History, no. 1.

Jones, D. W., 1988 *War and Economy in the Age of William III and Marlborough.* Oxford: Basil Blackwell.

Juillard, Etienne and Henri Nonn, 1976 *Espaces et régions en Europe Occidentale.* Paris: Editions du Centre National de la Recherche Scientifique.

Kann, Robert A., 1980 *A History of the Habsburg Empire, 1526–1918.* Berkeley, California: University of California Press. First published in 1974.

Keeney, Barnaby C., 1947 "Military Service and the Development of Nationalism in England, 1272–1327," *Speculum* 4: 534–49.

Kellenbenz, Hermann, 1975 ed., *Agrarisches Nebengewerbe und Formen der Reagrarisierung im Spätmittelalter und 19./20. Jahrhundert.* Stuttgart: Gustav Fischer.

—— 1976 *The Rise of the European Economy. An Economic History of Continental Europe from the Fifteenth to the Eighteenth Century.* London: Wiedenfeld and Nicolson.

—— 1981 "Marchands de l'Allemagne du Sud, médiateurs entre le Nord-Est et l'Occident européen," in *Actes du Colloque Franco-Polonais d'Histoire*. Nice: Laboratoire d'Histoire Quantitative, Université de Nice.

Kelly, John Dunham, 1988 "Fiji Indians and Political Discourse in Fiji: from the Pacific Romance to the Coups," *Journal of Historical Sociology* 1: 399–422.

Kennedy, Gavin, 1974 *The Military in the Third World*. London: Duckworth.

Kennedy, Paul, 1987 *The Rise and Fall of the Great Powers. Economic Change and Military Conflict from 1500 to 2000*. New York: Random House.

Kennedy, William, 1964 *English Taxation 1640–1799. An Essay on Policy and Opinion*. New York: Augustus Kelley. First published in 1913.

Keohane, Robert O., 1986 ed., *Neorealism and its Critics*. New York: Columbia University Press.

—— and Joseph S. Nye, Jr. 1975 "International Interdependence and Integration," vol. VIII, 363–414 in Fred I. Greenstein and Nelson W. Polsby, eds, *Handbook of Political Science*. Reading, Massachusetts: Addison-Wesley.

Kettering, Sharon, 1986 *Patrons, Brokers, and Clients in Seventeenth-Century France*. New York: Oxford University Press.

Kick, Edward L., 1983 "World-System Properties and Military Intervention-Internal War Linkages," *Journal of Political and Military Sociology* 11: 185–208.

—— and David Kiefer, 1987 "The Influence of the World System on War in the Third World," *International Journal of Sociology and Social Policy* 7: 34–48.

Kidron, Michael and Dan Smith, 1983 *The War Atlas, Armed Conflict – Armed Peace*. New York: Simon and Schuster.

Kiernan, V. G., 1973 "Conscription and Society in Europe before the War of 1914–18," in M. R. D. Foot, ed., *War and Society: Historical Essays in Honour and Memory of J. R. Western, 1928–1971*. London: Elek Books.

Kim, Kyung-Won, 1970 *Revolution and International System*. New York: New York University Press.

Kindleberger, Charles P., 1984 *A Financial History of Western Europe*. London: Allen & Unwin.

Kinzer, Stephen, 1989 "Guatemala: What Has Democracy Wrought?" *New York Times Magazine*, March 26, 1989: 32–4, 50–1.

Klare, Michael T. and Cynthia Arnson, 1981 *Supplying Repression. U.S. Support for Authoritarian Regimes Abroad*. Washington DC: Institute for Policy Studies.

Klaveren, Jacob van, 1960 "Fiskalismus – Merkantilismus – Korruption: Drei Aspekte der Finanz- und Wirtschaftspolitik während des Ancien Regime," *Vierteljahrschrift für Sozial- und Wirtschaftsgeschichte* 47: 333–53.

Kirchheimer, Otto, 1965 "Confining Conditions and Revolutionary Breakthroughs," *American Political Science Review* 59: 964–74.

Kliot, Nurit and Stanley Waterman, 1983 eds, *Pluralism and Political Geography*. London: Croom Helm.

Koblik, Steven, 1975 *Sweden's Development from Poverty to Affluence, 1750–1970*. Minneapolis, Minnesota: University of Minnesota Press.

Kohut, Zenon E., 1988 *Russian Centralism and Ukrainian Autonomy. Imperial*

Absorption of the Hetmanate, 1760s–1830s. Cambridge: Harvard University Press for the Harvard Ukrainian Research Institute.

Konvitz, Joseph W., 1985 *The Urban Millennium: The City-Building Process from the Early Middle Ages to the Present*. Carbondale, Illinois: Southern Illinois University Press.

Korpi, Walter, 1983 *The Democratic Class Struggle*. London: Routledge and Kegan Paul.

Krasner, Steven D., 1978 *Defending the National Interest. Raw Materials Investments and U.S. Foreign Policy*. Princeton, New Jersey: Princeton University Press.

—— 1985 *Structural Conflict. The Third World Against Global Liberalism*. Berkeley, California: University of California Press.

Krekic, Barisa, 1972 *Dubrovnik in the 14th and 15th Centuries: A City Between East and West*. Norman, Oklahoma: University of Oklahoma Press.

—— 1987 ed., *Urban Society of Eastern Europe in Premodern Times*. Berkeley, California: University of California Press.

Kriedte, Peter, 1982 "Die Stadt im Prozess der europäischen Proto-Industrialisierung," in Pierre Deyon and Franklin Mendels, eds, *Proto-Industrialisation: Théorie et réalité*. Lille: Université des Arts, Lettres, et Sciences Humaines.

—— 1983 *Peasants, Landlords and Merchant Capitalists. Europe and the World Economy, 1500–1800*. Cambridge: Cambridge University Press.

—— Hans Medick and Jurgen Schlumbohm, 1977 *Industrialisierung vor der Industrialisierung. Gewerbliche Warenproduktion auf dem Land in der Formationsperiode des Kapitalismus*. Göttingen: Vandenhoeck and Ruprecht.

Kula, Witold, 1960 "Secteurs et régions arriérés de l'économie du capitalisme naissant," *Studi Storici* 1: 569–85.

Kyle, Jörgen, 1988 "Peasant Elite? A Case Study of the Relations between Rural Society and the Swedish Assignment System in the Eighteenth Century," in Magnus Mörner and Thommy Svensson, eds, *Classes, Strata and Elites. Essays on Social Stratification in Nordic and Third World History*. Göteborg: Department of History, University of Göteborg. Report No. 34.

Lachmann, Richard, 1987 *From Manor to Market. Structural Change in England, 1536–1640*. Madison, Wisconsin: University of Wisconsin Press.

Ladero Quesado, Miguel Angel, 1970 "Les finances royales de Castille à la veille des temps modernes," *Annales; Economies, Sociétés, Civilisations* 25: 775–88.

Ladewig Petersen, E., 1983 "War, Finance and the Growth of Absolutism: Some Aspects of the European Integration of 17th Century Denmark," in Goran Rystad, ed., *Europe and Scandinavia: Aspects of the Process of Integration in the 17th Century*. Lund: Esselte Studium.

Lane, Frederic C., 1958 "Economic Consequences of Organized Violence," *Journal of Economic History* 18: 401–17.

—— 1966 "The Economic Meaning of War and Protection," in *Venice and History: The Collected Papers of Frederic C. Lane*. Baltimore, Maryland: Johns Hopkins University Press. Originally published in 1942.

—— 1973a *Venice, a Maritime Republic*. Baltimore, Maryland: Johns Hopkins University Press.

—— 1973b "Naval Actions and Fleet Organization, 1499–1502," in J. R. Hale, ed., *Renaissance Venice*. London: Faber and Faber.

Lang, James, 1979 *Portuguese Brazil. The King's Plantation*. New York: Academic Press.

Langer, William L., 1969 *Political and Social Upheaval, 1832–1852*. New York: Harper and Row.

Lapidus, Ira, 1967 *Muslim Cities in the Later Middle Ages*. Cambridge: Harvard University Press.

—— 1973 "The Evolution of Muslim Urban Society," *Comparative Studies in Society and History* 15: 21–50.

Laqueur, Walter, 1968 "Revolution," *International Encyclopedia of the Social Sciences* 13: 501–7.

Larson, Reidar, 1970 *Theories of Revolution, from Marx to the First Russian Revolution*. Stockholm: Almqvist & Wiksell.

Launius, Michael A., 1985 "The State and Industrial Labor in South Korea," *Bulletin of Concerned Asian Scholars* 16: 2–10.

Lebrun, François and Roger Dupuy, 1987 eds, *Les résistances à la Révolution*. Paris: Imago.

Lee, Su-Hoon, 1988 *State-Building in the Contemporary Third World*. Boulder, Colorado: Westview.

Le Goff, T. J. A. and D. M. G. Sutherland, 1984 "Religion and Rural Revolt in the French Revolution: An Overview," in János M. Bak and Gerhard Benecke, eds, *Religion and Rural Revolt*. Manchester: Manchester University Press.

Léon, Pierre, François Crouzet and Raymond Gascon, 1972 eds, *L'Industrialisation en Europe au XIXe siècle. Cartographie et typologie*. Paris: Editions du Centre National de la Recherche Scientifique.

Lepetit, Bernard, 1982 "Fonction administrative et armature urbaine: Remarques sur la distribution des chefs-lieux de subdélégation en France à la fin de l'Ancien Régime," *Institut d'Histoire Economique et Sociale de l'Université de Paris I, Recherches et Travaux*, 11: 19–34.

—— 1988 *Les villes dans la France moderne (1740–1840)*. Paris: Albin Michel.

Levack, Brian P., 1987 *The Formation of the British State. England, Scotland, and the Union, 1603–1707*. Oxford: Clarendon Press.

Levi, Margaret, 1983 "The Predatory Theory of Rule," in Michael Hechter, ed., *The Microfoundations of Macrosociology*. Philadelphia, Pennsylvania: Temple University Press.

—— 1988 *Of Rule and Revenue*. Berkeley, California: University of California Press.

Levine, David, 1987 *Reproducing Families. The Political Economy of English Population History*. Cambridge: Cambridge University Press.

Levine, Steven, 1988 "War Settlement and State Structure: The Case of China and the Termination of World War II," Working Paper 62, Center for Studies of Social Change, New School for Social Research.

Levy, Jack S., 1983 *War in the Modern Great Power System, 1495–1975*. Lexington, Kentucky: University Press of Kentucky.

—— 1989 "The Causes of War: A Review of Theories and Evidence," forthcoming in Philip Tetlock et al., eds, *Behavior, Society, and Nuclear War*. New York: Oxford University Press.

Lewis, Archibald R., 1988 *Nomads and Crusaders A.D. 1000–1368*. Bloomington, Indiana: Indiana University Press.

—— and Timothy J. Runyan, 1988 *European Naval and Maritime History, 300–1500*. Bloomington, Indiana: Indiana University Press.

Lewis, Gwynne, 1978 *The Second Vendée: The Continuity of Counter-Revolution in the Department of the Gard, 1789–1815*. Oxford: Clarendon Press.

—— and Colin Lucas, 1983 eds, *Beyond the Terror. Essays in French Regional and Social History, 1794–1815*. Cambridge: Cambridge University Press.

Lewis, John Wilson, 1974 ed., *Peasant Rebellion and Communist Revolution in Asia*. Stanford, California: Stanford University Press.

Lindegren, Jan, 1985 "The Swedish 'Military State', 1560–1720," *Scandinavian Journal of History* 10: 305–36.

Lindner, Rudi Paul, 1981 "Nomadism, Horses and Huns," *Past and Present* 92: 3–19.

—— 1983 *Nomads and Ottomans in Medieval Anatolia*. Bloomington, Indiana: Research Institute for Inner Asian Studies, Indiana University.

Livet, Georges and Bernard Vogler, 1983 eds, *Pouvoir, ville, et société en Europe, 1650–1750*. Paris: Ophrys.

Löwy, Michael, 1989 "Internationalisme, nationalisme et anti-impérialisme," *Critique Communiste* 87: 31–42.

Luard, Evan, 1987 *War in International Society*. New Haven, Connecticut: Yale University Press.

Lucas, Colin, 1973 *The Structure of the Terror. The Example of Claude Javogues and the Loire*. Oxford: Oxford University Press.

—— 1988 "The Crowd and Politics between *Ancien Régime* and Revolution in France," *Journal of Modern History* 60: 421–57.

Luckham, Robin, 1971 *The Nigerian Military. A Sociological Analysis of Authority & Revolt, 1960–1967*. Cambridge: Cambridge University Press.

—— 1981 "Armament Culture," *Alternatives* 10: 1–44.

Lüdtke, Alf, 1980 "Genesis und Durchsetzung des modernen Staates: Zur Analyse von Herrschaft und Verwaltung," *Archiv für Sozialgeschichte* 20: 470–91.

Luterbacher, Urs and Michael D. Ward, 1985 eds, *Dynamic Models of International Conflict*. Boulder, Colorado: Lynne Rienner.

Lynn, John 1984 *The Bayonets of the Republic. Motivation and Tactics in the Army of Revolutionary France, 1791–94*. Urbana, Illinois: University of Illinois Press.

—— 1989 "Introduction: The Pattern of Army Growth, 1445–1945," unpublished paper, University of Illinois Champaign-Urbana.

Lyons, G. M., 1961 "Exigences militaires et budgets militaires aux U.S.A.," *Revue Française de Sociologie* 2: 66–74.

Lyons, Martyn, 1980 *Révolution et Terreur à Toulouse*. Toulouse: Privat.

Mackie, J. P., 1964 *A History of Scotland*. Baltimore: Penguin.

Mack Smith, Dennis, 1968a *A History of Sicily. Medieval Sicily, 800–1713*. London: Chatto & Windus.

—— 1968b *A History of Sicily. Modern Sicily after 1713.* London: Chatto & Windus.

McNeill, William H., 1964 *Europe's Steppe Frontier, 1500–1800.* Chicago, Illinois: University of Chicago Press.

—— 1976 *Plagues and Peoples.* Garden City, New York: Anchor/Doubleday.

—— 1982 *The Pursuit of Power. Technology, Armed Force and Society since A.D. 1000.* Chicago Illinois: University of Chicago Press.

Maland, David, 1980 *Europe at War, 1600–1650.* Totowa, New Jersey: Rowman and Littlefield.

Mallett, M. E., 1974 *Mercenaries and their Masters. Warfare in Renaissance Italy.* Totowa, New Jersey: Rowman and Littlefield.

—— and J. R. Hale, 1984 *The Military Organization of a Renaissance State. Venice, c. 1400 to 1617.* Cambridge: Cambridge University Press.

Mandel, Robert, 1980 "Roots of the Modern Interstate Border Dispute," *Journal of Conflict Resolution* 24: 427–54.

Maniruzzaman, Talukder, 1987 *Military Withdrawal from Politics. A Comparative Study.* Cambridge, Massachusetts: Ballinger.

Mann, Michael, 1986 *The Sources of Social Power. I. A History of Power from the Beginning to A.D. 1760.* Cambridge: Cambridge University Press.

—— 1988 *States, War and Capitalism.* Oxford: Basil Blackwell.

Maravall, José Antonio, 1972 *Estado Moderno y Mentalidad Social (Siglos XV a XVII).* Madrid: Revista de Occidente. 2 vols.

Margadant, Ted, 1979 *French Peasants in Revolt. The Insurrection of 1851.* Princeton, New Jersey: Princeton University Press.

—— 1988a "Towns, Taxes, and State-Formation in the French Revolution," paper presented to the Irvine Seminar on Social History and Theory, April 1988.

—— 1988b "Politics, Class, and Community in the French Revolution: An Urban Perspective," paper presented to conference on Revolutions in Comparison, University of California, Los Angeles, 1988.

Markoff, John, 1986 "Contexts and Forms of Rural Revolt. France in 1789," *Journal of Conflict Resolution* 30: 253–89.

—— 1985 "The Social Geography of Rural Revolt at the Beginning of the French Revolution," *American Sociological Review* 50: 761–81.

—— and Silvio R. Duncan Baretta, 1986 "What We Don't Know About the Coups: Observations on Recent South American Politics," *Armed Forces and Society* 12: 207–35.

Martin, Jean-Clément 1987. *La Vendée et la France.* Paris: Le Seuil.

Martines, Lauro, 1988 *Power and Imagination. City-States in Renaissance Italy.* Baltimore, Maryland: Johns Hopkins University Press. First published in 1979.

Marx, Karl, 1970–1972 *Capital. A Critique of Political Economy.* London: Lawrence and Wishart. 3 vols.

Maschke, Eric and Jurgen Sydow, 1974 eds, *Stadt und Umland. Protokoll der X. Arbeitstagung des Arbeitskreises für sudwestdeutsche Stadtgeschichts forschung.* Stuttgart:

Kohlhammer. Veröffentlichungen der Kommission für Geschichtliche Landeskunde in Baden-Württemberg, Reihe B, 82.

Mauersberg, Hans, 1960 *Wirtschafts- und Sozialgeschichte zentraleuropäischer Städte in neurer Zeit.* Göttingen: Vandenhoeck and Ruprecht.

Mayer, Arno, 1981 *The Persistence of the Old Regime.* New York: Pantheon.

Mendels, Franklin, 1978 "Aux origines de la proto-industrialisation," *Bulletin du Centre d'Histoire Economique et Sociale de la Région Lyonnaise* 2: 1–25.

—— 1980 "Seasons and Regions in Agriculture and Industry during the Process of Industrialization," in Sidney Pollard, ed., *Region und Industrialisierung: Studien zur Rollen der Region in der Wirtschaftsgeschichte der letzten zwei Jahrhunderte.* Göttingen: Vandenhoeck and Ruprecht.

Merrington, John, 1975 "Town and Country in the Transition to Capitalism," *New Left Review* 93: 71–92.

Meyer, David R., 1986a "System of Cities Dynamics in Newly Industrializing Nations," *Studies in Comparative International Development* 21: 3–22.

—— 1986b "The World System of Cities: Relations Between International Financial Metropolises and South American Cities," *Social Forces* 64: 553–81.

Meyer, Jean, 1983 *Le poids de l'Etat.* Paris: Presses Universitaires de France.

—— et al., 1983 *Etudes sur les villes en Europe Occidentale.* Paris: Société d'Edition d'Enseignement Superieur. 2 vols.

Meyer, John W., 1980 "The World Polity and the Authority of the Nation-State," in Albert Bergesen, ed., *Studies of the Modern World-System.* New York: Academic Press.

Michaud, Claude, 1981 "Finances et guerres de religion en France," *Revue d'Histoire Moderne et Contemporaine* 28: 572–96.

Midlarsky, Manus, 1986 ed., *Inequality and Contemporary Revolutions.* Denver, Colorado: Graduate School of International Studies, University of Denver. Monograph Series in World Affairs, vol. 22, book 2.

Migdal, Joel, 1974 *Peasants, Politics, and Revolution. Pressures toward Political and Social Change in the Third World.* Princeton, New Jersey: Princeton University Press.

Miller, Edward, 1975 "War, Taxation, and the English Economy in the Late Thirteenth and Early Fourteenth Centuries," in J. M. Winter, ed., *War and Economic Development. Essays in Memory of David Joslin.* Cambridge: Cambridge University Press.

Milward, Alan S. and S. B. Saul, 1973 *The Economic Development of Continental Europe, 1780–1870.* London: Allen & Unwin.

Mitchell, B. R., 1975 *European Historical Statistics 1750–1970.* New York: Columbia University Press.

Moberg, Carl-Axel, 1962 "Northern Europe," in Robert J. Braidwood and Gordon R. Willey, eds, *Courses toward Urban Life. Archeological Considerations of Some Cultural Alternates.* Chicago, Illinois: Aldine.

Modelski, George, 1978 "The Long Cycle of Global Politics and the Nation-State," *Comparative Studies in Society and History* 20: 214–35.

—— and William R. Thompson, 1988 *Seapower in Global Politics, 1494–1993*. Seattle, Washington: University of Washington Press.

Mollat, Michel, and Philippe Wolff, 1973 *The Popular Revolutions of the Late Middle Ages*. London: Allen & Unwin.

Moore, Jr Barrington, 1966 *Social Origins of Dictatorship and Democracy*. Boston, Massachusetts: Beacon.

Moote, A. Lloyd, 1971 *The Revolt of the Judges: The Parlement of Paris and the Fronde*. Princeton, New Jersey: Princeton University Press.

Moraw, Peter, 1989 "Cities and Citizenry as Factors of State Formation in the Roman-German Empire of the Late Middle Ages," forthcoming in *Theory and Society*.

Mosca, Gaetano, 1939 *The Ruling Class (Elementi di Scienza Politica)*. New York: McGraw-Hill.

Moul, William Brian, 1988 "Balances of Power and the Escalation to War of Serious Disputes among the European Great Powers, 1815–1939: Some Evidence," *American Journal of Political Science* 32: 241–75.

Mueller, John, 1988 "The Essential Irrelevance of Nuclear Weapons," *International Security* 13: 55–79.

Mumford, Lewis, 1961 *The City in History. Its Origins, Its Transformations, and Its Prospects*. New York: Harcourt, Brace & World.

—— 1970 *The Myth of the Machine. The Pentagon of Power*. New York: Harcourt Brace Jovanovich.

Nef, John U., 1952 *War and Human Progress*. Cambridge: Cambridge University Press.

Nelkin, Dorothy, 1967 "The Economic and Social Setting of Military Takeovers in Africa," *Journal of Asian and African Studies* 2: 230–44.

Nicholas, David M., 1968 "Town and Countryside: Social and Economic Tensions in Fourteenth-Century Flanders," *Comparative Studies in Society and History* 10: 458–85.

Nichols, Glenn O., 1987 "Intermediaries and the Development of English Government Borrowing: The Case of Sir John James and Major Robert Huntington, 1675–79," *Business History* 29: 28–46.

Nicolas, Jean, 1985 ed., *Mouvements populaires et conscience sociale, XVIe–XIXe siècles*. Paris: Maloine.

Nilsson, Sven A., 1988 "Imperial Sweden: Nation-Building, War and Social Change," in Sven A. Nilsson et al., *The Age of New Sweden*. Stockholm: Livrustkammaren.

North, Douglass C., 1981 *Structure and Change in Economic History*. New York: W. W. Norton.

—— and Robert Paul Thomas, 1973 *The Rise of the Western World. A New Economic History*. Cambridge: Cambridge University Press.

Nunn, Frederick M., 1971 "The Latin American Military Establishment: Some Thoughts on the Origins of its Socio-Political Role and an Illustrative Bibliographical Essay," *The Americas* 28: 135–51.

O'Donnell, Guillermo, 1972 *Modernización y autoritarismo*. Buenos Aires: Paidos.

—— 1980 "Comparative Historical Formations in the State Apparatus and Socio-economic Change in the Third World," *International Social Science Journal* 32: 717–29.

Olson, Mancur, 1982 *The Rise and Decline of Nations. Economic Growth, Stagflation, and Social Rigidities*. New Haven, Connecticut: Yale University Press.

Oquist, Paul, 1980 *Violence, Conflict, and Politics in Colombia*. New York: Academic Press.

Organski, A. F. K., 1965 *The Stages of Political Development*. New York: Knopf.

—— and Jacek Kugler, 1980 *The War Ledger*. Chicago, Illinois: University of Chicago Press.

Österberg, Eva and Dag Lindström, 1988 *Crime and Social Control in Medieval and Early Modern Swedish Towns*. Stockhom: Almqvist & Wiksell. Studia Historica Upsaliensia, 152.

Owusu, Maxwell, 1989 "Rebellion, Revolution, and Tradition: Reinterpreting Coups in Ghana," *Comparative Studies in Society and History* 31: 372–97.

Ozouf-Marignier, Marie-Vic, 1986 "De l'universalisme constituant aux intérêts locaux: le débat sur la formation des départements en France (1789–1790)," *Annales; Economies, Sociétés, Civilisations* 41: 1193–1214.

Paddison, Ronan, 1983 *The Fragmented State. The Political Geography of Power*. Oxford: Basil Blackwell.

Palmer, Stanley H., 1988 *Police and Protest in England and Ireland 1780–1850*. Cambridge: Cambridge University Press.

Pamlenyi, Ervin, 1975 ed., *A History of Hungary*. London: Collet's.

Parker, Geoffrey, 1972 *The Army of Flanders and the Spanish Road, 1567–1659*. Cambridge: Cambridge University Press.

—— 1973 "Mutiny and Discontent in the Spanish Army of Flanders 1572–1607," *Past and Present* 58: 3–37.

—— 1975 "War and Economic Change: The Economic Costs of the Dutch Revolt," in J. M. Winter, ed., *War and Economic Development. Essays in Memory of David Joslin*. Cambridge: Cambridge University Press.

—— 1976 "The 'Military Revolution,' 1560–1660 – a Myth?" *Journal of Modern History* 48: 195–214.

—— 1988 *The Military Revolution. Military Innovation and the Rise of the West, 1500–1800*. Cambridge: Cambridge University Press.

Parker, William and Eric L. Jones, 1975 eds, *European Peasants and their Markets*. Princeton, New Jersey: Princeton University Press.

Parkinson, C. Northcote, 1957 *Parkinson's Law and Other Studies in Administration*. Boston, Massachusetts: Houghton Mifflin.

Parry, J. H., 1961 *The Establishment of the European Hegemony, 1415–1715. Trade and Exploration in the age of the Renaissance*. New York: Harper and Row. Third edition.

—— 1966 *The Spanish Seaborne Empire*. New York: Knopf.

Patten, John, 1973 *Rural–Urban Migration in Pre-Industrial England*. Oxford: School of Geography. Occasional Papers, No. 6.

Peacock, Alan T. and Jack Wiseman, 1961 *The Growth of Public Expenditure in the United Kingdom*. Princeton, New Jersey: Princeton University Press.

Pepper, Simon and Nicholas Adams, 1986 *Firearms and Fortifications. Military Architecture and Siege Warfare in Sixteenth-Century Siena*. Chicago, Illinois: University of Chicago Press.

Perlmutter, Amos, 1981 *Political Roles and Military Rulers*. London: Frank Cass.

Petitfrère, Claude, 1988 "The Origins of the Civil War in the Vendée," *French History* 2: 187–207.

Pitcher, Donald Edgar, 1972 *An Historical Geography of the Ottoman Empire from Earliest Times to the End of the Sixteenth Century*. Leiden: Brill.

Platzhoff, Walter, 1928 *Geschichte des europäischen Staatensystems 1559–1660*. Munich and Berlin: Oldenbourg.

Plumb, J. H., 1967 *The Origins of Political Stability. England 1675–1725*. Boston, Massachusetts: Houghton Mifflin.

Poggi, Gianfranco, 1978 *The Development of the Modern State*. Stanford, California: Stanford University Press.

Polisensky, Josef V., 1978 *War and Society in Europe, 1618–1648*. Cambridge: Cambridge University Press.

Pounds, Norman J. G., 1973 *An Historical Geography of Europe 450 B.C.–A.D. 1330*. Cambridge: Cambridge University Press.

—— 1979 *An Historical Geography of Europe, 1500–1840*. Cambridge: Cambridge University Press.

—— and Sue Simons Ball, 1964 "Core-Areas and the Development of the European States System," *Annals of the Association of American Geographers* 54: 24–40.

Powers, James F., 1988 *A Society Organized for War. The Iberian Municipal Militias in the Central Middle Ages, 1000–1284*. Berkeley, California: University of California Press.

Pryor, John H., 1988 *Geography, Technology, and War. Studies in the Maritime History of the Mediterranean 649–1571*. Cambridge: Cambridge University Press.

Pullan, Brian, 1971 *Rich and Poor in Renaissance Venice*. Oxford: Basil Blackwell.

Pye, Lucian, 1960 "The Politics of Southeast Asia," in Gabriel A. Almond and James S. Coleman, eds, *The Politics of the Developing Areas*. Princeton, New Jersey: Princeton University Press.

Quester, George H., 1975 "The World Political System," vol. VIII, 199–246 in Fred I. Greenstein and Nelson W. Polsby, eds, *Handbook of Political Science*. Reading, Massachusetts: Addison-Wesley.

Raeff, Marc, 1983 *The Well-Ordered Police State. Social and Institutional Change through Law in the Germanies and Russia, 1600–1800*. New Haven, Connecticut, Yale University Press.

Rambaud, Placide and Monique Vincienne, 1964 *Les transformations d'une société rurale. La Maurienne (1561–1962)*. Paris: Armand Colin. Ecole Pratique des Hautes Etudes (VIe Section), Centre d'Etudes Economiques, Etudes et Mémoires, 59.

Ramsay, G. D., 1975 *The City of London in International Politics at the Accession of Elizabeth Tudor*. Manchester: Manchester University Press.

—— 1986 *The Queen's Merchants and the Revolt of the Netherlands*. Manchester: Manchester University Press.

Rapoport, David C., 1982 "The Praetorian Army: Insecurity, Venality, and Impotence," in Roman Kolkowicz and Andrzej Korbonski, eds, *Soldiers, Peasants, and Bureaucrats: Civil–Military Relations in Communist and Modernizing Societies*. London: Routledge and Kegan Paul.

Rasler, Karen A. and William R. Thompson, 1983 "Global Wars, Public Debts, and the Long Cycle," *World Politics* 35: 489–516.

—— 1985a "War Making and State Making: Governmental Expenditures, Tax Revenues, and Global Wars," *American Political Science Review* 79: 491–507.

—— 1985b "War and the Economic Growth of Major Powers," *American Journal of Political Science* 29: 513–38.

—— 1988 "Defense Burdens, Capital Formation, and Economic Growth. The Systemic Leader Case," *Journal of Conflict Resolution* 32: 61–86.

—— 1989 *War and Statemaking: The Shaping of the Global Powers*. Boston, Massachusetts: Unwin Hyman.

Ratajczyk, Leonard, 1987 "Evolution of the Polish Armed Forces, 1764–1921," in Stephen Fischer-Galati and Béla K. Király, eds, *Essays on War and Society in East Central Europe, 1740–1920*. Boulder, Colorado: Social Science Monographs.

Redlich, Fritz, 1964–1965 *The German Military Enterpriser and His Work Force*. Wiesbaden: Steiner. 2 vols. *Vierteljahrschrift für Sozial- und Wirtschaftsgeschichte*, Beiheften 47, 48.

Reinhard, Marcel, André Armengaud and Jacques Dupâquier, 1968 *Histoire générale de la population mondiale*. Paris: Montchrestien.

Renouard, Yves, 1958 "1212–1216. Comment les traits durables de l'Europe occidentale moderne se sont définis au début du XIIIe siècle," *Annales de l'Université de Paris 1958*: 5–21.

Reuter, Timothy, 1978 "Introduction" to Timothy Reuter, ed., *The Medieval Nobility*. Amsterdam: North-Holland.

Reynolds, Susan, 1984 *Kingdoms and Communities in Western Europe, 900–1300*. Oxford: Clarendon Press.

Rian, Oystein, 1985 "State and Society in Seventeenth-century Norway," *Scandinavian Journal of History* 10: 337–63.

Rice, Condoleezza, 1988 "The Impact of World War II on Soviet State and Society," Working Paper 69, Center for Studies of Social Change, New School for Social Research.

Ringrose, David R., 1983 *Madrid and the Spanish Economy, 1560–1850*. Berkeley, California: University of California Press.

Roberts, Michael, 1979 *The Swedish Imperial Experience*. Cambridge: Cambridge University Press.

Robinson, E. A. G., 1969 ed., *Backward Areas in Advanced Countries*. London: Macmillan.

Roider, Karl, 1987 "Origins of Wars in the Balkans, 1660–1792," in Jeremy Black, ed., *The Origins of War in Early Modern Europe*. Edinburgh: John Donald.

Rokkan, Stein, 1975 "Dimensions of State Formation and Nation-Building: A Possible Paradigm for Research on Variations within Europe," in Charles Tilly, ed., *The Formation of National States in Western Europe*. Princeton, New Jersey: Princeton University Press.

—— and Derek W. Urwin, 1982 eds, *The Politics of Territorial Identity. Studies in European Regionalism*. Beverly Hills, California: Sage.

Roksandic, Drago, 1988 "Agrarian Ideologies and Theories of Modernization in Yugoslavia, 1918–1941," paper presented to the Conference on Models of Development and Theories of Modernization in Eastern Europe Between the World Wars, Ráckeve, Hungary.

Romano, Salvatore Franceso, 1963 *Storia della mafia*. Milan: Sugar.

Roscoe, Paul B. and Robert B. Graber, 1988 eds, "Circumscription and the Evolution of Society," special issue of *American Behavioral Scientist* 31: 403–511.

Rosenau, James N., 1970 *The Adaptation of National Societies: A Theory of Political System Behavior and Transformation*. New York: McCaleb-Seiler.

Rosenberg, Hans, 1958 *Bureaucracy, Aristocracy, and Autocracy. The Prussian Experience 1660–1815*. Cambridge: Harvard University Press.

Rosenberg, Harriet G., 1988 *A Negotiated World: Three Centuries of Change in a French Alpine Community*. Toronto: University of Toronto Press.

Rosenberg, William G. and Marilyn B. Young, 1982 *Transforming Russia and China. Revolutionary Struggles in the Twentieth Century*. New York: Oxford University Press.

Rothenberg, Gunther E., 1988 "The Origins, Causes, and Extension of the Wars of the French Revolution and Napoleon," *Journal of Interdisciplinary History* 18: 771–94.

Roubaud, François, 1983 "Partition économique de la France dans la première moitié du XIXe siècle (1830–1840)," Institut d'Histoire Economique et Sociale de l'Université de Paris I Panthéon-Sorbonne. *Recherches et Travaux* 12: 33–58.

Rouquié, Alain, 1987 *The Military and the State in Latin America*. Berkeley, California: University of California Press.

Rule, James B., 1988 *Theories of Civil Violence*. Berkeley, California: University of California Press.

Ruloff, Dieter, 1985 *Wie Kriege beginnen*. Munich: C. H. Beck.

Russell, Conrad S. R., 1982 "Monarchies, Wars, and Estates in England, France, and Spain, c. 1580–c. 1640," *Legislative Studies Quarterly* 7: 205–20.

Russell, D. E. H., 1974 *Rebellion, Revolution, and Armed Force*. New York: Academic Press.

Russell, Jocelyne G., 1986 *Peacemaking in the Renaissance*. Philadelphia, Pennsylvania: University of Pennsylvania Press.

Russell, Josiah Cox, 1972 *Medieval Regions and their Cities*. Newton Abbot: David & Charles.

Russett, Bruce, 1970 *What Price Vigilance? The Burdens of National Defense*. New Haven, Connecticut: Yale University Press.

Rystad, Goran, 1983 ed., *Europe and Scandinavia: Aspects of the Process of Integration in the 17th Century*. Lund: Esselte Studium.

Sales, Núria, 1974 *Sobre esclavos, reclutas y mercaderes de quíntos*. Madrid: Ariel.

—— 1986 "Servei militar i societat: la desigaultat enfront del servei obligatori, segles XVII–XX," *L'Avenç* 98: 721–8.

Scammell, G. V., 1981 *The World Encompassed. The First European Maritime Empires c. 800–1650*. London: Methuen.

Schama, Simon, 1975 "The Exigencies of War and the Politics of Taxation in the Netherlands 1795–1810," in J. M. Winter, ed., *War and Economic Development. Essays in Memory of David Joslin*. Cambridge: Cambridge University Press.

Schevill, Ferdinand, 1963 *Medieval and Renaissance Florence*. New York: Harper Torchbooks, 2 vols. First published in 1936.

Schissler, Hanna, 1978 *Preussische Agrargesellschaft im Wandel. Wirtschaftliche, gesellschaftliche und politische Transformationsprozesse von 1763 bis 1847*. Göttingen: Vandenhoeck and Ruprecht.

Schmal, H., 1981 ed., *Patterns of European Urbanization since 1500*. London: Croom Helm.

Schmoller, Gustav, 1896 "Die Epochen der Getreidehandelsverfassung und -politik," *Schmollers Jahrbuch* 20: 695–744.

Schram, Stuart R., 1985 ed., *The Scope of State Power in China*. Published for European Science Foundation by School of Oriental and African Studies, University of London and the Chinese University Press of Hong Kong.

—— 1987 ed., *Foundations and Limits of State Power in China*. Published for European Science Foundation by School of Oriental and African Studies, University of London and the Chinese University Press of Hong Kong.

Schultz, Patrick, 1982 *La décentralisation administrative dans le département du Nord (1790–1793)*. Lille: Presses Universitaires de Lille.

Schulze, Hagen, 1987 ed., *Nation-Building in Central Europe*. Leamington Spa: Berg.

Schumpeter, Joseph, 1955 *Imperialism, Social Classes*. New York: Meridian.

Schwartz, Robert M., 1988 *Policing the Poor in Eighteenth-Century France*. Chapel Hill, North Carolina: University of North Carolina Press.

Scott, James, 1985 *Weapons of the Weak. Everyday Forms of Peasant Resistance*. New Haven, Connecticut: Yale University Press.

Scott, William, 1973 *Terror and Repression in Revolutionary Marseilles*. New York: Barnes and Noble.

Searle, Eleanor, 1988 *Predatory Kinship and the Creation of Norman Power, 840–1066*. Berkeley, California: University of California Press.

Sedoc-Dahlberg, Betty, 1986 "Interest Groups and the Military Regime in Suriname," in Alma H. Young and Dion E. Phillips, eds, *Militarization in the Non-Hispanic Caribbean*. Boulder, Colorado: Lynne Rienner.

Segal, Daniel A., 1988 "Nationalism, Comparatively Speaking," *Journal of Historical Sociology* 1: 301–21.

Shennan, J. H., 1974 *The Origins of the Modern European State, 1450–1725*. London: Hutchinson University Library.

Shils, Edward, 1962 *Political Development in the New States*. The Hague: Mouton.

Shue, Vivienne, 1988 *The Reach of the State. Sketches of the Chinese Body Politic*. Stanford, California: Stanford University Press.

Sid-Ahmed, Mohamed, 1984 "Trends in the Middle East," *Alternatives* 10: 139–60.

Sivard, Ruth Leger, 1974–1988 *World Military and Social Expenditures*. Washington, DC: World Priorities. Annual publication.

Skinner, G. W., 1964 "Marketing and Social Structure in Rural China," *Journal of Asian Studies* 24: 3–43.

—— 1977 ed., *The City in Late Imperial China*. Stanford, California: Stanford University Press.

—— 1985 "The Structure of Chinese History," *Journal of Asian Studies* 44: 271–92.

Skocpol, Theda, 1979 *States and Social Revolutions: A Comparative Analysis of France, Russia, and China*. Cambridge: Cambridge University Press.

Small, Melvin and J. David Singer, 1982 *Resort to Arms. International and Civil Wars, 1816–1980*. Beverly Hills, California: Sage.

Smith, Adam, 1910 *The Wealth of Nations*. London: Dent. 2 vols. First published in 1778.

Smith, C. T., 1967 *An Historical Geography of Western Europe before 1800*. London: Longmans.

Smith, Carol A., 1976 "Analyzing Regional Systems," in Carol A. Smith, ed., *Regional Analysis*. Vol 2: Social Systems. New York: Academic Press.

Sorokin, Pitirim A., 1962 *Social and Cultural Dynamics. III. Fluctuation of Social Relationships, War, and Revolution*. New York: Bedminster. First published in 1937.

Spuler, Bertold, 1977 *Rulers and Governments of the World*. London: Bowker. 3 vols.

Steensgaard, Niels, 1974 *The Asian Trade Revolution of the Seventeenth Century*. Chicago, Illinois: University of Chicago Press.

—— 1981 "Asian Trade and World Market: Orders of Magnitude in 'The Long Seventeenth Century'," in *Actes du Colloque Franco-Polonais d'Histoire*. Nice: Laboratoire d'Histoire Quantitative, Université de Nice.

Stein, Arthur A., 1978 *The Nation at War*. Baltimore, Maryland: Johns Hopkins University Press.

—— 1988 "War Settlement, State Structures, and National Security Policy," Working Paper 60, Center for Studies of Social Change, New School for Social Research.

—— and Bruce M. Russett, 1980 "Evaluating War: Outcomes and Consequences," in Ted Robert Gurr, ed., *Handbook of Political Conflict: Theory and Research*. New York: Free Press.

Stepan, Alfred, 1988 *Rethinking Military Politics. Brazil and the Southern Cone*. Princeton, New Jersey: Princeton University Press.

Stinchcombe, Arthur L., 1963 "Institutions of Privacy in the Determination of Police Administrative Practice," *American Journal of Sociology* 69: 150–60.

—— 1983 *Economic Sociology*. New York: Academic Press.

Stoessinger, John G., 1974 *Why Nations Go to War*. New York: St Martin's.

Stohl, Michael, 1976 *War and Domestic Political Violence. The American Capacity for Repression and Reaction*. Beverly Hills, California: Sage.

Stoianovich, Traian, 1970 "Model and Mirror of the Premodern Balkan City," *Studia Balcanica. III. La Ville Balkanique XVe–XIXe siècle*, 83–110.

—— 1981 "Mode de production maghrébin de commandement ponctuel," in *Actes du Colloque Franco-Polonais d'Histoire*. Nice: Laboratoire d'Histoire Quantitative, Université de Nice.

—— 1989 "The Segmentary State and *La Grande Nation*," in Eugene D. Genovese and Leonard Hochberg, eds, *Geographic Perspectives in History*. Oxford: Basil Blackwell.

Stone, Bailey, 1981 *The Parlement of Paris, 1774–1789*. Chapel Hill, North Carolina: University of North Carolina Press.

Stone, Lawrence, 1947 "State Control in Sixteenth-Century England," *Economic History Review* 17: 103–20.

—— 1965 *The Crisis of the Aristocracy, 1558–1641*. Oxford: Clarendon Press.

—— 1983 "Interpersonal Violence in English Society, 1300–1980," *Past and Present* 101: 22–33.

Strayer, Joseph, 1970 *On the Medieval Origins of the Modern State*. Princeton, New Jersey: Princeton University Press.

Sundin, Jan and Eric Soderlund, 1979 eds, *Time, Space and Man: Essays in Microdemography*. Stockholm: Almqvist & Wilksell International.

Sutton, F. X., 1959 "Representation and the Nature of Political Systems," *Comparative Studies in Society and History* 2: 1–10.

Tanter, Richard, 1984 "Trends in Asia," *Alternatives* 10: 161–91.

Taylor, A. J. P., 1985 *How Wars End*. London: Hamish Hamilton.

Taylor, Peter J., 1981 "Political Geography and the World-Economy" in Alan D. Burnett and Peter J. Taylor, eds, *The Politics of Territorial Identity*. New York: Wiley.

Taylor, Stan, 1984 *Social Science and Revolutions*. New York: St Martin's.

Tenenti, Alberto, 1967 *Piracy and the Decline of Venice, 1580–1615*. Berkeley, California: University of California Press.

Thee, Marek, 1984 "Militarization in the United States and the Soviet Union: The Deepening Trends," *Alternatives* 10: 93–114.

Therborn, Goran, 1978 *What Does the Ruling Class Do When It Rules?* London: NLB.

Thibon, Christian, 1987 "L'ordre public villageois: le cas du Pays de Sault (1848–1914)," in *Société de la Révolution de 1848 et des Révolutions du XIXe Siècle, Maintien de l'ordre et polices en France et en Europe au XIXe siècle*. Paris: Créaphis.

Thomas, George M. and John W. Meyer, 1980 "Regime Changes and State Power in an Intensifying World-State-System," in Albert Bergesen, ed., *Studies of the Modern World System*. New York: Academic Press.

——, ——, Francisco O. Ramirez and Jeanne Gobalet, 1979 "Maintaining National Boundaries in the World System: The Rise of Centralist Regimes," in John W. Meyer and Michael T. Hannan, eds, *National Development and the World System. Educational, Economic, and Political Change, 1950–1970.* Chicago, Illinois: University of Chicago Press.

Thompson, I. A. A., 1976 *War and Government in Habsburg Spain 1560–1620.* London: Athlone Press.

—— 1982 "Crown and Cortes in Castile, 1590–1665," *Parlements, Estates and Representation* 2: 29–45.

Thompson, William R., 1988 *On Global War. Historical-Structural Approaches to World Politics.* Columbia, South Carolina: University of South Carolina Press.

—— and Gary Zuk, 1986 "World Power and the Strategic Trap of Territorial Commitments," *International Studies Quarterly* 30: 249–67.

Tilly, Charles, 1983 "Flows of Capital and Forms of Industry in Europe, 1500–1900," *Theory and Society* 12: 123–43.

—— 1984 "Demographic Origins of the European Proletariat" in David Levine, ed., *Proletarianization and Family Life.* Orlando, Florida: Academic Press.

—— 1985a "War and the Power of Warmakers in Western Europe and Elsewhere" in Peter Wallensteen, Johan Galtung and Carlos Portales, eds, *Global Militarization.* Boulder, Colorado: Westview Press.

—— 1985b "War Making and State Making as Organized Crime" In Peter Evans, Dietrich Rueschemeyer and Theda Skocpol, eds, *Bringing the State Back In.* Cambridge: Cambridge University Press.

—— 1986 *The Contentious French.* Cambridge: Belknap.

—— Louise A. Tilly and Richard Tilly, 1975 *The Rebellious Century, 1830–1930.* Cambridge: Harvard University Press.

Tilly, Louise A., 1971 "The Food Riot as a Form of Political Conflict in France," *Journal of Interdisciplinary History* 2: 23–57.

Timberlake, Michael, 1985 ed., *Urbanization in the World-Economy.* Orlando, Florida: Academic Press.

Torres i Sans, Xavier, 1988 "Guerra privada y bandolerismo en la Cataluña del Barroco," *Historia Social* 1: 5–18.

Torsvik, Per, 1981 ed., *Mobilization, Center-Periphery Structures and Nation-Building. A Volume in Commemoration of Stein Rokkan.* Bergen: Universitetsforlaget.

Tracy, James D., 1985 *A Financial Revolution in the Habsburg Netherlands. Renten and Renteniers in the County of Holland, 1515–1565.* Berkeley, California: University of California Press.

Treasure, Geoffrey, 1985 *The Making of Modern Europe 1648–1780.* London: Methuen.

Trexler, Richard C., 1980 *Public Life in Renaissance Florence.* New York: Academic Press.

Trotsky, Leon, 1965 *History of the Russian Revolution.* London: Gollancz. 2 vols.

Tucci, Ugo, 1981 "Entre Orient et Occident: L'Age vénitien des épices," in *Actes du Colloque Franco-Polonais d'Histoire.* Nice: Laboratoire d'Histoire Quantitative, Université de Nice.

Turner, Bryan S., 1988 "Religion and State Formation: A Commentary on Recent Debates," *Journal of Historical Sociology* 1: 322–33.

Ultee, Maarten, 1986 ed., *Adapting to Conditions. War and Society in the Eighteenth Century*. Alabama: University of Alabama Press.

Urlanis, B. Ts., 1960 *Voin'i i narodo-naselenie Evrop'i*. Moscow: Izdatel'stvo Sotsial'no-ekonomicheskoy literatur'i.

Van Creveld, Martin, 1977 *Supplying War. Logistics from Wallenstein to Patton*. Cambridge: Cambridge University Press.

—— 1989 *Technology and War From 2000 B.C. to the Present*. New York: Free Press.

Vaner, Semih, 1987 "The Army," in Irvin C. Schick and Ertugrul Ahmet Tonak, eds, *Turkey in Transition: New Perspectives*. New York: Oxford University Press.

Verhulst, Adriaan, 1989 "The Origins of Towns in the Low Countries and the Pirenne Thesis," *Past and Present* 122: 3–35.

Vilar, Pierre, 1962 *La Catalogne dans l'Espagne moderne. Recherches sur les fondements économiques des structures nationales*. Paris: SEVPEN. 3 vols.

Vovelle, Michel, 1987 ed., *Bourgeoisies de province et Révolution*. Grenoble: Presses Universitaires de Grenoble, 1987.

Vries, Jan de, 1973 "On the Modernity of the Dutch Republic," *Journal of Economic History* 33: 191–202.

—— 1974 *The Dutch Rural Economy in the Golden Age, 1500–1700*. New Haven, Connecticut: Yale University Press.

—— 1973 "On the Modernity of the Dutch Republic," *Journal of Economic History* 33: 191–202.

—— 1976 *The Economy of Europe in an Age of Crisis, 1600–1750*. Cambridge: Cambridge University Press.

—— 1978 "Barges and Capitalism. Passenger transportation in the Dutch economy, 1632–1839," *A. A. G. Bijdragen* 21: 33–398.

—— 1984 *European Urbanization, 1500–1800*. Cambridge: Harvard University Press.

Wakeman, Jr, Frederic, 1985 *The Great Enterprise. The Manchu Reconstruction of Imperial Order in Seventeenth-Century China*. Berkeley, California: University of California Press. 2 vols.

Waldmann, Peter, 1989 *Ethnischer Radikalismus. Ursachen und Folgen gewaltsamer Minderheitenkonflikte*. Opladen: Westdeutscher Verlag.

Waley, Daniel, 1969 *The Italian City-Republics*. New York: McGraw-Hill. World University Library.

Walker, Mack, 1971 *German Home Towns. Community, State, and General Estate 1648–1871*. Ithaca, New York: Cornell University Press.

Wallensteen, Peter, Johan Galtung and Carlos Portales, 1985 eds, *Global Militarization*. Boulder, Colorado: Westview.

Wallerstein, Immanuel, 1974–1988 *The Modern World System*. 3 vols. New York, and Orlando, Florida: Academic Press.

—— 1979 *The Capitalist World-Economy*. Cambridge: Cambridge University Press.

Waltz, Kenneth N., 1979 *Theory of International Politics*. New York: Random House.

—— 1988 "The Origins of War in Neorealist Theory," *Journal of Interdisciplinary History* 18: 615–28.

Watkins, Susan Cotts, 1989 *From Provinces into Nations*. Princeton, New Jersey: Princeton University Press.

Watson, J. Steven, 1960 *The Reign of George III, 1760–1815*. Oxford: Clarendon Press. Oxford History of England, vol. 12.

Webber, Carolyn and Aaron Wildavsky, 1986 *A History of Taxation and Expenditure in the Western World*. New York: Simon & Schuster.

Weber, Max, 1972 *Wirtschaft und Gesellschaft*. Tübingen: Mohr. Fifth edition.

Wedgewood, C. V., 1964 *The Thirty Years War*. London: Jonathan Cape. First published in 1938.

Wendt, Alexander E., 1987 "The Agent-Structure Problem in International Relations Theory," *International Organization* 41: 335–70.

Werner, Ernst, 1985 *Die Geburt einer Grossmacht – die Osmanen (1300–1481)*. Vienna: Böhlhaus.

Wheatcroft, Andrew, 1983 *The World Atlas of Revolutions*. London: Hamish Hamilton.

Whitney, Joseph B. R., 1970 *China: Area, Administration, and Nation Building*. Chicago: Department of Geography, University of Chicago. Research Paper 123.

Wickham, Chris, 1988 "The Uniqueness of the East," in Jean Baechler, John A. Hall and Michael Mann, eds, *Europe and the Rise of Capitalism*. Oxford: Basil Blackwell.

Wijn, J W., 1970 "Military Forces and Warfare 1610–1648," in J. P. Cooper, ed., *The New Cambridge Modern History. Vol. 4: The Decline of Spain and the Thirty Years War, 1609–48/59*. Cambridge: Cambridge University Press.

Wilkenfeld, Jonathan, 1973 ed., *Conflict Behavior and Linkage Politics*. New York: David McKay.

Wilson, Charles, 1968 *The Dutch Republic and The Civilisation of the Seventeenth Century*. New York: McGraw-Hill. World University Library.

Winberg, Christer, 1978 "Population Growth and Proletarianization. The Transformation of Social Structures in Rural Sweden During the Agrarian Revolution," in Sune Akerman, ed., *Chance and Change. Social and Economic Studies in Historical Demography in the Baltic Area*. Odense: Odense University Press.

Winter, J. M., 1986 *The Great War and the British People*. Cambridge: Harvard University Press.

Witt, Peter-Christian, 1987 ed., *Wealth and Taxation in Central Europe*. Leamington Spa: Berg.

Wong, R. Bin., 1983 "Les émeutes de subsistances en Chine et en Europe Occidentale," *Annales; Economies, Sociétés, Civilisations* 38: 234–58.

—— and Peter C. Perdue, 1983 "Famine's Foes in Ch'ing China," *Harvard Journal of Asiatic Studies* 43: 291–332.

Wright, Quincy, 1965 *A Study of War*. Chicago, Illinois: University of Chicago Press. Revised edn.

Wrigley, E. A., 1969 *Population and History*. New York: McGraw-Hill.

—— and R. S. Schofield, 1981 *The Population History of England, 1541–1871. A Reconstruction*. Cambridge: Harvard University Press.

Wyczanski, Andrzej, 1981 "La frontière de l'unité européenne au XVIème siècle: Liens – cadres – contenu," in *Actes du Colloque Franco-Polonais d'Histoire*. Nice: Laboratoire d'Histoire Quantitative, Université de Nice.

Wyrobisz, Andrezej, 1989 "Power and Towns in the Polish Gentry Commonwealth: The Polish-Lithuanian State in the 16th and 17th Centuries," forthcoming in *Theory and Society*.

Young, Alma H. and Dion E. Phillips, 1986 eds, *Militarization in the Non-Hispanic Caribbean*. Boulder, Colorado: Lynne Rienner.

Zagorin, Perez, 1982 *Rebels and Rulers, 1500–1660*. Cambridge: Cambridge University Press. 2 vols.

Zimmerman, Ekkart, 1983 *Political Violence, Crises and Revolutions*. Cambridge: Schenkman.

Zinnes, Dina, 1980 "Why War? Evidence on the Outbreak of International Conflict," in Ted Robert Gurr, ed., *Handbook of Political Conflict*. New York: Free Press.

Zolberg, Aristide, 1968 "The Structure of Political Conflict in the New States of Tropical Africa," *American Political Science Review* 62: 70–87.

—— 1978 "Belgium" in Raymond Grew, ed., *Crises of Political Development in Europe and the United States*. Princeton, New Jersey: Princeton University Press.

—— 1980 "Strategic Interactions and the Formation of Modern States: France and England," *International Social Science Journal* 32: 687–716.

—— 1981 "International Migrations in Political Perspective," in Mary M. Kritz, Charles B. Keely, and Silvano M. Tomasi, eds, *Global Trends in Migration. Theory and Research on International Population Movements*. Staten Island, New York: Center for Migration Studies.

—— 1987 "Beyond the Nation-State: Comparative Politics in Global Perspective," in Jan Berting and Wim Blockmans, eds, *Beyond Progress and Development. Macro-Political and Macro-Societal Change*. Aldershot: Avebury.

Index